XQuery

Priscilla Walmsley

O'REILLY®

Beijing · Cambridge · Farnham · Köln · Paris · Sebastopol · Taipei · Tokyo

XQuery
by Priscilla Walmsley

Copyright © 2007 Priscilla Walmsley. All rights reserved.
Printed in the United States of America.

Published by O'Reilly Media, Inc., 1005 Gravenstein Highway North, Sebastopol, CA 95472.

O'Reilly books may be purchased for educational, business, or sales promotional use. Online editions are also available for most titles (*safari.oreilly.com*). For more information, contact our corporate/institutional sales department: (800) 998-9938 or *corporate@oreilly.com*.

Editor: Simon St.Laurent
Production Editor: Lydia Onofrei
Proofreader: Lydia Onofrei
Indexer: Ellen Troutman-Zaig

Cover Designer: Karen Montgomery
Interior Designer: David Futato
Illustrators: Robert Romano and Jessamyn Read

Printing History:

April 2007: First Edition.

 This book uses RepKover™, a durable and flexible lay-flat binding.

ISBN-10: 0-596-00634-9
ISBN-13: 978-0-596-00634-1
[M]

XQuery

Other XML resources from O'Reilly

Related titles

XSLT
Learning XSLT
XSLT Cookbook™
XML in a Nutshell
Learning XML

Developing Feeds with RSS
and Atom
Java™ and XML
XSLT 1.0 Pocket Reference
XML Hacks™

XML Books Resource Center

xml.oreilly.com is a complete catalog of O'Reilly's books on XML and related technologies, including sample chapters and code examples.

XML.com helps you discover XML and learn how this Internet technology can solve real-world problems in information management and electronic commerce.

Conferences

O'Reilly brings diverse innovators together to nurture the ideas that spark revolutionary industries. We specialize in documenting the latest tools and systems, translating the innovator's knowledge into useful skills for those in the trenches. Visit *conferences.oreilly.com* for our upcoming events.

Safari Bookshelf (*safari.oreilly.com*) is the premier online reference library for programmers and IT professionals. Conduct searches across more than 1,000 books. Subscribers can zero in on answers to time-critical questions in a matter of seconds. Read the books on your Bookshelf from cover to cover or simply flip to the page you need. Try it today for free.

Table of Contents

Preface

This book provides complete coverage of the W3C XQuery 1.0 standard that was finalized in January 2007. In addition, it provides the background knowledge in namespaces, schemas, built-in types, and regular expressions that is relevant to writing XML queries.

This book is designed for query writers who have some knowledge of XML basics but not necessarily advanced knowledge of XML-related technologies. It can be used as a tutorial, by reading it cover to cover, and as a reference, by using the comprehensive index and appendixes.

Contents of This Book

The book is organized into six parts:

1. Chapters 1 and 2 provide a high-level overview and quick tour of XQuery.
2. Chapters 3–9 provide enough information to write sophisticated queries, without being bogged down by the details of types, namespaces, and schemas.
3. Chapters 10–15 introduce some advanced concepts for users who want to take advantage of modularity, namespaces, typing, and schemas.
4. Chapters 16–23 provide guidelines for working with specific types of data, such as numbers, strings, dates, URIs, and processing instructions.
5. Chapters 24 and 25 describe XQuery's relationship to SQL and XSLT.
6. Appendixes A, B, and C provide a complete alphabetical reference to the built-in functions, types, and error messages.

Reading the Syntax Diagrams

This book includes syntax diagrams as an option for readers who want a more visual representation of XQuery expression syntax. Each syntax diagram is accompanied by

explanatory text and examples. Figure P-1 illustrates the components of a syntax diagram, showing the schema import syntax as an example.

Figure P-1. Example syntax diagram

Rules for interpreting the syntax diagrams are:

- Parts of the diagram in `constant width` font are literal values. In Figure P-1, `import schema` and `at` should appear literally in your query.

- Quotes that appear in syntax diagrams also must appear in your query. Figure P-1 shows that the *<namespace-name>* must be surrounded by quotes, whereas the *<prefix>* must not. Either single or double quotes can be used in XQuery, but only double quotes are included in the diagrams for simplicity.

- Where you can specify a value, such as a name, a descriptive name for that value appears in constant width italic and is surrounded by angle brackets. Figure P-1 shows that you fill in the *<namespace-name>*, *<prefix>*, and *<location>* with your own values.

- Multiple options are indicated by parallel lines in the diagram. Figure P-1 shows that you may choose to specify a namespace prefix or `default element namespace`.

- Optional parts of the expression are indicated by an arrow that bypasses the main arrow. In Figure P-1, it is not necessary to include the `namespace` *<prefix>* `=` or the `default element namespace` keywords.

- Repeating parts of an expression are indicated by an arrow that returns to the beginning. Figure P-1 shows that you can specify multiple *<location>*s (preceded by commas) as part of the at clause.

Conventions Used in This Book

`Constant width` is used for:

- Code examples and fragments

- Anything that might appear in an XML document, including element names, tags, attribute values, and processing instructions

- Anything that might appear in a program, including keywords, operators, method names, class names, and literals

Constant width bold is used for:

- Emphasis in code examples and fragments

Italic is used for:

- New terms where they are defined
- Emphasis in body text
- Pathnames, filenames, and program names
- Host and domain names

 This icon indicates a tip, suggestion, or general note.

 This icon indicates a warning or caution.

 This icon indicates a situation where compatibility issues may cause surprises.

Significant code fragments, complete programs, and documents are generally placed into a separate paragraph like this:

```
for $prod as element(*,ProductType) in doc("catalog.xml")/catalog/*
order by $prod/name
return $prod/name
```

Using Code Examples

This book is here to help you get your job done. In general, you may use the code in this book in your programs and documentation. You do not need to contact us for permission unless you're reproducing a significant portion of the code. For example, writing a program that uses several chunks of code from this book does not require permission. Selling or distributing a CD-ROM of examples from O'Reilly books does require permission. Answering a question by citing this book and quoting example code does not require permission. Incorporating a significant amount of example code from this book into your product's documentation does require permission.

We appreciate, but do not require, attribution. An attribution usually includes the title, author, publisher, and ISBN. For example: "*XQuery* by Priscilla Walmsley. Copyright 2007 Priscilla Walmsley, 978-0-596-00634-1."

If you feel your use of code examples falls outside fair use or the permission given above, feel free to contact us at *permissions@oreilly.com*.

Useful Functions

This book contains a series of illustrative examples that are labeled Useful Function. What sets them apart from regular examples is that they are likely to be directly useful in your own queries. They range from string functions like substring-after-last and replace-first to functions that modify elements and attributes, such as add-attribute.

The useful functions included in this book are part of a large library of XQuery functions called the FunctX XQuery Library, which is available at *http://www. xqueryfunctions.com*. This library contains a wide variety of reusable XQuery functions that can be searched or browsed by category. It also includes detailed descriptions and example function calls.

We'd Like to Hear from You

Please address comments and questions concerning this book to the publisher:

> O'Reilly Media, Inc.
> 1005 Gravenstein Highway North
> Sebastopol, CA 95472
> 800-998-9938 (in the United States or Canada)
> 707-829-0515 (international or local)
> 707-829-0104 (fax)

We have a web page for this book, where we list errata, examples, and any additional information. You can access this page at:

> *http://www.oreilly.com/catalog/9780596006341*

To comment or ask technical questions about this book, send email to:

> *bookquestions@oreilly.com.*

For more information about our books, conferences, Resource Centers, and the O'Reilly Network, see our web site at:

> *http://www.oreilly.com.*

Acknowledgments

I am deeply indebted to Michael Kay, not only for his detailed review of this book, but also for his excellent Saxon XQuery implementation, without which I would not have been able to reliably test the examples.

Ron Bourret, Bob DuCharme, Tim Finney, Ashok Malhotra, Darin McBeath, Peter Meggitt, Shannon Shiflett, and Bruno J. Walmsley (my father) provided extremely helpful comments on, and assistance with, this book.

This project would not have been possible without Simon St.Laurent, who provided editorial guidance and championed the book within O'Reilly. Thanks, Simon!

Finally, I would like to thank Doug, my partner, my love, for his constant support and encouragement during the busy years I have spent writing this book.

Introduction to XQuery

This chapter provides background on the purpose and capabilities of XQuery. It also gives a quick introduction to the features of XQuery that are covered in more detail later in the book. It is designed to provide a basic familiarity with the most commonly used kinds of expressions, without getting too bogged down in the details.

What Is XQuery?

The use of XML has exploded in recent years. An enormous amount of information is now stored in XML, both in XML databases and in documents on a filesystem. This includes highly structured data, such as sales figures, semistructured data such as product catalogs and yellow pages, and relatively unstructured data such as letters and books. Even more information is passed between systems as transitory XML documents.

All of this data is used for a variety of purposes. For example, sales figures may be useful for compiling financial statements that may be published on the Web, reporting results to the tax authorities, calculating bonuses for salespeople, or creating internal reports for planning. For each of these uses, we are interested in different elements of the data and expect it to be formatted and transformed according to our needs.

XQuery is a query language designed by the W3C to address these needs. It allows you to select the XML data elements of interest, reorganize and possibly transform them, and return the results in a structure of your choosing.

Capabilities of XQuery

XQuery has a rich set of features that allow many different types of operations on XML data and documents, including:

- Selecting information based on specific criteria
- Filtering out unwanted information

- Searching for information within a document or set of documents
- Joining data from multiple documents or collections of documents
- Sorting, grouping, and aggregating data
- Transforming and restructuring XML data into another XML vocabulary or structure
- Performing arithmetic calculations on numbers and dates
- Manipulating strings to reformat text

As you can see, XQuery can be used not just to extract sections of XML documents, but also to manipulate and transform the results. One capability that XQuery 1.0 does not provide is updates, which would be particularly useful in the case of XML data stored in databases. This is under development for a future version of XQuery.

Uses for XQuery

There are as many reasons to query XML as there are reasons to use XML. Some examples of common uses for the XQuery language are:

- Extracting information from a relational database for use in a web service
- Generating reports on data stored in a database for presentation on the Web as XHTML
- Searching textual documents in a native XML database and presenting the results
- Pulling data from databases or packaged software and transforming it for application integration
- Combining content from traditionally non-XML sources to implement content management and delivery
- Ad hoc querying of standalone XML documents for the purposes of testing or research

Processing Scenarios

XQuery's sweet spot is querying bodies of XML content that are stored in databases. For this reason, it is sometimes called the "SQL of XML." Some of the earliest XQuery implementations were in native XML database products. The term "native XML database" generally refers to a database that is designed for XML content from the ground up, as opposed to a traditionally relational database. Rather than being oriented around tables and columns, its data model is based on hierarchical documents and collections of documents.

Native XML databases are most often used for narrative content and other data that is less predictable than what you would typically store in a relational database. Examples

of native XML database products that support XQuery are Berkeley DB XML, eXist (which is open source), MarkLogic Server, TigerLogic XDMS, and X-Hive/DB. These products provide the traditional capabilities of databases, such as data storage, indexing, querying, loading, extracting, backup, and recovery. Most of them also provide some added value in addition to their database capabilities. For example, they might provide advanced full-text searching functionality, document conversion services, or end-user interfaces.

Major relational database products, including Oracle 10g, IBM DB2 9, and Microsoft SQL Server 2005, also have support for XML and XQuery. Early implementations of XML in relational databases involved storing XML in table columns as blobs or character strings and providing query access to those columns. However, these vendors are increasingly blurring the line between native XML databases and relational databases with new features that allow you to store XML natively.

Other XQuery processors are not embedded in a database product, but work independently. They might be used on physical XML documents stored as files on a file system or on the Web. They might also operate on XML data that is passed in memory from some other process. The most notable product in this category is Saxon, which has both open source and commercial versions.

Easing into XQuery

The rest of this chapter takes you through a set of example queries, each of which builds on the previous one. Three XML documents are used repeatedly as input documents to the query examples throughout the book. They will be used so frequently that it may be worth printing them from the companion web site so that you can view them alongside the examples.

These three examples are quite simplistic, but they are useful for educational purposes because they are easy to learn and remember while looking at query examples. In reality, most XQuery queries will be executed against much more complex documents, and often against multiple documents as a group. However, in order to keep the examples reasonably concise and clear, this book will work with smaller documents that have a representative mix of XML characteristics.

The catalog.xml document is a product catalog containing general information about products (Example 1-1).

Example 1-1. Product catalog input document (catalog.xml)

```
<catalog>
  <product dept="WMN">
    <number>557</number>
    <name language="en">Fleece Pullover</name>
    <colorChoices>navy black</colorChoices>
  </product>
```

Example 1-1. Product catalog input document (catalog.xml) (continued)

```
  <product dept="ACC">
    <number>563</number>
    <name language="en">Floppy Sun Hat</name>
  </product>
  <product dept="ACC">
    <number>443</number>
    <name language="en">Deluxe Travel Bag</name>
  </product>
  <product dept="MEN">
    <number>784</number>
    <name language="en">Cotton Dress Shirt</name>
    <colorChoices>white gray</colorChoices>
    <desc>Our <i>favorite</i> shirt!</desc>
  </product>
</catalog>
```

The prices.xml document contains prices for the products, based on effective dates (Example 1-2).

Example 1-2. Price information input document (prices.xml)

```
<prices>
  <priceList effDate="2006-11-15">
    <prod num="557">
      <price currency="USD">29.99</price>
      <discount type="CLR">10.00</discount>
    </prod>
    <prod num="563">
      <price currency="USD">69.99</price>
    </prod>
    <prod num="443">
      <price currency="USD">39.99</price>
      <discount type="CLR">3.99</discount>
    </prod>
  </priceList>
</prices>
```

The order.xml document is a simple order containing a list of products ordered (referenced by a number that matches the number used in catalog.xml), along with quantities and colors (Example 1-3).

Example 1-3. Order input document (order.xml)

```
<order num="00299432" date="2006-09-15" cust="0221A">
  <item dept="WMN" num="557" quantity="1" color="navy"/>
  <item dept="ACC" num="563" quantity="1"/>
  <item dept="ACC" num="443" quantity="2"/>
  <item dept="MEN" num="784" quantity="1" color="white"/>
  <item dept="MEN" num="784" quantity="1" color="gray"/>
  <item dept="WMN" num="557" quantity="1" color="black"/>
</order>
```

Path Expressions

The most straightforward kind of query simply selects elements or attributes from an input document. This type of query is known as a path expression. For example, the path expression:

```
doc("catalog.xml")/catalog/product
```

will select all the product elements from the catalog.xml document.

Path expressions are used to traverse an XML tree to select elements and attributes of interest. They are similar to paths used for filenames in many operating systems. They consist of a series of steps, separated by slashes, that traverse the elements and attributes in the XML documents. In this example, there are three steps:

1. doc("catalog.xml") calls an XQuery function named doc, passing it the name of the file to open
2. catalog selects the catalog element, the outermost element of the document
3. product selects all the product children of catalog

The result of the query will be the four product elements, exactly as they appear (with the same attributes and contents) in the input document. Example 1-4 shows the complete result.

Example 1-4. Four product elements selected from the catalog

```
<product dept="WMN">
  <number>557</number>
  <name language="en">Fleece Pullover</name>
  <colorChoices>navy black</colorChoices>
</product>
<product dept="ACC">
  <number>563</number>
  <name language="en">Floppy Sun Hat</name>
</product>
<product dept="ACC">
  <number>443</number>
  <name language="en">Deluxe Travel Bag</name>
</product>
<product dept="MEN">
  <number>784</number>
  <name language="en">Cotton Dress Shirt</name>
  <colorChoices>white gray</colorChoices>
  <desc>Our <i>favorite</i> shirt!</desc>
</product>
```

Path expressions can also return attributes, using the @ symbol. For example, the path expression:

```
doc("catalog.xml")/*/product/@dept
```

will return the four dept attributes in the input document. The asterisk (*) can be used as a wildcard to indicate any element name. In this example, the path will return any product children of the outermost element, regardless of the outermost element's name. Alternatively, you can use a double slash (//) to return product elements that appear anywhere in the catalog document, as in:

```
doc("catalog.xml")//product/@dept
```

In addition to traversing the XML document, a path expression can contain predicates that filter out elements or attributes that do not meet a particular criterion. Predicates are indicated by square brackets. For example, the path expression:

```
doc("catalog.xml")/catalog/product[@dept = "ACC"]
```

contains a predicate. It selects only those product elements whose dept attribute value is ACC.

When a predicate contains a number, it serves as an index. For example:

```
doc("catalog.xml")/catalog/product[2]
```

will return the second product element in the catalog.

Path expressions are convenient because of their compact, easy-to-remember syntax. However, they have a limitation: they can only return elements and attributes as they appear in input documents. Any elements selected in a path expression appear in the results with the same names, the same attributes and contents, and in the same order as in the input document. When you select the product elements, you get them with all of their children and with their dept attributes. Path expressions are covered in detail in Chapter 4.

FLWORs

The basic structure of many (but not all) queries is the FLWOR expression. FLWOR (pronounced "flower") stands for "for, let, where, order by, return", the keywords used in the expression.

FLWORs, unlike path expressions, allow you to manipulate, transform, and sort your results. Example 1-5 shows a simple FLWOR that returns the names of all products in the ACC department.

Example 1-5. Simple FLWOR

Query
```
for $prod in doc("catalog.xml")/catalog/product
where $prod/@dept = "ACC"
order by $prod/name
return $prod/name
```
Results
```
<name language="en">Deluxe Travel Bag</name>
<name language="en">Floppy Sun Hat</name>
```

As you can see, the FLWOR is made up of several parts:

for

> This clause sets up an iteration through the product nodes, and the rest of the FLWOR is evaluated once for each of the four products. Each time, a variable named $prod is bound to a different product element. Dollar signs are used to indicate variable names in XQuery.

where

> This clause selects only products in the ACC department. This has the same effect as a predicate ([@dept = "ACC"]) in a path expression.

order by

> This clause sorts the results by product name, something that is not possible with path expressions.

return

> This clause indicates that the product element's name children should be returned.

The let clause (the L in FLWOR) is used to set the value of a variable. Unlike a for clause, it does not set up an iteration. Example 1-6 shows a FLWOR that returns the same result as Example 1-5. The second line is a let clause that assigns the product element's name child to a variable called $name. The $name variable is then referenced later in the FLWOR, in both the order by clause and the return clause.

Example 1-6. Adding a let clause

```
for $product in doc("catalog.xml")/catalog/product
let $name := $product/name
where $product/@dept = "ACC"
order by $name
return $name
```

The let clause serves as a programmatic convenience that avoids repeating the same expression multiple times. Using some implementations, it can also improve performance, because the expression is evaluated only once instead of each time it is needed.

This chapter has provided only very basic examples of FLWORs. In fact, FLWORs can become quite complex. Multiple for clauses are permitted, which set up iterations within iterations. In addition, complex expressions can be used in any of the clauses. FLWORs are discussed in detail in Chapter 6. Even more advanced examples of FLWORs are provided in Chapter 9.

Adding XML Elements and Attributes

Sometimes you want to reorganize or transform the elements in the input documents into differently named or structured elements. XML constructors can be used to create elements and attributes that appear in the query results.

Adding Elements

Suppose you want to wrap the results of your query in a different XML vocabulary, for example XHTML. You can do this using a familiar XML-like syntax. To wrap the name elements in a ul element, for instance, you can use the query shown in Example 1-7. The ul element represents an unordered list in XHTML.

Example 1-7. Wrapping results in a new element

```
Query
<ul>{
  for $product in doc("catalog.xml")/catalog/product
  where $product/@dept='ACC'
  order by $product/name
  return $product/name
}</ul>
Results
<ul>
  <name language="en">Deluxe Travel Bag</name>
  <name language="en">Floppy Sun Hat</name>
</ul>
```

This example is the same as Example 1-5, with the addition of the first and last lines. In the query, the ul start tag and end tag, and everything in between, is known as an element constructor. The curly braces around the content of the ul element signify that it is an expression (known as an enclosed expression) that is to be evaluated. In this case, the enclosed expression returns two elements, which become children of ul.

Any content in an element constructor that is not inside curly braces appears in the results as is. For example:

```
<h1>There are {count(doc("catalog.xml")//product)} products.</h1>
```

will return the result:

```
<h1>There are 4 products.</h1>
```

The content outside the curly braces, namely the strings "There are " and " products." appear literally in the results, as textual content of the ul element.

The element constructor does not need to be the outermost expression in the query. You can include element constructors at various places in your query. For example, if you want to wrap each resulting name element in its own li element, you could use the query shown in Example 1-8. An li element represents a list item in XHTML.

Example 1-8. Element constructor in FLWOR return clause

```
Query
<ul>{
  for $product in doc("catalog.xml")/catalog/product
  where $product/@dept='ACC'
  order by $product/name
```

Example 1-8. Element constructor in FLWOR return clause (continued)

```
   return <li>{$product/name}</li>
}</ul>
```
Results
```
<ul>
   <li><name language="en">Deluxe Travel Bag</name></li>
   <li><name language="en">Floppy Sun Hat</name></li>
</ul>
```

Here, the li element constructor appears in the return clause of a FLWOR. Since the return clause is evaluated once for each iteration of the for clause, two li elements appear in the results, each with a name element as its child.

However, suppose you don't want to include the name elements at all, just their contents. You can do this by calling a built-in function called data, which extracts the contents of an element. This is shown in Example 1-9.

Example 1-9. Using the data function

Query
```
<ul>{
   for $product in doc("catalog.xml")/catalog/product
   where $product/@dept='ACC'
   order by $product/name
   return <li>{data($product/name)}</li>
}</ul>
```
Results
```
<ul>
   <li>Deluxe Travel Bag</li>
   <li>Floppy Sun Hat</li>
</ul>
```

Now no name elements appear in the results. In fact, no elements at all from the input document appear.

Adding Attributes

You can also add your own attributes to results using an XML-like syntax. Example 1-10 adds attributes to the ul and li elements.

Example 1-10. Adding attributes to results

```
Query
<ul type="square">{
   for $product in doc("catalog.xml")/catalog/product
   where $product/@dept='ACC'
   order by $product/name
   return <li class="{$product/@dept}">{data($product/name)}</li>
}</ul>
```

Example 1-10. Adding attributes to results (continued)

Results
```
<ul type="square">
  <li class="ACC">Deluxe Travel Bag</li>
  <li class="ACC">Floppy Sun Hat</li>
</ul>
```

As you can see, attribute values, like element content, can either be literal text or enclosed expressions. The ul element constructor has an attribute type that is included as is in the results, while the li element constructor has an attribute class whose value is an enclosed expression delimited by curly braces. In attribute values, unlike element content, you don't need to use the data function to extract the value: it happens automatically.

The constructors shown in these examples are known as *direct constructors*, because they use an XML-like syntax. You can also construct elements and attributes with dynamically determined names, using computed constructors. Chapter 5 provides detailed coverage of XML constructors.

Functions

There are over 100 functions built into XQuery, covering a broad range of functionality. Functions can be used to manipulate strings and dates, perform mathematical calculations, combine sequences of elements, and perform many other useful jobs. You can also define your own functions, either in the query itself, or in an external library.

Both built-in and user-defined functions can be called from almost any place in a query. For instance, Example 1-9 calls the doc function in a for clause, and the data function in an enclosed expression. Chapter 8 explains how to call functions and also describes how to write your own user-defined functions. Appendix A lists all of the built-in functions and explains each of them in detail.

Joins

One of the major benefits of FLWORs is that they can easily join data from multiple sources. For example, suppose you want to join information from your product catalog (catalog.xml) and your order (order.xml). You want a list of all the items in the order, along with their number, name, and quantity.

The name comes from the product catalog, and the quantity comes from the order. The product number appears in both input documents, so it is used to join the two sources. Example 1-11 shows a FLWOR that performs this join.

Example 1-11. Joining multiple input documents

Query
```
for $item in doc("order.xml")//item
let $name := doc("catalog.xml")//product[number = $item/@num]/name
return <item num="{$item/@num}"
             name="{$name}"
             quan="{$item/@quantity}"/>
```
Results
```
<item num="557" name="Fleece Pullover" quan="1"/>
<item num="563" name="Floppy Sun Hat" quan="1"/>
<item num="443" name="Deluxe Travel Bag" quan="2"/>
<item num="784" name="Cotton Dress Shirt" quan="1"/>
<item num="784" name="Cotton Dress Shirt" quan="1"/>
<item num="557" name="Fleece Pullover" quan="1"/>
```

The for clause sets up an iteration through each item from the order. For each item, the let clause goes to the product catalog and gets the name of the product. It does this by finding the product element whose number child equals the item's num attribute, and selecting its name child. Because the FLWOR iterated six times, the results contain one new item element for each of the six item elements in the order document. Joins are covered in Chapter 6.

Aggregating and Grouping Values

One common use for XQuery is to summarize and group XML data. It is sometimes useful to find the sum, average, or maximum of a sequence of values, grouped by a particular value. For example, suppose you want to know the number of items contained in an order, grouped by department. The query shown in Example 1-12 accomplishes this. It uses a for clause to iterate over the list of distinct departments, a let clause to bind $items to the item elements for a particular department, and the sum function to calculate the totals of the quantity attribute values for the items in $items.

Example 1-12. Aggregating values

Query
```
for $d in distinct-values(doc("order.xml")//item/@dept)
let $items := doc("order.xml")//item[@dept = $d]
order by $d
return <department name="{$d}" totQuantity="{sum($items/@quantity)}"/>
```
Results
```
<department name="ACC" totQuantity="3"/>
<department name="MEN" totQuantity="2"/>
<department name="WMN" totQuantity="2"/>
```

Chapter 7 covers joining, sorting, grouping, and aggregating values in detail.

CHAPTER 2
XQuery Foundations

This chapter provides a brief overview of the foundations of XQuery: its design, its place among XML-related standards, and its processing model. It also discusses the underlying data model behind XQuery and the use of types and namespaces in queries.

The Design of the XQuery Language

The XML Query Working Group of the World Wide Web Consortium (W3C) began work on XQuery in 1999. It used as a starting point an XML query language called Quilt, which was itself influenced by two earlier XML query languages: XQL and XML-QL.

The working group set out to design a language that would:

- Be useful for both highly structured and semistructured documents
- Be protocol-independent, allowing a query to be evaluated on any system with predictable results
- Be a declarative language rather than a procedural one
- Be strongly typed, allowing queries to be "compiled" to identify possible errors and to optimize evaluation of the query
- Allow querying across collections of documents
- Use and share as much as possible with appropriate W3C recommendations, such as XML 1.0, Namespaces, XML Schema, and XPath

The XQuery recommendation includes 11 separate documents and over 1,000 printed pages. These documents are listed (with links) at the public XQuery web site at *http://www.w3.org/XML/Query*. The various recommendation documents are generally designed to be used by implementers of XQuery software, and they vary in readability and accessibility.

XQuery in Context

XQuery is dependent on or related to a number of other technologies, particularly XPath, XSLT, SQL, and XML Schema. This section explains how XQuery fits in with these technologies.

XQuery and XPath

XPath started out as a language for selecting elements and attributes from an XML document while traversing its hierarchy and filtering out unwanted content. XPath 1.0 is a fairly simple yet useful recommendation that specifies path expressions and a limited set of functions. XPath 2.0 has become much more than that, encompassing a wide variety of expressions and functions, not just path expressions.

XQuery 1.0 and XPath 2.0 overlap to a very large degree. They have the same data model and the same set of built-in functions and operators. XPath 2.0 is essentially a subset of XQuery 1.0. XQuery has a number of features that are not included in XPath, such as FLWORs and XML constructors. This is because these features are not relevant to selecting, but instead have to do with structuring or sorting query results.

The two languages are consistent in that any expression that is valid in both languages evaluates to the same value using both languages.

XPath 2.0 was built with the intention that it would be as backward-compatible with XPath 1.0 as possible. Almost all XPath 1.0 expressions are still valid in XPath 2.0, with a few slight differences in the way values are handled. These differences are identified in Chapter 25.

XQuery Versus XSLT

XSLT is a W3C language for transforming XML documents into other XML documents or, indeed, documents of any kind. There is a lot of overlap in the capabilities of XQuery and XSLT. In fact, the XSLT 2.0 standard is based upon XPath 2.0, so it has the same data model and supports all the same built-in functions and operators as XQuery, as well as many of the same expressions.

Some of the differences between XQuery and XSLT are:

- XSLT implementations are generally optimized for transforming entire documents; they load the entire input document into memory. XQuery is optimized for selecting fragments of data, for example, from a database. It is designed to be scalable and to take advantage of database features such as indexes for optimization.

- XQuery has a more compact non-XML syntax, which is sometimes easier to read and write (and embed in program code) than the XML syntax of XSLT.

- XQuery is designed to select from a collection of documents as opposed to a single document. FLWORs make it easy to join information across (and within) documents. Also, XSLT 2.0 stylesheets can operate on multiple documents, but XSLT processors are not particularly optimized for this less common use case.

Generally, when transforming an entire XML document from one XML vocabulary to another, it makes more sense to use XSLT. When your main focus is selecting a subset of data from an XML document or database, you should use XQuery. The relationship between XQuery and XSLT is explored further in Chapter 25.

XQuery Versus SQL

XQuery borrows ideas from SQL, and many of the designers of XQuery were also designers of SQL. The line between XQuery and SQL may seem clear; XQuery is for XML, and SQL is for relational data. However, increasingly this line is blurred, because relational database vendors are putting XML frontends on their products and allowing XML to be stored in traditionally relational databases.

XQuery is unlikely to replace SQL for the highly structured data that is traditionally stored in relational databases. Most likely, the two will coexist, with XQuery being used to query less-structured data, or data that is destined for an XML-based application, and SQL continuing to be used for highly structured relational data.

Chapter 24 compares XQuery and SQL, and describes how they can be used together.

XQuery and XML Schema

XML Schema is a W3C standard for defining schemas, that can be used to validate XML documents and to assign types to XML elements and attributes. XQuery uses the type system of XML Schema, which includes built-in types that represent common datatypes such as decimal, date, and string. XML Schema also specifies a language for defining your own types based on the built-in types.

If an input document to a query has a schema, the types can be used when evaluating expressions on the input data. For example, if your item element has a quantity attribute, and you know from the schema that the type of the quantity attribute is xs:integer, you can perform sorts or other operations on that attribute's value without converting it to an integer in the query. This also has the advantages of allowing the processor to better optimize the query and to catch errors earlier.

XQuery users are not required to use schemas. It is entirely possible to write a complete query with no mention of schemas or any of the schema types. However, a rich set of functions and operators are provided that generally operate on typed data, so it is useful to understand the type system and use the built-in types, even if no schema is present. Chapter 13 covers schemas in more detail.

Processing Queries

A simple example of a processing model for XQuery is shown in Figure 2-1. This section describes the various components of this model.

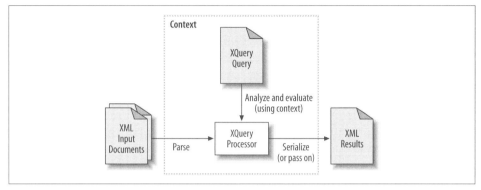

Figure 2-1. A Basic XQuery processor

XML Input Documents

Throughout this book, the term *input document* is used to refer to the XML data that is being queried. The data that is being queried can, in fact, take a number of different forms, for example:

- Text files that are XML documents
- Fragments of XML documents that are retrieved from the Web using a URI
- A collection of XML documents that are associated with a particular URI
- Data stored in native XML databases
- Data stored in relational databases that have an XML frontend
- In-memory XML documents

Some queries use a hardcoded link to the location of the input document(s), using the doc or collection function in the query. Other queries operate on a set of input data that is set by the processor at the time the query is evaluated.

Whether it is physically stored as an XML document or not, an input document must conform to other constraints on XML documents. For example, an element may not have two attributes with the same name, and element and attribute names may not contain special characters other than dashes, underscores, and periods.

The Query

An XQuery query could be contained in a text file, embedded in program code or in a query library, generated dynamically by program code, or input by the user on a

command line or in a dialog box. Queries can also be composed from multiple files, known as *modules*.

A query is made up of two parts: a *prolog* and a *body*. The query prolog is an optional section that appears at the beginning of a query. Despite its name, the prolog is often much larger than the body. The prolog can contain various declarations, separated by semicolons, that affect settings used in evaluating the query. This includes namespace declarations, imports of schemas, variable declarations, function declarations, and others. These declarations are discussed in relevant sections throughout the book and summarized in Chapter 12.

The query body is a single expression, but that expression can consist of a sequence of one or more expressions that are separated by commas. Example 2-1 shows a query with a prolog (the first three lines), and a body (the last two lines) that contains two element constructor expressions separated by a comma.

Example 2-1. A query with prolog and body

```
declare boundary-space preserve;
declare namespace prod = "http://datypic.com/prod";
declare variable $catalog := doc("catalog.xml")//catalog;

<firstResult>{count($catalog/product)}</firstResult>,
<prod:secondResult>{$catalog/product/number}</prod:secondResult>
```

The result of this query will be a `firstResult` element followed by a `prod:secondResult` element. If the comma after `firstResult` were not there, it would be a syntax error because there would be two separate expressions in the query body.

The Context

A query is not evaluated in a vacuum. The query context consists of a collection of information that affects the evaluation of the query. Some of these values can be set by the processor outside the scope of the query, while others are set in the query prolog. The context includes such values as:

- Current date and time, and the implicit time zone
- Names and values of variables that are bound outside the query or in the prolog
- External (non-XQuery) function libraries
- The context item, which determines the context for path expressions in the query

The Query Processor

The query processor is the software that parses, analyzes, and evaluates the query. The analysis and evaluation phases are roughly equivalent to compiling and executing program code. The analysis phase finds syntax errors and other static errors that

do not depend on the input data. The evaluation phase actually evaluates the results of the query based on input documents, possibly raising dynamic errors for situations like missing input documents or division by zero. Either phase may raise type errors, which result when a value is encountered that has a different type than expected. All errors in XQuery all have eight-character names, such as XPST0001, and they are described in detail in Appendix C.

There are a number of implementations of XQuery. Some are open source, while others are available commercially from major vendors. Many are listed at the official XQuery web site at *http://www.w3.org/XML/Query*. This book does not delve into all the details of individual XQuery implementations but points out features that are implementation-defined or implementation-dependent, meaning that they may vary by implementation.

The Results of the Query

The query processor returns a sequence of values as the results. Depending on the implementation, these results can then be written to a physical XML file, sent to a user interface, or passed to another application for further processing.

Writing the results to a physical XML document is known as *serialization*. There may be some variations in the way different implementations serialize the results of the query. These variations have to do with whitespace, the encoding used, and the ordering of the attributes. The implementation you use may allow you to have some control over these choices.

The XQuery Data Model

XQuery has a data model that is used to define formally all the values used within queries, including those from the input document(s), those in the results, and any intermediate values. The XQuery data model is officially known as the XQuery 1.0 and XPath 2.0 Data Model, or XDM. It is not simply the same as the Infoset (the W3C model for XML documents) because it has to support values that are not complete XML documents, such as sequences of elements (without a single outermost element) and atomic values.

Understanding the XQuery data model is analogous to understanding tables, columns, and rows when learning SQL. It describes the structure of both the inputs and outputs of the query. It is not necessary to become an expert on the intricacies of the data model to write XML queries, but it *is* essential to understand the basic components:

Node
 An XML construct such as an element or attribute

Atomic value
 A simple data value with no markup associated with it

Item
A generic term that refers to either a node or an atomic value

Sequence
An ordered list of zero, one, or more items

The relationship among these components is depicted in Figure 2-2.

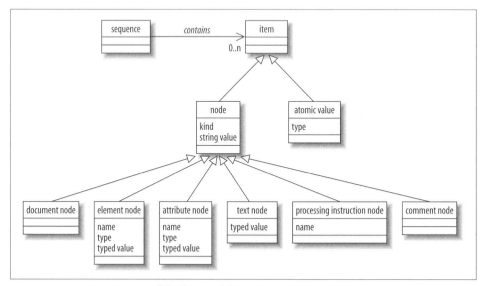

Figure 2-2. Basic components of the data model

Nodes

Nodes are used to represent XML constructs such as elements and attributes. Nodes are returned by many expressions, including path expressions and constructors. For example, the path expression doc("catalog.xml")/catalog/product returns four product element nodes.

Node kinds

XQuery uses six kinds of nodes:[*]

Element nodes
Represent an XML element

Attribute nodes
Represent an XML attribute

[*] The data model also allows for namespace nodes, but the XQuery language does not provide any way to access them or perform any operations on them. Therefore, they are not discussed directly in this book. Chapter 10 provides complete coverage of namespaces in XQuery.

Document nodes
> Represent an entire XML document (not its outermost element)

Text nodes
> Represent some character data content of an element

Processing instruction nodes
> Represent an XML processing instruction

Comment nodes
> Represent an XML comment

Most of this book focuses on element and attribute nodes, the ones most often used within queries. Generally, the book refers to them simply as "elements" and "attributes" rather than "element nodes" and "attribute nodes," unless a special emphasis on the data model is required. The other node kinds are discussed in Chapter 21.

The node hierarchy

An XML document (or document fragment) is made up of a hierarchy of nodes. For example, suppose you have the document shown in Example 2-2.

Example 2-2. Small XML example

```
<catalog xmlns="http://datypic.com/cat">
  <product dept="MEN" xmlns="http://datypic.com/prod">
    <number>784</number>
    <name language="en">Cotton Dress Shirt</name>
    <colorChoices>white gray</colorChoices>
    <desc>Our <i>favorite</i> shirt!</desc>
  </product>
</catalog>
```

When translated to the XQuery data model, it looks like the diagram in Figure 2-3.[*]

The node family

A family analogy is used to describe the relationships between nodes in the hierarchy. Each node can have a number of different kinds of relatives:

Children
> An element may have zero, one, or several other elements as its children. It can also have text, comment, and processing instruction children. Attributes are not considered children of an element. A document node can have an element child (the outermost element), as well as comment and processing instruction children.

[*] The figure is actually slightly oversimplified because, in the absence of a DTD or schema, there will also be text nodes for the line breaks and spaces in between elements.

Parent

> The parent of an element is either another element or a document node. The parent of an attribute is the element that carries it.*

Ancestors

> Ancestors are a node's parent, parent's parent, etc.

Descendants

> Descendants are a node's children, children's children, etc.

Siblings

> A node's siblings are the other children of its parent. Attributes are not considered to be siblings.

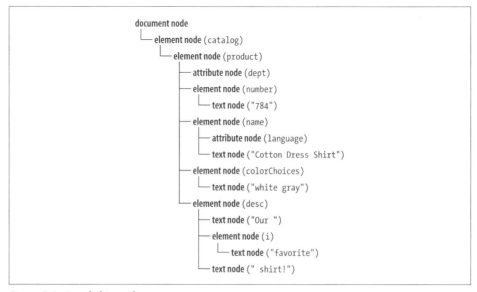

Figure 2-3. A node hierarchy

Roots, documents, and elements

A lot of confusion surrounds the term *root* in XML processing, because it's used to mean several different things. XML 1.0 uses the term *root element*, synonymous with *document element*, to mean the top-level, outermost element in a document. Every well-formed XML document must have a single element at the top level. In Example 2-2, the root element or document element is the catalog element.

XPath 1.0, by contrast, does not use the term *root element* and instead would call the catalog element the *document element*. XPath 1.0 has a separate concept of a *root*

* Even though attributes are not considered children of elements, elements *are* considered parents of attributes!

node, which is equivalent to a *document node* in XQuery (and XPath 2.0). A root node represents the entire document and would be the parent of the catalog element in our example.

This terminology made sense in XPath 1.0, where the input to a query was always expected to be a complete, well-formed XML document. However, the XQuery 1.0/ XPath 2.0 data model allows for inputs that are not complete documents. For example, the input might be a document fragment, a sequence of multiple elements, or even a sequence of processing instruction nodes. Therefore, the root is not one special kind of node; it could be one of several different kinds of nodes.

In order to avoid confusion, this book does not use either of the terms *root element* or *document element*. Instead, when referring to the top-level element, it uses the term *outermost element*. The term *root* is reserved for whatever node might be at the top of a hierarchy, which may be a document node (in the case of a complete XML document), or an element or other kind of node (in the case of a document fragment).

Node identity and name

Every node has a unique identity. You may have two XML elements in the input document that contain the exact same data, but that does not mean they have the same identity. Note that identity is unique to each node and is assigned by the query processor. Identity values cannot be retrieved, but identities can be compared with the is operator.

In addition to their identity, element and attribute nodes have names. These names can be accessed using the built-in functions node-name, name, and local-name.

String and typed values of nodes

There are two kinds of values for a node: string and typed. All nodes have a string value. The *string value* of an element node is its character data content and that of all its descendant elements concatenated together. The string value of an attribute node is simply the attribute value.

The string value of a node can be accessed using the string function. For example:

```
string(doc("catalog.xml")/catalog/product[4]/number)
```

returns the string 784, while:

```
string(<desc>Our <i>favorite</i> shirt!</desc>)
```

returns the string Our favorite shirt!, without the i start and end tags.

Element and attribute nodes also both have a typed value that takes into account their type, if any. An element or attribute might have a particular type if it has been validated with a schema. The typed value of a node can be accessed using the data function. For example:

```
data(doc("catalog.xml")/catalog/product[4]/number)
```

returns the integer 784, if the number element is declared in a schema to be an integer. If it is not declared in the schema, its typed value is still 784, but the value is considered to be *untyped* (meaning it does not have a specified type).

Atomic Values

An atomic value is a simple data value such as 784 or ACC, with no markup, and no association with any particular element or attribute. An atomic value can have a specific type, such as xs:integer or xs:string, or it can be untyped.*

Atomic values can be extracted from element or attribute nodes using the string and data functions described in the previous section. They can also be created from literals in queries. For example, in the expression @dept = 'ACC', the string ACC is an atomic value.

The line between a node and an atomic value that it contains is often blurred. That is because all functions and operators that expect to have atomic values as their operands also accept nodes. For example, you can call the substring function as follows:

```
doc("catalog.xml")//product[4]/substring(name, 1, 15)
```

The function expects a string atomic value as the first argument, but you can pass it an element node (name). In this case, the atomic value is automatically extracted from the node in a process known as atomization.

Atomic values don't have identity. It's not meaningful (or possible) to ask whether a and a are the same string or different strings; you can only ask whether they are equal.

Sequences

Sequences are ordered collections of items. A sequence can contain zero, one, or many items. Each item in a sequence can be either an atomic value or a node.

The most common way that sequences are created is that they are returned from expressions or functions that return sequences. For example, the expression doc("catalog.xml")/catalog/product returns a sequence of four items, which happen to be product element nodes.

A sequence can also be created explicitly using a sequence constructor. The syntax of a sequence constructor is a series of values, delimited by commas, surrounded by parentheses. For example, the expression (1, 2, 3) creates a sequence consisting of those three atomic values.

* Technically, if an atomic value is untyped, it is assigned a generic type called xs:untypedAtomic.

You can also use expressions in sequence constructors. For example, the expression:

```
(doc("catalog.xml")/catalog/product, 1, 2, 3)
```

results in a seven-item sequence containing the four product element nodes, plus the three atomic values 1, 2, and 3, in that order.

 Unlike node-sets in XPath 1.0, sequences in XQuery (and XPath 2.0) are ordered, and the order is not necessarily the same as the document order. Another difference from XPath 1.0 is that sequences can contain duplicate nodes.

Sequences do not have names, although they may be bound to a named variable. For example, the let clause:

```
let $prodList := doc("catalog.xml")/catalog/product
```

binds the sequence of four product elements to the variable $prodList.

A sequence with only one item is known as a singleton sequence. There is no difference between a singleton sequence and the item it contains. Therefore, any of the functions or operators that can operate on sequences can also operate on items, which are treated as singleton sequences.

A sequence with zero items is known as the empty sequence. In XQuery, the empty sequence is different from a zero-length string (i.e., "") or a zero value. Many of the built-in functions and operations accept the empty sequence as an argument, and have defined behavior for handling it. Some expressions will return the empty sequence, such as doc("catalog.xml")//foo, if there are no foo elements in the document.

Sequences cannot be nested within other sequences; there is only one level of items. If a sequence is inserted into another sequence, the items of the inserted sequence become full-fledged items of the new sequence. For example:

```
(10, (20, 30), 40)
```

is equivalent to:

```
(10, 20, 30, 40)
```

Quite a few functions and operators in XQuery operate on sequences. Some of the most used functions on sequences are the aggregation functions (min, max, avg, sum). In addition, union, except, and intersect expressions allow sequences to be combined. There are also a number of functions that operate generically on any sequence, such as index-of and insert-before.

Like atomic values, sequences have no identity. You can't ask whether (1,2,3) and (1,2,3) are the same sequence; you can only compare their contents.

Types

XQuery is a strongly typed language, meaning that each function and operator expects its arguments or operands to be of a particular type. This section provides some basic information about types that is useful to any query author. More detailed coverage of types in XQuery can be found in Chapter 11.

The XQuery type system is based on that of XML Schema. XML Schema has built-in simple types representing common datatypes such as xs:integer, xs:string, and xs:date. The xs: prefix is used to indicate that these types are defined in the XML Schema specification. Types are assigned to items in the input document during schema validation, which is optional. If no schema is used, the items are untyped.

The type system of XQuery is not as rigid as it may sound, since there are a number of type conversions that happen automatically. Most notably, items that are untyped are automatically cast to the type required by a particular operation. Casting involves converting a value from one type to another following specified rules. For example, the function call:

```
doc("order.xml")/order/substring(@num, 1, 4)
```

does not require that the num attribute be declared to be of type xs:string. If it is untyped, it is cast to xs:string. In fact, if you do not plan to use a schema, you can in most cases use XQuery without any regard for types. However, if you do use a schema and the num attribute is declared to be of type xs:integer, you cannot use the preceding substring example without explicitly converting the value of the num attribute to xs:string, as in:

```
doc("order.xml")/order/substring(xs:string(@num), 1, 4)
```

Namespaces

Namespaces are used to identify the vocabulary to which XML elements and attributes belong, and to disambiguate names from different vocabularies. This section provides a brief overview of the use of namespaces in XQuery for those who expect to be writing queries with basic use of namespaces. More detailed coverage of namespaces, including a complete explanation of the use of namespaces in XML documents, can be found in Chapter 10.

Many of the names used in a query are namespace-qualified, including those of:

* Elements and attributes from an input document
* Elements and attributes in the query results
* Functions, variables, and types

Example 2-3 shows an input document that contains a namespace declaration, a special attribute whose name starts with xmlns. The prod prefix is mapped to the namespace http://datypic.com/prod. This means that any element or attribute name in the document that is prefixed with prod is in that namespace.

Example 2-3. Input document with namespaces (prod_ns.xml)

```
<prod:product xmlns:prod="http://datypic.com/prod">
  <prod:number>563</prod:number>
  <prod:name language="en">Floppy Sun Hat</prod:name>
</prod:product>
```

Example 2-4 shows a query (and its results) that might be used to select the products from the input document.

Example 2-4. Querying with namespaces

Query
```
declare namespace prod = "http://datypic.com/prod";
for $product in doc("prod_ns.xml")/prod:product
return $product/prod:name
```
Results
```
<prod:name xmlns:prod="http://datypic.com/prod"
           language="en">Floppy Sun Hat</prod:name>
```

The namespace declaration that appears in the first line of the query maps the namespace http://datypic.com/prod to the prefix prod. The prod prefix is then used in the body of the query to refer to elements in the input document. The namespace (not the prefix) is considered to be a significant part of the name of an element or attribute, so the namespace URIs (if any) in the query and input document must match exactly. The prefixes themselves are technically irrelevant; they do not have to be the same in the input document and the query.

CHAPTER 3

Expressions: XQuery Building Blocks

The basic unit of evaluation in the XQuery language is the expression. A query contains expressions that can be made up of a number of sub-expressions, which may themselves be composed from other sub-expressions. This chapter explains the XQuery syntax, and covers the most basic types of expressions that can be used in queries: literals, variables, function calls, and comments.

Categories of Expressions

A query can range in complexity from a single expression such as 2+3, to a complex composite expression like a FLWOR. Within a FLWOR, there may be other expressions, such as $prodDept = "ACC", which is a comparison expression, and doc("catalog.xml")/catalog/product, which is a path expression. Within these expressions, there are further expressions, such as "ACC", which is a literal, and $prodDept, which is a variable reference.

The categories of expressions available are summarized in Table 3-1, along with the number of the chapter that covers them. Every expression evaluates to a sequence, which may be a single atomic value, a single node, the empty sequence, or multiple atomic values and/or nodes.

Table 3-1. Categories of expressions

Category	Description	Operators or keywords	Chapter
Primary	The basics: literals, variables, function calls, and parenthesized expressions		3
Comparison	Comparison based on value, node identity, or document order	=, !=, <, <=, >, >=, eq, ne, lt, le, gt, ge, is, <<, >>	3
Conditional	If-then-else expressions	if, then, else	3
Logical	Boolean and/or operators	or, and	3
Path	Selecting nodes from XML documents	/, //, .., ., child::, etc.	4
Constructor	Adding XML to the results	<, >, element, attribute	5

Table 3-1. Categories of expressions (continued)

Category	Description	Operators or keywords	Chapter	
FLWOR	Controlling the selection and processing of nodes	`for, let, where, order by, return`	6	
Quantified	Determining whether sequences fulfill specific conditions	`some, every, in, satisfies`	6	
Sequence-related	Creating and combining sequences	`to, union (), intersect, except`	9
Type-related	Casting and validating values based on type	`instance of, typeswitch, cast as, castable, treat, validate`	11, 14	
Arithmetic	Adding, subtracting, multiplying, and dividing	`+, -, *, div, idiv, mod`	16	

Keywords and Names

The XQuery language uses a number of keywords and symbols in its expressions. All of the keywords are case-sensitive, and they are generally lowercase. In some cases, a symbol (such as *) or keyword (such as in) has several meanings, depending on the context. The XQuery grammar is defined in such a way that these multiuse operators are never ambiguous.

Names are used in XQuery to identify elements, attributes, types, variables, and functions. These names must conform to the rules for XML qualified names, meaning that they can start with a letter or underscore and contain letters, digits, underscores, dashes, and periods. Like the keywords, they are also case-sensitive. Because there are no reserved words in the XQuery language, a name (for example, a variable or function name) used in a query may be the same as any of the keywords, without any ambiguity arising.

All names used in XQuery are namespace-qualified names. This means that they can be prefixed in order to associate them with a namespace name, and that they may be affected by default namespace declarations.

Whitespace in Queries

Whitespace (spaces, tabs, and line breaks) is allowed almost anywhere in a query to break up expressions and make queries more readable. You are required to use whitespace to separate keywords from each other—for example, order by cannot be written as orderby. Extra whitespace is acceptable, as in order by. By contrast, you are not required to use whitespace as a separator when using nonword symbols such as = and (. For example, you can use a=b or a = b.

In most cases, whitespace used in queries has no significance. Whitespace *is* significant in quoted strings, e.g., in the expression "contains spaces", and in constructed elements and attributes.

No special end-of-line characters are required in the XQuery language as they might be in some programming languages. Newline and carriage return characters are treated like any other whitespace.

Literals

Literals are simply constant values that are directly represented in a query, such as "ACC" and 29.99. They can be used in expressions anywhere a constant value is needed, for example the strings in the comparison expression:

```
if ($department = "ACC") then "accessories" else "other"
```

or the numbers 1 and 30 in the function call:

```
substring($name, 1, 30)
```

There are two kinds of literals: *string literals*, which must be enclosed in single or double quotes, and *numeric literals*, which must not. Numeric literals can take the form of simple integers, such as 1, decimal numbers, such as 1.5, or floating-point numbers, such as 1.5E2. The processor makes assumptions about the type of a numeric literal based on its format.

You can also use type constructors to convert your literal values to the desired type. For example, to include a literal date in an expression, you can use xs:date("2006-05-03"). For literal Boolean values, you can use the expressions true() and false().

Variables

Variables in XQuery are identified by names that are preceded by a dollar sign ($).[*] The names (not including the dollar sign) must conform to the definition of an XML-qualified name. This means that they can be prefixed, in which case they are associated with the namespace mapped to that prefix. If they are not prefixed, they are not associated with any namespace.

When a query is evaluated, a variable is bound to a particular value. That value may be any sequence, including a single node, a single atomic value, the empty sequence, or multiple nodes and/or atomic values. Once the variable is bound to a value, its value does not change. One consequence of this is that you cannot assign a new value to the variable as you can in most procedural languages. Instead, you must use a new variable.

[*] Variable names are most often preceded immediately by the dollar sign, but the XQuery syntax allows for whitespace between the dollar sign and the variable name.

Variables can be bound in several kinds of expressions: in global variable declarations, for or let clauses of a FLWOR, quantified expressions, or typeswitch expressions. For example, evaluation of the FLWOR:

```
for $prod in doc("catalog.xml")/catalog/product
return $prod/number
```

binds the $prod variable to a node returned by the path expression doc("catalog.xml")/catalog/product. The variable is then referenced in the return clause. Function declarations also bind variables to values. For example, the function declaration:

```
declare function local:addTwo ($value as xs:integer) as xs:integer
    { $value + 2 };
```

binds the $value variable to the value of the argument passed to it. In this case, the $value variable is referenced in the function body.

Function Calls

Function calls are another building block of queries. A typical function call might look like:

```
substring($prodName, 1, 5)
```

where the name of the function is substring and there are three arguments, separated by commas and surrounded by parentheses. The first argument is a variable reference, whereas the other two are numeric literals.

The XQuery language has over 100 built-in functions, detailed in Appendix A. Chapter 8 explains the details of how to read function signatures and call them. It also explains how to define your own functions.

Comments

XQuery comments, delimited by (: and :), can be added to any query to provide more information about the query itself. These comments are ignored during processing. XQuery comments can contain any text, including XML markup. For example:

```
(: This query returns the <number> children :)
```

XQuery comments can appear anywhere insignificant whitespace is allowed in a query. If they appear within quoted strings, or directly in the content of element constructors, they are not interpreted as comments. XQuery comments can be nested within other XQuery comments.

You can also include XML comments, delimited by <!-- and -->, in your queries. Unlike XQuery comments, these comments appear in the result document. They can include expressions that are evaluated, making them a useful debugging tool. XML comments are discussed further in Chapter 21.

Evaluation Order and Parentheses

A query can contain many nested expressions that are not necessarily delimited by parentheses. Therefore, it is important to understand which expressions are evaluated first. In most cases, the evaluation order (also known as the precedence) of expressions is straightforward. For example, in the expression:

```
if ($x < 12 and $y > 0) then $x + $y else $x - $y
```

it is easy to see that the if, then, and else keywords are all parts of the same expression that should be evaluated as a whole after all the sub-expressions have been evaluated. In the cases where it is not obvious, this book explains the evaluation order of that type of expression. For example, any and operators are evaluated before or operators, so that:

```
true() and true() or false() and false()
```

is the same as:

```
(true() and true()) or (false() and false())
```

If there is doubt in your mind regarding which expression is evaluated first, it is likely that others reading your query will be uncertain too. In this case, it is best to surround the expressions in question with parentheses. For example, you can change the previous if-then-else expression to:

```
if (($x < 12) and ($y > 0)) then ($x + $y) else ($x - $y)
```

The meaning is exactly the same, but the evaluation order is clearer. Parentheses can also be used to change the evaluation order. For example, if you change the true/false example to:

```
true() and (true() or false()) and false()
```

it now has a different value (false) because the or expression is evaluated first.

Comparison Expressions

Comparison expressions are used to compare values. There are three kinds of comparison expressions: general, value, and node.

General Comparisons

General comparisons are used for comparing atomic values or nodes that contain atomic values. Table 3-2 shows some examples of general comparisons. They use the operators = (equal to), != (not equal to), < (less than), <= (less than or equal to), > (greater than), and >= (greater than or equal to). Unlike in XSLT, you don't need to escape the < operator as <; in fact, it won't be recognized if you do.

Table 3-2. General comparisons

Example	Value
doc("catalog.xml")/catalog/product[2]/name = 'Floppy Sun Hat'	true
doc("catalog.xml")/catalog/product[4]/number < 500	false
1 > 2	false
() = (1, 2)	false
(2, 5) > (1, 3)	true
(1, "a") = (2, "b")	Type error

If either operand is the empty sequence, the expression evaluates to false.

General comparisons on multi-item sequences

General comparisons can operate on sequences of more than one item, as well as empty sequences. If one or both of the operands is a sequence of more than one item, the expression evaluates to true if the corresponding value comparison is true for any combination of two items from the two sequences. For example, the expression (2, 5) < (1, 3) returns true if one or more of the following conditions is true:

- 2 is less than 1
- 2 is less than 3
- 5 is less than 1
- 5 is less than 3

This example returns true because 2 is less than 3. The expression (2, 5) > (1, 3) also returns true because there are values in the first sequence that are greater than values in the second sequence.

General comparisons are useful for determining if any values in a sequence meet a particular criterion. For example, if you want to determine whether any of the products are in the ACC department, you can use the expression:

 doc("catalog.xml")/catalog/product/@dept = 'ACC'

This expression is true if *at least one* of the four dept attributes is equal to ACC.

General comparisons and types

When comparing two values, their types are taken into account. Values of like types (e.g., both numeric, or both derived from the same primitive type) can always be tested for equality using the = and != operators. However, a few types[*] do not allow their values to be compared using the other comparison operators such as < and >=. The processor may raise a type error if the two operands contain any incomparable values, as shown in the last row of Table 3-2.

[*] These types are xs:hexBinary, xs:base64Binary, xs:NOTATION, xs:QName, xs:duration, and all the date component types starting with g.

When comparing any two of the atomic values in each operand, if one value is typed, and the other is untyped, the untyped value is cast to the other value's type (or to xs:double if the specific type is numeric). For example, you can compare the untyped value of a number element with the xs:integer 500, as long as the number element's content can be cast to xs:double. If both operands are untyped, they are compared as strings.

Parentheses or Curly Braces?

One of the more confusing aspects of XQuery syntax to newcomers is the interaction of parentheses, commas, and curly braces ({ and }). Curly braces appear in very specific kinds of expressions, namely XML constructors, validate expressions, ordered and unordered expressions, and pragmas. Each of these kinds of expressions is discussed later in this book.

In the case of element and attribute constructors, commas can be used within curly braces to separate multiple expressions. For example, in the expression:

```
<myNewEl>{"a", "b", "c"}</myNewEl>
```

commas are used to separate the three expressions.

Parentheses are part of the syntax of specific kinds of expressions, too, such as function calls and around if expressions. In addition, parentheses, unlike curly braces, can be added around any expression to change the evaluation order, or simply to visually format a query.

Parentheses are also commonly used to construct sequences of multiple items. This is useful in cases where only one expression is expected but multiple values are desired. For example, an else expression can only consist of one expression, so if you would like to return two elements, you need to put them together as a sequence constructor, as in:

```
if (not($prod))
then (<empty/>)
else (<name>{data($prod/name)}</name>,
      <num>{data($prod/number)}</num>)
```

The parentheses around the name and num elements, and the comma that separates them, are used to combine them into a single expression. If they were omitted, the query processor would consider the num element to be outside the if-then-else expression.

At the top level of a query, you can omit the parentheses and just list individual expressions separated by commas. For example, to return all the product elements of the catalog, followed by all of the item elements from the order, your entire query can be:

```
doc("catalog.xml")//product, doc("order.xml")//item
```

The comma is used to separate the two expressions. All of the results of the first expression will appear first, followed by the results of the second expression.

Value Comparisons

Value comparisons differ fundamentally from general comparisons in that they can only operate on single atomic values. They use the operators eq (equal to), ne (not equal to), lt (less than), le (less than or equal to), gt (greater than), and ge (greater than or equal to). Table 3-3 shows some examples.

Table 3-3. Value comparisons

Example	Value
3 **gt** 4	false
"abc" **lt** "def"	true
doc("catalog.xml")/catalog/product[4]/ number lt 500	Type error, if number is untyped or nonnumeric
<a>3 gt <z>2</z>	true
<a>03 gt <z>2</z>	false, since a and z are untyped and treated like strings
(1, 2) eq (1, 2)	Type error

Unlike general comparisons, if either operand is the empty sequence, the empty sequence is returned. In this respect, the empty sequence behaves like null in SQL.

Each operand of a value comparison must be either a single atomic value, a single node that contains a single atomic value, or the empty sequence. If either operand is a sequence of more than one item, a type error is raised. For example, the expression:

```
doc("catalog.xml")/catalog/product/@dept eq 'ACC'
```

raises an error, because the path expression on the left side of the operator returns more than one dept attribute. The difference between general and value comparisons is especially important in the predicates of path expressions.

When comparing typed values, value comparisons have similar restrictions to general comparisons. The two operands must have comparable types. For example, you cannot compare the string "4" with the integer 3. In this case, one value must be explicitly cast to the other's type, as in:

```
xs:integer("4") gt 3
```

However, value comparisons treat untyped data differently from general comparisons. Untyped values are always treated like strings by value comparisons. This means that if you have two untyped elements that contain numbers, they will be compared as strings unless you explicitly cast them to numbers. For example, the expression:

```
xs:integer($prodNum1) gt xs:integer($prodNum2)
```

explicitly casts the two variables to the type xs:integer.

You also must perform an explicit cast if you are comparing the value of an untyped element to a numeric literal. For example, the expression:

```
doc("catalog.xml")/catalog/product[1]/number gt 1
```

will raise a type error if the number element is untyped, because you are essentially comparing a string to a number. Because of these complexities, you may prefer to use general comparisons if you are using untyped data.

USEFUL FUNCTION

between-inclusive

There is no built-in between function in XQuery, but you can easily write one:

```
declare namespace functx = "http://www.functx.com";
declare function functx:between-inclusive
  ($value as xs:anyAtomicType, $minValue as xs:anyAtomicType,
   $maxValue as xs:anyAtomicType) as xs:boolean  {

    $value >= $minValue and $value <= $maxValue

};
```

This function accepts any atomic value and an upper and lower bound. It does a simple value comparison and returns true if the value is between the bounds. To call this function, you might use the following function call to test whether a product number is between 1 and 500:

```
functx:between-inclusive ($prod/number, 1, 500)
```

This function is the first of many "useful functions" that are included in this book. You can use them not just as examples but also directly in your queries. The source for these functions (and many more) can be found at *http://www.xqueryfunctions.com*.

Node Comparisons

Another type of comparison is the node comparison. To determine whether two operands are actually the same node, you can use the is operator. Each of the operands must be a single node, or the empty sequence. If one of the operands is the empty sequence, the result is the empty sequence.

The is operator compares the nodes based on their *identity* rather than by any value they may contain. To compare the contents and attributes of two nodes, you can use the deep-equal built-in function instead.

Table 3-4 shows some examples of node comparisons. They assume that the variables $n1 and $n2 are bound to two different nodes.

Table 3-4. Node comparisons

Example	Value
`$n1 is $n2`	false
`$n1 is $n1`	true
`doc("catalog.xml")/catalog/product[1] is` `doc("catalog.xml")//product[number = 557]`	true
`doc("catalog.xml")/catalog/product[2]/@dept is` `doc("catalog.xml")/catalog/product[3]/@dept`	false

In the last example of the table, even though the second and third products have the same value for their dept attributes, they are two distinct attribute nodes.

Conditional (if-then-else) Expressions

XQuery allows conditional expressions using the keywords if, then, and else. The syntax of a conditional expression is shown in Figure 3-1.

Figure 3-1. Syntax of a conditional expression

The expression after the if keyword is known as the test expression. It must be enclosed in parentheses. If the test expression evaluates to true, the value of the entire conditional expression is the value of the then expression. Otherwise, it is the value of the else expression.

Example 3-1 shows a conditional expression (embedded in a FLWOR).

Example 3-1. Conditional expression

Query
```
for $prod in (doc("catalog.xml")/catalog/product)
return if ($prod/@dept = 'ACC')
       then <accessoryNum>{data($prod/number)}</accessoryNum>
       else <otherNum>{data($prod/number)}</otherNum>
```
Results
```
<otherNum>557</otherNum>
<accessoryNum>563</accessoryNum>
<accessoryNum>443</accessoryNum>
<otherNum>784</otherNum>
```

If the then expression and else expression are single expressions, they are not required to be in parentheses. However, to return the results of multiple expressions, they need to be concatenated together using a sequence constructor. For example, if in Example 3-1 you wanted to return an accessoryName element in addition to accessoryNum, you would be required to separate the two elements by commas and

surround them with parentheses, effectively constructing a sequence of two elements. This is shown in Example 3-2.

Example 3-2. Conditional expression returning multiple expressions

Query
```
for $prod in (doc("catalog.xml")/catalog/product)
return if ($prod/@dept = 'ACC')
       then (<accessoryNum>{data($prod/number)}</accessoryNum>,
            <accessoryName>{data($prod/name)}</accessoryName>)
       else <otherNum>{data($prod/number)}</otherNum>
```
Results
```
<otherNum>557</otherNum>
<accessoryNum>563</accessoryNum>
<accessoryName>Floppy Sun Hat</accessoryName>
<accessoryNum>443</accessoryNum>
<accessoryName>Deluxe Travel Bag</accessoryName>
<otherNum>784</otherNum>
```

The else keyword and the else expression are required. However, if you want the else expression to evaluate to nothing, it can simply be () (the empty sequence).

Conditional Expressions and Effective Boolean Values

The test expression is interpreted as an xs:boolean value by calculating its effective Boolean value. This means that if it evaluates to the xs:boolean value false, the number 0 or NaN, a zero-length string, or the empty sequence, it is considered false. Otherwise, it is generally considered true. For example, the expression:

```
if (doc("order.xml")//item) then "Item List: " else ""
```

returns the string Item List: if there are any item elements in the order document. The if expression doc("order.xml")//item returns a sequence of element nodes rather than a Boolean value, but its effective Boolean value is true. Effective Boolean values are discussed in more detail in Chapter 11.

Nesting Conditional Expressions

You can also nest conditional expressions, as shown in Example 3-3. This provides an "else if" construct.

Example 3-3. Nested conditional expressions

Query
```
for $prod in (doc("catalog.xml")/catalog/product)
return if ($prod/@dept = 'ACC')
       then <accessory>{data($prod/number)}</accessory>
       else if ($prod/@dept = 'WMN')
            then <womens>{data($prod/number)}</womens>
            else if ($prod/@dept = 'MEN')
                 then <mens>{data($prod/number)}</mens>
                 else <other>{data($prod/number)}</other>
```

Example 3-3. Nested conditional expressions (continued)

Results
```
<womens>557</womens>
<accessory>563</accessory>
<accessory>443</accessory>
<mens>784</mens>
```

Logical (and/or) Expressions

Logical expressions combine Boolean values using the operators and and or. They are most often used in conditional (if-then-else) expressions, where clauses of FLWORs and path expression predicates. However, they can be used anywhere a Boolean value is expected.

For example, when used in a conditional expression:

```
if ($isDiscounted and $discount > 10) then 10 else $discount
```

an and expression returns true if both of its operands are true. An or expression evaluates to true if one or both of its operands is true.

As with conditional test expressions, the effective Boolean value of each of the operands is evaluated. This means that if the operand expression evaluates to a Boolean false value, the number 0 or NaN, a zero-length string, or the empty sequence, it is considered false; otherwise, it is generally considered true. For example:

```
$order/item and $numItems
```

returns true if there is at least one item child of $order, and $numItems (assuming it is numberic) is not equal to 0 or NaN (i.e., not a number).

Evaluation Order of Logical Expressions

The logical operators have lower precedence than comparison operators do, so you can use:

```
if ($x < 12 and $y > 15) then ...
```

without parenthesizing the two comparison expressions.

You can also chain multiple and and or expressions together. The and operator takes precedence over the or operator. Therefore:

```
true() and true() or false() and false()
```

is the same as:

```
(true() and true()) or (false() and false())
```

and evaluates to true. It is *not* equal to:

```
true() and (true() or false()) and false()
```

which evaluates to false.

Negating a Boolean Value

You can negate any Boolean value by using the not function, which turns false to true and true to false. Because not is a function rather than a keyword, you are required to use parentheses around the value that you are negating.

The function accepts a sequence of items, from which it calculates the effective Boolean value before negating it. This means that if the argument evaluates to the xs: boolean value false, the number 0 or NaN, a zero-length string, or the empty sequence, the not function returns true. In most other cases, it returns false.

Table 3-5 shows some examples of the not function.

Table 3-5. Examples of the not function

Example	Return value
not(true())	false
not($numItems > 0)	false if $numItems > 0
not(doc("catalog.xml")/catalog/ product)	false if there is at least one product child of catalog in catalog.xml
not(())	true
not("")	true

There is a subtle but important difference between using the != operator and calling the not function with an expression that uses the = operator. For example, the expression $prod/@dept != 'ACC' returns:

- true if the $prod element has a dept attribute that is not equal to ACC
- false if it has a dept attribute that is equal to ACC
- false if it does not have a dept attribute

On the other hand, not($prod/@dept = 'ACC') will return true in the third case—that is, if the $prod element does not have a dept attribute. This is because the $prod/ @dept expression returns the empty sequence, which results in the comparison evaluating to false. The not function will negate this and return true.

Navigating Input Documents Using Paths

Path expressions are used to navigate input documents to select elements and attributes of interest. This chapter explains how to use path expressions to select elements and attributes from an input document and apply predicates to filter those results. It also covers the different methods of accessing input documents.

Path Expressions

A path expression is made up of one or more steps that are separated by a slash (/) or double slashes (//). For example, the path:

```
doc("catalog.xml")/catalog/product
```

selects all the product children of the catalog element in the catalog.xml document. Table 4-1 shows some other simple path expressions.

Table 4-1. Simple path expressions

Example	Explanation
doc("catalog.xml")/catalog	The catalog element that is the outermost element of the document
doc("catalog.xml")//product	All product elements anywhere in the document
doc("catalog.xml")//product/@dept	All dept attributes of product elements in the document
doc("catalog.xml")/catalog/*	All child elements of the catalog element
doc("catalog.xml")/catalog/*/number	All number elements that are grandchildren of the catalog element

Path expressions return nodes in document order. This means that the examples in Table 4-1 return the product elements in the same order that they appear in the catalog.xml document. More information on document order and on sorting results differently can be found in Chapter 7.

Path Expressions and Context

A path expression is always evaluated relative to a particular context item, which serves as the starting point for the relative path. Some path expressions start with a step that sets the context item, as in:

```
doc("catalog.xml")/catalog/product/number
```

The function call doc("catalog.xml") returns the document node of the catalog.xml document, which becomes the context item. When the context item is a node (as opposed to an atomic value), it is called the *context node*. The rest of the path is evaluated relative to it. Another example is:

```
$catalog/product/number
```

where the value of the variable $catalog sets the context. The variable must select zero, one or more nodes, which become the context nodes for the rest of the expression.

A path expression can also be relative. For example, it can also simply start with a name, as in:

```
product/number
```

This means that the path expression will be evaluated relative to the current context node, which must have been previously determined outside the expression. It may have been set by the processor outside the scope of the query, or in an outer expression.

Steps and changing context

The context item changes with each step. A step returns a sequence of zero, one, or more nodes that serve as the context items for evaluating the next step. For example, in:

```
doc("catalog.xml")/catalog/product/number
```

the doc("catalog.xml") step returns one document node that serves as the context item when evaluating the catalog step. The catalog step is evaluated using the document node as the current context node, returning a sequence of one catalog element child of the document node. This catalog element then serves as the context node for evaluation of the product step, which returns the sequence of product children of catalog.

The final step, number, is evaluated in turn for each product child in this sequence. During this process, the processor keeps track of three things:

- The context node itself—for example, the product element that is currently being processed
- The context sequence, which is the sequence of items currently being processed—for example, all the product elements
- The position of the context node within the context sequence, which can be used to retrieve nodes based on their position

Steps

As we have seen in previous examples, steps in a path can simply be primary expressions like function calls (doc("catalog.xml")) or variable references ($catalog). Any expression that returns nodes can be on the lefthand side of the slash operator.

Another kind of step is the *axis step*, which allows you to navigate around the XML node hierarchy. There are two kinds of axis steps:

Forward step
> This step selects descendents or nodes appearing after the context node (or the context node itself).

Reverse step
> This step selects ancestors or nodes appearing before the context node (or the context node itself).

In the examples so far, catalog, product, and @dept are all axis steps (that happen to be forward steps). The syntax of an axis step is shown in Figure 4-1.

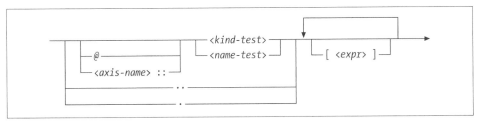

Figure 4-1. Syntax of a step in a path expression

Axes

Each forward or reverse step has an *axis*, which defines the direction and relationship of the selected nodes. For example, the child:: axis (a forward axis) can be used to indicate that only child nodes should be selected, while the parent:: axis (a reverse axis) can be used to indicate that only the parent node should be selected. The 12 axes are listed in Table 4-2.

Table 4-2. Axes

Axis	Meaning
self::	The context node itself.
child::	Children of the context node. Attributes are not considered children of an element. This is the default axis if none is specified.
descendant::	All descendants of the context node (children, children of children, etc.). Attributes are not considered descendants.
descendant-or-self::	The context node and its descendants.
attribute::	Attributes of the context node (if any).

Table 4-2. Axes (continued)

Axis	Meaning
following::	All nodes that follow the context node in the document, minus the context node's descendants.
following-sibling::	All siblings of the context node that follow it. Attributes of the same element are not considered siblings.
parent::	The parent of the context node (if any). This is either the element or the document node that contains it. The parent of an attribute is its element, even though it is not considered a child of that element.
ancestor::	All ancestors of the context node (parent, parent of the parent, etc.).
ancestor-or-self::	The context node and all its ancestors.
preceding::	All nodes that precede the context node in the document, minus the context node's ancestors.
preceding-sibling::	All the siblings of the context node that precede it. Attributes of the same element are not considered siblings.

An additional forward axis, namespace, is supported (but deprecated) by XPath 2.0 but not supported at all by XQuery 1.0. It allows you to access the in-scope namespaces of a node.

Implementations are not required to support the following axes: following, following-sibling, ancestor, ancestor-or-self, preceding, and preceding-sibling.

Node Tests

In addition to having an axis, each axis step has a node test. The *node test* indicates which of the nodes (by name or node kind) to select, along the specified axis. For example, child::product only selects product element children of the context node. It does not select other kinds of children (for example, text nodes), or other product elements that are not children of the context node.

Node name tests

In previous examples, most of the node tests were based on names, such as product and dept. These are known as name tests. The syntax of a node name test is shown in Figure 4-2.

Figure 4-2. Syntax of a node name test

Node name tests and namespaces

Names used in node tests are *qualified names*, meaning that they are affected by namespace declarations. A namespace declaration is in scope if it appears in an outer element, or in the query prolog. The names may be prefixed or unprefixed. If a name is prefixed, its prefix must be mapped to a namespace using a namespace declaration.

If an element name is unprefixed, and there is an in-scope default namespace declared, it is considered to be in that namespace; otherwise, it is in no namespace. Attribute names, on the other hand, are not affected by default namespace declarations.

Use of namespace prefixes in path expressions is depicted in Example 4-1, where the prod prefix is first mapped to the namespace, and then used in the steps prod:product and prod:number. Keep in mind that the prefix is just serving as a proxy for the namespace name. It is not important that the prefixes in the path expressions match the prefixes in the input document; it is only important that the prefixes map to the same namespace. In Example 4-1, you could use the prefix pr instead of prod in the query, as long as you used it consistently throughout the query.

Example 4-1. Prefixed name tests

```
Input document (prod_ns.xml)
<prod:product xmlns:prod="http://datypic.com/prod">
  <prod:number>563</prod:number>
  <prod:name language="en">Floppy Sun Hat</prod:name>
</prod:product>
Query
declare namespace prod = "http://datypic.com/prod";
<prod:prodList>{
  doc("prod_ns.xml")/prod:product/prod:number
}</prod:prodList>
Results
<prod:prodList xmlns:prod="http://datypic.com/prod">
  <prod:number>563</prod:number>
</prod:prodList>
```

Node name tests and wildcards

You can use wildcards to match names. The step child::* (abbreviated simply *) can be used to select all element children, regardless of name. Likewise, @* (or attribute::*) can be used to select all attributes, regardless of name.

In addition, wildcards can be used for just the namespace and/or local part of a name. The step prod:* selects all child elements in the namespace mapped to the prefix prod, and the step *:product selects all product child elements that are in any namespace, or no namespace.

Node kind tests

In addition to the tests based on node name, you can test based on node kind. The syntax of a node kind test is shown in Figure 4-3.

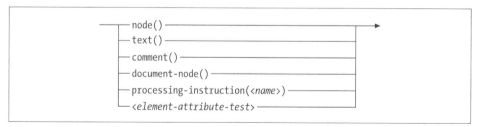

Figure 4-3. Syntax of a node kind test[a]

[a] The detailed syntax of `<element-attribute-test>` is shown in Figure 13-4.

The test `node()` will retrieve all different kinds of nodes. You can specify `node()` as the entire step, and it will default to the `child::` axis. In this case, it will bring back child element, text, comment, and processing-instruction nodes (but not attributes, because they are not considered children). This is in contrast to *, which selects child *element* nodes only.

You can also use `node()` in conjunction with the axes. For example, `ancestor::node()` returns all ancestor element nodes and the document node (if it exists). This is different from `ancestor::*`, which returns ancestor element nodes only. You can even use `attribute::node()`, which will return attribute nodes, but this is not often used because it means the same as `@*`.

Four other kind tests, `text()`, `comment()`, `processing-instruction()`, and `document-node()`, are discussed in Chapter 21.

If you are using schemas, you can also test elements and attributes based on their type using node kind tests. For example, you can specify `element(*, ProductType)` to return all elements whose type is `ProductType`, or `element(product, ProductType)` to return all elements named `product` whose type is `ProductType`. This is discussed further in the section "Sequence Types and Schemas" in Chapter 13.

Abbreviated Syntax

Some axes and steps can be abbreviated, as shown in Table 4-3. The abbreviations "." and ".." are used as the entire step (with no node test). "." represents the current context node itself, regardless of its node kind. Likewise, the step ".." represents the parent node, which could be either an element node or a document node.

Table 4-3. Abbreviations

Abbreviation	Meaning
.	self::node()
..	parent::node()
@	attribute::
//	/descendant-or-self::node()/

The @ abbreviation, on the other hand, replaces the axis only, so it is used along with a node test or wildcard. For example, you can use @dept to select dept attributes, or @* to select all attributes.

The // abbreviation is a shorthand to indicate a descendant anywhere in a tree. For example, catalog//number will match all number elements at any level among the descendants of catalog. You can start a path with .// if you want to limit the selection to descendants of the current context node.

Table 4-4 shows additional examples of abbreviated and unabbreviated syntax.

Table 4-4. Abbreviated and unabbreviated syntax examples

Unabbreviated syntax	Abbreviated equivalent
child::product	product
child::*	*
self::node()	.
attribute::dept	@dept
attribute::*	@*
descendant::product	.//product
child::product/descendant::name	product//name
parent::node/number	../number

Other Expressions As Steps

In addition to axis steps, other expressions can also be used as steps. You have already seen this in use in:

```
doc("catalog.xml")/catalog/product/number
```

where doc("catalog.xml") is a function call that is used as a step. You can include more complex expressions, for example:

```
doc("catalog.xml")/catalog/product/(number | name)
```

which uses the parenthesized expression (number | name) to select all number and name elements. The | operator is a union operator; it selects the union of two sets of nodes.

If the expression in a step contains an operator with lower precedence than /, it needs to be in parentheses. Some other examples of more complex steps are provided in Table 4-5.

Table 4-5. More complex steps (examples start with doc("catalog.xml")/catalog/)

Example	Meaning
product/(number \| name)	All number AND name children of product.
product/(* except number)	All children of product except number. See "Combining Results" in Chapter 9 for more information on the \| and except operators.
product/ (if (desc) then desc else name)	For each product element, the desc child if it exists; otherwise, the name child.
product/substring(name,1,30)	A sequence of xs:string values that are substrings of product names.

The last step (and only the last step) in a path may return atomic values rather than nodes. The last example in Table 4-5 will return a sequence of atomic values that are the substrings of the product names. An error is raised if a step that is *not* the last returns atomic values. For example:

```
product/substring(name,1,30)/replace(.,' ','-')
```

will raise an error because the substring step returns atomic values, and it is not the last step.

Predicates

Predicates are used in a path expression to filter the results to contain only nodes that meet specific criteria. Using a predicate, you can, for example, select only the elements that have a certain value for an attribute or child element, using a predicate like [@dept = "ACC"]. You can also select only elements that *have* a particular attribute child element, using a predicate such as [color], or elements that occur in a particular position within their parent, using a predicate such as [3].

The syntax of a predicate is simply an expression in square brackets ([and]). Table 4-6 shows some examples of predicates.

Table 4-6. Predicates (examples start with doc("catalog.xml")/catalog/)

Example	Meaning
product[name = "Floppy Sun Hat"]	All product elements that have a name child whose value is equal to Floppy Sun Hat
product[number < 500]	All product elements that have a number child whose value is less than 500
product[@dept = "ACC"]	All product elements that have a dept attribute whose value is ACC
product[desc]	All product elements that have at least one desc child
product[@dept]	All product elements that have a dept attribute
product[@dept]/number	All number children of product elements that have a dept attribute

If the expression evaluates to anything other than a number, its effective Boolean value is determined. This means that if it evaluates to the xs:boolean value false, the number 0 or NaN, a zero-length string, or the empty sequence, it is considered false. In most other cases, it is considered true. If the effective Boolean value is true for a particular node, that node is returned. If it is false, the node is not returned.

If the expression evaluates to a number, it is interpreted as the position as described in "Using Positions in Predicates" later in this chapter.

As you can see from the last example, the predicate is not required to appear at the end of the path expression; it can appear at the end of any step.

Note that product[number] is different from product/number. While both expressions filter out products that have no number child, in the former expression, the product element is returned. In the latter case, the number element is returned.

Comparisons in Predicates

The examples in the previous section use general comparison operators like = and <. You can also use the corresponding value comparison operators, such as eq and lt, but you should be aware of the difference. Value comparison operators only allow a single value, while general comparison operators allow sequences of zero, one, or more values. Therefore, the path expression:

```
doc("prices.xml")//priceList[@effDate eq '2006-11-15']
```

is acceptable, because each priceList element can have only one effDate attribute. However, if you wanted to find all the priceList elements that contain the product 557, you might try the expression:

```
doc("prices.xml")//priceList[prod/@num eq 557]
```

This will raise an error because the expression prod/@num returns more than one value per priceList. By contrast:

```
doc("prices.xml")//priceList[prod/@num = 557]
```

returns a priceList if it has *at least one* prod child whose num attribute is equal to 557. It might have other prod children whose numbers are not equal to 557.

In both cases, if a particular priceList does not have any prod children with num attributes, it does not return that priceList, but it does not raise an error.

Another difference is that value comparison operators treat all untyped data like strings. If we fixed the previous problem with eq by returning prod nodes instead, as in:

```
doc("prices.xml")//priceList/prod[@num eq 557]
```

it would still raise an error if no schema were present, because it treats the num attribute like a string, which can't be compared to a number. The = operator, on the other hand, will cast the value of the num attribute to xs:integer and then compare it to 557, as you would expect.

For these reasons, general comparison operators are easier to use than value comparison operators in predicates when children are untyped or repeating. The down side of general comparison operators is that they also make it less likely that the processor will catch any mistakes you make. In addition, they may be more expensive to evaluate because it's harder for the processor to make use of indexes.

Using Positions in Predicates

Another use of predicates is to specify the numeric position of an item within the sequence of items currently being processed. These are sometimes called, predictably, *positional predicates*. For example, if you want the fourth product in the catalog, you can specify:

```
doc("catalog.xml")/catalog/product[4]
```

Any predicate expression that evaluates to an integer will be considered a positional predicate. If you specify a number that is greater than the number of items in the context sequence, it does not raise an error; it simply does not return any nodes. For example:

```
doc("catalog.xml")/catalog/product[99]
```

returns the empty sequence.

Understanding positional predicates

With positional predicates, it is important to understand that the position is the position within the current sequence of items being processed, not the position of an element relative to its parent's children. Consider the expression:

```
doc("catalog.xml")/catalog/product/name[1]
```

This expression refers to the first name child of each product; the step name[1] is evaluated once for every product element. It does not necessarily mean that the name element is the first child of product.

It also does not return the first name element that appears in the document as a whole. If you wanted just the first name element in the document, you could use the expression:

```
(doc("catalog.xml")/catalog/product/name)[1]
```

because the parentheses change the order of evaluation. First, all the name elements are returned; then, the first one of those is selected. Alternatively, you could use:

```
doc("catalog.xml")/catalog/descendant::name[1]
```

because the sequence of descendants is evaluated first, then the predicate is applied. However, this is different from the abbreviated expression:

```
doc("catalog.xml")/catalog//name[1]
```

which, like the first example, returns the first name child of each of the products. That's because it's an abbreviation for:

```
doc("catalog.xml")/catalog/descendant-or-self::node( )/name[1]
```

The position and last functions

The position and last functions are also useful when writing predicates based on position. The position function returns the position of the context item within the context sequence (the current sequence of items being processed). The function takes no arguments and returns an integer representing the position (starting with 1, not 0) of the context item. For example:

```
doc("catalog.xml")/catalog/product[position( ) < 3]
```

returns the first two product children of catalog. You could also select the first two children of each product, with any name, using:

```
doc("catalog.xml")/catalog/product/*[position( ) < 3]
```

by using the wildcard *. Note that the predicate [position() = 3] is equivalent to the predicate [3], so the position function is not very useful in this case.

 When using positional predicates, you should be aware that the to keyword does not work as you might expect when used in predicates. If you want the first three products, it may be tempting to use the syntax:

```
doc("catalog.xml")/catalog/product[1 to 3]
```

However, this will raise an error* because the predicate evaluates to multiple numbers instead of a single one. You can, however, use the syntax:

```
doc("catalog.xml")/catalog/product[position( ) = (1 to 3)]
```

You can also use the subsequence function to limit the results based on position, as in:

```
doc("catalog.xml")/catalog/subsequence(product, 1, 3)
```

The last function returns the number of nodes in the current sequence. It takes no arguments and returns an integer representing the number of items. The last function is useful for testing whether an item is the last one in the sequence. For example, catalog/product[last()] returns the last product child of catalog.

Table 4-7 shows some examples of predicates that use the position of the item. The descriptions assume that there is only one catalog element, which is the case in the catalog.xml example.

* Although several implementations erroneously support this construct.

Table 4-7. Position in predicates (examples start with doc("catalog.xml")/catalog/)

Example	Description
product[2]	The second product child of catalog
product[position() = 2]	The second product child of catalog
product[position() > 1]	All product children of catalog after the first one
product[last()-1]	The second to last product child of catalog
product[last()]	The last product child of catalog
*[2]	The second child of catalog, regardless of name
product[3]/*[2]	The second child of the third product child of catalog

In XQuery, it's very unusual to use the position or last functions anywhere except within a predicate. It's not an error, however, as long as the context item is defined. For example, a/last() returns the same number as count(a).

Positional predicates and reverse axes

Oddly, positional predicates have the opposite meaning when using reverse axes such as ancestor, ancestor-or-self, preceding, or preceding-sibling. These axes, like all axes, return nodes in document order. For example, the expression:

```
doc("catalog.xml")//i/ancestor::*
```

returns the ancestors of the i element in document order, namely the catalog element, followed by the fourth product element, followed by the desc element. However, if you use a positional predicate, as in:

```
doc("catalog.xml")//i/ancestor::*[1]
```

you might expect to get the catalog element, but you will actually get the nearest ancestor, the desc element. The expression:

```
doc("catalog.xml")//i/ancestor::*[last( )]
```

will give you the catalog element.

Using Multiple Predicates

Multiple predicates can be chained together to filter items based on more than one constraint. For example:

```
doc("catalog.xml")/catalog/product[number < 500][@dept = "ACC"]
```

selects only product elements with a number child whose value is less than 500 *and* whose dept attribute is equal to ACC. This can also be equivalently expressed as:

```
doc("catalog.xml")/catalog/product[number < 500 and @dept = "ACC"]
```

It is sometimes useful to combine the positional predicates with other predicates, as in:

```
doc("catalog.xml")/catalog/product[@dept = "ACC"][2]
```

which represents "the second product child that has a dept attribute whose value is ACC," namely the third product element. The order of the predicates is significant. If the previous example is changed to:

```
doc("catalog.xml")/catalog/product[2][@dept = "ACC"]
```

it means something different, namely "the second product child, if it has a dept attribute whose value is ACC." This is because the predicate changes the context, and the context node for the second predicate in this case is the second product element.

More Complex Predicates

So far, the examples of predicates have been simple path expressions, comparison expressions, and numbers. In fact, any expression is allowed in a predicate, making it a very flexible construct. For example, predicates can contain function calls, as in:

```
doc("catalog.xml")/catalog/product[contains(@dept, "A")]
```

which returns all product children whose dept attribute contains the letter A. They can contain conditional expressions, as in:

```
doc("catalog.xml")/catalog/product[if ($descFilter)
                            then desc else true()]
```

which filters product elements based on their desc child only if the variable $descFilter is true. They can also contain expressions that combine sequences, as in:

```
doc("catalog.xml")/catalog/product[* except number]
```

which returns all product children that have at least one child other than number. General comparisons with multiple values can be used, as in:

```
doc("catalog.xml")/catalog/product[@dept = ("ACC", "WMN", "MEN")]
```

which returns products whose dept attribute value is any of those three values. This is similar to a SQL "in" clause.

To retrieve every third product child of catalog, you could use the expression:

```
doc("catalog.xml")/catalog/product[position() mod 3 = 0]
```

because it selects all the products whose position is divisible by 3.

Predicates can even contain path expressions that themselves have predicates. For example:

```
doc("catalog.xml")/catalog/product[*[3][self::colorChoices]]
```

can be used to find all product elements whose third child element is colorChoices. The *[3][self::colorChoices] is part of a separate path expression that is itself within a predicate. *[3] selects the third child element of product, and [self:: colorChoices] is a way of testing the name of the current context element.

Predicates are not limited to use with path expressions. They can be used with any sequence. For example:

```
(1 to 100)[. mod  5 = 0]
```

can be used to return the integers from 1 to 100 that are divisible by 5. Another example is:

```
(@price, 0.0)[1]
```

which selects the price attribute if it exists, or the decimal value 0.0 otherwise.

Dynamic Paths

It is a common requirement that the paths in your query will not be static but will instead be calculated based on some input to the query. For example, if you want to provide users with a search capability where they choose the elements in the input document to search, you can't use a static path in your query. XQuery does not provide any built-in support for evaluating dynamic paths, but you do have a couple of alternatives.

For simple paths, it is easy enough to test for an element's name using the name function instead of including it directly as a step in the path. For example, if the name of the element to search and its value are bound to the variables $elementName and $searchValue, you can use a path like:

```
doc("catalog.xml")//*[name() = $elementName][. = $searchValue]
```

If the dynamic path is more complex than a simple element or attribute name, you can use an implementation-specific function. Most XQuery implementations provide a function for dynamic evaluation of paths or entire queries. For example, in Saxon, it is the saxon:evaluate function, while in Mark Logic it is called xdmp:eval. In Saxon, I could use the following expression to get the same results as the previous example:

```
saxon:evaluate(concat('doc("catalog.xml")//',$elementName,
                      '[. = "',$searchValue,'"]'))
```

Input Documents

A single query can access many input documents. The term *input document* is used in this book to mean any XML data that is being queried. Technically, it might not be an entire XML document; it might be a document fragment, such as an element or sequence of elements, possibly with children. Alternatively, it might not be a physical XML file at all; it might be data retrieved from an XML database, or an in-memory XML representation that was generated from non-XML data.

If the input document is physically stored in XML syntax, it must be well-formed XML. This means that it must comply with XML syntax rules, such as that every start tag has an end tag, there is no overlap among elements, and special characters are used appropriately. It must also use namespaces appropriately. This means that if colons are used in element or attribute names, the part before the colon must be a prefix that is mapped to a namespace using a namespace declaration.

Whether it is physically stored as an XML document or not, an input document must conform to other constraints on XML documents. For example, an element may not have two attributes with the same name, and element and attribute names may not contain special characters other than dashes, underscores, and periods.

There are four ways that input documents could be accessed from within a query. They are described in the next four sections.

Accessing a Single Document

The doc function can be used to open one input document based on its URI. It takes as an argument a single URI as a string, and returns the document node of the resource associated with the specified URI.

Implementations interpret the URI passed to the doc function in different ways. Some, like Saxon, will dereference the URI, that is, go out to the URL and retrieve the resource at that location. For example, using Saxon:

```
doc("http://datypic.com/order.xml")
```

will return the document node of the document that can be found at the URL http://datypic.com/order.xml.

Other implementations, such as those embedded in XML databases, consider the URIs to be just names. The processor might take the name and look it up in an internal catalog to find the document associated with that name. The doc function is covered in detail in Appendix A.

Accessing a Collection

The collection function returns the nodes that make up a collection. A collection may be a sequence of nodes of any kind, identified by a URI. Exactly how the URI is associated with the nodes is defined by the implementation. For example, one implementation might accept a URI that is the name of a directory on a filesystem, and return the document nodes of the XML documents stored in that directory. Another implementation might associate a URI with a particular database. A third might allow you to specify the URI of an XML document that contains URIs for all the XML documents in the collection.

The function takes as an argument a single URI. For example, the function call:

```
collection("http://datypic.com/orders")
```

might return all the document nodes of the XML documents associated with the collection http://datypic.com/orders. It is also possible to use the function without any parameters, as in collection(), to retrieve a default collection as defined by the implementation.

 Some XQuery implementations support a function called input, with no arguments. This function appeared in earlier drafts of the XQuery recommendation but is no longer part of the standard. It is equivalent to calling the collection function with no arguments.

Setting the Context Node Outside the Query

The context node can be set by the processor outside the query. In this case, it may not be necessary to use the doc or collection functions, unless you want to open secondary data sources.

For example, a hypothetical XQuery implementation might allow you to set the context node in the Java code that executes the query, as in:

```
Document catalogDocument = new Document(File("catalog.xml"));
String query = "catalog/product[@dept = 'ACC']";
List productElements = catalogDocument.evaluateXQuery(query);
```

In that case, the XQuery expression catalog/product might be evaluated in the context of the catalog document node itself. If the processor had not set the context node, a path expression starting with catalog/product would not be valid.

Another implementation might allow you to select a document to query in a user interface, in which case it uses that document as the context node.

Using Variables

The processor can bind external variables to input documents or document fragments. These variables can then be used in the query to access the input document. For example, an implementation might allow an external variable named $input to be defined, and allow the user to specify a document to be associated with that variable. The hypothetical query processor could be invoked from the command line using:

```
xquery -input catalog.xml
```

and the query could use expressions like $input/catalog/product to retrieve the product elements. The name $input is provided as an example; the implementation could use any name for the variable.

You should consult the documentation for your XQuery implementation to determine which of these four methods are appropriate for accessing input documents.

A Closer Look at Context

The processor can set the context node outside the query. Alternatively, the context node can be set by an outer expression. In XQuery, the *only* operators that change the context node are the slash and the square brackets used in predicates.* For example:

```
doc("catalog.xml")/catalog/product/(if (desc) then desc else name)
```

In this case, the if expression uses the paths desc and name. Because it is entirely contained in one step of another (outer) path expression, it is evaluated with the context node being the product element. Therefore, desc and name are tested as children of product.

In some cases, no context node is defined. This might occur if the processor does not set the context node outside the scope of the query, as described earlier in "Setting the Context Node Outside the Query" and there is no outer expression that sets the context. In addition, the context node is never defined inside the body of a function. In these cases, using a relative path such as desc raises an error.

Working with the Context Node

It is sometimes useful to be able to reference the context node, either in a step or in a predicate. A prior example retrieved product elements whose number child is less than 500 using the expression:

```
doc("catalog.xml")/catalog/product[number < 500]
```

Suppose, instead, you want to retrieve the number child itself. You can do this using the expression:

```
doc("catalog.xml")/catalog/product/number[. < 500]
```

The period (.) is used to represent the context node itself in predicates and in paths. You can also use the period as a parameter to functions, as in:

```
doc("catalog.xml")/catalog/product/name[starts-with(., "T")]
```

which passes the context item to the starts-with function. Some functions, when they are not passed any arguments, automatically use the context node. For example:

```
doc("catalog.xml")/catalog/product/desc[string-length( ) > 20]
```

uses the string-length function to test the length of the desc value. It was not necessary to pass the "." to the string-length function. This is because the defined behavior of this particular function is such that if no argument is passed to the function, it defaults to the context node.

* This is in contrast to XSLT, where several kinds of expressions change the context node, including the xsl:for-each element and template matching.

Accessing the Root

When the context node is part of a complete XML document, the root is a document node (*not* the outermost element). However, XQuery also allows nodes to participate in tree fragments, which can be rooted at any kind of node.

There are several ways of accessing the root of the current context node. When a path expression starts with one forward slash, as in:

```
/catalog/product
```

the path is evaluated relative to the root of the tree containing the current context node. For example, if the current context node is a number element in the catalog.xml document, the path /catalog/product retrieves all product children of catalog in catalog.xml.

When a path expression starts with two forward slashes, as in:

```
//product/number
```

it is referring to any product element in the tree containing the current context node. Starting an expression with / or // is allowed only if the current context node is part of a complete XML document (with a document node at its root). / can also be used as an expression in its own right, to refer to the root of the tree containing the context node (provided this is a document node).

The root function also returns the root of the tree containing a node. It can be used in conjunction with path expressions to find siblings and other elements that are in the same document. For example, root($myNode)//product retrieves all product elements that are in the same document (or document fragment) as $myNode. When using the root function, it's *not* necessary for the tree to be rooted at a document node.

Adding Elements and Attributes to Results

Most queries include some XML elements and attributes that structure the results. In the previous chapter, we saw how to use path expressions to copy elements and attributes from input documents. After a brief review of this technique, this chapter explains how you can create entirely new elements and attributes and include them in your results.

There are two ways to create new elements and attributes: direct constructors and computed constructors. *Direct constructors*, which use an XML-like syntax, are useful for creating elements and attributes whose names are fixed. *Computed constructors*, on the other hand, allow for names that are generated dynamically in the query.

Including Elements and Attributes from the Input Document

Some queries simply include elements and attributes from the input document in the results. Example 5-1 includes certain selected name elements in the results.

Example 5-1. Including elements from the input document

Query
```
for $prod in doc("catalog.xml")/catalog/product[@dept = 'ACC']
return $prod/name
```
Results
```
<name language="en">Floppy Sun Hat</name>
<name language="en">Deluxe Travel Bag</name>
```

Note that because the entire name element is returned, the results include the name elements, not just their atomic values. In fact, if the query returns elements that have attributes and descendants, they are all part of the results. This is exhibited in Example 5-2.

Example 5-2. Including complex elements from the input document

Query
```
for $prod in doc("catalog.xml")/catalog/product[@dept = 'ACC']
return $prod
```
Results
```
<product dept="ACC">
  <number>563</number>
  <name language="en">Floppy Sun Hat</name>
</product>
<product dept="ACC">
  <number>443</number>
  <name language="en">Deluxe Travel Bag</name>
</product>
```

The product elements are included as they appear in the input document, with all attributes and children. If they are in a namespace in the input document, they will be in that same namespace in the results. There is no opportunity to add or remove children or attributes, or change the namespace name, when using path expressions. Techniques for making such modifications are covered later in this chapter.

Direct Element Constructors

You can also insert your own XML elements and attributes into the query results using XML constructors. There are two kinds of XML constructors: direct constructors, which use familiar XML-like syntax, and computed constructors, that allow you to generate dynamically the XML names used in the results.

A direct element constructor is a constructor of the first kind; it specifies an XML element (optionally with attributes) using XML-like syntax, as shown in Example 5-3. The result of the query is an XHTML fragment that presents the selected data.

Example 5-3. Constructing elements using XML-like syntax

Query
```
<html>
  <h1>Product Catalog</h1>
  <ul>{
    for $prod in doc("catalog.xml")/catalog/product
    return <li>number: {data($prod/number)}, name: {data($prod/name)}</li>
  }</ul>
</html>
```
Results
```
<html>
  <h1>Product Catalog</h1>
  <ul>
    <li>number: 557, name: Fleece Pullover</li>
    <li>number: 563, name: Floppy Sun Hat</li>
    <li>number: 443, name: Deluxe Travel Bag</li>
    <li>number: 784, name: Cotton Dress Shirt</li>
  </ul>
</html>
```

The h1, ul, and li elements appear in the results as XML elements. The h1 element constructor simply contains literal characters Product Catalog, which appear in the results as the content of h1. The ul element constructor, on the other hand, contains another XQuery expression enclosed in curly braces. This is known as an enclosed expression, and its value becomes the content of the ul element in the results. In this case, the enclosed expression evaluates to a sequence of li elements, which then appear as children of the ul element in the results. An enclosed expression may also evaluate to one or more atomic values, which appear in the results as character data.

The li element constructor contains a combination of both literal characters (the strings number: and , name:) and enclosed expressions, each of which evaluates to an atomic value. Any element constructor content outside curly braces is considered a literal, no matter how much it looks like an expression.

Direct element constructors use a syntax that looks very much like XML. The tags use the same angle-bracket syntax, the names must be valid XML names, and every start tag must have a matching end tag that is properly nested. In addition, prefixed names can be used, and even namespace declarations included. As with regular XML, the attributes of a direct element constructor must have unique names. But there are a few differences from real XML. For example, expressions within curly braces can use the < operator without escaping it.

As shown in Example 5-3, element constructors can contain literal characters, other element constructors, and enclosed expressions, in any combination.

Containing Literal Characters

Literal characters are characters that appear outside of enclosed expressions in element constructor content. Literal characters from Example 5-3 include the string Product Catalog in the h1 element constructor, and the string , name: in the li element constructor.

In addition, the literal characters can include character and predefined entity references such as and < and CDATA sections (described in Chapter 21). As in XML content, the literal characters may not include unescaped less-than (<) or ampersand (&) characters; they must be escaped using < and &, respectively.

When a curly brace is to be included literally in the content of an element, it must be escaped by doubling it, that is, {{ for the left curly brace, or }} for the right.

Containing Other Element Constructors

Direct element constructors can also contain other direct element constructors. In Example 5-4, the html element constructor contains constructors for h1 and ul. They are included directly within the content of html, without curly braces. No special separator is used between them. The p element constructor contains a combination of character

data content, a direct element constructor (for the element i), and an enclosed expression. As you can see, these three things can be intermingled as necessary.

Example 5-4. Embedded direct element constructors

Query
```
<html>
  <h1>Product Catalog</h1>
  <p>A <i>huge</i> list of {count(doc("catalog.xml")//product)} products.</p>
</html>
```
Results
```
<html>
  <h1>Product Catalog</h1>
  <p>A <i>huge</i> list of 4 products.</p>
</html>
```

Containing Enclosed Expressions

In Example 5-3, the enclosed expression of the ul element evaluates to a sequence of elements. In fact, it is possible for the enclosed expression to evaluate to a sequence of attributes or other nodes, atomic values, or even a combination of nodes and atomic values. It can even evaluate to a document node, in which case that document node is replaced by its children.

Enclosed expressions that evaluate to elements

As you have seen with the li elements, elements in the sequence become children of the element being constructed (in this case, ul). Atomic values, on the other hand, become character data content. If the enclosed expression evaluates to a sequence of both elements and atomic values, as shown in Example 5-5, the result element has mixed content, with the order of the child elements and character data preserved.

Example 5-5. Enclosed expressions that evaluate to elements

Query
```
for $prod in doc("catalog.xml")/catalog/product
return <li>number: {$prod/number}</li>
```
Results
```
<li>number: <number>557</number></li>
<li>number: <number>563</number></li>
<li>number: <number>443</number></li>
<li>number: <number>784</number></li>
```

The prior examples used the data function in enclosed expressions to extract the values of the elements number and name. In this example, the number element is included without applying the data function. The results are somewhat different; instead of just the number value itself, the entire number element is included.

Enclosed expressions that evaluate to attributes

If an element constructor contains an enclosed expression that evaluates to one or more attributes, these attributes become attributes of the element under construction. This is exhibited in Example 5-6, where the enclosed expression {$prod/@dept} has been added at the beginning of the li constructor content.

Example 5-6. Enclosed expressions that evaluate to attributes

```
Query
for $prod in doc("catalog.xml")/catalog/product
return <li>{$prod/@dept}number: {$prod/number}</li>
Results
<li dept="WMN">number: <number>557</number></li>
<li dept="ACC">number: <number>563</number></li>
<li dept="ACC">number: <number>443</number></li>
<li dept="MEN">number: <number>784</number></li>
```

The dept attribute appears in the results as an attribute of the li element rather than as content of the element. If the example had used the data function within the enclosed expression, the value of the dept attribute would have been the first character data content of the li element.

Enclosed expressions that evaluate to attributes must appear first in the element constructor content, before any other kinds of nodes.

Enclosed expressions that evaluate to atomic values

If an enclosed expression evaluates to one or more atomic values, those values are simply cast to xs:string and included as character data content of the element. When adjacent atomic values appear in the expression sequence, they are separated by a space in the element content. For example:

```
<li>{"x", "y", "z"}</li>
```

will return x y z, with spaces. To avoid this, you can use three separate expressions, as in:

```
<li>{"x"}{"y"}{"z"}</li>
```

Another option is to use the concat function to concatenate them together into a single expression, as in:

```
<li>{concat("x", "y", "z")}</li>
```

Enclosed expressions with multiple subexpressions

Enclosed expressions may include more than one subexpression inside the curly braces, using commas as separators. In Example 5-7, the enclosed expression in the li constructor contains four different subexpressions, separated by commas.

Example 5-7. Enclosed expressions with multiple subexpressions

Query
```
for $prod in doc("catalog.xml")/catalog/product
return <li>{$prod/@dept,"string",5+3,$prod/number}</li>
```
Results
```
<li dept="WMN">string 8<number>557</number></li>
<li dept="ACC">string 8<number>563</number></li>
<li dept="ACC">string 8<number>443</number></li>
<li dept="MEN">string 8<number>784</number></li>
```

The first subexpression, $prod/@dept, evaluates to an attribute, and therefore becomes an attribute of li.

The next two subexpressions, "string" and 5+3, evaluate to atomic values: a string and an integer, respectively. Note that they are separated by a space in the results.

The final subexpression, $prod/number, is an element, which is *not* separated from the atomic values by a space.

Specifying Attributes Directly

You have seen how attributes can be included with the result elements by including enclosed expressions that evaluate to attributes. Attributes can also be constructed directly using XML-like syntax. Attribute values can be specified using literal text or enclosed expressions, or a combination of the two.

In Example 5-8, class and dep attributes are added to the h1 and li elements, respectively. The class attribute of h1 simply includes literal text that is repeated in the results. The dep attribute of li, on the other hand, includes an enclosed expression that evaluates to the value of the dept attribute of that item. Do not let the quotes around the expression fool you; anything in curly braces is evaluated as an enclosed expression.

Example 5-8. Specifying attributes directly using XML-like syntax

Query
```
<html>
<h1 class="itemHdr">Product Catalog</h1>
<ul>{
  for $prod in doc("catalog.xml")/catalog/product
  return <li dep="{$prod/@dept}">number: {data($prod/number)
         }, name: {data($prod/name)}</li>
}</ul>
</html>
```
Results
```
<html>
<h1 class="itemHdr">Product Catalog</h1>
<ul>
  <li dep="WMN">number: 557, name: Fleece Pullover</li>
  <li dep="ACC">number: 563, name: Floppy Sun Hat</li>
```

```
  <li dep="ACC">number: 443, name: Deluxe Travel Bag</li>
  <li dep="MEN">number: 784, name: Cotton Dress Shirt</li>
</ul>
</html>
```

Note that the dep attribute will appear regardless of whether there is a dept attribute of the $prod element. If the $prod element has no dept attribute, the dep attribute's value will be a zero-length string. This is in contrast to Example 5-7, where li will have a dept attribute only if $prod has a dept attribute.

If literal text is used in a direct attribute constructor, it follows similar rules to the literal text in element constructors. Also, as with XML syntax, quote characters in attribute values must be escaped if they match the kind of quotes (single or double) used to delimit that value. However, you don't need to escape quotes appearing in an expression inside curly braces. The following example is valid because the inner pair of double quotes is inside curly braces:

```
  <li dep="{substring-after($prod/@dept, "-")}"/>
```

The evaluation of enclosed expressions in attribute values is slightly different from those in element content. Because attributes cannot themselves have children or attributes, the attribute value must evaluate to an atomic value. Therefore, if an enclosed expression in an attribute value evaluates to one or more elements or attributes, the value of the node(s) is extracted and converted to a string.

In Example 5-8, the enclosed expression {$prod/@dept} for the dep attribute of li evaluates to an attribute. The processor did not attempt to add a dept attribute to the dep attribute (which would not make sense). Instead, it extracted the value of the dept attribute and used this as the value of the dep attribute.

Just as in XML, you can specify multiple attributes on an element, as long as they have unique names. The order of the attributes is never considered significant in XML, so your attributes might not appear in your result document in the same order as you specified them in the query. There is no way to force the processor to preserve attribute order.

Declaring Namespaces in Direct Constructors

In addition to regular attributes, you can also include namespace declarations in direct element constructors. These namespace declaration attributes affect the element itself and all its descendants, and override any namespace declarations in the prolog or in outer element constructors. Example 5-9 shows the use of a namespace declaration in an element constructor. This is discussed in detail in the section "Namespace Declarations in Element Constructors" in Chapter 10.

Example 5-9. Using a namespace declaration in a constructor

Query
```
<xhtml:html xmlns:xhtml="http://www.w3.org/1999/xhtml">
  <xhtml:h1 class="itemHdr">Product Catalog</xhtml:h1>
  <xhtml:ul>{
    for $prod in doc("catalog.xml")/catalog/product
    return <xhtml:li class="{$prod/@dept}">number: {
                            data($prod/number)}</xhtml:li>
  }</xhtml:ul>
</xhtml:html>
```
Results
```
<xhtml:html xmlns:xhtml="http://www.w3.org/1999/xhtml">
  <xhtml:h1 class="itemHdr">Product Catalog</xhtml:h1>
  <xhtml:ul>
    <xhtml:li class="WMN">number: 557</xhtml:li>
    <xhtml:li class="ACC">number: 563</xhtml:li>
    <xhtml:li class="ACC">number: 443</xhtml:li>
    <xhtml:li class="MEN">number: 784</xhtml:li>
  </xhtml:ul>
</xhtml:html>
```

Use Case: Modifying an Element from the Input Document

Suppose you want to include elements from the input document but want to make minor modifications such as adding or removing a child or attribute. To do this, a new element must be created using a constructor. For example, suppose you want to include product elements from the input document, but add an additional attribute id that is equal to the letter P plus the product number. The query shown in Example 5-10 accomplishes this.

Example 5-10. Adding an attribute to an element

Query
```
for $prod in doc("catalog.xml")/catalog/product[@dept = 'ACC']
return <product id="P{$prod/number}">
          {$prod/(@*, *)}
       </product>
```
Results
```
<product dept="ACC" id="P563">
  <number>563</number>
  <name language="en">Floppy Sun Hat</name>
</product>
<product dept="ACC" id="P443">
  <number>443</number>
  <name language="en">Deluxe Travel Bag</name>
</product>
```

The query makes a new copy of the product element, which contains the enclosed expression {$prod/(@*, *)} to copy all of the attributes and child elements from the original product element. You could also use the broader expression {$prod/(@*, node())} to copy *all* the child nodes of the element, including text, comments, and processing instructions.

As another example, suppose you want to copy some product elements from the input document but remove the number child. This can be accomplished using the query in Example 5-11. The enclosed expression $prod/(@*, * except number) selects all the attributes and all of the child elements of product except number.

Example 5-11. Removing a child from an element

Query
```
for $prod in doc("catalog.xml")/catalog/product[@dept = 'ACC']
return <product>
          {$prod/(@*, * except number)}
       </product>
```
Results
```
<product dept="ACC">
  <name language="en">Floppy Sun Hat</name>
</product>
<product dept="ACC">
  <name language="en">Deluxe Travel Bag</name>
</product>
```

Additional examples of making "modifications" to elements and attributes can be found in the section "Copying Input Elements with Modifications" in Chapter 9.

Direct Element Constructors and Whitespace

Whitespace is often used in direct element constructors. For example, you may use line breaks and tabs to indent result XML elements for readability, or spaces to separate enclosed expressions. Sometimes the query author intends for whitespace to be significant (included in the results); sometimes it is just used for formatting the query for visual presentation.

Boundary whitespace

Boundary whitespace is whitespace that occurs by itself (without any nonwhitespace characters) in direct element constructors. It may appear between two element constructor tags, between two enclosed expressions, or between a tag and an enclosed expression. It can be made up of any of the XML whitespace characters, namely space, tab, carriage return, and line feed.

For example, in the constructor shown in Example 5-12, there is boundary whitespace in the ul constructor between the ul start tag and the left curly brace, as well as between the right curly brace and the ul end tag. In the li constructor, there is boundary whitespace between the li start tag and the b start tag, between the b end tag and the left curly brace, and between the right curly brace and the li end tag.

Example 5-12. Constructor with boundary whitespace

```
<ul>
  {  <li>  <b> number:</b> { $prod/number }  </li>   }
</ul>
```

With boundary whitespace discarded,[*] the results look something like:

```
<ul><li><b> number:</b><number>557</number></li></ul>
```

Note that the whitespace before the text `number:` is not discarded because it appears with other characters.

Whitespace inside enclosed expressions that is not in quotes is never considered significant. It is simply the normal whitespace allowed by XQuery syntax. In the `ul` constructor, the spaces between the left curly brace and the `li` start tag fall into this category. It is not technically considered boundary whitespace, and it is always discarded.

There is no boundary whitespace in attribute values. For example, in the expression:

```
<product dept="     {$d}     "/>
```

the whitespace between the quotes and the enclosed expression is considered significant and therefore is preserved. The expression:

```
<product dept="{     $d     }"/>
```

has no boundary whitespace either, only whitespace in an enclosed expression. This whitespace is *not* preserved. Line breaks are never preserved in attribute values; they are converted to spaces. This is a standard feature of XML itself, known as attribute value normalization.

The boundary-space declaration

By default, a query processor discards all boundary whitespace. Sometimes you want to preserve the boundary whitespace in your query results because it is significant. The boundary-space declaration, specified in the query prolog, instructs the processor how to handle boundary whitespace in direct element constructors.[†] Its syntax is shown in Figure 5-1.

The two valid values are:

`preserve`
> This value results in boundary whitespace being preserved.

`strip`
> This value results in boundary whitespace being deleted.

The default is `strip`. For example, the boundary-space declaration:

```
declare boundary-space preserve;
```

[*] Although the boundary whitespace will be discarded, if you choose to serialize your results, your processor may add whitespace to indent them. Therefore, your results may vary.

[†] By contrast, the `xml:space` attribute on a constructed element has no effect on boundary whitespace.

Figure 5-1. Syntax of a boundary-space declaration

causes whitespace to be preserved. With this boundary-space declaration, the result of the constructor in Example 5-12 becomes:

```
<ul>
  <li>  <b> number:</b> <number>557</number>  </li>
</ul>
```

Table 5-1 shows some additional examples of results with and without preserved whitespace.

Table 5-1. Stripping boundary whitespace

Expression	Value with boundary whitespace preserved	Value with boundary whitespace stripped
`<e>` `<c></c>` `</e>`	`<e>` `<c></c>` `</e>`	`<e><c></c></e>`
`<e> {"x"} </e>`	`<e> x </e>`	`<e>x</e>`
`<e> {()} </e>`	`<e> </e>`	`<e></e>`
`<e>{"x"} {"y"}</e>`	`<e>x y</e>`	`<e>xy</e>`
`<e> x {"y"}</e>`	`<e> x y</e>`	`<e> x y</e>`
`<e>{" x "}</e>`	`<e> x </e>`	`<e> x </e>`
`<e>{ "x" }</e>`	`<e>x</e>`	`<e>x</e>`
`<e> {"x"}</e>`	`<e> x</e>`	`<e> x</e>`
`<e> </e>`	`<e> </e>`	`<e></e>`

Forcing boundary whitespace preservation

If you don't want to preserve all whitespace but wish to preserve it in one or more specific elements, you can do this in one of two ways. The first way is to include an enclosed expression that evaluates to whitespace. For example, `<e>{" x "}</e>` evaluates to `<e> x </e>`, regardless of the boundary-space declaration. This is because the whitespace is part of the value of the expression (the literal string).

Another method is to use a character reference to a whitespace character. Whitespace that is the result of a character reference is always considered significant. For example, `<e> {"x"}</e>` always evaluates to `<e> x</e>`. Character references are described further in the section "XML Entity and Character References" in Chapter 21.

Computed Constructors

Generally, if you know the element or attribute name that you want to use in your results, you can use XML-like syntax as described in the previous sections. However, sometimes you may want to compute the name dynamically, so you cannot include the literal names in the query. In this case, you use computed constructors. This can be useful when:

- You want to simply copy elements from the input document (regardless of name) but make minor changes to their content. For example, to add an id attribute to every element, or to move all the elements to a different namespace.

- You want to turn content from the input document into element or attribute names. For example, you want to create an element whose name is the value of the dept attribute in the input document, without a predefined list of elements.

- You want to look up element names in a separate dictionary, e.g., for language translation purposes.

You can use computed constructors for elements, attributes, and other kinds of nodes.

Computed Element Constructors

A computed element constructor uses the keyword element, followed by a name and some content in curly braces. The syntax of a computed element constructor is shown in Figure 5-2.

Figure 5-2. Syntax of a computed element constructor

Example 5-13 shows a query that is equivalent to Example 5-3, except that it uses computed element constructors instead of direct ones.

Example 5-13. Simple computed constructor

Query
```
element html {
  element h1 { "Product Catalog" },
  element ul {
    for $prod in doc("catalog.xml")/catalog/product
    return element li {"number:",data($prod/number),", name:",data($prod/name)}
  }
}
```
Results
```
<html>
  <h1>Product Catalog</h1>
  <ul>
```

Example 5-13. Simple computed constructor (continued)

```
      <li>number: 557 , name: Fleece Pullover</li>
      <li>number: 563 , name: Floppy Sun Hat</li>
      <li>number: 443 , name: Deluxe Travel Bag</li>
      <li>number: 784 , name: Cotton Dress Shirt</li>
  </ul>
</html>
```

Names of computed element constructors

The name in a computed element constructor is represented by either a qualified name or an expression (in curly braces) that evaluates to a qualified name. This is then followed by an enclosed expression (also in curly braces) that contains the content of the element. For example, the constructor:

```
element h1 { "Product Catalog" }
```

uses a literal name to construct the element `<h1>Product Catalog</h1>`, while:

```
element {concat("h",$level)}  { "Product Catalog" }
```

uses an expression, enclosed in curly braces, to dynamically generate the name by concatenating the literal h with a variable value.

You could also copy the name of the new node from an existing node, using the node-name function. For example:

```
element {node-name($myNode)}  { "contents" }
```

will give the new element the same name as the node that is bound to the `$myNode` variable.

The expression used for the name can be untyped, or it can be either an `xs:QName` (which is what node-name returns) or an `xs:string` value. It can even be a node, in which case it is atomized to extract its typed value (not its name).

Default namespace declarations apply to element constructors. If you do not prefix your names, and you declare a default element namespace (e.g., in an outer expression or in the query prolog), the new elements are considered to be in that namespace.

Content of computed element constructors

After the name, the next part of the computed element constructor is an enclosed expression that contains the contents of the element, including attributes, character data, and child elements. As with direct XML constructors, any elements returned by the enclosed expression become children of the new element, attributes become attributes, and atomic values become character data content. Computed constructors have the same rule that the attributes must appear *before* any elements or character data.

The syntax is slightly different for computed constructors in that there can only be one pair of curly braces, containing the attributes and contents of the element. If several expressions are needed for the attributes, child elements, and character data content, they are separated by commas. For example, when using a direct element constructor, you can construct the li element this way:

```
<li>number: {data($prod/number)} , name: {data($prod/name)}</li>
```

where you intersperse literal text and enclosed expressions. To create an identical li element using a computed constructor, you would use the syntax:

```
element li {"number:", data($prod/number), ", name:", data($prod/name)}
```

Note that the literal text is in quotes and is separated from the expressions by commas. Also, the expressions, such as data($prod/number), are not themselves enclosed in curly braces as they were with the direct constructor.

The values of each of the four expressions in the li constructor will be separated by spaces in the results. If you do not wish to have those spaces in the results, you can use the concat function to concatenate the values together, as in:

```
element li {concat("number:", data($prod/number), ", name:", data($prod/name))}
```

If you want the constructed element to be empty, you can put nothing between the curly braces (as in { }), but the braces are still required.

Computed Attribute Constructors

A computed attribute constructor has syntax identical to a computed element constructor, except that it uses the keyword attribute. Its syntax is shown in Figure 5-3.

Figure 5-3. Syntax of a computed attribute constructor

For example, the constructors:

```
attribute myattr  { $prod/@dept }
```

and:

```
attribute {concat("my", "attr")}  { $prod/@dept }
```

both construct an attribute whose name is myattr and whose value is the same as the dept attribute of $prod. As with direct attribute constructors, any elements or attributes that are returned by the expression have their values extracted and converted to strings.

Computed attribute constructors are not just for use in computed element constructors. They can be used in direct element constructors as well, if they are included in an enclosed expression. For example, the expression:

```
<result>{attribute {concat("my", "attr")}  { "xyz" } }</result>
```

will return the result:

```
<result myattr="xyz"/>
```

You cannot construct namespace declarations using computed attribute constructors. If the name specified for an attribute constructor is xmlns, or a name whose prefix is xmlns, an error is raised. For example, the following constructor is invalid:

```
attribute xmlns:prod { "http://datypic.com/prod" }
```

Instead, you should declare the namespace in the query prolog or in an outer direct element constructor.

Use Case: Turning Content to Markup

One application of computed constructors is to transform content into markup. For example, suppose you want to create a product catalog that has the names of the departments as element names instead of attribute values. The query in Example 5-14 can be used for this purpose.

Example 5-14. Turning content into markup

Query
```
for $dept in distinct-values(doc("catalog.xml")/catalog/product/@dept)
return element {$dept}
              {doc("catalog.xml")/catalog/product[@dept = $dept]/name}
```
Results
```
<WMN>
  <name language="en">Fleece Pullover</name>
</WMN>
<ACC>
  <name language="en">Floppy Sun Hat</name>
  <name language="en">Deluxe Travel Bag</name>
</ACC>
<MEN>
  <name language="en">Cotton Dress Shirt</name>
</MEN>
```

In the results, the department names are now element names. The second expression in curly braces returns all the name elements for products in that department.

Computed constructors are also useful to recursively process elements regardless of their name. Example 5-10 showed how to add an id attribute to a product element. Suppose you wanted to add an id attribute to every element in a document, regardless of its name. It is necessary to use computed constructors for this, because you will not know the name of the constructed elements in advance. "Copying Input Elements with Modifications" in Chapter 9 shows some further examples of using computed constructors to generically handle elements with any name.

Selecting and Joining Using FLWORs

This chapter describes the facilities in XQuery for selecting, filtering, and joining data from one or more input documents. It covers the syntax of FLWORs (for, let, where, order by, return) and quantitative expressions.

Selecting with Path Expressions

Chapter 4 described how to use path expressions to select elements from input documents. For example, the expression:

```
doc("catalog.xml")//product[@dept = "ACC"]/name
```

can be used to select the names of all the products in the ACC department. You can add multiple predicates (expressions in square brackets) to filter the results based on more than one criterion. You can even add logical and other expressions to predicates, as in:

```
doc("catalog.xml")//product[@dept = "ACC" or @dept = "WMN"]/name
```

A path expression can be the entire content of a query; there is no requirement that there be a FLWOR expression in every query. Path expressions are useful for queries where no new elements and attributes are being constructed and the results don't need to be sorted. A path expression can be preferable to a FLWOR because it is more compact and some implementations will be able to evaluate it faster.

FLWOR Expressions

FLWOR expressions, also known simply as FLWORs, are used for queries that are more complex. In addition to allowing more readable and structured selections, they allow functionality such as joining data from multiple sources, constructing new elements and attributes, evaluating functions on intermediate values, and sorting results.

FLWOR (pronounced "flower"), stands for "for, let, where, order by, return," the keywords that are used in the expression. Example 6-1 shows a FLWOR that is equivalent to the second path expression from the previous section.

Example 6-1. FLWOR

```
for $prod in doc("catalog.xml")//product
let $prodDept := $prod/@dept
where $prodDept = "ACC" or $prodDept = "WMN"
return $prod/name
```

Of course, this is far more verbose, and for such a simple example, the path expression is preferable. However, this example is useful as an illustration before moving on to examples that are more complex. As you can see, the FLWOR is made up of several parts:

for
> This clause sets up an iteration through the product elements returned by the path expression. The variable $prod is bound, in turn, to each product in the sequence. The rest of the FLWOR is evaluated once for each product, in this case, four times.

let
> This clause binds the $prodDept variable to the value of the dept attribute.

where
> This clause selects elements whose dept attribute is equal to ACC or WMN.

return
> This clause returns the name child of each of the three product elements that pass the where clause.

The overall syntax of a FLWOR is shown in Figure 6-1. The details of the syntax of the for and let clauses are provided in the following sections.

Figure 6-1. Syntax of a FLWOR

There can be multiple for and let clauses, in any order, followed by an optional where clause, followed by an optional order by clause, followed by the required return clause. A FLWOR must have at least one for or let clause.

FLWORs can be the whole query, or they can appear in other expressions such as in the return clause of another FLWOR or even in a function call, as in:

```
max(for $prod in doc("catalog.xml")//product
    return xs:integer($prod/number))
```

The for and return keywords are aligned vertically here to make the structure of the FLWOR more obvious. This is generally good practice, though not always possible.

Let's take a closer look at the clauses that make up the FLWOR. The order by clause is covered in Chapter 7.

 XPath 2.0 does not support FLWORs, but instead supports a simplified subset called for expressions, which can only have one for clause and a return clause. Any for expression is also a valid FLWOR that returns the same results.

The for Clause

A for clause, whose syntax is shown in Figure 6-2, sets up an iteration that allows the rest of the FLWOR to be evaluated multiple times, once for each item in the sequence returned by the expression after the in keyword. This sequence, also known as the *binding sequence*, can evaluate to any sequence of zero, one or more items. In the previous example, it was a sequence of product elements, but it could also be atomic values, or nodes of any kind, or a mixture of items. If the binding sequence is the empty sequence, the rest of the FLWOR is simply not evaluated (it iterates zero times).

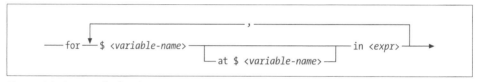

Figure 6-2. Syntax of a for clause[a]

[a] The at clause, which allows for positional variables, is described in "Working with Positions and Sequence Numbers" in Chapter 9. An additional as clause, useful for static typing, is allowed as part of the first variable declaration; this is described in "Type Declarations in FLWORs" in Chapter 14.

The FLWOR expression with its for clause is similar to loops in procedural languages such as C. However, one key difference is that in XQuery, because it is a functional language, the iterations are considered to be in no particular order. They do not necessarily occur sequentially, one after the other. One manifestation of this is that you cannot keep variable counters that are incremented with each iteration, or continuously append to the end of a string variable with each iteration. "Working with Positions and Sequence Numbers" in Chapter 9 provides more information about simulating counters.

Range expressions

Another useful technique is to supply a sequence of integers in the for clause in order to specify the number of times to iterate. This can be accomplished through a range expression, which creates a sequence of consecutive integers. For example, the

range expression 1 to 3 evaluates to a sequence of integers (1, 2, 3). The FLWOR shown in Example 6-2 iterates three times and returns three oneEval elements.

Example 6-2. Using a range expression

Query
```
for $i in 1 to 3
return <oneEval>{$i}</oneEval>
```
Result
```
<oneEval>1</oneEval>
<oneEval>2</oneEval>
<oneEval>3</oneEval>
```

Range expressions can be included within parenthesized expressions, as in (1 to 3, 6, 8 to 10). They can also use variables, as in 1 to $prodCount. Each of the expressions before and after the to keyword must evaluate to an integer.

If the first integer is greater than the second, as in 3 to 1, or if either operand is the empty sequence, the expression evaluates to the empty sequence. The reason for this is to ensure that for $i in 1 to count($seq) does the expected thing even if $seq is an empty sequence.

You can use the reverse function if you want to descend in value, as in:

```
for $i in reverse(1 to 3)
```

You can also increment by some value other than 1 using an expression like:

```
for $i in (1 to 100)[. mod 2 = 0]
```

which gives you every other number (2, 4, 6, etc.) up to 100.

Multiple for clauses

You can use multiple for clauses in a FLWOR, which is similar to nested loops in a programming language. The result is that the rest of the FLWOR is evaluated for every combination of the values of the variables. Example 6-3 shows a query with two for clauses, and demonstrates the order of the results.

Example 6-3. Multiple for clauses

Query
```
for $i in (1, 2)
for $j in ("a", "b")
return <oneEval>i is {$i} and j is {$j}</oneEval>
```
Result
```
<oneEval>i is 1 and j is a</oneEval>
<oneEval>i is 1 and j is b</oneEval>
<oneEval>i is 2 and j is a</oneEval>
<oneEval>i is 2 and j is b</oneEval>
```

The order is significant; it uses the first value of the first variable ($i) and iterates over the values of the second variable ($j), then takes the second value of $i and iterates over the values of $j.

Also, multiple variables can be bound in a single for clause, separated by commas. This has the same effect as using multiple for clauses. The example shown in Example 6-4 returns the same results as Example 6-3. This syntax is shorter but can be less clear in the case of complex expressions.

Example 6-4. Multiple variable bindings in one for clause

```
for $i in (1, 2), $j in ("a", "b")
return <oneEval>i is {$i} and j is {$j}</oneEval>
```

Specifying multiple variable bindings (or multiple for clauses) is especially useful for joining data. This is described further in the section "Joins," later in this chapter.

The let Clause

A let clause is a convenient way to bind a variable to a value. Unlike a for clause, a let clause does not result in iteration; it binds the whole sequence to the variable rather than binding each item in turn. The let clause serves as a programmatic convenience that avoids repeating the same expression multiple times. Using some implementations, it can also improve performance, because the expression is evaluated only once instead of each time it is needed.

The syntax of a let clause is shown in Figure 6-3.

Figure 6-3. Syntax of a let clause

To illustrate the difference between for and let clauses, compare Example 6-5 with Example 6-2.

Example 6-5. Using a let clause with a range expression

Query
```
let $i := (1 to 3)
return <oneEval>{$i}</oneEval>
```
Result
```
<oneEval>1 2 3<oneEval>
```

The FLWOR with the let clause returns only a single oneEval element, because no iteration takes place and the return clause is evaluated only once.

One or more let clauses can be intermingled with one or more for clauses. Each of the let and for clauses may reference a variable bound in any previous clause. The only requirement is that they all appear before any where, order by, or return clauses of that FLWOR. Example 6-6 shows such a FLWOR.

Example 6-6. Intermingled for and let clauses

```
let $doc := doc("catalog.xml")
for $prod in $doc//product
let $prodDept := $prod/@dept
let $prodName := $prod/name
where $prodDept = "ACC" or $prodDept = "WMN"
return $prodName
```

As with for clauses, adjacent let clauses can be represented using a slightly short-ened syntax that replaces the let keyword with a comma, as in:

```
let $prodDept := $prod/@dept, $prodName := $prod/name
```

Another handy use for the let clause is to perform several functions or operations in order. For example, suppose I want to take a string and replace all instances of at with @, replace all instances of dot with a period (.), and remove any remaining spaces. I could write the expression:

```
replace(replace(replace($myString,'at','@'),'dot','.'),' ','')
```

but that is difficult to read and debug, especially as more functions are added. An alternative is the expression:

```
let $myString2 := replace($myString,'at','@')
let $myString3 := replace($myString2,'dot','.')
let $myString4 := replace($myString3,' ','')
return $myString4
```

which makes the query clearer.

The where Clause

The where clause is used to specify criteria that filter the results of the FLWOR. The where clause can reference variables that were bound by a for or let clause. For example:

```
where $prodDept = "ACC" or $prodDept = "WMN"
```

references the $prodDept variable. In addition to expressing complex filters, the where clause is also very useful for joins.

Only one where clause can be included per FLWOR, but it can be composed of many expressions joined by and and or keywords, as shown in Example 6-7.

Example 6-7. A where clause with multiple expressions

```
for $prod in doc("catalog.xml")//product
let $prodDept := $prod/@dept
where $prod/number > 100
      and starts-with($prod/name, "F")
      and exists($prod/colorChoices)
      and ($prodDept = "ACC" or $prodDept = "WMN")
return $prod
```

Note that when using paths within the where clause, they need to start with an expression that sets the context. For example, it has to say $prod/number > 100 rather than just number > 100. Otherwise, the processor does not know where to look for the number child.

The effective Boolean value of the where expression is calculated. This means that if the where expression evaluates to a Boolean value false, a zero-length string, the number 0 or NaN, or the empty sequence, it is considered false, and the return expression is not evaluated. If the effective Boolean value is true, the return expression *is* evaluated. For example, you could use:

```
where $prod/name
```

which returns true if $prod has a name child, and false if it does not. As another example, you could use:

```
where $numProds
```

which returns true if $numProds is a numeric value that is not zero (and not NaN). However, these types of expressions are somewhat cryptic, and it is preferable to use clearer expressions, such as:

```
where exists($prod/name)
and $numProds > 0
```

The return Clause

The return clause consists of the return keyword followed by the single expression that is to be returned. It is evaluated once for each iteration, assuming the where expression evaluated to true. The result value of the entire FLWOR is a sequence of items returned by each evaluation of the return clause. For example, the value of the entire FLWOR:

```
for $i in (1 to 3)
return <oneEval>{$i}</oneEval>
```

is a sequence of three oneEval elements, one for each time the return clause was evaluated.

If more than one expression is to be included in the return clause, they can be combined in a sequence. For example, the FLWOR:

```
for $i in (1 to 3)
return (<one>{$i}</one>, <two>{$i}</two>)
```

returns a sequence of six elements, two for each time the return clause is evaluated. The parentheses and comma are used in the return clause to indicate that a sequence of the two elements should be returned. If no parentheses or comma were used, the two element constructors would not be considered part of the FLWOR.

The Scope of Variables

When a variable is bound in a for or let clause, it can be referenced anywhere in that FLWOR after the clause that binds it. For example, if it is bound in a let clause, it can be referenced anywhere in the FLWOR after that let clause. This includes other subsequent let or for clauses, the where clause, or the return clause. It cannot be referenced in a for clause that precedes the let clause, and it should not be referenced in the let clause itself, as in:

```
let $count := $count + 1
```

This is not illegal, but it will have unexpected results, as described in "Adding Sequence Numbers to Results" in Chapter 9.

If you bind two variables with the same name with the same containing expression, such as two for or let clauses that are part of the same FLWOR, you may again get unexpected results. This is because it will create two separate variables with the same name, where the second masks the first and makes it inaccessible.

Quantified Expressions

A quantified expression determines whether some or all of the items in a sequence meet a particular condition. For example, if you want to know whether any of the items in an order are from the accessory department, you can use the expression shown in Example 6-8. This expression will return true.

Example 6-8. Quantified expression using the some keyword

```
some $dept in doc("catalog.xml")//product/@dept
satisfies ($dept = "ACC")
```

Alternatively, if you want to know if *every* item in an order is from the accessory department, you can simply change the word some to every, as shown in Example 6-9. This expression will return false.

Example 6-9. Quantified expression using the every keyword

```
every $dept in doc("catalog.xml")//product/@dept
satisfies ($dept = "ACC")
```

A quantified expression always evaluates to a Boolean value (true or false). As such, it is not useful for selecting the elements or attributes that meet certain criteria, but rather for simply determining whether any exist. Quantified expressions can generally be easily rewritten as FLWORs or even as simple path expressions. However, the quantified expression can be more compact and easier for implementations to optimize.

A quantified expression is made of several parts:

- A quantifier (the keyword some or every)
- One or more in clauses that bind variables to sequences
- A satisfies clause that contains the test expression

The syntax of a quantified expression is shown in Figure 6-4.

Figure 6-4. Syntax of a quantified expression[a]

[a] An additional as clause, useful for static typing, is allowed as part of the variable declaration; this is described in "Type Declarations in Quantified Expressions" in Chapter 14.

The processor tests the satisfies expression (using its effective Boolean value) for every item in the sequence. If the quantifier is some, it returns true if the satisfies expression is true for any of the items. If the quantifier is every, it returns true only if the satisfies expression is true for all items. If there are no items in the sequence, an expression with some always returns false, while an expression with every always returns true.

You can use the not function with a quantified expression to express "not any" (none), and "not every." Example 6-10 returns true if *none* of the product elements have a dept attribute equal to ACC. For our particular catalog, this returns false.

Example 6-10. Combining the not function with a quantified expression

```
not(some $dept in doc("catalog.xml")//product/@dept
    satisfies ($dept = "ACC"))
```

Binding Multiple Variables

You can bind multiple variables in a quantified expression by separating the clauses with commas. As with the for clauses of FLWORs, the result is that every combination of the items in the sequences is taken. Example 6-11 returns true because there is a combination of values (where $i is 3 and $j is 10) where the satisfies expression is true.

Example 6-11. Binding multiple variables in a quantified expression

```
some $i in (1 to 3), $j in (10, 11)
  satisfies $j - $i = 7
```

Selecting Distinct Values

The `distinct-values` function selects distinct atomic values from a sequence. For example, the function call:

```
distinct-values(doc("catalog.xml")//product/@dept)
```

returns all the distinct values of the dept attribute, namely ("WMN", "ACC", "MEN"). This function determines whether two values are distinct based on their value equality using the eq operator.

It is also common to select a distinct set of combinations of values. For example, you might want to select all the distinct department/product number combinations from the product catalog. You cannot use the `distinct-values` function directly for this, because it accepts only one sequence of atomic values, not multiple sequences of multiple values. Instead, you could use the expression shown in Example 6-12.

Example 6-12. Distinctness on a combination of values

Query
```
let $prods := doc("catalog.xml")//product
for $d in distinct-values($prods/@dept),
    $n in distinct-values($prods[@dept = $d]/number)
return <result dept="{$d}" number="{$n}"/>
```
Results
```
<result dept="WMN" number="557"/>
<result dept="ACC" number="563"/>
<result dept="ACC" number="443"/>
<result dept="MEN" number="784"/>
```

For each distinct department, assigned to $d, it generates a list of distinct product numbers *within that department* using the predicate [@dept = $d]. It then returns the resulting combination of values as a `result` element. The order in which the values are returned is implementation-dependent, so it can be unpredictable.

Additional data items can be added by adding for clauses with the appropriate predicates.

Joins

One of the major benefits of FLWORs is that they can easily join data from multiple sources. For example, suppose you want to join information from your product catalog (catalog.xml) and your order (order.xml). You want a list of all the items in the order, along with their number, name, and quantity. Example 6-13 shows a FLWOR that performs this join.

distinct-deep

Suppose you want to find distinct elements based on all of their children and attributes. You could use an expression similar to the one shown in Example 6-12, but it could get complicated if there are many elements and attributes to compare. Also, you would be required to know the names of all the attributes and child elements in advance. A more generic function, shown here, can be used to select distinct nodes based on all of their contents:

```
declare namespace functx = "http://www.functx.com";
declare function functx:distinct-deep ($nodes as node()*) as node( )*
  {
    for $x in (1 to count($nodes))
    let $node := $nodes[$x]
    let $restOfNodes := subsequence($nodes, $x + 1)
    return if (some $otherNode in $restOfNodes satisfies
             (deep-equal($otherNode, $node)))
           then ( )
           else $node
  };
```

For each node in a sequence, the function determines whether the node has the same contents as any nodes that occur later in the sequence. Any nodes that have later matches are eliminated. The function makes use of the deep-equal function, which compares two elements based on their attributes and children. It is also a good example of the usefulness of quantified expressions.

For example, suppose your product catalog is very large, and you suspect that there are duplicate entries that need to be eliminated from the query results. The function call:

```
functx:distinct-deep(doc("catalog.xml")//product)
```

returns only distinct product elements, based on all of their content and attributes.

Example 6-13. Two-way join in a predicate

Query
```
for $item in doc("order.xml")//item,
    $product in doc("catalog.xml")//product[number = $item/@num]
return <item num="{$item/@num}"
            name="{$product/name}"
            quan="{$item/@quantity}"/>
```
Results
```
<item num="557" name="Fleece Pullover" quan="1"/>
<item num="563" name="Floppy Sun Hat" quan="1"/>
<item num="443" name="Deluxe Travel Bag" quan="2"/>
<item num="784" name="Cotton Dress Shirt" quan="1"/>
<item num="784" name="Cotton Dress Shirt" quan="1"/>
<item num="557" name="Fleece Pullover" quan="1"/>
```

The first part of the for clause selects each item from the order, and the second part selects the matching product element from the catalog.xml document, using a predicate to identify the one whose number matches the item's num attribute. Another way to accomplish the same thing is by using a where clause instead of a predicate, as shown in Example 6-14. This query yields the same results.

Example 6-14. Two-way join in a where clause

```
for $item in doc("order.xml")//item,
    $product in doc("catalog.xml")//product
where $item/@num = $product/number
return <item num="{$item/@num}"
            name="{$product/name}"
            quan="{$item/@quantity}"/>
```

Whether to use a predicate or a where clause is a matter of personal preference. When many conditions apply, a where clause can be more readable. However, for simple conditions, a predicate may be preferable because it is less verbose. In some implementations, predicates perform faster than where clauses.

Three-Way Joins

Joins can be extended to allow more than two sources to be joined together. For example, suppose that, along with catalog.xml and order.xml, you also want to join the prices.xml document, which contains current pricing information for each product.

The query shown in Example 6-15 joins the prices.xml document with the others to provide pricing information in the results. It uses two expressions in the where clause to implement the two joins.

Example 6-15. Three-way join in a where clause

Query
```
for $item in doc("order.xml")//item,
    $product in doc("catalog.xml")//product,
    $price in doc("prices.xml")//prices/priceList/prod
where $item/@num = $product/number and $product/number = $price/@num
return <item num="{$item/@num}"
            name="{$product/name}"
            price="{$price/price}"/>
```
Results
```
<item num="557" name="Fleece Pullover" price="29.99"/>
<item num="563" name="Floppy Sun Hat" price="69.99"/>
<item num="443" name="Deluxe Travel Bag" price="39.99"/>
<item num="557" name="Fleece Pullover" price="29.99"/>
```

Outer Joins

The previous join examples in this section are known as *inner joins*; the results do not include items without matching products or products without matching items. Suppose you want to create a list of products and join it with the price information. Even if there is no price, you still want to include the product in the list. This is known in relational databases as an *outer join*.

The query in Example 6-16 performs this join. It uses two FLWORs, one embedded in the return clause of the other. The outer FLWOR returns the list of products, regardless of the availability of price information. The inner FLWOR selects the price, if it is available.

Example 6-16. Outer join

Query
```
for $product in doc("catalog.xml")//product
return <product number="{$product/number}">{
              attribute price
                 {for $price in doc("prices.xml")//prices/priceList/prod
                  where $product/number = $price/@num
                  return $price/price}
  }</product>
```
Results
```
<product number="557" price="29.99"/>
<product number="563" price="69.99"/>
<product number="443" price="39.99"/>
<product number="784" price=""/>
```

Product 784 doesn't have a corresponding price in the prices.xml document, so the price attribute has an empty value for that product.

Joins and Types

The where clauses in the join examples use the = operator to determine whether two values are equal. Keep in mind that XQuery considers type when determining whether two values are equal. If schemas are not used with these documents, both values are untyped, and the join shown in Example 6-16 compares the values as strings. Unless they are cast to numeric types, the join does not consider different representations of the same number equal, for example 0557 and 557.

On the other hand, if number in catalog.xml is declared as an xs:integer, and the num attribute in prices.xml is declared as an xs:string, the join will not work. One value would have to be explicitly cast to the other's type, as in:

```
where $product/number = xs:integer($price/@num)
```

Sorting and Grouping

This chapter explains how to sort and group data from input documents. It covers sorting in FLWORs, grouping results together, and calculating summary values using the aggregation functions.

Sorting in XQuery

Path expressions, which are most often used to select elements and attributes from input documents, always return items in document order. FLWORs by default return results based on the order of the sequence specified in the for clause, which is also often document order if a path expression was used.

The only way to sort data in an order other than document order is by using the order by clause of the FLWOR. Therefore, in some cases it is necessary to use a FLWOR where it would not otherwise be necessary. For example, if you simply want to select all of your items from an order, you can use the path expression doc("order.xml")//item. However, if you want to sort those items based on their num attribute, you have to use a FLWOR.

The order by Clause

Example 7-1 shows an order by clause in a FLWOR.

Example 7-1. The order by clause

```
for $item in doc("order.xml")//item
order by $item/@num
return $item
```

The results will be sorted by item number. The syntax of an order by clause is shown in Figure 7-1.

The order by clause is made up of one or more ordering specifications, separated by commas, each of which consists of an expression and an optional modifier. The

expression can only return one value for each item being sorted. In Example 7-1, there is only one num attribute of $item. If instead, you had specified order by $item/@*, which selects all attributes of item, a type error would have been raised because more than one value is returned by that expression.

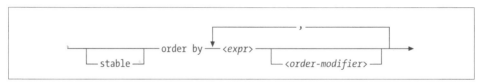

Figure 7-1. Syntax of an order by clause[a]

[a] The syntax of *<order-modifier>* is shown in Figure 7-2.

Unlike SQL, XQuery allows you to order by a value that is not returned by the expression. For example, you can order by $item/@dept and only return $item/@num in the results.

Using multiple ordering specifications

In order to sort on more than one expression, you can include multiple ordering specifications, as shown in Example 7-2.

Example 7-2. Using multiple ordering specifications

```
for $item in doc("order.xml")//item
order by $item/@dept, $item/@num
return $item
```

This sorts the results first by department, then by item number. An unlimited number of ordering specifications can be included.

Sorting and types

When sorting values, the processor considers their type. All the values returned by a single ordering specification expression must have comparable types. For example, they could be all xs:integer or all xs:string. They could also be a mix of xs:integer and xs:decimal, since values of these two types can be compared.

However, if integer values are mixed with string values, a type error is raised. It is acceptable, of course, for different ordering specifications to sort on values of different types; in Example 7-2, item numbers could be integers while departments are strings.

Untyped values are treated like strings. If your values are untyped but you want them to be treated as numeric for sorting purposes, you can use the number function, as in:

```
order by number($item/@num)
```

This allows the untyped value 10 to come after the untyped value 9. If they were treated as strings, the value 10 would come before 9.

Order modifiers

Several order modifiers can optionally be specified for each ordering specification.

- ascending and descending specify the sort direction. The default is ascending.
- empty greatest and empty least specify how to sort the empty sequence.
- collation, followed by a collation URI in quotes, specifies a collation used to determine the sort order of strings. Collations are described in detail in Chapter 17.

The syntax of an order modifier is shown in Figure 7-2.

Figure 7-2. Syntax of an order modifier

Order modifiers apply to only one order specification. For example, if you specify:

```
order by $item/@dept, $item/@num descending
```

the descending modifier applies only to $item/@num, not to $item/@dept. If you want both to be sorted in descending order, you have to specify:

```
order by $item/@dept descending, $item/@num descending
```

Empty order

The order modifiers empty greatest and empty least indicate whether the empty sequence and NaN should be considered a low value or a high value. If empty greatest is specified, the empty sequence is greater than NaN, and NaN is greater than all other values. If empty least is specified, the opposite is true; the empty sequence is less than NaN, and NaN is less than all other values. Note that this applies to the empty sequence and NaN only, not to zero-length strings.

You can also specify the default behavior for all order by clauses in the query prolog, using an empty order declaration, whose syntax is shown in Figure 7-3.

Figure 7-3. Syntax of an empty order declaration

Example 7-3 shows a query that uses an empty order declaration and sorts the results by the color attributes. Because the greatest option is chosen, the items with no color attribute appear last in the results.

Example 7-3. Using an empty order declaration

Query
```
declare default order empty greatest;
for $item in doc("order.xml")//item
order by $item/@color
return $item
```
Results
```
<item dept="WMN" num="557" quantity="1" color="black"/>
<item dept="MEN" num="784" quantity="1" color="gray"/>
<item dept="WMN" num="557" quantity="1" color="navy"/>
<item dept="MEN" num="784" quantity="1" color="white"/>
<item dept="ACC" num="563" quantity="1"/>
<item dept="ACC" num="443" quantity="2"/>
```

The setting in the empty order declaration applies unless it is overridden by an order modifier in an individual ordering specification. The empty order declaration in the prolog applies only when an order by clause is present; otherwise, the results are not sorted. If no empty order declaration is present, the default order for empty sequences is implementation-defined.

Stable ordering

When you sort on $item/@num, several values may be returned that have the same sort value. If stable ordering is not in use, the implementation is free to return those values that have equal sort values in any order. If you want those with equal sort values to be sorted in the order of the input sequence, or if you simply want to ensure that every implementation returns the values in the same order for the query, you can use the stable keyword before the keywords order by. For example, if you specify:

```
stable order by $item/@num
```

the items with the same num value are always returned in the order returned by the for expression, within the sorted results.

More complex order specifications

So far, the order specifications have been simple path expressions. You can sort based on almost any expression, as long as it only returns a single item. For example, you could sort on the result of a function call, such as:

```
order by substring($item/@dept, 2, 2)
```

which sorts on a substring of the department, or you could sort on a conditional expression, as in:

```
order by (if ($item/@color) then $item/@color else "unknown")
```

which sorts on the color if it exists or the string unknown if it does not. In addition, you could use a path expression that refers to a completely different XML document, as in:

```
order by doc("catalog.xml")//product[number = $item/@num]/name
```

which orders the results based on a name it looks up in the `catalog.xml` document.

A common requirement is to parameterize the sort key—that is, to decide at runtime what sort key to use. In some cases you can use:

```
order by $item/@*[name( )=$param]
```

In other cases you may need to use an extension function, as described in "Dynamic Paths" in Chapter 4.

Document Order

Every XML document (or document fragment) has an order, known as *document order*, which defines the sequence of nodes. Document order is significant because certain expressions return nodes in document order. Additionally, document order is used when determining whether one node precedes another. Note that, unlike in XPath 1.0, items in sequences are not always arranged in document order; it depends on how the sequence was constructed.

Document order defined

The document order of a set of nodes is:

- The document node itself
- Each element node in order of the appearance of its first tag, followed by:
 — Its attribute nodes, in an implementation-dependent order
 — Its children (text nodes, child elements, comments, and processing instructions) in the order they appear

Sorting a sequence of nodes in document order will remove any duplicate nodes.

If a sequence containing nodes from more than one document is sorted in document order, it is arbitrary (implementation-dependent) which document comes first, but all of the nodes from one document come before all of the nodes from the other document. For nodes that are not part of a document, such as those that are constructed in your query, the order is implementation-dependent, but stable.

There is no such thing as a document order on atomic values.

Sorting in document order

Certain kinds of expressions, including path expressions and operators that combine sequences (|, union, intersect, and except), return nodes in document order automatically. For example, the path expression:

```
doc("catalog.xml")//product/(number | name)
```

retrieves the number and name children of product, in document order. If you want all the number children to appear before all the name children, you need to use a sequence constructor, as in:

```
(doc("catalog.xml")//product/number , doc("catalog.xml")//product/name)
```

which uses parentheses and a comma. This sequence constructor maintains the order of the items, putting all the results of the first expression first in the sequence, and all the results of the second expression next.

If you have a sequence of nodes that are not in document order, but you want them to be, you can simply use the expression:

```
$mySequence/.
```

where $mySequence is a sequence of nodes. The / operator means that it is a path expression, which always returns nodes in document order.

Inadvertent resorting in document order

If you have used an order by clause to sort the results of a FLWOR, you should use caution when using the resulting sequence in another expression, since the results may be resorted to document order. The example shown in Example 7-4 first sorts the products in order by product number, then returns their names in li elements.

Example 7-4. Inadvertent resorting in document order

```
let $sortedProds := for $prod in doc("catalog.xml")//product
                    order by $prod/number
                    return $prod
for $prodName in $sortedProds/name
return <li>{string($prodName)}</li>
```

However, this query returns the products in document order, not product number order. This is because the expression $sortedProds/name resorts the nodes back to document order. In this case, the expression can easily be rewritten as shown in Example 7-5. In more complex queries, the error might be more subtle.

Example 7-5. FLWOR without inadvertent resorting

```
for $prod in doc("catalog.xml")//product
order by $prod/number
return <li>{string($prod/name)}</li>
```

Order Comparisons

Two nodes can be compared based on their relative position in document order using the << and >> operators. For example, $n1 << $n2 returns true if $n1 precedes $n2 in document order. According to the definition of document order, a parent precedes its children.

Each of the operands of the << and >> operators must be a single node, or the empty sequence. If one of the operators is the empty sequence, the result of the comparison is the empty sequence.

Example 7-6 shows a FLWOR that makes use of an order comparison in its where clause. For each product, it checks whether there are any other products later in the document that are in the same department. If so, it returns the product element. Specifically, it binds the $prods variable to a sequence of all four product elements. In the where clause, it uses predicates to choose from the $prods sequence those that are in the same department as the current $prod, and then gets the last of those. If the current $prod precedes that last product in the department, the expression evaluates to true, and the product is selected.

In the case of catalog.xml, only the second product element is returned because it appears before another product in the same department (ACC).

Example 7-6. Using an order comparison

```
let $prods := doc("catalog.xml")//product
for $prod in $prods
where $prod << $prods[@dept = $prod/@dept][last()]
return $prod
```

Reversing the Order

The reverse function reverses the order of items in a sequence. For example:

```
reverse(doc("catalog.xml")//product)
```

returns the product elements in reverse document order. The function is not just for reversing document order; it can reverse any sequence. For example:

```
reverse((6, 2, 3))
```

returns the sequence (3, 2, 6).

Indicating That Order Is Not Significant

As described in the previous section, several kinds of expressions return results in document order. In cases where the order of the results does not matter, the processor may be much more efficient if it does not have to keep track of order. This is especially true for FLWORs that perform joins. For example, processing multiple

variable bindings in a for clause might be significantly faster if the processor can decide which variable binding controls the join without regard to the order of the results.

To make a query more efficient, there are three ways for a query author to indicate that order is not significant: the unordered function, the unordered expression, and the ordering mode declaration.

The unordered function

A query author can tell the processor that order does not matter for an individual expression by enclosing it in a call to the unordered function, as shown in Example 7-7. The unordered function takes as an argument any sequence of items, and returns those same items in an undetermined order. Rather than being a function that performs some operation on its argument, it is more a signal to the processor to evaluate the expression without regard to order.

Example 7-7. Using the unordered function

```
unordered(
for $item in doc("order.xml")//item,
    $product in doc("catalog.xml")//product
where $item/@num = $product/number
return <item number="{$item/@num}"
            name="{$product/name}"
            quantity="{$item/@quantity}"/>
)
```

The unordered expression

An unordered expression is similar to a call to the unordered function, except that it affects not just the main expression passed as an argument, but also every embedded expression. The syntax of an unordered expression is similar, but it uses curly braces instead of the parentheses, as shown in Example 7-8.

Example 7-8. An unordered expression

```
unordered {
for $item in doc("order.xml")//item,
    $product in doc("catalog.xml")//product
where $item/@num = $product/number
return <item number="{$item/@num}"
            name="{$product/name}"
            quantity="{$item/@quantity}"/>
}
```

Similarly, an ordered expression will allow you to specify that order matters in a certain section of your query. This is generally unnecessary except to override an ordering mode declaration as described in the next section.

The ordering mode declaration

You can specify whether order is significant for an entire query in the query prolog, using an ordering mode declaration, whose syntax is shown in Figure 7-4.

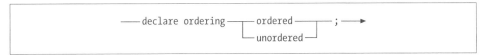

Figure 7-4. Syntax of an ordering mode declaration

For example, the prolog declaration:

```
declare ordering unordered;
```

allows the processor to disregard order for the scope of the entire query, unless it is overridden by an ordered expression or an order by clause. If no ordering mode declaration is present, the default is ordered.

Grouping

Queries are often written to summarize or organize information into categories. For example, suppose you want your list of items to be grouped by department. This can be accomplished using nested FLWORs, as shown in Example 7-9.

Example 7-9. Grouping by department

Query
```
for $d in distinct-values(doc("order.xml")//item/@dept)
let $items := doc("order.xml")//item[@dept = $d]
order by $d
return <department code="{$d}">{
         for $i in $items
         order by $i/@num
         return $i
      }</department>
```

Results
```
<department code="ACC">
  <item dept="ACC" num="443" quantity="2"/>
  <item dept="ACC" num="563" quantity="1"/>
</department>
<department code="MEN">
  <item dept="MEN" num="784" quantity="1" color="white"/>
  <item dept="MEN" num="784" quantity="1" color="gray"/>
</department>
<department code="WMN">
  <item dept="WMN" num="557" quantity="1" color="navy"/>
  <item dept="WMN" num="557" quantity="1" color="black"/>
</department>
```

In this example, the variable $d is iteratively bound to each of the distinct values for department code, namely WMN, ACC, and MEN. For each department, the variable $items is bound to all the items that have the particular department code $d. Because $items is bound in a let clause rather than a for clause, the *entire sequence* of items (for a single department) is bound to $items, not each item individually. The order by clause causes the results to be sorted by department.

The inner FLWOR is used simply to sort $items by item number. If the order of the items within a department is not a concern, the entire inner FLWOR can simply be replaced by $items, which returns the items in document order.

Aggregating Values

In addition to simply regrouping items, it is often desirable to perform calculations on the groups. For example, suppose you want to know the number of item elements in a department, or the sum of the quantities for a department. This type of aggregation can be performed using the aggregation functions. Example 7-10 shows some of these functions in action.

Example 7-10. Aggregation

Query
```
for $d in distinct-values(doc("order.xml")//item/@dept)
let $items := doc("order.xml")//item[@dept = $d]
order by $d
return <department code="{$d}"
                   numItems="{count($items)}"
                   distinctItemNums="{count(distinct-values($items/@num))}"
                   totQuant="{sum($items/@quantity)}"/>
```
Results
```
<department code="ACC" numItems="2" distinctItemNums="2" totQuant="3"/>
<department code="MEN" numItems="2" distinctItemNums="1" totQuant="2"/>
<department code="WMN" numItems="2" distinctItemNums="1" totQuant="2"/>
```

Here is how the aggregation functions work:

count

> This function is used to determine the number of items in the sequence. In Example 7-10, the count function is used to calculate the value of numItems, which is the number of items in the department. It is also used to calculate the value of distinctItemNums. In the latter case, the count function is combined with the distinct-values function to count only the unique numbers in that department.

sum

> This function is used to determine the total value of the items in a sequence. In Example 7-10, the sum function is used to calculate the value of totQuant, the sum of all the quantity attributes for that department.

min *and* max

These functions are used to determine the minimum and maximum values of the items in the sequence.

avg

This function is used to determine the average value of the items in a sequence.

The sum and avg functions accept values that are all numeric, all xs:yearMonthDuration values, or all xs:dayTimeDuration values. The max and min functions accept values of any type that is ordered (i.e., values can be compared using < and >). This includes strings, dates, and many other types.

The sum, min, max, and avg functions treat untyped data as numeric. This means that if you are not using a schema, and you want to find a maximum string value, you need to use an expression like:

```
max(doc("order.xml")//item/string(@dept))
```

which uses the string function to convert each value to xs:string before the comparison.

USEFUL FUNCTION

max-string

If you are going to be finding the maximum value of many untyped strings, it may be useful to define a function like this one:

```
declare namespace functx = "http://www.functx.com";
declare function functx:max-string ($stringSeq as xs:string*) as xs:string?{
   max($stringSeq)
};
```

Unlike the max function, it accepts an argument of type xs:string*, which means that untyped values are cast to xs:string automatically. You can call this function with:

```
functx:max-string(doc("order.xml")//item/@dept)
```

Ignoring "Missing" Values

The sequence passed to an aggregation function may contain nodes that are zero-length strings, even though the user might think of them as "missing" values. For example, the minimum value of the color attribute in order.xml is black. However, if there had been an item with a color attribute whose value was a zero-length string (as in color=""), the min function would have returned a zero-length string.

min-non-empty-string

Suppose you want to find the minimum string value, but you do not want a zero-length string to count. You can use this function:

```
declare namespace functx = "http://www.functx.com";
declare function functx:min-non-empty-string
($stringSeq as xs:string*) as xs:string? {
   min($stringSeq[. != ''])
};
```

This function is similar to the `max-string` useful function, but it eliminates all zero-length strings from consideration.

Counting "Missing" Values

On the other hand, there may be cases where you want "missing" values to be taken into consideration, but they are not. For example, the avg function ignores any absent nodes. If you want the average product discount, and you use:

```
avg(doc("prices.xml")//discount)
```

you get the average of the two discount values. It does not take into account the fact that there are three products, and that you might want the discount to be counted as zero for the product with no discount child. To count absent discount children as zero, you need to calculate the average explicitly, using:

```
sum(doc("prices.xml")//prod/discount)
       div count(doc("prices.xml")//prod)
```

On the other hand, if a prod had an empty discount child (i.e., `<discount></discount>`), it would be considered a zero-length string and the avg function would raise an error because this value is not of a numeric or duration type. In that case, you would have to test for missing values using:

```
avg(doc("prices.xml")//prod/discount[. != ""])
```

Aggregating on Multiple Values

So far, the aggregation examples assume that you want to group on one value, the dept attribute. Suppose you want to group on two values: the dept attribute *and* the num attribute. You would like to know the number of items and total quantity for each department/product number combination. This could be accomplished using the query shown in Example 7-11.

USEFUL FUNCTION

avg-empty-is-zero

The avg-empty-is-zero function, shown here, can alleviate the problems with counting missing values in averages:

```
declare namespace functx = "http://www.functx.com";
declare function functx:avg-empty-is-zero
 ($allNodes as node()*, $values as xs:anyAtomicType*) as xs:double {
   if (empty($allNodes))
   then 0
   else sum($values[. != ""]) div count($allNodes)
};
```

It takes as its first argument the entire sequence of items for which the average should be calculated (in this case, the sequence of prod elements). The second argument is the sequence of values to be averaged. If you use the function call:

```
let $prods := doc("prices.xml")//prod
return (functx:avg-empty-is-zero($prods, $prods/discount))
```

it returns 4.66333, which is the average of 10.00 and 3.99 (the two discount values), and 0 for the prod element that does not have a discount child. The function would have returned the same result if the discount child were present but empty.

Example 7-11. Aggregation on multiple values

Query
```
let $allItems := doc("order.xml")//item
for $d in distinct-values($allItems/@dept)
for $n in distinct-values($allItems[@dept = $d]/@num)
let $items := $allItems[@dept = $d and @num = $n]
order by $d, $n
return <group dept="{$d}" num="{$n}"
             numItems="{count($items)}"
             totQuant="{sum($items/@quantity)}"/>
```
Results
```
<group dept="ACC" num="443" numItems="1" totQuant="2"/>
<group dept="ACC" num="563" numItems="1" totQuant="1"/>
<group dept="MEN" num="784" numItems="2" totQuant="2"/>
<group dept="WMN" num="557" numItems="2" totQuant="2"/>
```

The query uses two for clauses to obtain two separate lists of distinct departments and distinct numbers. Using two for clauses results in the rest of the FLWOR being evaluated once for every possible combination of department and product number. The second for clause uses a predicate to choose only numbers that exist in that particular department.

The let clause binds $items to a list of items that exist for that department/number combination. If any items exist in $items, the return clause returns a group element with the summarized information for that combination.

Constraining and Sorting on Aggregated Values

In addition to returning aggregated values in the query results, you can constrain and sort the results on the aggregated values. Suppose you want to return the similar results to those shown in Example 7-11, but you only want the groups whose total quantity (totQuant) is greater than 1, and you want the results sorted by the number of items (numItems). The query shown in Example 7-12 accomplishes this.

Example 7-12. Constraining and sorting on aggregated values

Query
```
let $allItems := doc("order.xml")//item
for $d in distinct-values($allItems/@dept)
for $n in distinct-values($allItems/@num)
let $items := $allItems[@dept = $d and @num = $n]
where sum($items/@quantity) > 1
order by count($items)
return if (exists($items))
        then <group dept="{$d}" num="{$n}" numItems="{count($items)}"
                    totQuant="{sum($items/@quantity)}"/>
        else ()
```
Results
```
<group dept="ACC" num="443" numItems="1" totQuant="2"/>
<group dept="WMN" num="557" numItems="2" totQuant="2"/>
<group dept="MEN" num="784" numItems="2" totQuant="2"/>
```

Adjusting the query was a simple matter of adding a where clause that tested the total quantity, and modifying the order by clause to use the number of items.

Functions

Functions are a useful feature of XQuery that allow a wide array of built-in functionality, as well as the ability to modularize and reuse parts of queries. There are two kinds of functions: built-in functions and user-defined functions.

Built-in Versus User-Defined Functions

The built-in functions are a standard set, defined in the Functions and Operators recommendation and supported by all XQuery implementations. A detailed description of each built-in function is provided in Appendix A, and most are also discussed at appropriate places in the book.

The Functions and Operators recommendation defines built-in operators in addition to functions. These operators are like functions, but they cannot be called directly from a query; instead, they back up a symbol or keyword in the XQuery language. For example, the `numeric-add` operator backs up the + sign when both operands are numeric. Because they are internal to the implementation, and not used by the query author, they are not discussed directly in this book.

A user-defined function is one that is specified by a query author, either in the query itself, or in an external library. The second half of this chapter explains how to define your own functions in detail.

Calling Functions

The syntax of a function call, shown in Figure 8-1, is the same whether it is a built-in function or a user-defined function. It is the qualified name of the function, followed by a parenthesized list of the arguments, separated by commas.[*] For example, to call the `substring` function, you might use:

```
substring($prodName, 1, 5)
```

[*] An argument is the actual value that is passed to a function, while a parameter is its definition.

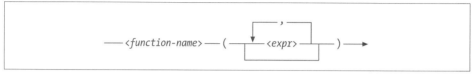

Figure 8-1. Syntax of a function call

Function calls can be included anywhere an expression is permitted. For example, you might include a function call in a let clause, as in:

```
let $name := substring($prodName, 1, 5)
```

or in element constructor content:

```
<name>{substring($prodName, 1, 5)}</name>
```

or in the predicate of a path expression:

```
doc("catalog.xml")/catalog/product[substring(name, 1, 5) = 'Short']
```

Function Names

Functions have namespace-qualified names. All of the built-in function names are in the XPath Functions Namespace, http://www.w3.org/2005/xpath-functions. Since this is the default namespace for functions, the built-in functions can be referenced without a namespace prefix (unless you have overridden the default function namespace, which is not recommended). Some XQuery users still prefer to use the fn prefix for these functions, but this is normally unnecessary.

If the function is user-defined, it *must* be called by its prefixed name. If a function is declared in the same query module, you can call it using the same prefixed name found in the declaration. Some functions may use the local prefix, a built-in prefix for locally declared functions. To call these functions, you use the local prefix in the name, as in:

```
declare function local:return2 () as xs:integer {2};
<size>{local:return2()}</size>
```

If the function is in a separate query module, it has a different namespace that needs to be declared. For example, if you are calling a function named discountPrice in the namespace http://datypic.com/prod, you must declare that namespace and use the appropriate prefix when calling the function, as in:

```
import module namespace prod = "http://datypic.com/prod"
                at "http://datypic.com/prod/module.xq";
<price>{prod:discountPrice()}</price>
```

Function Signatures

A function signature is used to describe the inputs and outputs of a function. For example, the signature of the built-in upper-case function is:

```
upper-case($arg as xs:string?) as xs:string
```

The signature indicates:

- The name of the function, in this case, upper-case.
- The list of parameters. In this case, there is only one, whose name is $arg and whose type is xs:string?. The question mark after xs:string indicates that the function accepts a single xs:string value or the empty sequence.
- The return type of the function, in this case, xs:string.

There may be several signatures associated with the same function name, with a different number of parameters. For example, there are two signatures for the substring function:

```
substring($sourceString as xs:string?,
          $startingLoc as xs:double) as xs:string
substring($sourceString as xs:string?,
          $startingLoc as xs:double,
          $length as xs:double) as xs:string
```

The second signature has one additional parameter, $length.

Argument Lists

When calling a function, there must be an argument for every parameter specified in the function signature. If there is more than one signature, as in the case of the substring function, the argument list may match either function signature. If the function does not take any arguments, the parentheses are still required, although there is nothing between them, as in:

```
current-date( )
```

You are not limited to simple variable names and literals in a function call. You can have complex, nested expressions that are evaluated before evaluation of the function. For example, the following function call has one argument that is itself a function call, and another argument that is a parenthesized conditional (if) expression:

```
concat(substring($name,1,$sublen), (if ($addT) then "T" else ""))
```

Calling a function never changes the value of any of the variables that are passed to it. In the preceding example, the value of $name does not change during evaluation of the substring function.

Argument lists and the empty sequence

Passing the empty sequence or a zero-length string for an argument is not the same as omitting an argument. For example:

```
substring($myString, 2)
```

is not the same as:

```
substring($myString, 2, ( ))
```

The first function call matches the first signature of substring, and therefore returns a substring of $myString starting at position 2. The second matches the second signature of substring, which takes three arguments. This function call raises a type error because the third argument of the substring function must be an xs:double value, and cannot be the empty sequence.

Conversely, if an argument can be the empty sequence, this does not mean it can be omitted. For example, the upper-case function expects one argument, which can be the empty sequence. It is not acceptable to use upper-case(), although it is acceptable to use upper-case(()), because the inner parentheses (()) represent the empty sequence.

Argument lists and sequences

The syntax of an argument list is similar to the syntax of a sequence constructor, and it is important not to confuse the two. Each expression in the argument list (separated by a comma) is considered a single argument. A sequence passed to a function is considered a single argument, not a list of arguments. Some functions expect sequences as arguments. For example, the max function, whose signature is:

```
max($arg as xs:anyAtomicType*) as xs:anyAtomicType?
```

expects *one* argument that is a sequence. Therefore, an appropriate call to max is:

```
max ((1, 2, 3))
```

not:

```
max (1, 2, 3)
```

which is attempting to pass it three arguments.

Conversely, it is not acceptable to pass a sequence to a function that expects several arguments that are atomic values. For example, in:

```
substring( ($myString, 2) )
```

the argument list contains only one argument, which happens to be a sequence of two items, because of the extra parentheses. This raises an error because the function expects two (or three) arguments.

You may want to pass a sequence of multiple items to a function to apply the function to each of those items. For example, to take the substring of each of the product names, you might be tempted to write:

```
substring( doc("catalog.xml")//name, 1, 3)
```

but this won't work because the first argument of substring is not allowed to contain more than one item. Instead, you could use a path expression, as in:

```
doc("catalog.xml")//name/substring( ., 1, 3 )
```

which will return a sequence of four strings: Fle, Flo, Del, and Cot.

Sequence Types

The types of parameters are expressed as sequence types, which specify both the number and type (and/or node kind) of items that make up the parameter. The most commonly used sequence types are the name of a specific atomic type, such as xs:integer, xs:double, xs:date, or xs:string. The sequence type xs:anyAtomicType, which matches any atomic value, can also be specified. Some of the built-in functions also use numeric to allow values of any numeric type.

Occurrence indicators are used to indicate how many items can be in a sequence. The occurrence indicators are:

? For zero or one items

* For zero, one, or many items

+ For one or many items

If no occurrence indicator is specified, it is assumed that it means one and only one. For example, a sequence type of xs:integer matches one and only one atomic value of type xs:integer. A sequence type of xs:string* matches a sequence that is either the empty sequence, or contains one or more atomic values of type xs:string. Sequence types are covered in detail in "Sequence Types" in Chapter 11.

Remember that there is no difference between an item, and a sequence that contains only that item. If a function expects xs:string* (a sequence of zero to many strings), it is perfectly acceptable to pass it a single string such as "xyz".

When you call a function, sometimes the type of an argument differs from the type specified in the function signature. For example, you may pass an xs:integer to a function that expects an xs:decimal. Alternatively, you may pass an element that contains a string to a function that expects just the string itself. XQuery defines rules, known as *function conversion rules*, for converting arguments to the expected type. The function conversion rules are covered in detail in "Function Conversion Rules" in Chapter 11.

Not all arguments can be converted using the function conversion rules, because function conversion does not involve straight casting from one type to another. For example, you cannot pass a string to a function that expects an integer. If you attempt to pass an argument that does not match the sequence type specified in the function signature, a type error is raised.

User-Defined Functions

XQuery allows you to create your own functions. This allows query fragments to be reused, and allows code libraries to be developed and reused by other parties. User-defined functions can also make a query more readable by separating out expressions and naming them. For a starter set of user-defined function examples, see *http://www.xqueryfunctions.com*.

Why Define Your Own Functions?

There are many good reasons for user-defined functions, such as:

Reuse

> If you are evaluating the same expression repeatedly, it makes sense to define it as a separate function, and then call it from multiple places. This has the advantage of being written (and maintained) only once. If you want to change the algorithm later—for example, to accept the empty sequence or to fix a bug—you can do it only in one place.

Clarity

> Functions make it clearer to the query reader what is going on. Having a function clearly named, with a set of named, typed parameters, serves as a form of documentation. It also physically separates it from the rest of the query, which makes it easier to decipher complex queries with many nested expressions.

Recursion

> It is virtually impossible to implement some algorithms without recursion. For example, if you want to generate a table of contents based on section headers, you can write a recursive function that processes section elements, their children, their grandchildren, and so on.

Managing change

> By encapsulating functionality such as "get all the orders for a product" into a user-defined function, applications become easier to adapt to subsequent schema changes.

Automatic type conversions

> The function conversion rules automatically perform some type promotions, casting, and atomization. These type conversions can be performed explicitly in the query, but sometimes it is cleaner simply to call a function.

Function Declarations

Functions are defined using function declarations, which can appear either in the query prolog or in an external library. Example 8-1 shows a function declaration in a query prolog. The function, called `local:discountPrice`, accepts three arguments: a price, a discount, and a maximum discount percent. It applies the lesser of the discount and the maximum discount to the price. The last line in the example is the query body, which consists of a call to the `discountPrice` function.

Example 8-1. A function declaration

```
declare function local:discountPrice(
  $price as xs:decimal?,
  $discount as xs:decimal?,
  $maxDiscountPct as xs:integer?) as xs:decimal?
```

Example 8-1. A function declaration (continued)

```
{
    let $maxDiscount := ($price * $maxDiscountPct) div 100
    let $actualDiscount := min(($maxDiscount, $discount))
    return ($price - $actualDiscount)
};

local:discountPrice($prod/price, $prod/discount, 15)
```

As you can see, a function declaration consists of several parts:

- The keywords `declare function` followed by the qualified function name
- A list of parameters enclosed in parentheses and separated by commas
- The return type of the function
- A function body enclosed in curly braces and followed by a semicolon

 A previous draft of the XQuery recommendation used the keywords `define function` instead of `declare function`. Some popular XQuery implementations still use the previous syntax.

The syntax of a function declaration is shown in Figure 8-2. The parameter list is optional, although the parentheses around the parameter list are required. The return type is also optional, but it is strongly encouraged.

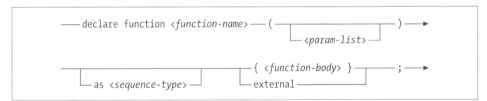

Figure 8-2. Syntax of a function declaration[a]

[a] The syntax of *<param-list>* is shown in Figure 8-3.

The Function Body

The function body is an expression enclosed in curly braces, which may contain any valid XQuery expressions, including FLWORs, path expressions, or any other XQuery expression. It does not have to contain a `return` clause; the return value is simply the value of the expression. You could have a function declaration as minimal as:

```
declare function local:get-pi( ) {3.141592653589};
```

Within a function body, a function can call other functions that are declared anywhere in the module, or in an imported module, regardless of the order of their declarations.

Once the function body has been evaluated, its value is converted to the return type using the function conversion rules described in "Function Conversion Rules" in Chapter 11. If the return type is not specified, it is assumed to be item*, that is, a possibly empty sequence of atomic values and nodes.

The Function Name

Each function is uniquely identified by its qualified name and its number of parameters. There can be more than one function declaration that has the same qualified name, as long as the number of parameters is different. The function name must be a valid XML name, meaning that it can start with a letter or underscore and contain letters, digits, underscores, dashes, and periods. Like other XML names, function names are case-sensitive.

All user-defined function names must be in a namespace. In the main query module, you can use any prefix that is declared in the prolog. You can also use the predefined prefix local, which puts the function in the namespace http://www.w3.org/2005/xquery-local-functions. It can then be called from within that main module using the prefix local. On the other hand, if a function is declared in a library module, its name must be in the target namespace of the module. Library modules are discussed in "Assembling Queries from Multiple Modules" in Chapter 12.

In addition, certain function names are reserved; these are listed in Table 8-1. It is not illegal to declare functions with these names, but when called they must be prefixed. As long as you have not overridden the default function namespace, this is not an issue. However, for clarity, it is best to avoid these function names.

Table 8-1. Reserved function names

attribute	if	schema-attribute
comment	item	schema-element
document-node	node	text
element	processing-instruction	typeswitch
empty-sequence		

The Parameter List

The syntax of a parameter list is shown in Figure 8-3. Each parameter has a unique name, and optionally a type. The name is expressed as a variable name, preceded by a dollar sign ($). When a function is called, the variable specified is bound to the value that is passed to it. For example, the function declaration:

```
declare function local:getProdNum ($prod as element()) as element( )
    { $prod/number };
```

binds the $prod variable to the value of the argument passed to it. The $prod variable can be referenced anywhere in the function body.

Figure 8-3. Syntax of a parameter list

The type is expressed as a sequence type, described earlier in this chapter. If no type is specified for a particular parameter, it allows any argument. However, it is best to specify a type, for the purposes of error checking and clarity. Some of the built-in functions use the keyword `numeric` to indicate that the argument may be of any numeric type. This keyword cannot be used in user-defined functions.

When the function is called, each argument value is converted to the appropriate type according to the function conversion rules.

Accepting arguments that are nodes versus atomic values

You may be faced with the decision of whether to accept a node that contains an atomic value, or to accept the atomic value itself. For example, in the declaration of `local:discountPrice`, you could have accepted the `price` and `discountPct` element instead of accepting their `xs:decimal` and `xs:integer` values. There are some cases where it is advantageous to pass the entire element as an argument, such as if:

- You want to access its attributes—for example, to access the `currency` attribute of `price`
- You need to access its parent or siblings

However, if you are interested in only a single data value, there are a number of reasons why it is generally better to accept the atomic value:

- It is more flexible, in that you can pass a node to a function that expects an atomic value, but you cannot pass an atomic value to a function that expects a node.
- You can be more specific about the desired type of the value, to ensure, for example, that it is an `xs:integer`.
- You don't have to cast untyped values to the desired type; this will happen automatically as part of the conversion.

Accepting arguments that are the empty sequence

You may have noticed that many of the XQuery built-in functions accept the empty sequence as arguments, as evidenced by the occurrence indicators * and ?. For example, the `substring` function accepts the empty sequence for its first argument and returns the empty sequence if the empty sequence is passed to it. This is a flexible

way of handling optional elements. If you want to take a substring of an optional number child, *if it exists*, you can simply specify:

```
substring ($product/number, 1, 5)
```

If the substring function were less flexible, and did not accept the empty sequence, you would be required to write:

```
if   ($product/number)
then substring ($product/number, 1, 5)
else ()
```

This can become quite cumbersome if you are nesting many function calls. Generally, your functions should be designed to be easily nested in this way as well.

It is also important to decide how you want the function to handle arguments that are the empty sequence, if they are allowed. In some cases, it is not appropriate simply to return the empty sequence. Using the local:discountPrice function from Example 8-1, suppose $discount is bound to the empty sequence, because $prod has no discount child. The function returns the empty sequence because all arithmetic operations on the empty sequence return the empty sequence.

It is more likely that you want the function to return the original price if no discount amount is provided. Example 8-2 shows a revised function declaration where special checking is done for the case where either $discount or $maxDiscountPct is the empty sequence.

Example 8-2. Handling the empty sequence

```
declare function local:discountPrice(
  $price as xs:decimal?,
  $discount as xs:decimal?,
  $maxDiscountPct as xs:integer?) as xs:double?
{
  let $newDiscount    := if ($discount) then $discount else 0
  let $maxDiscount    := if ($maxDiscountPct)
                            then ($price * $maxDiscountPct) div 100
                            else 0
  let $actualDiscount := min(($maxDiscount, $discount))
  return ($price - $actualDiscount)
};
local:discountPrice($prod/price, $prod/discount, 15)
```

Functions and Context

Inside a function body, there is no context item, even if there is one in the part of the query that contained the function call. For example, the function shown in Example 8-3 is designed to return all the products with numbers whose second digit is greater than 5. You might think that because the function is called in an expression where the context is the product element, the function can use the simple expression number to access the number child of that product. However, since the

function does not inherit the context item from the main body of the query, the processor does not have a context in which to evaluate number.

Example 8-3. Invalid use of context in a function body

```
declare function local:prod2ndDigit() as xs:string? {
    substring(number, 2, 1)
};
doc("catalog.xml")//product[local:prod2ndDigit() > '5']
```

Instead, the relevant node must be passed to the function as an argument. Example 8-4 shows a revised function that correctly accepts the desired product element as an argument and uses a path expression ($prod/number) to find the number child. The product element is passed to the function using a period (.), shorthand for the context item.

Example 8-4. Passing the context item to the function

```
declare function local:prod2ndDigit($prod as element()?) as xs:string? {
    substring($prod/number, 2, 1)
};
doc("catalog.xml")//product[local:prod2ndDigit(.) > '5']
```

Recursive Functions

Functions can recursively call themselves. For example, suppose you want to count the number of descendant elements of an element (not just the immediate children, but all the descendants). You could accomplish this using the function shown in Example 8-5.

Example 8-5. A recursive function

```
declare namespace functx = "http://www.functx.com";
declare function functx:num-descendant-elements
  ($el as element()) as xs:integer {
    sum(for $child in $el/*
        return functx:num-descendant-elements($child) + 1)
};
```

The functx:num-descendant-elements function recursively calls itself to determine how many element children the element has, how many children its children has, and so on. The only caveat is that there must be a level at which the function stops calling itself. In this case, it will eventually reach an element that has no children, so the return clause will not be evaluated. On the other hand, declaring a function such as:

```
declare function local:addItUp () { 1 + local:addItUp() };
```

results in an infinite loop, which will possibly end with an "out of memory" or "stack full" error.

You can also declare mutually recursive functions that call each other. Chapter 9 explores the use of recursive functions for making modifications to element structures.

Advanced Queries

Now that you are an expert on the syntax of XQuery expressions, let's look at some more-advanced queries. This chapter describes syntax and techniques for some commonly requested query capabilities. You may have these same requirements for your queries, but even if you don't, this chapter will show you some creative ways to apply XQuery syntax.

Copying Input Elements with Modifications

Often you will want to include elements from an input document, but with minor modifications. For example, you may wish to eliminate or add attributes, or change their names. However, the XQuery language does not have specific update capability, nor does it have any special functions or operators that perform these minor modifications. For example, there is no direct syntax that means "select all the product elements, but leave out their dept attributes."

The good news is that you can accomplish these modifications by "reconstructing" the elements. For example, you can write a query to construct a new product element and include all the children and attributes (except dept) of the original product element in the input document. Even better, you can write a user-defined function that uses computed constructors to handle these modifications in the general case. This section describes some common modifications and provides useful functions to handle these cases.

Note that these functions are intended to change the way elements and attributes appear in the results of a query, not to update them in an XML database. To update your XML database, you should use the implementation-specific update functions of your processor, since there is no standard XQuery update syntax yet.

Adding Attributes to an Element

To add an attribute to an element, you could use a function like the one shown in Example 9-1. It takes as arguments an element, along with an attribute name and value, and returns a newly constructed element with that attribute added.

Example 9-1. Useful function: add-attribute

```
declare namespace functx = "http://www.functx.com";
declare function functx:add-attribute
 ($element as element( ), $name as xs:string,
  $value as xs:anyAtomicType?) as element( ) {
   element { node-name($element)}
          { attribute {$name} {$value},
            $element/@*,
            $element/node( ) }
};
```

The function makes use of computed constructors to create dynamically a new element with the same name as the original element passed to the function. It also uses a computed constructor to create the attribute, specifying its name and value as expressions.

It then copies the attribute and child nodes from the original element. The expression node() is used rather than * because node() will return text, processing instruction, and comment nodes in addition to child elements. However, node() does not return attributes, so a separate expression @* is used to copy those.

The expression:

```
doc("catalog.xml")//product/functx:add-attribute(., "xml:lang", "en")
```

uses this function to return all of the product elements from the catalog, with an additional xml:lang="en" attribute.

Removing Attributes from an Element

Removing attributes also requires the original element to be reconstructed. Example 9-2 shows a function that "removes" attributes from a single element. It does this by reconstructing the element, copying the content and all of the attributes except those whose names are specified in the second argument.

Example 9-2. Useful function: remove-attribute

```
declare namespace functx = "http://www.functx.com";
declare function functx:remove-attributes
 ($element as element(), $names as xs:string*) as element() {
```

Example 9-2. Useful function: remove-attribute (continued)

```
    element { node-name($element)}
            { $element/@*[not(name() = $names)],
              $element/node() }
};
```

The function will accept a sequence of strings that represent attribute names to remove. For example, the expression:

```
    doc("order.xml")//item/functx:remove-attributes(., ("quantity", "color"))
```

returns all of the item elements from the order document, minus the quantity and color attributes. The extra parentheses are necessary around the "quantity" and "color" strings to combine them into a single argument that is a sequence of two items. Otherwise, they would be considered two separate arguments.

Notice that the predicate [not(name() = $names)] does not need to explicitly iterate through each of the strings in the $names sequence. This is because the = operator, unlike the eq operator, can be used on lists of values. The comparison will return true for every attribute name that is equal to any one of the strings in $names. Using the not function means that the predicate will allow through only the attributes whose names do *not* match any of the strings in $names.

It may seem simpler to use the != operator rather than the not function, but that does not have the same meaning. If the predicate were [name() != $names], it would return all the attributes whose names don't match *either* quantity or color. This means that it will return *all* the attributes, since no single attribute name will match both strings.

Removing Attributes from All Descendants

You could go further and remove attributes from an element as well as remove all of its descendants. The recursive function functx:remove-attributes-deep, shown in Example 9-3, accomplishes this.

Example 9-3. Useful function: remove-attribute-deep

```
declare namespace functx = "http://www.functx.com";
declare function functx:remove-attributes-deep
 ($element as element(), $names as xs:string*) as element() {
   element { node-name($element)}
           { $element/@*[not(name() = $names)],
             for $child in $element/node()
             return if ($child instance of element())
                    then functx:remove-attributes-deep($child, $names)
                    else $child }
};
```

This function uses an algorithm similar to the previous example, but it differs in the way it processes the children. Instead of simply copying all the child nodes, the function uses

a FLWOR to iterate through them. If a child is an element, it recursively calls itself to process that child. If the child is not an element (for example, if it is a text or processing-instruction node), the function returns it as is. Iterating through all of the child nodes in a single FLWOR preserves their original order in the results.

Removing Child Elements

The three previous functions relate to adding and removing attributes, and they could apply equally to child elements. For example, the function in Example 9-4 could be used to eliminate certain elements from a document by name. It is very similar to remove-attribute-deep, in Example 9-3, except that it removes child elements instead of the attributes.

Example 9-4. Useful function: remove-elements-deep

```
declare namespace functx = "http://www.functx.com";
declare function functx:remove-elements-deep
 ($element as element(), $names as xs:string*) as element() {
   element {node-name($element)}
           {$element/@*,
            for $child in $element/node()
            return if ($child instance of element())
                   then if ($child[name() = $names])
                        then ()
                        else functx:remove-elements-deep($child, $names)
                   else $child }
};
```

Another common use case is to remove certain elements but keep their contents. For example, if you want to remove any inline formatting from the desc element in the product catalog, you will want to remove any i or b tags, but keep the content of those elements. You can use the function shown in Example 9-5 for that.

Example 9-5. Useful function: remove-elements-not-contents

```
declare namespace functx = "http://www.functx.com";
declare function functx:remove-elements-not-contents
 ($element as element(), $names as xs:string*) as element() {
   element {node-name($element)}
           {$element/@*,
            for $child in $element/node()
            return if ($child instance of element())
                   then if ($child[name() = $names])
                        then $child/node()
                        else functx:remove-elements-not-contents($child, $names)
                   else $child }
};
```

Changing Names

Another minor modification is to change the names of certain elements. This could be useful for implementing changes to an XML vocabulary or for language translation.

For example, suppose you want to preserve the structure of the order document but want to change the name order to purchaseOrder, and the name item to purchasedItem. Since the document is very simple, this could be done in a hardcoded way using direct constructors. However, there may be situations where the document is more complex and you do not know exactly where these elements appear, or they appear in a variety of places in different document types.

You can modify names more flexibly using the function shown in Example 9-6.

Example 9-6. Useful function: change-elem-names

```
declare function local:change-elem-names
  ($nodes as node( )*, $old-names as xs:string+,
   $new-names as xs:string+) as node( )* {

  if (count($old-names) != count($new-names))
  then error(xs:QName("Different_Number_Of_Names"))
  else for $node in $nodes
      return if ($node instance of element( ))
          then let $newName :=
                  if (local-name($node) = $old-names)
                  then $new-names[index-of($old-names, local-name($node))]
                  else local-name($node)
               return element {$newName}
                 {$node/@*,
                  local:change-elem-names($node/node( ),
                                          $old-names, $new-names)}
          else $node
};
```

Like the remove-attribute-deep function, change-elem-names calls itself recursively to traverse the entire XML document. Every time it finds an element, it figures out what its new name should be and assigns it to the variable $newName. If it finds its original name in the $old-names sequence, it selects the name in $new-names that is in the same position. Otherwise, it uses the original name. It then reconstructs the element using the new name, copies all of its attributes, and recursively calls itself to process all of its children.

Example 9-7 calls the change-elem-names function with sequences of old and new names. It returns the same data and basic structure as the order.xml document, except with the two names changed.

Example 9-7. Using the change-elem-names function

Query
```
let $order := doc("order.xml")/order
```

Example 9-7. Using the change-elem-names function (continued)

```
let $oldNames := ("order", "item")
let $newNames := ("purchaseOrder", "purchasedItem")
return local:change-elem-names($order, $oldNames, $newNames)
```
Results
```
<purchaseOrder num="00299432" date="2006-09-15" cust="0221A">
  <purchasedItem dept="WMN" num="557" quantity="1" color="navy"/>
  <purchasedItem dept="ACC" num="563" quantity="1"/>
  <purchasedItem dept="ACC" num="443" quantity="2"/>
  <purchasedItem dept="MEN" num="784" quantity="1" color="white"/>
  <purchasedItem dept="MEN" num="784" quantity="1" color="gray"/>
  <purchasedItem dept="WMN" num="557" quantity="1" color="black"/>
</purchaseOrder>
```

Another common function is to change the namespace of an element or attribute. An example of this is shown in "Constructing Qualified Names" in Chapter 20.

Working with Positions and Sequence Numbers

Determining positions and generating sequence numbers are sometimes challenging to query authors who are accustomed to procedural programming languages. Because XQuery is a declarative rather than a procedural language, it is not possible to use familiar techniques like counters. In addition, the sorting and filtering of results can interfere with sequence numbers. This section describes some techniques for working with positions and sequence numbers.

Adding Sequence Numbers to Results

Suppose you want to return a list of product names preceded by a sequence number. Your first approach might be to use a variable as a counter, as shown in Example 9-8. However, the results are not what you might expect. This is because the return clause for each iteration is evaluated in parallel rather than sequentially. This means that you cannot make changes to the value of a variable in one iteration, and expect it to affect the next iteration of the for clause. At the beginning of every iteration, the $count variable is equal to 0.

Example 9-8. Attempting to use a counter variable

Query
```
let $count := 0
for $prod in doc("catalog.xml")//product[@dept = ("ACC", "WMN")]
let $count := $count + 1
return <p>{$count}. {data($prod/name)}</p>
```
Results
```
<p>1. Fleece Pullover</p>
<p>1. Floppy Sun Hat</p>
<p>1. Deluxe Travel Bag</p>
```

Another temptation might be to use the position function, as shown in Example 9-9. However, this will return the same results as the previous example. In XQuery, unlike in XSLT, the position function only has meaning inside a predicate in a path expression. In this case, the value assigned to $prod is no longer in the context of three product items; therefore, it has no relative sequence number within that sequence.

Example 9-9. Attempting to use the position function

```
for $prod in doc("catalog.xml")//product[@dept = ("ACC", "WMN")]
return <p>{$prod/position()}. {data($prod/name)}</p>
```

Luckily, FLWORs have a special syntax that enables you to define a positional variable in the for clause. This variable, which is followed by the keyword at, is bound to an integer representing the iteration number, as shown in Example 9-10.

Example 9-10. Using a positional variable in a for clause

Query
```
for $prod at $count in doc("catalog.xml")//product[@dept = ("ACC", "WMN")]
return <p>{$count}. {data($prod/name)}</p>
```
Results
```
<p>1. Fleece Pullover</p>
<p>2. Floppy Sun Hat</p>
<p>3. Deluxe Travel Bag</p>
```

However, the positional variable in the at clause does not always work. For example, suppose you wanted to use both where and order by clauses in your FLWOR. This interferes with the sequencing, as shown in Example 9-11. First, the numbers are not in ascending order. This is because the results are ordered *after* the positional number is evaluated. Another problem is that the sequence numbers are 2, 3, and 4 instead of 1, 2, and 3. This is because there are four product elements returned in the for clause, and the first one was eliminated by the where clause.

Example 9-11. Attempting to use a positional variable with a where clause

Query
```
for $prod at $count in doc("catalog.xml")//product
where $prod/@dept = ("ACC", "MEN")
order by $prod/name
return <p>{$count}. {data($prod/name)}</p>
```
Results
```
<p>4. Cotton Dress Shirt</p>
<p>3. Deluxe Travel Bag</p>
<p>2. Floppy Sun Hat</p>
```

One way to resolve this is by embedding a second FLWOR in the let clause, as shown in Example 9-12. This embedded FLWOR returns all the products sorted and filtered appropriately. Then, the for clause contained in the main FLWOR uses the positional variable on the sorted sequence.

Example 9-12. Embedding the where clause

Query
```
let $sortedProds := for $prod in doc("catalog.xml")//product
                    where $prod/@dept = "ACC" or $prod/@dept = "MEN"
                    order by $prod/name
                    return $prod
for $sortedProd at $count in $sortedProds
return <p>{$count}. {data($sortedProd/name)}</p>
```
Results
```
<p>1. Cotton Dress Shirt</p>
<p>2. Deluxe Travel Bag</p>
<p>3. Floppy Sun Hat</p>
```

Testing for the Last Item

Sometimes it is also useful to test whether an item is last in a sequence. Earlier in this chapter, we saw that the position function is not useful unless it is in a predicate. The same is true of the last function, which limits its usefulness when testing for the last item, for example, in a FLWOR.

Suppose you want to concatenate the names of the products together, separated by commas. At the end of the last product name, you want to specify a period instead of a comma.[*] The best approach is to assign the number of items to a variable in a let clause, as shown in Example 9-13.

Example 9-13. Testing for the last item

Query
```
<p>{ let $prods := doc("catalog.xml")//product
     let $numProds := count($prods)
     for $prod at $count in $prods
     return if ($count = $numProds)
            then concat($prod/name,".")
            else concat($prod/name,",")
}</p>
```
Results
```
<p>Fleece Pullover, Floppy Sun Hat, Deluxe Travel Bag, Cotton Dress Shirt.</p>
```

The $numProds variable is bound to the number of products. A positional variable, $count, is used to keep track of the iteration number. When the $count variable equals the $numProds variable, you have arrived at the last item in the sequence.

Another approach is to use the is operator to determine whether the current $prod element is the last one in the sequence. This query is shown in Example 9-14. In this case, it is not necessary to count the number of items or to use a positional variable. The results are the same as in Example 9-13.

[*] Actually, this particular example would be best accomplished using the string-join function. However, the example is useful for illustrative purposes.

Example 9-14. Testing for the last item using the is operator

```
<p>{ let $prods := doc("catalog.xml")//product
     for $prod in $prods
     return if ($prod is $prods[last()])
            then concat($prod/name,".")
            else concat($prod/name,", ")
}</p>
```

Combining Results

Your query results may consist of several FLWORs or other expressions that each return a result sequence. In addition, the sequences you use in your for and let clauses may be composed from more than one sequence.

There are four ways to combine two or more sequences to form a third sequence. They differ in which items are selected, whether their order is affected, whether duplicates are eliminated, and whether atomic values are allowed in the sequences.

Sequence Constructors

The first way to merge two sequences is simply to create a third sequence that is the concatenation of the first two. This is known as a sequence constructor, and it uses parentheses and commas to concatenate two sequences together. For example:

```
let $prods := doc("catalog.xml")//product
let $items := doc("order.xml")//item
return ($prods, $items)
```

returns a sequence that is the concatenation of two other sequences, $prods and $items. The items in $prods are first in the sequence, then the items in $items, in the order they appear in that sequence. No attempt is made to eliminate duplicates or sort the items in any way.

Note that concatenation is the only way to combine sequences that contain atomic values; union, intersect, and except work on sequences that contain nodes only.

The union Expression

Another approach to combining sequences of nodes is via a union expression, which is indicated by the keyword union or the vertical bar character (|). The two operators have the exact same meaning. The resulting nodes are rearranged into document order. Path expressions such as:

```
doc("catalog.xml")//product/(number | name)
```

use the vertical bar operator to select the union of the number children and the name children of product. An equivalent alternative is to use the vertical bar operator to separate two entire multistep path expressions, as in:

```
doc("catalog.xml")//product/number | doc("catalog.xml")//product/name
```

Unlike simple concatenation, using a union expression eliminates duplicate nodes. Duplicates are determined based on node identity, not typed value or string value. That means an expression like:

```
doc("catalog.xml")//product/@dept | doc("order.xml")//item/@dept
```

results in all 10 dept attributes (four from catalog.xml and six from order.xml), because it does not eliminate the duplicate department *values*.

A union eliminates duplicate nodes not just between the sequences, but also within either of the original sequences.

The intersect Expression

An intersect expression results in a sequence that contains only those nodes that are in both of the original sequences. As with union expressions, duplicate nodes (based on node identity) are eliminated, and the resulting nodes are rearranged into document order. For example, the expression:

```
let $prods := doc("catalog.xml")//product
return $prods[@dept = "ACC"] intersect $prods[number = 443]
```

returns the third product element in the catalog.

The except Expression

An except expression results in a sequence that contains only nodes that are in the first sequence, but not in the second. As with union expressions, duplicate values (based on node identity) are eliminated, and the resulting nodes are rearranged into document order. For example, the expression:

```
doc("catalog.xml")//product/(* except number)
```

returns all the element children of product except for number elements. The parentheses are required because the slash (/) operator has precedence over the except operator. Without the parentheses, it would be interpreted as two separate path expressions: doc("catalog.xml")//product/* and number. This is equally true for the other operators in this section.

Using Intermediate XML Documents

When we think of XML structures, we tend to think of the input documents and the results. However, XQuery also allows you to create intermediate XML structures in your queries that are not included in the results. This can be useful for many reasons, among them creating lookup tables and narrowing down input documents to reduce complexity or improve performance.

Creating Lookup Tables

Suppose you want to create a summary of the product catalog that lists the departments. However, you would like to convert the department codes to more descriptive names. You could use the query shown in Example 9-15 to accomplish this.

Example 9-15. Converting values without a lookup table

Query
```
let $cat := doc("catalog.xml")/catalog
for $dept in distinct-values($cat/product/@dept)
return  <li>Department: {if ($dept = "ACC")
                         then "Accessories"
                         else if ($dept = "MEN")
                             then "Menswear"
                             else if ($dept = "WMN")
                                 then "Womens"
                                 else ()
              } ({$dept})</li>
```
Results
```
<li>Department: Womens  (WMN)</li>
<li>Department: Accessories  (ACC)</li>
<li>Department: Menswear  (MEN)</li>
```

This gives the desired results, namely a descriptive name for the department, with the department code in parentheses. However, the query is somewhat cluttered, and anyone maintaining the query would have to be careful to insert any new department codes in the right place, using the right XQuery syntax. A more elegant solution is shown in Example 9-16, which uses an intermediate XML structure as a lookup table. It has the same results as the previous example.

Example 9-16. Converting values with a lookup table

```
let $deptNames := <deptNames>
                    <dept code="ACC" name="Accessories"/>
                    <dept code="MEN" name="Menswear"/>
                    <dept code="WMN" name="Womens"/>
                  </deptNames>
let $cat := doc("catalog.xml")/catalog
for $dept in distinct-values($cat/product/@dept)
return <li>Department: {data($deptNames/dept[@code = $dept]/@name)
              } ({$dept})</li>
```

Just as you can use path expressions on the input documents, you can use them to traverse the intermediate XML structure. So, the expression $deptNames/dept[@code = $dept]/@name traverses the deptNames structure looking for the department name where the code matches the department code in question.

This solution is easier to maintain and it makes the mappings more obvious. Of course, if this is a general-purpose and unchanging lookup table that might be used in many queries, it can alternatively be stored as a separate XML document that is referenced using the doc function.

Reducing Complexity

In the previous example, the intermediate XML was hardcoded into the query. You can also build a temporary XML structure in the query, based on values from the input data. This can be handy to reduce the complexity of an input document before performing further querying or transformation on it.

Suppose you want to perform a join on the product catalog and the order. With the results of the join, you want to create an HTML table that formats the information. While this can probably be done in one FLWOR, it may be easier to write (and read!) a query that does it in two steps.

Such a query is shown in Example 9-17. It constructs a series of item elements that have attributes representing all the data items from the join. It binds the variable $tempResults to the six resulting item elements using a let clause. Within the return clause, it uses an embedded FLWOR to iterate through the item elements and turn them into table rows (tr elements).

Example 9-17. Reducing complexity

Query
```
let $tempResults:= for $item in doc("order.xml")//item,
                       $product in doc("catalog.xml")//product
                   where $item/@num = $product/number
                   return <item num="{$item/@num}" name="{$product/name}"
                               color="{$item/@color}"
                               quant="{$item/@quantity}"/>
return <table>
        <tr>
          <th>#</th><th>Name</th><th>Color</th><th>Quan</th>
        </tr>
        {for $lineItem in $tempResults
         return <tr>
                  <td>{data($lineItem/@num)}</td>
                  <td>{data($lineItem/@name)}</td>
                  <td>{data($lineItem/@color)}</td>
                  <td>{data($lineItem/@quant)}</td>
                </tr>
        }
     </table>
```

Value of $tempResults
```
<item num="557" color="navy" name="Fleece Pullover" quant="1"/>
<item num="563" color="" name="Floppy Sun Hat" quant="1"/>
<item num="443" color="" name="Deluxe Travel Bag" quant="2"/>
<item num="784" color="white" name="Cotton Dress Shirt" quant="1"/>
<item num="784" color="gray" name="Cotton Dress Shirt" quant="1"/>
<item num="557" color="black" name="Fleece Pullover" quant="1"/>
```

Partial Results
```
<table>
   <tr>
      <th>#</th><th>Name</th><th>Color</th><th>Quan</th>
   </tr>
```

Example 9-17. Reducing complexity (continued)

```
    <tr>
      <td>557</td>
      <td>Fleece Pullover</td>
      <td>navy</td>
      <td>1</td>
    </tr>
    <!-- ... -->
</table>
```

In this case, the example input documents are fairly simple, so this approach may be overkill. However, as documents and the joins between them become more complex, intermediate XML results can be very useful in simplifying queries.

This technique is sometimes called pipelining. Rather than putting the whole pipeline in one query, you could also consider chaining together a sequence of separate queries. This makes it easier to reuse each of the queries in different pipelines. A good use case for pipelining is to handle variants of the input vocabulary—for example, different flavors of RSS. Rather than have one query that handles all the variations, you can build a pipeline in which you first convert a particular variant to your chosen "canonical form," and then operate on that. It's also possible to combine XQuery with other technologies (such as XSLT) using pipelines, where different technologies are used to implement different steps in the pipeline.

Namespaces and XQuery

Namespaces are an important part of XML, and it is essential to understand the concepts behind namespaces in order to query XML documents that use them. This chapter first provides a refresher on namespaces in XML input documents in general. It then covers the use of namespaces in queries: how to declare and refer to them, and how to control their appearance in your results.

XML Namespaces

Namespaces are used to identify the vocabulary to which XML elements and attributes belong, and to disambiguate names from different vocabularies. For example, both of the XHTML and XSL-FO vocabularies have a table element, but it has a different structure in each vocabulary. Some XML documents combine elements from multiple vocabularies, and namespaces make it possible to distinguish between them.

Namespaces are defined by a W3C recommendation called *Namespaces in XML*. Two versions are available: 1.0 and 1.1. XQuery implementations may support either version; you should check with your product's documentation to determine which version is supported.

Namespace URIs

A namespace is identified by a URI (Uniform Resource Identifier) reference.[*] A namespace URI is most commonly an HTTP URL, such as `http://datypic.com/prod`. It could also be a Uniform Resource Name (URN), which might take the form `urn:prod-datypic-com`.

[*] Or IRI (International Resource Identifier) reference if your processor supports Namespaces 1.1. IRIs allow a wider, more international set of characters. The term *URI* is used in this book (and in the XQuery specification) to mean "URI or IRI."

The use of a URI helps to ensure the uniqueness of the name. If a person owns the domain name datypic.com, he is likely to have some control over that domain and not use duplicate or conflicting namespace URIs within that domain. By contrast, if namespaces could be defined as any string, the likelihood of collisions would be much higher. For this reason, using relative URI references (such as prod or ../prod) is discouraged in Namespaces 1.0 and deprecated in Namespaces 1.1.

However, the use of URIs for namespaces has created some confusion. Most people, seeing a namespace http://datypic.com/prod, assume that they can access that URL in a browser and expect to get something back: a description of the namespace, or perhaps a schema. This is not necessarily the case; there is no requirement for a namespace URI to be dereferencable. No parser, schema validator, or query tool would dereference that URL expecting to retrieve any useful information. Instead, the URI serves simply as a name.

For two namespace URIs to be considered the same, they must have the exact same characters. Although http://datypic.com/prod and http://datypic.com/prod/ (with a trailing slash) would be considered "equivalent" by most people, they are considered to be different namespace URIs. Likewise, namespace URIs are case-sensitive, so http://datypic.com/prod is different from http://DATYPIC.COM/prod.

Declaring Namespaces

Namespaces are declared in XML documents using namespace declarations. A namespace declaration, which looks similar to an attribute, maps a short prefix to a namespace name. That prefix is then used before element and attribute names to indicate that they are in a particular namespace. Example 10-1 shows a document that contains two namespace declarations.

Example 10-1. Namespace declarations

```
<cat:catalog xmlns:cat="http://datypic.com/cat"
             xmlns:prod="http://datypic.com/prod">
  <cat:number>1446</cat:number>
  <prod:product>
    <prod:number>563</prod:number>
    <prod:name prod:language="en">Floppy Sun Hat</prod:name>
  </prod:product>
</cat:catalog>
```

The first namespace declaration maps the prefix cat to the namespace http://datypic.com/cat, while the second maps the prefix prod to the namespace http://datypic.com/prod. The cat and prod prefixes precede the names of elements and attributes in the document to indicate their namespace. There are two different number elements, in different namespaces. The one attribute in the document, language, is also prefixed, indicating that it is in the http://datypic.com/prod namespace.

It is important to understand that the prefixes are arbitrary and have no technical significance. Although some XML languages have conventional prefixes, such as xsl for XSLT, you can actually choose any prefix you want for your XML documents. The document shown in Example 10-2 is considered the equivalent of Example 10-1.

Example 10-2. Alternate prefixes

```
<foo:catalog xmlns:foo="http://datypic.com/cat"
             xmlns:bar="http://datypic.com/prod">
  <foo:number>1446</foo:number>
  <bar:product>
    <bar:number>563</bar:number>
    <bar:name bar:language="en">Floppy Sun Hat</bar:name>
  </bar:product>
</foo:catalog>
```

Prefixes must follow the same rules as XML names, in that they must start with a letter or underscore, and can only contain certain letters. They also may not start with the letters xml in upper- or lowercase. Generally, prefixes are kept short for clarity, usually two to four characters.

Default Namespace Declarations

You can also designate a particular namespace as the default, meaning that any unprefixed elements are in that namespace. To declare a default namespace, you simply leave the colon and prefix off the xmlns in the namespace declaration. In this example:

```
<product xmlns="http://datypic.com/prod">
  <number>563</number>
  <name language="en">Floppy Sun Hat</name>
</product>
```

the product, number, and name elements are in the http://datypic.com/prod namespace, because they are unprefixed and that is the default namespace. Default namespace declarations and regular namespace declarations can be used together in documents.

However, default namespace declarations do not apply to unprefixed attribute names. Therefore, the language attribute is not in any namespace, even though you might expect it to be in the default namespace.

Namespaces and Attributes

An attribute name can also be in a namespace. This is less common than an element in a namespace, because often attributes are considered to be indirectly associated with the namespace of the element they are on, and therefore don't need to be put in a namespace themselves. For example, general-purpose attributes in the XSLT and XML Schema vocabularies are never prefixed.

However, certain attributes, sometimes referred to informally as *global attributes*, can appear in many different vocabularies and are therefore in namespaces. Examples include the xml:lang attribute, which can be used in any XML document to indicate natural language, and the xsi:schemaLocation attribute, which identifies the location of the schema for a document. It makes sense that these attributes should be in namespaces because they appear on elements that are in different namespaces.

If an attribute name is prefixed, it is associated with the namespace that is mapped to that prefix. A significant difference between elements and attributes, however, is that default namespace declarations do not apply to attribute names. Therefore, an unprefixed attribute name is always in *no* namespace, not the default namespace. It may seem that an attribute should automatically be in the namespace of the element that carries it, but it is considered to be in no namespace for the purposes of querying and even schema validation.

The product element shown in Example 10-3 has two attributes: app:id and dept. The app:id attribute is, as you would expect, in the http://datypic.com/app namespace. The dept attribute, because it is not prefixed, is in no namespace. This is true regardless of the fact that there is a default namespace declaration that applies to the product element itself.

Example 10-3. Namespaces and attributes

```
<product xmlns="http://datypic.com/prod"
         xmlns:app="http://datypic.com/app"
         app:id="P123" dept="ACC">
...
</product>
```

Namespace Declarations and Scope

Namespace declarations are not required to appear in the outermost element of an XML document; they can appear on any element. The scope of a namespace declaration is the element on which it appears and any attributes or descendants of that element. In Example 10-4, there are two namespace declarations: one on catalog and one on product. The scope of the second namespace declaration is indicated in bold font; the prod prefix cannot be used outside this scope.

Example 10-4. Namespace declarations and scope (cat_ns.xml)

```
<catalog xmlns="http://datypic.com/cat">
  <number>1446</number>
  <prod:product xmlns:prod="http://datypic.com/prod">
    <prod:number>563</prod:number>
    <prod:name language="en">Floppy Sun Hat</prod:name>
  </prod:product>
</catalog>
```

If a namespace declaration appears in the scope of another namespace declaration with the same prefix, it overrides it. This is not recommended for namespace declarations with prefixes because it is confusing. However, it is also possible to override the default namespace, which can be useful when a document consists of several subtrees in different namespaces. Example 10-5 shows an example of this, where the product element and its descendants are in a separate namespace but do not need to be prefixed.

Example 10-5. Overriding the default namespace

```
<catalog xmlns="http://datypic.com/cat">
  <number>1446</number>
  <product xmlns="http://datypic.com/prod"
    <number>563</number>
    <name language="en">Floppy Sun Hat</name>
  </product>
</catalog>
```

When using Namespaces 1.1, the namespace specified can be a zero-length string, as in xmlns:prod="". This has the effect of *undeclaring* the namespace mapped to prod; that prefix will no longer be available for use in that scope. Undeclaring prefixes is not permitted in Namespaces 1.0.

As with regular namespace declarations, you can specify a zero-length string as the default namespace, as in xmlns="". This undeclares the default namespace.

Namespaces and XQuery

Now that you have seen how namespaces are used in XML documents, let's look at how they are used in queries. Namespace-qualified names are used in queries in a number of ways:

- The input documents may contain elements and attributes that are in one or more namespaces.
- The query may construct new elements and attributes that are in one or more namespaces.
- The functions that are declared and/or called in a query have qualified names. This includes user-defined functions and XQuery built-in functions.
- The types used in a query have qualified names that are used, for example, in function signatures and in the constructors that create new values of that type.
 — Built-in types are in the XML Schema Namespace, and are conventionally prefixed with xs:.
 — User-defined types are in the target namespace of the schema document in which they are defined.
- The variables used in a query have qualified names. Many variables will have no namespace and no prefix, but the names are still considered qualified names.

Namespace Declarations in Queries

There are three ways that namespaces are mapped to prefixes in XQuery queries:

- Some namespaces are predeclared; no explicit namespace declaration is necessary to associate a prefix with the namespace.
- Namespace declarations can appear in the query prolog.
- Namespace declarations can appear in direct XML constructors.

The examples in this section use the input document cat_ns.xml shown in Example 10-4.

Predeclared Namespaces

For convenience, five commonly used namespace declarations are built into the XQuery recommendation. They are listed in Table 10-1. The five prefixes can be used anywhere in a query even if they are not explicitly declared by a namespace declaration. These prefixes are also used throughout this book to represent the appropriate namespaces.

Table 10-1. Predeclared namespaces

Prefix	Namespace	Uses
xml	http://www.w3.org/XML/1998/namespace	XML attributes such as xml:lang and xml:space
xs	http://www.w3.org/2001/XMLSchema	XML Schema built-in types and their constructors
xsi	http://www.w3.org/2001/XMLSchema-instance	XML Schema instance attributes such as xsi:type and xsi:nil
fn	http://www.w3.org/2005/xpath-functions	XPath Functions Namespace: the default namespace of all built-in functions
local	http://www.w3.org/2005/xquery-local-functions	Functions declared in a main module that are not in a specific namespace

In addition, your XQuery implementation may predeclare other namespaces for use within your queries or allow users to predeclare other namespaces by means of an API. Consult the documentation for your implementation to determine what, if any, other namespaces are predeclared.

Prolog Namespace Declarations

Namespaces can be declared in the query prolog. The syntax of a namespace declaration in the query prolog, shown in Figure 10-1, is different from a typical XML namespace declaration. For example:

```
declare namespace cat = "http://datypic.com/cat";
```

maps the prefix cat to the namespace http://datypic.com/cat.

```
                    ─── declare namespace <prefix> = "<namespace-name>" ; ───▶
```

Figure 10-1. Syntax of a prolog namespace declaration

This mapping applies to all names in the entire query, including element names, attribute names, function names, variable names, and type names.

Example 10-6 makes use of two prolog namespace declarations:

- The rep prefix is mapped to a namespace that is to be used for a newly constructed element, report. The report constructor uses a prefix to indicate that it is that namespace.

- The prod prefix is mapped to a namespace used in the input document. This declaration is necessary so that the path expression step prod:product can associate the name product with the correct namespace.

Note that the http://datypic.com/cat namespace does not need to be declared in the query (even though it is used in the input document), because it is not used in any names in the query itself. It does appear in the results, even though it is not associated with any names in the results. This is explained further in "Controlling Namespace Declarations in Your Results," later in this chapter.

Example 10-6. Prolog namespace declarations

Query
```
declare namespace rep = "http://datypic.com/report";
declare namespace prod = "http://datypic.com/prod";
<rep:report> {
  doc("cat_ns.xml")//prod:product
} </rep:report>
```
Results
```
<rep:report xmlns:rep="http://datypic.com/report">
   <prod:product xmlns="http://datypic.com/cat"
                 xmlns:prod="http://datypic.com/prod">
         <prod:number>563</prod:number>
         <prod:name language="en">Floppy Sun Hat</prod:name>
      </prod:product>
</rep:report>
```

The namespace name in a namespace declaration must be a literal value (in quotes), not a variable reference or other evaluated expression. The value should be a syntactically valid absolute URI.

Default namespace declarations in the prolog

You can also declare default namespaces in the prolog, using the syntax shown in Figure 10-2. There are two different default namespace declarations, one for elements and types, and the other for functions.

Figure 10-2. Syntax of a prolog default namespace declaration

For example:

```
declare default element namespace "http://datypic.com/cat";
```

would make `http://datypic.com/cat` the default namespace for elements and types. This means that anywhere an unprefixed element or type name is used in the query (for example, in element constructors and path expressions), it is assumed to be in that namespace.

This is shown in Example 10-7, which is the same as Example 10-6 except with an added default namespace declaration and a new step `catalog` in the path expression. The results are the same as those returned by Example 10-6. In this case, because `catalog` is unprefixed, the processor will look for a catalog element in the default element namespace, `http://datypic.com/cat`.

Example 10-7. Prolog default namespace declaration

```
declare default element namespace "http://datypic.com/cat";
declare namespace rep = "http://datypic.com/report";
declare namespace prod = "http://datypic.com/prod";
<rep:report> {
  doc("cat_ns.xml")/catalog/prod:product
} </rep:report>
```

In Example 10-7, it just so happens that the namespace declarations in the query match the namespace declarations in the input document. The namespace `http://datypic.com/prod` is mapped to the `prod` prefix, and `http://datypic.com/cat` is the default, in both places.

However, it is not necessary for the prefixes to match. Example 10-8 shows an equivalent query where a different prefix is used for the namespace `http://datypic.com/prod`, and `http://datypic.com/cat` now has a prefix associated with it too. Note that the prefixes declared in the query (`prod2` and `cat`) are used in the path expression, not those from the input document. In fact, it would be illegal to use the `prod` prefix in this query, because it is not declared in the query itself.

Example 10-8. Namespace declarations in query different from input document

```
declare namespace rep = "http://datypic.com/report";
declare namespace cat = "http://datypic.com/cat";
declare namespace prod2 = "http://datypic.com/prod";
<rep:report> {
  doc("cat_ns.xml")/cat:catalog/prod2:product
} </rep:report>
```

Example 10-8 yields the same results as Example 10-7. It is worth noting that the prod prefix (from the input document) is used in the results rather than prod2 (from the query).

As with a regular XML default namespace declaration, a prolog default element namespace declaration does not apply to attribute names, nor does it apply to variable names or function names.

Only one default element namespace declaration may appear in the query prolog. If the string literal is a zero-length string, unprefixed element and type names are considered to be in no namespace.

The default function namespace declaration

You can also declare a default namespace for functions, using the same syntax, but with the keyword function. For example:

```
declare default function namespace "http://datypic.com/funclib";
```

This means that all unprefixed functions that are called or declared within that query (including type constructors) are assumed to be in that namespace. If you specify a zero-length string, the default will be "no namespace." Only one default function namespace declaration may appear in the query prolog.

If no default function namespace is declared, the default is the XPath Functions Namespace, http://www.w3.org/2005/xpath-functions. In general, it is best not to override this, because if you do, you are required to prefix all calls to the built-in functions such as substring and max.

Other prolog namespace declarations

For convenience, other prolog declarations can bind namespaces to prefixes, namely schema imports, module declarations, and module imports. For example:

```
import module namespace strings = "http://datypic.com/strings"
                  at "http://datypic.com/strings/lib.xq";
```

will bind the http://datypic.com/strings namespace to the strings prefix. These types of declarations are covered in Chapters 12 and 13.

Namespace Declarations in Element Constructors

Namespaces can also be declared in direct element constructors, using the regular XML attributes whose names start with xmlns. These are known as namespace declaration attributes in XQuery, and are shown in Example 10-9.

Example 10-9. Using namespace declaration attributes

Query
```
<rep:report xmlns="http://datypic.com/cat">
```

Example 10-9. Using namespace declaration attributes (continued)

```
          xmlns:prod="http://datypic.com/prod"
          xmlns:rep="http://datypic.com/report"> {
  doc("cat_ns.xml")/catalog/prod:product
} </rep:report>
```

Results
```
<rep:report xmlns:rep="http://datypic.com/report"
          xmlns:prod="http://datypic.com/prod"
          xmlns="http://datypic.com/cat">
  <prod:product>
    <prod:number>563</prod:number>
    <prod:name language="en">Floppy Sun Hat</prod:name>
  </prod:product>
</rep:report>
```

The location of the namespace declarations in the results of Example 10-9 are different from those of Example 10-7, although the two results are technically equivalent. This subtle difference is explained in "Controlling Namespace Declarations in Your Results," later in this chapter.

As with prolog namespace declarations, the namespace name used in a namespace declaration attribute must be a literal value, not an enclosed expression, and it should be a syntactically valid absolute URI. Namespace declaration attributes with prefixes whose values are zero-length strings, such as `xmlns:cat=""`, are only allowed if the implementation supports Namespaces 1.1.

The Impact and Scope of Namespace Declarations

As in XML documents, namespace declarations in queries have a scope and a set of names to which they are applicable. This section describes the scope and impact of namespace declarations in XQuery, whether they are in the prolog or in direct element constructors.

Scope of namespace declarations

The scope of a namespace declaration in an element constructor is the constructor itself (including any other attributes, whether they appear before or after the namespace declaration). Much like regular XML documents, namespace declarations in child element constructors can override the namespace declarations of the outer constructors. However, this is not recommended.

The scope of a prolog namespace declaration is the entire query module. However, prolog namespace declarations can also be overridden, by namespace declarations in an element constructor. For example, if in Example 10-7 you placed a default namespace declaration in the report start tag, it would be in scope until the report end tag (including any attributes of report), overriding the default namespace declaration in the prolog.

Names affected by namespace declarations

Whether namespace declarations appear in the prolog or in a direct element constructor, they have similar rules regarding the names on which they have an effect. Namespace declarations that specify a prefix (i.e., ones that are not default namespace declarations) allow that prefix to be used with any qualified name, namely:

- The element and attribute names that are constructed in the query, like `rep:report`
- The element and attribute names from the input document that are used in path expressions, such as `cat:catalog` and `prod:product`
- Type names that are used in function signatures and in type-related expressions such as constructors or `instance of` expressions
- The names of functions, in both function calls and function declarations
- The names of variables, both when they are bound and when they are referenced

Default element namespace declarations affect only element and type names. They do not affect attribute, variable, or function names. Attribute and variable names, when they appear unprefixed, are considered to be in no namespace, not the default element namespace. Unprefixed function names are in the default *function* namespace.

 The fact that element names in XQuery paths are affected by default namespace declarations is different from XSLT. In XSLT, a default namespace declaration does *not* affect element names in path expressions. For example, in XQuery:

```
<abc xmlns="xyz">{$root/d/e}</abc>
```

the processor will look for the d and e elements in the xyz namespace. In XSLT:

```
<abc xmlns="xyz">
  <xsl:copy-of select="$root/d/e"/>
</abc>
```

the processor will look for the d and e elements in *no* namespace.

These rules governing the impact of namespace declarations on names are summarized in Table 10-2.

Table 10-2. Impact of namespace declarations on names

Variety of namespace declaration	Element	Attribute	Type	Function/type constructor	Variable
Predeclared namespaces	y	y	y	y	y
Prolog namespace declaration (with prefix)	y	y	y	y	y
Prolog default element namespace	y		y		

Table 10-2. Impact of namespace declarations on names (continued)

Variety of namespace declaration	Element	Attribute	Type	Function/type constructor	Variable
Prolog default function namespace				y	
Namespace declaration attribute (with prefix)	y	y	y	y	y
Namespace declaration attribute (default)	y		y		

Namespace declarations and input elements

It is important to understand that namespace declarations in a query affect only names that are explicitly specified in that query, not those of any child elements that might be included from the input document. Example 10-10 shows a query that copies some elements from an input document into a newly constructed element. It uses the input document prod_ns.xml shown in Example 10-11. The input document elements (names and name) are in the http://datypic.com/prod namespace, while the constructed report element is in the http://datypic.com/report namespace.

Example 10-10. Namespace declaration impact on input elements

Query
```
<report xmlns="http://datypic.com/report">
  <firstChild/>
  {doc("prod_ns.xml")/*}
</report>
```
Results
```
<report xmlns="http://datypic.com/report">
  <firstChild/>
  <prod:product xmlns:prod="http://datypic.com/prod">
    <prod:number>563</prod:number>
    <prod:name language="en">Floppy Sun Hat</prod:name>
  </prod:product>
</report>
```

In the results, report and firstChild are in the default namespace specified in the query. However, the product, number, and name elements are still in their original namespace from the input document. They do not become part of the default http://datypic.com/prodreport namespace. This would be true even if they were in no namespace in the input document. Copying an element never changes its namespace.

Example 10-11. Simple product example in namespace (prod_ns.xml)

```
<prod:product xmlns:prod="http://datypic.com/prod">
  <prod:number>563</prod:number>
  <prod:name language="en">Floppy Sun Hat</prod:name>
</prod:product>
```

Controlling Namespace Declarations in Your Results

If you take the results of your query and serialize them as an XML document, you may be surprised by the way the namespace declarations appear. The number and location of namespace declarations in your results is not always intuitive. However, it can be controlled somewhat by how you declare namespaces in your query and by the use of settings in the prolog.

This section describes how you can control the appearance of namespace declarations in your results. None of these techniques affects the real meaning of the results; they are simply cosmetic. If you are unconcerned with the appearance of namespace declarations, you can skip this section.

In-Scope Versus Statically Known Namespaces

This chapter describes how you can declare namespaces in the prolog or in direct element constructors. Which one you choose will not affect the actual namespaces of the elements and attributes in the results. However, it can affect the way the results will be serialized, in particular the number and location of the namespace declarations.

The difference has to do with statically known namespaces and in-scope namespaces.

Statically known namespaces are all the namespaces that are known at any given point in a query. This includes the predeclared namespaces, those that were declared in the prolog, and those that were declared using a namespace declaration attribute in an element constructor that is in scope.

In-scope namespaces, on the other hand, are namespaces that are currently in scope for a particular element. For an element from the input document, the in-scope namespaces are all the namespaces that are declared on that element or on any of its ancestors. Likewise, for an element being constructed in a query, they include the namespaces that are declared using a namespace declaration attribute on that element constructor or one of its ancestors. For a newly constructed element, the in-scope namespaces are a subset of the statically known namespaces. The in-scope namespaces may include predeclared namespaces, or ones that are declared in the prolog, but *only* if those namespaces are used in the name of that element, one of its ancestors, or one of its attributes.

Only in-scope namespaces, not all of the statically known namespaces become part of the results. Therefore, whether you declare a namespace in the prolog or in an element constructor can affect whether (and where) its declaration appears in your results. It can also affect which prefix is used, since although the prefix is not technically significant, the XQuery processor will keep track of prefixes used in input documents and queries and use them in the result documents.

Examples 10-12 and 10-13 illustrate this subtle difference. These examples use the input document shown in Example 10-11.

Example 10-12 shows a query where three different namespace declaration attributes appear in the report element constructor. Namespaces that are declared in constructors are always part of the in-scope namespaces, so the report element has three in-scope namespaces. As a result, all three namespace declarations appear in the report element in the results. The namespace that is mapped to the cat prefix is not used anywhere in the results, but its declaration nevertheless appears because it is one of the in-scope namespaces.

Example 10-12. Using XML namespace declarations

Query
```
<report xmlns="http://datypic.com/report"
            xmlns:cat="http://datypic.com/cat"
            xmlns:prod="http://datypic.com/prod"> {
  for $product in doc("prod_ns.xml")/prod:product
  return <lineItem>
            {$product/prod:number}
            {$product/prod:name}
         </lineItem>
} </report>
```
Results
```
<report xmlns:prod="http://datypic.com/prod"
        xmlns:cat="http://datypic.com/cat"
        xmlns="http://datypic.com/report">
  <lineItem>
    <prod:number>563</prod:number>
    <prod:name language="en">Floppy Sun Hat</prod:name>
  </lineItem>
</report>
```

Example 10-13, on the other hand, declares the three namespaces in the prolog. Prolog namespace declarations are not included in the in-scope namespaces unless they are specifically used by the element in question. Therefore, in this case, the report element has only one in-scope namespace, the one that is used as part of its name, namely the default element namespace http://datypic.com/report. Consequently, in the results, you only see one namespace declaration on the report element.

The prod:number and prod:name elements are in the prod namespace, so the prod declaration is added to the in-scope namespaces of each of these elements. The prod namespace is declared on both the prod:number and prod:name elements, rather than on the report element, because it is not one of the in-scope namespaces for the report element.

The prod:number and prod:name elements also have the http://datypic.com/report namespace in scope, since it is used by an ancestor. However, the declaration for http://datypic.com/report does not need to be repeated on the prod:number and prod:name elements, since the declaration already appears on the report element.

Example 10-13. Prolog namespace declarations

Query
```
declare default element namespace "http://datypic.com/report";
declare namespace cat = "http://datypic.com/cat";
declare namespace prod = "http://datypic.com/prod";
<report> {
  for $product in doc("prod_ns.xml")/prod:product
  return <lineItem>
            {$product/prod:number}
            {$product/prod:name}
         </lineItem>
} </report>
```
Results
```
<report xmlns="http://datypic.com/report">
   <lineItem>
      <prod:number xmlns:prod="http://datypic.com/prod">
            563</prod:number>
      <prod:name xmlns:prod="http://datypic.com/prod"
            language="en">Floppy Sun Hat</prod:name>
   </lineItem>
</report>
```

As you can see, your choice of how to declare the namespaces can affect their location in the result document. Example 10-14 shows a balance between the two approaches. The cat namespace is declared in the prolog because it is not intended to appear in the results. (Perhaps it does need to be declared—for example, if it is used in a function or variable name.) The prod namespace declaration is included in the report constructor so that it only appears once in the results rather than being repeated for each of the prod:number and prod:name elements.

Example 10-14. A balanced approach

Query
```
declare namespace cat = "http://datypic.com/cat";
<report xmlns="http://datypic.com/report"
        xmlns:prod="http://datypic.com/prod"> {
  for $product in doc("prod_ns.xml")/prod:product
  return <lineItem>
            {$product/prod:number}
            {$product/prod:name}
         </lineItem>
} </report>
```
Results
```
<report xmlns:prod="http://datypic.com/prod"
        xmlns="http://datypic.com/report">
   <lineItem>
     <prod:number>563</prod:number>
     <prod:name language="en">Floppy Sun Hat</prod:name>
   </lineItem>
</report>
```

Controlling the Copying of Namespace Declarations

In addition to the considerations discussed in the previous section, there is another way to control the placement of namespace declarations in your results. A word of caution: the facilities described here interact in subtle ways, and not all products implement them correctly.

The copy-namespaces declaration, which appears in the query prolog, controls the appearance of namespace declarations. Specifically, it applies to the case where you construct a new element, and include elements from the input document as children of your new element. It controls whether namespace declarations are inherited from parent constructors, and/or preserved from input documents. Its syntax is shown in Figure 10-3.

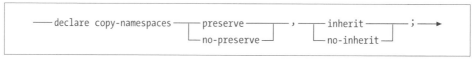

Figure 10-3. Syntax of a copy-namespaces declaration

It consists of two settings (both required), separated by a comma. For example:

```
declare copy-namespaces no-preserve, inherit;
```

If no copy-namespaces declaration is provided, the default values are determined by your implementation. They may have been specified by the user outside the scope of the query or set automatically by the processor.

The first setting, either preserve or no-preserve, controls whether unused namespace declarations are included from the input document. *Unused* here means "not used in the name of the element or its attributes." Namespace declarations that are being used are always included from the input document, regardless of the setting of preserve or no-preserve. Generally, no-preserve is preferred, since there is not much point in copying unused namespace declarations.

> One reason to choose preserve is if your element *content* (or attribute values) contains namespace-sensitive values, such as qualified names. Namespaces used in content (as opposed to in element/attribute names) are not considered to be "used." If you choose no-preserve, and the prefixes in the content are dependent on those nonpreserved declarations, an error may be raised when you try to validate or use the output document, because there may be an undeclared prefix.

The second setting, either inherit or no-inherit, controls whether the in-scope namespace declarations are copied from an outer constructor in the query to elements that are being copied (usually from the input document). Choosing inherit usually results in a less cluttered result document. If this value is set to no-inherit, unused namespaces declared on ancestor elements are explicitly undeclared on the

copied element. The main reason for this is to stop namespaces from a content enve-lope (for example, a SOAP header) from bleeding into the content: if the namespaces are undeclared in the content, the recipient can extract the content without the enve-lope namespaces having polluted the message body.

Undeclaring prefixes is only allowed in Namespaces 1.1, so no-inherit is essentially ignored if your implementation does not support Namespaces 1.1.

Note that these settings affect in-scope namespaces only, not statically known namespaces. They apply to both default namespace declarations and those that use prefixes.

Examples 10-16 and 10-17 exhibit the differences in these settings. They use the input document shown in Example 10-15, which has three different namespaces declared.

Example 10-15. Multinamespace input document (cat_ns2.xml)

```
<cat:catalog xmlns:cat="http://datypic.com/cat"
        xmlns:prod="http://datypic.com/prod"
        xmlns:ord="http://datypic.com/ord">
  <prod:product>
    <prod:number>563</prod:number>
    <prod:name language="en">Floppy Sun Hat</prod:name>
  </prod:product>
</cat:catalog>
```

Example 10-16 shows a query that uses the settings no-preserve and inherit. This combination of settings usually results in the fewest surprises. The query returns a report element that contains a product element copied from the input document. The report element has three namespace declaration attributes, and therefore has three in-scope namespaces.

Example 10-16. Query with no-preserve, inherit

Query
```
declare copy-namespaces no-preserve, inherit;
<report xmlns="http://datypic.com/report"
        xmlns:cat="http://datypic.com/cat"
        xmlns:prodnew="http://datypic.com/prod"> {
  doc("cat_ns2.xml")//prodnew:product
} </report>
```
Results
```
<report xmlns="http://datypic.com/report"
          xmlns:cat="http://datypic.com/cat"
          xmlns:prodnew="http://datypic.com/prod">
  <prod:product xmlns:prod="http://datypic.com/prod">
    <prod:number>563</prod:number>
    <prod:name language="en">Floppy Sun Hat</prod:name>
  </prod:product>
</report>
```

In the results, the only namespace declaration preserved from the input document is the one that the `product` element is actually using (because it is part of its name). This is because the `no-preserve` setting meant that unused namespace declarations were not copied from the input document.

Because `inherit` is chosen, the `product` element has declarations for the default (`report`) and cat namespaces in scope, even though it doesn't use them.

Note that even though the `http://datypic.com/prod` namespace is declared (with the prefix `prodnew`) in the `report` start tag, it is redeclared in the `product` start tag with a different prefix, and it is the `prod` prefix that is used. This is because nodes that are included from the input document will always use the prefixes that come from the input document. No combination of copy-namespaces settings will allow the `prodnew` prefix to be used for the `product` element instead of the `prod` prefix. To change any aspect of the element name, whether prefix, URI, or local name, you need to construct a new element rather than copying the original.

Example 10-17 shows the exact same query but with the opposite settings: `preserve` and `no-inherit`. In this case, all three namespace declarations from the input document are preserved (prod, ord, and cat), even though the cat and ord namespaces are not used. The cat namespace declaration is not written out in the `product` start tag because it has the same prefix and namespace as the one in the `report` start tag. The serialization process takes care of eliminating duplicate namespace declarations that are in the same scope.

Because `no-inherit` is chosen, the `product` element should not inherit the default (`report`) and `prodnew` namespace declarations from the `report` element. Therefore, they are undeclared.

Example 10-17. Query with preserve, no-inherit

Query
```
declare copy-namespaces preserve, no-inherit;
<report xmlns="http://datypic.com/report"
        xmlns:cat="http://datypic.com/cat"
        xmlns:prodnew="http://datypic.com/prod"> {
  doc("cat_ns2.xml")//prodnew:product
} </report>
```
Results
```
<report xmlns="http://datypic.com/report"
      xmlns:cat="http://datypic.com/cat"
      xmlns:prodnew"http://datypic.com/prod">
  <prod:product xmlns:prod="http://datypic.com/prod"
             xmlns:ord="http://datypic.com/ord"
             xmlns=""
             xmlns:prodnew="">
    <prod:number>563</prod:number>
    <prod:name language="en">Floppy Sun Hat</prod:name>
  </prod:product>
</report>
```

A Closer Look at Types

Chapter 2 briefly introduced the use of types in XQuery. This chapter delves deeper into the XQuery type system and its set of built-in types. It explains the automatic type conversions performed by the processors and describes the expressions that are relevant to types, namely type constructors, cast and castable expressions, and instance of expressions.

The XQuery Type System

XQuery is a strongly typed language, meaning that each function and operator is expecting its arguments or operands to be of a particular type. This means, for example, that you cannot perform arithmetic operations on strings, without explicitly telling the processor to treat your strings like numbers. This is similar to some common object-oriented programming languages, like Java and C#. It is in contrast to most scripting languages, like JavaScript, which will automatically coerce values to the appropriate type.

Advantages of a Strong Type System

There are several advantages to a strong type system. One of them is the early and reliable identification of errors in a query. Potential errors in the query can be determined before the query is even executed. For example, if you are trying to double a value that is a string (e.g., a product name), there is probably an error in the query. In addition, a type system allows for the identification of errors in the values of input data. This identification of errors can make queries easier to debug, and results in more reliable queries that are able to handle a variety of input data. This is especially true if schemas are used, because schema types can help identify possible errors. A schema allows the processor to tell you that the product name is a string and that you should not be trying to double it. Based on a schema, the processor can also tell you when you've specified a path that will never return any elements—for example, because of a misspelling or an invalid chain of steps.

Another advantage of a strong type system is optimization. Implementations can optimize performance if they know more about the types of data. This too is especially true if schemas are used, because schema types can help a processor find specific elements. If your schema says that all number elements appear as children of product elements, your processor only has to look in one place for the number elements you have requested in your query. If it knows that there is always only one number per product, it can further optimize certain comparison operations.

A strong type system has its disadvantages, too. One is that it can complicate query authoring, because more attention is being paid to types. For example, if you know you want to treat a numeric value like a string, you have to explicitly cast it to xs: string in order to perform string-related operations. Also, supporting an extensive type system can put a burden on implementers of the standard. This is why the more complex features—schema awareness and static typing—are optional features of the standard that will not be available in all implementations.

Do You Need to Care About Types?

If you do not use schemas, your input data will be untyped. Usually, this means that you, as a query author, do not need to be especially concerned about types. Because of the type conversions described in "Automatic Type Conversions," later in this chapter, the processor will usually "do the right thing" with your data.

For example, you may pass an untyped price element to the round function, or multiply it by two. In these cases, the processor will automatically assume that the content of the price element is numeric, and convert it to a numeric type. Likewise, calling the substring function with a name element will assume that name contains a string.

There is the occasional "gotcha," though. One example is comparing two untyped values using general comparison operators (e.g., < or =). If the values are untyped, they are compared as strings. Therefore, if you compare the untyped price element <price>123.99</price> with the untyped price element <price>99.99</price>, the second will be considered greater because the string value starts with a greater digit. Similarly, order by clauses in FLWORs assume that untyped values are strings rather than numbers. In both of these cases, the prices need to be explicitly converted to numbers in order to be sorted or compared as numbers. Casting is described in "Constructors and Casting," later in this chapter.

With untyped text values, you need to be concerned when using the max and min functions. These two functions treat untyped data as if it is numeric. Therefore, the expression:

```
max(doc("catalog.xml")//name)
```

will raise an error. Instead, you need to cast the names to `xs:string`. One way to do this is to use the `string` function, as in:

```
max(doc("catalog.xml")//name/string())
```

If you *do* use schemas, you will be able to get more of the benefits of strong typing, but you will need to pay more attention to types when writing your query. Unlike some weakly typed languages, XQuery will not automatically convert values of one type to an unrelated type (for example, a string to a number). So, if your schema for some reason declares the `price` element to be of type `xs:string`, you will not be able to perform arithmetic operations, or call functions like `round`, on your price without explicitly casting it to a numeric type.

The Built-in Types

A wide array of atomic types is built into XQuery. These simple types, shown in Figure 11-1, represent common datatypes such as strings, numbers, dates, and times. The built-in types are identified by qualified names that are prefixed with xs, because they are defined in the XML Schema Namespace. You can use all of these built-in types in your queries whether or not the implementation is actually schema-aware, and whether or not you are using schemas to validate your source or result documents.

Nineteen of the built-in types are primitive, meaning that they are the top level of the type hierarchy. Each primitive type has a value space, which describes all its valid values, and a set of lexical representations for each value in the value space. There is one lexical representation, the canonical representation, that maps one-to-one with each value in the value space. The canonical representation is important because it is the format used when a value is serialized or cast as a string.[*]

For example, the primitive type `xs:integer` has a value that is equal to 12 in its value space. This value has multiple lexical representations that map to the same value, such as 12, +12, and 012. The canonical representation is 12. Some primitive types, such as `xs:date`, only have one lexical representation, which becomes, by default, the canonical representation.

The rest of the built-in types are derived (directly or indirectly) from one of the primitive types. The derived built-in types (and indeed, user-defined types) inherit the qualities of the primitive type from which they are derived, including their value space (possibly restricted), lexical representations, and canonical representations. Their values can also be substituted for each other. For example, the `insert-before` function expects a value of type `xs:integer` for its second argument. Nevertheless, it accepts a value of any type derived from `xs:integer`, such as `xs:positiveInteger` or `xs:long`.

[*] There are three exceptions: `xs:decimal`, `xs:float`, and `xs:double` values, when cast to `xs:string`, may differ slightly from the canonical representation defined in XML Schema. See Appendix B for details.

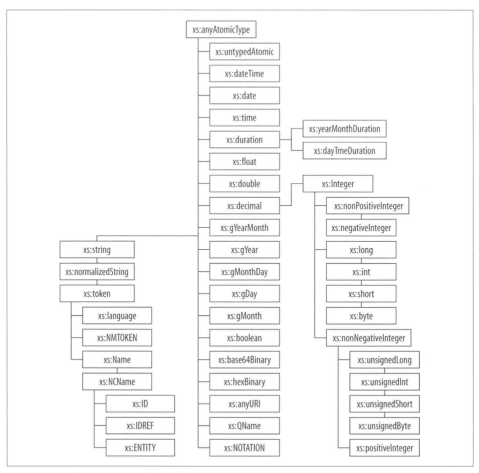

Figure 11-1. The atomic type hierarchy

At the top of the built-in atomic type hierarchy is xs:anyAtomicType. This type encompasses all of the other atomic types. No values ever actually have the type xs: anyAtomicType; they always have a more specific type. However, this type name can be used as a placeholder for all other atomic types. For example, the `distinct-values` function signature specifies that its argument is xs:anyAtomicType. This means that atomic values of any type can be passed to this function.

All of the built-in types are covered in detail in Appendix B, with a description, lexical representations, and examples. In practice, you are likely to need only a handful of these built-in types.

Types, Nodes, and Atomic Values

Element and attribute nodes, as well as atomic values, all have types associated with them. Sequences don't technically have types, although they can be matched to sequence types, as described later in this chapter.

Nodes and Types

All element and attribute nodes have type annotations, which indicate the type of their content. An element or attribute can come to be annotated with a specific type when it is validated against a schema. This might occur when the document is first opened, or as the result of a validate expression. Schema validation is discussed further in Chapter 13.

If an element or attribute has not been validated and does not have a specific type, it is automatically assigned a generic type, namely xs:untyped (for elements) or xs:untypedAtomic (for attributes). Sometimes these nodes are referred to as untyped, despite the fact that they do have a type, albeit a generic one.

Attributes, and most elements, also have a typed value.* This typed value is an atomic value extracted from the node, taking into account the node's type annotation. For example, if the number element has been validated and given the type xs:integer, its typed value is 784 (type xs:integer). If the number element is untyped, its typed value is 784 (type xs:untypedAtomic). The data function allows you to retrieve the typed value of a node.

Atomic Values and Types

Every atomic value has a type. An atomic value might have a specific type because:

- It is extracted from an element or attribute that has a type annotation. This can be done explicitly using the data function, or automatically using many functions and operators.

- It is the result of a constructor function or a cast expression.

- It is the value of a literal expression. Literals surrounded by single or double quotes are considered to have the type xs:string, whereas nonquoted numeric values have the type xs:integer, xs:decimal, or xs:double, depending on their format.

- It is the result of an expression or function that returns a value of a particular type—for example, a comparison expression returns an xs:boolean value, and the count function returns an xs:integer.

* Technically, other kinds of nodes have typed values, too, but they are less useful.

A value might not have a specific type if it was extracted from an untyped element or attribute. In this case, it is automatically assigned the generic type xs:untypedAtomic. Untyped atomic values can be used wherever a typed value can be used, and they are usually cast to the required type automatically. This is because every function and expression has rules for casting untyped values to an appropriate type.

Type Checking in XQuery

Because XQuery is a strongly typed language, an XQuery processor verifies that all items are of the appropriate type and raises type errors when they are not. There are two phases to processing a query: the static analysis phase and the dynamic evaluation phase, both of which have type-checking components.

The Static Analysis Phase

During the static analysis phase, the processor checks the query itself, along with any related schemas, for static errors, without regard to the input documents. It is roughly equivalent to *compiling* the query; that is, checking for syntax errors and other errors that will occur regardless of the input document. The processor raises static errors during the static analysis phase. Examples of static errors include:

- Syntax errors, such as invalid keywords or mismatched brackets
- Referring to a variable or calling a function that has not been declared
- Using namespace prefixes that are not declared

Some implementations support an optional static typing feature, which means that they evaluate the types of expressions in a query during the static analysis phase. This allows errors in the query to be caught early and more reliably, and can help optimize queries. A number of expressions, functions and syntactic constructs are available solely to support static typing. These are discussed in Chapter 14.

Implementations that don't claim to support the static typing feature might also do static analysis in order to reduce the amount of runtime type checking needs. It's always a good idea to declare the types of your variables, function parameters, and function return types to give the processor as much information as possible.

The Dynamic Evaluation Phase

During the dynamic evaluation phase, the processor checks the query again, this time with the data from the input document. Some expressions that did not result in errors during the analysis phase will in fact result in errors during the evaluation phase. For example, the expression sum(doc("catalog.xml")//number) might pass the static analysis phase if number is untyped; the processor has no way of knowing whether all the contents of the number elements will be numeric values. However, it will raise a dynamic error in the evaluation phase if any of the number elements contains a value that cannot be cast to a numeric type, such as the string abc.

Automatic Type Conversions

In XQuery, each function and operator expects its arguments to be of a particular type. However, this is not as rigid as it may sound since there are a number of type conversions that happen automatically. They are discussed in this section.

Subtype Substitution

Functions and operators that expect a value of a particular type also accept a value of one of its derived types. This is known as subtype substitution. For example, the upper-case function expects an xs:string as an argument, but you can pass a value whose type is derived by restriction from xs:string, such as xs:NMTOKEN. This also works for complex types. A function expecting an element of type ProductType also accepts an element of type UmbrellaType, if UmbrellaType is derived by restriction from ProductType. Note that the value retains its original type; it is not actually cast to another type.

Type Promotion

When two values of different numeric types are compared or used in the same operation, one is promoted to the type of the other. An xs:decimal value can be promoted to the xs:float or xs:double type, and an xs:float value can be promoted to the xs:double type. For example, the expression 1.0 + 1.2E0 adds an xs:decimal value (1.0) to an xs:double value. The xs:decimal value is promoted to xs:double before the expression is evaluated. Numeric type promotion happens automatically in arithmetic expressions, comparison expressions, and function calls.

In addition, values of type xs:anyURI are automatically promoted to xs:string in comparison expressions and function calls. Unlike subtype substitution, type promotion results in the type of a value changing.

Casting of Untyped Values

In some cases, an untyped value is automatically cast to a specific type. This occurs in function calls, as well as in comparison and arithmetic expressions. For example, if you call the upper-case function with an untyped value, it is automatically cast to xs:string. If you add an untyped value to a number, as in <a>3 + 2, the untyped value 3 is cast to xs:integer, and the expression returns 5.

Note that typed values are *not* automatically cast. For example, "3" + 2 will not automatically cast the string 3 to the number 3, even though this is theoretically possible. One exception is the concat function, which automatically casts its arguments to strings. But that's special behavior of this particular function, not something that happens implicitly on the function call.

Atomization

Atomization occurs when a function or operator expects an atomic value and receives a node instead. Specifically, it is used in:

- Arithmetic operations
- Comparisons
- Function calls and returns
- Cast expressions and constructors
- Name expressions in computed constructors

Atomization involves extracting the typed value of one or more elements or attributes to return one or more atomic values. For example:

```
<el>3</el> + 5
```

returns the value 8 because the value 3 is extracted from the el element during atomization. Also:

```
substring(<e2>query</e2>, 2, 3)
```

returns uer because the string query is extracted from the e2 element. These two examples work if e1 and e2 are untyped, because their so-called typed values would be instances of xs:untypedAtomic, and would be cast to the type required by the operation. They would work equally well if e1 had the type xs:integer, and e2 had the type xs:string, in which case no casting would need to take place.

Effective Boolean Value

It is often useful to treat a sequence as a Boolean value. For example, if you want to determine whether your catalog element contains any products whose price is less than $20, you might use the expression:

```
if (doc("prices.xml")//prod[price < 20])
then <bargain-bin>{local:getBargains()}</bargain-bin>
else ()
```

In this case, the result of the path expression doc("prices.xml")//prod[price < 20] is a sequence of elements that match the criteria. However, the if expression simply needs a yes/no answer regarding whether there are any elements that match the criteria. In this case, the sequence is automatically converted to its effective Boolean value, which essentially indicates whether it is empty.

Sequences are automatically interpreted as Boolean values in:

- Conditional (if-then-else) expressions
- Logical (and/or) expressions
- where clauses of FLWORs

- Quantified (some/every) expressions
- The argument to the not function
- The predicates of path expressions

In addition, the boolean function can be used to explicitly convert a sequence to its effective Boolean value. The effective Boolean value of a sequence is false if it is:

- The empty sequence
- A single, atomic value of type xs:boolean that is equal to false
- A single, atomic value of type xs:string that is a zero-length string ("")
- A single, atomic value with a numeric type that is equal to 0 or NaN

The effective Boolean value is undefined on a sequence of more than one item whose first item is an atomic value, and on individual atomic values whose type is not numeric, untyped, or xs:string. If the processor attempts to evaluate the effective Boolean value, and it is undefined, a type error is raised.

In all other cases, the effective Boolean value is true. This includes a sequence of one or more items whose first item is a node or a single atomic value other than those described in the preceding list. Table 11-1 shows some examples.

Table 11-1. Examples of effective Boolean value

Example	Effective Boolean value
()	false
false()	false
true()	true
""	false
"false"	true
"x"	true
0	false
xs:float("NaN")	false
(false() or false())	false
doc("prices.xml")/*	true
<a>false	true
(false(), false(), false())	Error
1, 2, 3	Error
xs:date("2007-01-15")	Error

Note that a node that contains a false atomic value is *not* the same thing as a false atomic value by itself. In the <a>false example in Table 11-1, the effective Boolean value is true because a is an element node, not an atomic value of type xs:boolean. This is true even if the a element is declared to be of type xs:boolean.

Function Conversion Rules

When you call a function, sometimes the type of an argument differs from the type specified in the function signature. For example, you can pass an xs:integer to a function that expects an xs:decimal. Alternatively, you can pass an element that contains a string to a function that expects just a string. XQuery defines rules, known as function conversion rules, for converting arguments to the expected type. These function conversion rules apply only if the function expects an atomic value (or sequence of atomic values).

In fact, these function conversion rules use the various methods of type conversion and matching that are described in the preceding sections. They are put together here to show the sequential process that takes place for each argument when a function is called.

1. Atomization is performed on the argument sequence, resulting in a sequence of atomic values.

2. Casting of untyped values is performed. For example, the untyped value 12 can be cast to xs:integer. As noted above, typed values are not cast to other types.

3. If the expected type is numeric or xs:string, type promotion may be performed. This means that a value of type xs:decimal can be promoted to xs:float, and xs:float can be promoted to xs:double. A value of type xs:anyURI can be promoted to xs:string.

Note that these rules do not cover converting a value to the base type from which its type is derived. For example, if an xs:unsignedInt value is passed to a function that expects an xs:integer, the value is not converted to xs:integer. However, subtype substitution does occur, and the function accepts this value.

The reverse is not true; you cannot pass an xs:integer value to a function that expects an xs:unsignedInt, even if the integer you pass meets all the tests for an xs:unsignedInt. The value must be explicitly cast to xs:unsignedInt.

As an example of the function conversion rules, if a function expects an argument of type xs:decimal?, it accepts any of the following:

- An atomic value of type xs:decimal

- The empty sequence, because the occurrence indicator (?) allows for it

- An atomic value of type dty:myDecimal (derived from xs:decimal) because the sequence type xs:decimal? matches derived types as well

- An atomic value of type xs:integer (derived from xs:decimal) because the sequence type xs:decimal? matches derived types as well

- An atomic value of type dty:myInteger (derived from xs:integer) because the sequence type xs:decimal? matches derived types as well

- An untyped atomic value, whose value is 12.5, because it is cast to xs:decimal (step 2)

- An element of type xs:decimal, because its value is extracted (step 1)

- An untyped attribute, whose value is 12, because its value is extracted (step 1) and cast to xs:decimal (step 2)

- An untyped element whose only content is 12.5, because its value is extracted (step 1) and cast to xs:decimal (step 2)

A function expecting xs:decimal* accepts a sequence of any combination of the above items. On the other hand, a function expecting xs:decimal? does *not* accept:

- An atomic value of type xs:string, even if its value is 12.5. This value must be explicitly cast to xs:decimal or a type error is raised.

- An atomic value of type xs:float, because type promotion only works in one direction.

- An untyped element whose only content is abc, because its value cannot be cast to xs:decimal.

- An untyped element with no content, because its value "" (not the empty sequence) cannot be cast to xs:decimal.

- A typed element whose type allows element-only content even if it has no children, because step 1 raises an error.

- A sequence of multiple xs:decimal values; only one item is allowed.

 In XPath 1.0, if a function expects a single item and is passed a sequence of multiple items, it uses the first item and discards the rest. In XQuery 1.0/XPath 2.0, this situation raises a type error instead.

Sequence Types

A sequence type is used in a query to specify the expected type of a sequence of zero, one, or more items. When declaring functions, sequence types are used to specify the types of the parameters as well as the return value. For example, the function declaration:

```
declare function local:getProdNums ($catalog as element( )) as xs:integer*
  {$catalog/product/xs:integer(number)};
```

uses two sequence types:

- element(), to specify that the $catalog parameter must be one (and only one) element

- xs:integer*, to specify that the return type of the function is zero to many xs: integer values

Sequence types are also used in many type-related expressions, such as the cast as, treat as, and instance of expressions. The syntax of a sequence type is shown in Figure 11-2.

Figure 11-2. Syntax of a sequence type[a]

[a] The detailed syntax of `<element-attribute-test>` is shown in Figure 13-4.

Occurrence Indicators

An occurrence indicator can be used at the end of a sequence type to indicate how many items can be in a sequence. The occurrence indicators are:

? For zero or one items

* For zero, one, or many items

+ For one or many items

If no occurrence indicator is specified, it is assumed that the sequence can have one and only one item. For example, a sequence type of xs:integer matches one and only one atomic value of type xs:integer. A sequence type of xs:string* matches a sequence that is either the empty sequence or contains one or more atomic values of type xs:string. A sequence type of node()? matches either the empty sequence or a single node.

Remember that there is no difference between an item and a sequence that contains only that item. If a function expects xs:string* (a sequence of zero to many strings), it is perfectly acceptable to pass it a single string without attempting to enclose it in a sequence in any way.

The empty sequence, which is a sequence containing zero items, only matches sequence types that use the occurrence indicator ? or *, or empty-sequence().

Generic Sequence Types

Follwing are some generic sequence types:

item()
 Matches either a node or an atomic value of any type

node()
 Matches a node of any kind

```
empty-sequence( )
```
> Matches the empty sequence

```
xs:anyAtomicType
```
> Matches an atomic value

Table 11-2 shows some examples of the generic sequence types.

Table 11-2. Examples of generic sequence types

Example	Explanation
node()*	A sequence of one or more nodes, or the empty sequence
item()?	One item (a node or an atomic value) or the empty sequence
xs:anyAtomicType+	A sequence of one or more atomic values (of any type)

These generic sequence types are useful because it is not possible to specify, for example, "one or more xs:string values or nodes." In this case, you would instead need to specify a more generic sequence type, namely item()+. They're also useful when defining generic functions such as reverse or count.

Atomic Type Names As Sequence Types

The sequence type can also be the qualified name of specific built-in or user-defined atomic types, such as xs:integer, xs:double, xs:date, xs:string, or prod:SizeType. This matches atomic values of that type or any type derived (directly or indirectly) from it. For example, the sequence type xs:integer also matches an atomic value of type xs:unsignedInt, because xs:unsignedInt is indirectly derived by restriction from xs:integer in the type hierarchy. The reverse is not true; the sequence type xs:unsignedInt does not match an xs:integer value; it must be explicitly cast.

These sequence types match atomic values only, not nodes that contain atomic values of the specified type.[*] An element that contains an integer would match element(*,xs:integer) (described in the next section) rather than xs:integer, for example. Table 11-3 shows some examples.

Table 11-3. Examples of sequence types based on type name

Example	Explanation
xs:integer	One atomic value of type xs:integer (or any type derived by restriction from xs:integer)
xs:integer?	One atomic value of type xs:integer (or any type derived by restriction from xs:integer), or the empty sequence
prod:NameType*	A sequence of one or more atomic values of type prod:NameType, or the empty sequence

[*] However, in function calls, nodes can be passed to functions expecting these kinds of atomic sequence types, because of atomization.

Atomic types used in sequence type expressions must be in the in-scope schema definitions. This means that if it is not a built-in type, it must have been imported from a schema.

Element and Attribute Tests

The sequence types element() and attribute() can be used to match any one element or attribute (respectively). An alternate syntax, with the same meaning, uses an asterisk, as in element(*) and attribute(*).

It is also possible to test for a specific name. For example, the sequence type:

```
element(prod:product)
```

matches any element whose name is prod:product.

When schemas are used, it is also possible to test elements and attributes based on their type annotations in addition to their names. This is described in "Sequence Types and Schemas" in Chapter 13.

Sequence types can be used to test for other node kinds, using document-node(), text(), comment(), and processing-instruction(). These sequence types are discussed in Chapter 21.

Sequence Type Matching

Sequence type matching is the process of determining whether a sequence of one or more items matches a specified sequence type, according to the rules specified in the preceding sections. Several kinds of expressions perform sequence type matching, such as the instance of expression described in this section.

Additional static-typing-related expressions, described in Chapter 14, also use the rules for sequence type matching. The typeswitch expression uses sequence type matching to control which expressions are evaluated. Other expressions, namely FLWOR expressions and quantified expressions, allow a sequence type to be specified to test whether values bound to variables match a particular sequence type.

The "instance of" Expression

To determine whether a sequence of one or more items matches a particular sequence type, you can use an instance of expression, whose syntax is shown in Figure 11-3.

```
──── <expr> ── instance of ── <sequence-type> ────▶
```

Figure 11-3. Syntax of an "instance of" expression

The instance of expression does not cast a value to the specified sequence type. It simply returns true or false, indicating whether the value matches that sequence type. Table 11-4 shows some examples of the instance of expression.

Table 11-4. Examples of "instance of" expressions

Example	Explanation
3 instance of xs:integer	true
3 instance of xs:decimal	true, because xs:integer is derived by restriction from xs:decimal
<x>{3}</x> instance of xs:integer	false, because the element node x is untyped, even though it happens to contain an integer
<x>{3}</x> instance of element()	true
<x>{3}</x> instance of node()	true
<x>{3}</x> instance of item()	true
(3, 4, 5) instance of xs:integer	false
(3, 4, 5) instance of xs:integer*	true
xs:float(3) instance of xs:double	false

Sequence type matching does not include numeric type promotion. For this reason, the last example in the table returns false.

Constructors and Casting

There are two mechanisms in XQuery for changing values from one type to another: constructors and casting.

Constructors

Constructors are functions used to construct atomic values with given types. For example, the constructor xs:date("2006-05-03") constructs an atomic value whose type is xs:date. The signature of this xs:date constructor function is:

```
xs:date($arg as xs:anyAtomicType?) as xs:date?
```

There is a constructor function for each of the built-in atomic types (both primitive and derived). The qualified name of the constructor is the same as the qualified name of the type. For the built-in types, constructor names are prefixed with xs to indicate that they are in the XML Schema namespace.

All of the constructor functions have a similar signature, in that they accept an atomic value and return an atomic value of the appropriate type. Because function arguments are atomized, you can pass a node to a constructor function, and its typed value is extracted. If you pass an empty sequence to a constructor, the result will be the empty sequence.

Unlike most other functions, constructor functions will accept arguments of any type and attempt to cast them to the appropriate type.* The argument value must have a type that can be cast to the new type; otherwise, a type error is raised. Values of almost all types can be cast to and from xs:string and xs:untypedAtomic. The specific rules for casting among types are described in "Casting Rules," later in this chapter.

In addition, the value must also be valid for the new type. For example, although the rules allow you to cast an xs:string value to xs:date, the expression xs:date("2006-13-02") raises an error because the month 13 is invalid.

Constructors also exist for all named user-defined atomic types that are in the in-scope schema definitions. If, in a schema, you have defined a type prod:SizeType that is derived from xs:integer by setting minInclusive to 0 and maxInclusive to 24, you can construct a value of this type using, for example:

```
prod:SizeType("10")
```

The qualified names must match, so the prefix prod must be mapped to the target namespace of the schema containing the SizeType definition. If the type name is in no namespace (the schema in which it is defined has no target namespace), you cannot use a constructor (unless you change the default function namespace, which is not recommended). You must use a cast expression instead.

The Cast Expression

Casting is the process of changing a value from one type to another. The cast expression can be used to cast a value to another type. It has the same meaning as the constructor expression; it is simply a different syntax. The only difference is that it can be used with a type name that is in no namespace. For example:

```
$myNum cast as xs:integer
```

casts the value of $myNum to the type xs:integer. It is equivalent to xs:integer($myNum). The syntax of a cast expression is shown in Figure 11-4.

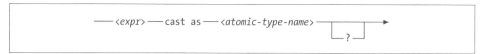

Figure 11-4. Syntax of a cast expression

The cast expression consists of the expression to be cast, known as the input expression, followed by the keywords cast as, followed by the qualified name of the target

* This is because constructor functions do not rely on function conversion rules to perform automatic casts; the signature accepts arguments of any type and it is part of the function's purpose to cast those values to the appropriate type.

type. Only a named atomic type can be specified, either a built-in type or a user-defined simple type whose definition is among the in-scope schema definitions.

The name of the atomic type may optionally be followed by a question mark as an occurrence indicator. In this case, the cast expression evaluates to the empty sequence if the input expression evaluates to the empty sequence. If no question mark is used, the input expression cannot evaluate to the empty sequence, or a type error is raised. This is in contrast to constructors, which always allow the empty sequence.

You cannot use the other occurrence indicators + and * because you cannot cast a sequence of more than one item using a cast expression. To cast more than one value, you could place your cast expression as the last step of a path, as in:

```
doc("catalog.xml")//number/(. cast as xs:string)
```

The input expression can evaluate to a node (in which case it is atomized to retrieve its typed value) or an atomic value. As with constructors, the value must have a type that allows casting to the target type, and it must also be a valid value of the target type.

The Castable Expression

The castable expression is used to determine whether a value can be cast to another specified atomic type. It is sometimes useful to determine this before the cast takes place to avoid dynamic errors, or to determine how the expression should be processed. For example:

```
if ($myNum castable as xs:integer)
then $myNum cast as xs:integer
else ()
```

evaluates to $myNum cast to xs:integer if that is valid, otherwise the empty sequence. If the castable expression had not been used to test this, and $myNum was not castable as an xs:integer, an error would have been raised. The syntax of a castable expression is shown in Figure 11-5.

Figure 11-5. Syntax of a castable expression

The castable expression consists of an expression, followed by the keywords castable as, followed by the qualified name of the target type. It evaluates to a Boolean value. As with the cast expression, you can use the question mark as an occurrence indicator. The castable expression determines not only whether the one type can be cast to the other type, but also whether that specific value is valid for that type.

Casting Rules

This section describes the rules for casting atomic values between specific types. These rules are used in cast expressions and constructors. In this section, the source type refers to the type of the original value that is being cast, and the target type refers to the type to which the value is being cast.

Casting among the primitive types

Specific rules exist for casting between each combination of two primitive types. These rules are discussed, along with the types themselves, in Appendix B. The rules can be summarized as follows:

- Values of any atomic type can be cast to and from `xs:string` and `xs:untypedAtomic` if the value is valid for the target type. See the next two sections for more information.
- A value of a numeric type can be cast to any other numeric type if the value is in the value space of the target type.
- A value of a date, time, or duration type can sometimes be cast to another date, time, or duration type.
- Other types (`xs:boolean`, `xs:QName`, `xs:NOTATION`, `xs:anyURI`, `xs:hexBinary`, and `xs:base64Binary`) have limited casting ability to and from types other than `xs:string` and `xs:untypedAtomic`. See Appendix B for more information on each type.

Casting to xs:string or xs:untypedAtomic

A value of type `xs:string` or `xs:untypedAtomic` can be cast to any other primitive type. For example, `xs:integer("12")` casts the `xs:string` value 12 to `xs:integer`. Of course, the string must represent a valid lexical representation of the target type. For example, `xs:integer("12.1")` raises an error because the lexical representation of `xs:integer` does not allow fractional parts.

When a value is cast from `xs:string` to another primitive type, whitespace is collapsed. Specifically, this means that every tab, carriage return, and line feed character is replaced by a single space; consecutive spaces are collapsed into one space; and leading and trailing spaces are removed. Therefore, `xs:integer(" 12 ")` is valid, even with the leading and trailing whitespace.

Casting to xs:string or xs:untypedAtomic

An atomic value of any type can be cast to `xs:string` or to `xs:untypedAtomic`. Some types have special rules about how their values are cast to `xs:string`. For example, integers have their leading zeros stripped. The rules (if any) for each type are described in Appendix B. Table 11-5 shows some examples of casting to `xs:string` and `xs:untypedAtomic`.

Table 11-5. Examples of casting to xs:string and xs:untypedAtomic

Expression	Value
xs:string("012")	"012"
xs:string(012)	"12"
xs:string(xs:float(12.3E2))	"1230"
xs:untypedAtomic(xs:float(12))	12 (of type xs:untypedAtomic)
xs:string(true())	"true"

Casting among derived types

Now that you have seen casting among the primitive types, let's look at derived types. There are three different cases.

The first case is that the source type is derived by restriction from the target type. In this case, the cast always succeeds because the source type is a subset of the target type. For example, an xs:byte value can always be cast to xs:integer.

The second case is that the source type and the target type are derived by restriction from the same primitive type. In this case, the cast succeeds as long as the value is in the value space of the target type. For example, xs:unsignedInt("60") can be cast to xs:byte, but xs:unsignedInt("6000") cannot, because 6000 is too large for xs:byte. This case also applies when the target type is derived by restriction from the source type. For example, xs:integer("25") can be cast to xs:unsignedInt, which is derived from it.

The third case is that the source type and the target type are derived by restriction from different primitive types—for example, if you want to cast a value of xs:unsignedInt to dty:myFloat, which is derived by restriction from xs:float. In this case, the casting process has three steps:

1. The value is cast to the primitive type from which it is derived, e.g., from xs:unsignedInt to xs:decimal.

2. The value is cast from that primitive type to the primitive type from which the target type is derived, e.g., from xs:decimal to xs:float.

3. The value is cast from that primitive type to the target type, e.g., from xs:float to dty:myFloat.

Queries, Prologs, and Modules

This chapter covers the structure of queries in more detail. It discusses the query prolog and its various declarations. It then describes how to assemble queries from multiple modules, declare global variables, and define external functions.

Structure of a Query: Prolog and Body

An XQuery query is made up of two parts: a prolog and a body. The query prolog is an optional section that appears at the beginning of a query. The prolog can contain various declarations that affect settings used in evaluating the query. This includes namespace declarations, imports of schemas, variable declarations, function declarations, and other setting values. In a query module of any size, the prolog is actually likely to be much larger than the body.

Example 12-1 shows a query with a prolog containing several different types of declarations.

Example 12-1. A query prolog

```
xquery version "1.0";
declare default element namespace "http://datypic.com/cat";
declare boundary-space preserve;
declare default collation "http://datypic.com/collation/custom";
declare namespace ord = "http://datypic.com/ord";
import schema namespace prod="http://datypic.com/prod"
                    at "http://datypic.com/prod.xsd";
declare function local:getProdNums
  ($catalog as element()) as xs:integer*
  {for $prod in $catalog/product
   return xs:integer($prod/number)};
```

The query body is a single expression, but that expression can consist of a sequence of one or more expressions that are separated by commas. Example 12-2 shows a query body that contains a sequence of two expressions, a constructed element, and

a FLWOR. The comma after the `title` element is used to separate the two expressions in the query body.

Example 12-2. A query body

```
<title>Order Report</title>,
(for $item in doc("order.xml")//item
 order by $item/@num
 return $item)
```

Prolog Declarations

The prolog consists of a series of declarations terminated by semicolon (;) characters. There are three distinct sections of the prolog.

The first declaration to appear in the query prolog is a version declaration, if it exists.

The second prolog section consists of setters, imports, and namespace declarations. Setters are the declarations listed in Table 12-1, along with a link to where they are covered fully in the book. Each kind of setter can only appear once. Imports and namespace declarations, listed in Table 12-2, can appear intermingled with setters in any order.

Table 12-1. Query prolog setters

Declaration	Description	Chapter
Boundary-space	How to process boundary whitespace in element constructors	5
Ordering mode	Whether the default order is document order or some implementation-dependent order	7
Empty order	Whether empty sequences should come first or last when ordered	7
Copy-namespaces	Whether nodes copied in constructors should copy namespaces from their parents	10
Construction	Whether nodes copied in constructors should be typed	13
Default collation	The default collation for string comparison	17
Base URI	The base URI of the static context	20

Table 12-2. Query prolog imports and namespace declarations

Declaration	Description	Chapter
Default namespace declaration	Maps unprefixed names to a namespace for the entire scope of the query	10
Namespace declaration	Maps a prefix to a namespace for the entire scope of the query	10
Module import	Imports a function module from a specified location	12
Schema import	Imports a schema definition from a specified location	13

The last section of the prolog consists of function, variable, and option declarations, listed in Table 12-3. They must appear after all the setters, imports, and namespace declarations.

Table 12-3. Query prolog variable and function declarations

Declaration	Description	Chapter
Function declaration	Declares a user-defined function	8
Variable declaration	Declares global variables	12
Option declaration	Declares implementation-specific parameters	23

It is important to note that your processor might also be setting these values. For example, different XQuery implementations can choose to build in different default collations or different sets of predefined functions. In addition, an implementation might allow the user to specify these values outside the query—for example, using a command-line interface. Prolog declarations override or augment the default settings defined outside the scope of the query.

The Version Declaration

The first of the declarations in Example 12-1 is a version declaration, whose syntax is shown in Figure 12-1. The version declaration is used to indicate the version of the XQuery language. `1.0` is the default (and the only allowed value), so it does not actually need to be explicitly specified, though it's recommended if you expect your query to be long-lived. If a version declaration does appear, it must appear first in the query, even before any comments.

Figure 12-1. Syntax of a version declaration

The version declaration also allows you to specify a character encoding for the query itself using the `encoding` keyword and a literal string. For example, the following version declaration specifies an encoding of UTF-8:

```
xquery version "1.0" encoding "UTF-8";
```

Other example values for the encoding include `UTF-16`, `ISO-8859-1`, and `US-ASCII`. The way encoding is handled is somewhat implementation-dependent, in that processors are allowed to ignore the encoding value specified in the query if they have other knowledge about the encoding.

Because the encoding of a file can easily change unintentionally—for example, when you save it using a text editor—it's safest to stick to using ASCII characters in the query, using numeric character references for any non-ASCII characters.

Assembling Queries from Multiple Modules

So far, all of this book's example queries were contained in one module, known as the main module. However, you can declare functions and variables in other modules and import them into the main module of the query. This is a very useful feature for:

- Reusing functions among many queries
- Creating standardized libraries that can be distributed to a variety of query users
- Organizing and reducing the size of query modules

The main module contains a query prolog followed by a query body, which is the main expression to be evaluated. In its prolog, the main module can import other modules known as library modules.

Not all implementations support the use of library modules; it is an optional feature.

Library Modules

Library modules differ from main modules in that they cannot have a query body, only a prolog. They also differ in that they must start with a module declaration, whose syntax is shown in Figure 12-2.

```
────module namespace <prefix> = "<namespace-name>" ;────▶
```

Figure 12-2. Syntax of a module declaration

The module declaration identifies the module as a library module. It also declares the target namespace of the module and maps it to a prefix. For example, the expression:

```
module namespace strings = "http://datypic.com/strings";
```

declares the target namespace of the module to be http://datypic.com/strings and binds that namespace to the prefix strings.

The target namespace must be a literal value in quotes, not an evaluated expression. It should be a syntactically valid absolute URI, and cannot be a zero-length string.

All of the functions and variables declared in that library module must be qualified with that same target namespace. This differs from main modules, which do not have target namespaces and allow you to declare variables and functions in a variety of namespaces.

This is shown in Example 12-3, where the variable and function names are prefixed with strings.

Example 12-3. Module

```
module namespace strings = "http://datypic.com/strings";
declare variable $strings:maxStringLength := 32;
declare function strings:trim($arg as xs:string?) as xs:string? {
  "function body here"
};
```

Importing a Library Module

Both main modules and library modules can import other library modules. Importing a library module allows its variables and functions to be referenced from the importing module. Only library modules can be imported; a main module can never be imported by another module.

A module import, which appears in the prolog, specifies the target namespace and location of the library module to be imported. Multiple module imports can appear in the query prolog. (The syntax of a module import is shown in Figure 12-3.)

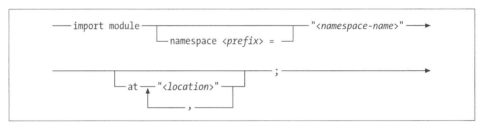

Figure 12-3. Syntax of a module import

For example, the declaration:

```
import module "http://datypic.com/strings"
        at "http://datypic.com/strings/lib.xq";
```

imports the module from `http://datypic.com/strings/lib.xq` whose target namespace is `http://datypic.com/strings`. The target namespace specified in the module import must match the target namespace of the library module that is being imported. The module location and namespace must be literal values in quotes (not evaluated expressions), and they should be syntactically valid absolute URIs.

Imported modules can have the same target namespace as the importing module, or they can have a different one. For convenience, it is also possible to map a namespace prefix directly in the module import. For example:

```
import module namespace strings = "http://datypic.com/strings"
               at "http://datypic.com/strings/lib.xq";
```

binds the prefix strings to the namespace, in addition to importing the module.

The at keyword and location are optional. If the processor has some other way to locate the module based on its target namespace, it can be omitted. In fact, the processor is not required to use the location even if it is provided.

Multiple module imports

It is possible to specify multiple module locations for the same target namespace in a single import, using commas to separate them, as in:

```
import module "http://datypic.com/strings"
            at "http://datypic.com/strings/lib.xq",
               "http://datypic.com/strings/lib2.xq";
```

This syntax is the only way to specify multiple imports for the same target namespace. If two *separate* module imports specify the same target namespace, an error is raised.

Function signatures and variable names must be unique across all modules that are used together (main or imported). Declaring two functions with the same qualified name and the same number of parameters raises an error, as does declaring two variables with the same qualified name. These errors are raised even if the two duplicate declarations are exactly the same.

Library modules can import other library modules, even ones with the same target namespace. However, circular module imports are not allowed unless all modules imported in the circle have the same target namespace. This means you need to plan the assignment of functions to modules with great care. For example, if you have a module for manipulating postal codes and another for manipulating geographical coordinates, and if each of these modules needs to reference functions in the other module, then you will have to either put them in the same namespace or move some shared components to a third, neutral namespace.

The behavior of a module import

It is important to understand that a module import *only* imports the function and variable declarations of the library module. It does not import any schemas or other modules that are imported in the prolog of the library module.

For example, suppose the strings.xq library module contains an import of a third module, called characters.xq. If the main module imports strings.xq, that does not mean that characters.xq is also imported into the main module. If the main module refers to the functions and variables of characters.xq directly, it needs to have a separate module import for characters.xq.

Likewise, if strings.xq imports a schema named stringtypes.xsd, the main module that imports strings.xq must also separately import the schema if it refers to any types from that schema. This is described further in the section "Schema Imports" in Chapter 13.

Variable Declarations

Variables can optionally be declared (and bound) in the query prolog. If a variable is bound within an expression in the query body, it does not have to be declared in the prolog as well. For example, you can use the expression `let $myInt := 2` in the query body without declaring `$myInt` in advance. `$myInt` is bound when the `let` expression is evaluated.

However, it is sometimes necessary to declare variables in the prolog, such as when:

- They are referenced in a function that is declared in that module
- They are referenced in other modules that import the module
- Their value is set by the processor outside the scope of the query

Declaring variables in the prolog can also be a useful way to define *constants*, or values that can be calculated up front and used throughout the query. It's important to remember that global variables (prolog-declared variables) are immutable, just like other XQuery variables.

Variable Declaration Syntax

The syntax of a variable declaration is shown in Figure 12-4. For example, the declaration:

```
declare variable $maxItems := 12;
```

binds the value 12 to the variable `$maxItems`.

Figure 12-4. Syntax of a variable declaration[a]

[a] The optional as clause, useful for static typing, is described in "Type Declarations in Global Variable Declarations" in Chapter 14.

 A previous draft of the XQuery recommendation specified the following syntax for variable declarations:

```
define variable $maxItems {12}
```

Some popular XQuery implementations still use this old syntax.

The Scope of Variables

The processor evaluates all variable declarations in the order they appear, before it evaluates the query body. When a variable declaration is evaluated, the variable is bound to a specific value.

After a variable is bound, you can reference that variable anywhere in the query. If a function body references a variable that is declared in the prolog, the function declaration must appear *after* the variable declaration. Similarly, if one global variable references another, the referencing variable must come after the referenced variable. This differs from functions referencing other functions, where forward references are allowed.

As with all other XQuery variables, a variable can only be bound once. Therefore, you cannot declare a variable in the prolog and then set its value later, for example, in a let expression. If you attempt to do this, it will be considered an entirely new variable with the same name and a smaller scope (the FLWOR).

Variable Names

Each variable declaration specifies a unique variable name. Variables have qualified names, meaning that they can be associated with a namespace. In the main module, variable declarations can have either unprefixed or prefixed names. If they have unprefixed names, they are not in any namespace, since variable names are not affected by default namespace declarations. If they are prefixed, they can be associated with any namespace that was also declared in the prolog.

In library modules, on the other hand, the names of declared variables must be in the target namespace of the module. Since default namespace declarations do not apply to variable names, this means that they must be prefixed, with a prefix mapped to the target namespace. This applies only to the variables that are declared in the prolog. If other variables are bound inside a function body, for example in let clauses, they can be in no namespace (unprefixed) or associated with a namespace other than the target namespace.

Initializing Expressions

The expression that specifies the value of the variable is known as the initializing expression. In the previous example, it was 12. It does not have to be a constant; it can be any valid XQuery expression. For example:

```
declare variable $firstNum := doc("catalog.xml")//product[1]/number;
```

binds the value of the first product number in the catalog to the $firstNum variable.

The initializing expression can call any function that is declared anywhere in the module or in an imported module. However, it can only reference variables that are declared before it. The following example is invalid because the initializing expression of $firstNum references a variable that is declared later:

```
declare variable $firstNum := $firstProd/number;
declare variable $firstProd := doc("catalog.xml")//product[1];
```

Neither can the declarations be circular. For example, an initializing expression cannot call a function that itself references the variable being initialized.

External Variables

External variables are variables whose values are bound by the processor outside the scope of the query. This is useful for parameterizing queries. For example, an external variable might allow a query user to specify the maximum number of items she wants returned from the query.

To declare an external variable, you use the keyword external instead of an initializing expression, as in:

```
declare variable $maxItems external;
```

In this case, the processor must have bound $maxItems to a value before the query is evaluated. Consult the documentation of your XQuery implementation to determine exactly how you can specify the values of external variables outside the query. It may allow them to be specified on a command-line interface or set programmatically.

Note that external variables are not the same thing as variables that are imported from other XQuery modules. Variables from imported modules do not need to be redeclared in the importing module.

Declaring External Functions

External functions can be provided by a particular XQuery implementation. They may be unique to that implementation or be part of a standard set of extensions defined by a user community. They may be implemented in XQuery or in another language; they simply need to be able to interface with a query using an XQuery function signature.

External functions may be declared with signatures in the query prolog. Their syntax starts out similar to a function declaration, but instead of a function body in curly braces, they use the keyword external. For example:

```
declare function ext:trim ($arg as xs:string?) as xs:string? external;
```

declares an external function named trim. Like other function names, the names of external functions must be prefixed. This example assumes that the ext prefix has been declared using a namespace declaration.

Note that external functions are not the same thing as user-defined functions that are imported from other modules. Functions declared in imported modules do not need to be redeclared in the importing module.

You should consult the documentation for your XQuery implementation to determine whether there are libraries of external functions that you can call, or whether you are able to write external functions of your own. Many processors are likely to provide the capability to write external functions written in procedural programming languages such as C# and Java. This creates the possibility of calling functions that have side effects. Even fairly innocent-looking functions, such as reading a record from a file, can have side effects (in this case, it changes the current position in the file). Such functions need great care because XQuery does not define the order of evaluation, and in some cases it may not call a function at all if the results aren't needed.

CHAPTER 13
Using Schemas with XQuery

Using schemas can result in queries that are better optimized and tested. This chapter first provides a brief overview of XML Schema. It then explains how schemas are used with queries, by importing schema definitions and taking advantage of schema-defined types.

What Is a Schema?

A schema is used to describe the structure and data content of XML documents. Example 13-1 shows a schema that might describe our catalog.xml sample document. This schema can be used to validate the catalog document, assuring that:

- Only approved elements and attributes are used
- The elements appear in the correct order
- All required elements are present
- All elements and attributes have valid values

In addition, it can provide information to the query processor about the types of the values in the document—for example, that product numbers are integers.

Example 13-1. Schema for catalog.xml

```
<xs:schema xmlns:xs="http://www.w3.org/2001/XMLSchema">
  <xs:element name="catalog" type="CatalogType"/>
  <xs:complexType name="CatalogType">
    <xs:sequence>
      <xs:element ref="product" maxOccurs="unbounded"/>
    </xs:sequence>
  </xs:complexType>
  <xs:element name="product" type="ProductType"/>
  <xs:complexType name="ProductType">
    <xs:sequence>
      <xs:element name="number" type="xs:integer"/>
      <xs:element name="name" type="NameType"/>
      <xs:element name="colorChoices" type="ColorListType" minOccurs="0"/>
      <xs:element name="desc" minOccurs="0"/>
```

Example 13-1. Schema for catalog.xml (continued)

```
    </xs:sequence>
    <xs:attribute name="dept" type="xs:string"/>
  </xs:complexType>
  <xs:simpleType name="ColorListType">
    <xs:list itemType="xs:string"/>
  </xs:simpleType>
  <xs:complexType name="NameType">
    <xs:simpleContent>
      <xs:extension base="xs:string">
        <xs:attribute name="language" type="LangType"/>
      </xs:extension>
    </xs:simpleContent>
  </xs:complexType>
  <xs:simpleType name="LangType">
    <xs:restriction base="xs:string">
      <xs:enumeration value="en"/>
      <xs:enumeration value="fr"/>
    </xs:restriction>
  </xs:simpleType>
</xs:schema>
```

Why Use Schemas with Queries?

There are a number of advantages of using schemas with queries:

Predictability

If an input document has been validated against a schema, its structure and data content are predictable. If the schema says that there will always be a number child of product, and your input document was validated, you can be sure that a number child will exist for each product. You do not need to check for its existence before you use it in an expression.

Type information for use in expressions

The schema provides type information to the query processor about the values in the instance document. For example, it can tell us that the number element contains an integer value. This is useful, for example, if you write a query that returns results sorted by number. The query processor will know that the number values should be sorted as integers and not strings, and will therefore sort 100 after 99. If they were sorted as strings, 100 would come before 99.

Identification of query errors

Schemas can be used in static analysis to determine the expected type of an expression. Using schemas, you might discover errors in the query that were not otherwise apparent. Schemas can also help you debug your queries more quickly and easily by providing more useful error messages. To use a SQL analogy, you wouldn't want a SQL statement that had a misspelled column name to come back with nothing instead of raising an error. Without XML schemas, this is exactly what your XQuery queries will do if you misspell an element name or specify an invalid path: return nothing.

Query optimization

The more a processor knows about the structure of the input documents, the more it can optimize access to them. For example, if a schema is present, an expression such as catalog//number is a simple matter of looking at the grandchildren of catalog and returning those named number. If no schema is present, every node of the document must be traversed to find number elements.

Special processing based on type

Type-related expressions, such as instance of and typeswitch, can be used on user-defined types in the schema. For example, you could write an expression that processes the product element differently depending on whether it is of type ShirtType, HatType, etc.

Validity of query results

A query might be designed to produce results that conform to a particular XML language, such as XHTML. Performing schema validation in the query ensures that the results are valid XHTML. If the query isn't generating valid XHTML, the query processor may be able to pinpoint the error in your query.

Some query users are not concerned about these benefits, and they feel that using schemas adds too much complexity. For these users, it is entirely possible to use XQuery without schemas. If no schema is present, all of the elements and attributes are untyped. This means that they are assigned generic types (xs:untyped and xs:untypedAtomic) that allow any content or value.

W3C XML Schema: A Brief Overview

The schema language supported directly by the XQuery recommendation is W3C XML Schema, which is a W3C Recommendation with two normative parts:[*]

Part 1 Structures

Defines a language for defining schemas, which express constraints on XML documents.

Part 2 Datatypes

Defines a rich set of built-in types that can be applied to XML documents through schemas, as well as through other mechanisms.

The XML Schema built-in types defined in Part 2 are the basis for the atomic types used in XQuery. Regardless of whether schemas are present, these types can be used in queries to represent common datatypes such as strings, numbers, dates, and times. All XQuery implementations support this basic set of types.

[*] Full coverage of XML Schema is outside the scope of this book. For detailed coverage, please see *Definitive XML Schema* by Priscilla Walmsley (Prentice Hall PTR).

XQuery also interacts with Part 1 of XML Schema. Schema definitions can be used in queries to validate input documents, intermediate values, and result elements.

XQuery does not currently provide specific support for other schema languages or validation mechanisms such as DTDs, RELAX NG, or Schematron. However, a processor can be written that validates a document using one of these schema languages and annotates its elements and attributes with appropriate types.

Element and Attribute Declarations

Elements and attributes are the most basic components of an XML document. The catalog schema has a declaration for each of the different kinds of elements and attributes in the catalog, such as `product`, `number`, and `dept`. Elements are declared in the schema using an `xs:element` element, while attributes are declared with `xs:attribute`.

Element and attribute declarations can be declared globally or locally. The `catalog` and `product` element declarations are global, meaning that they appear as a child of `xs:schema` in the schema document. The other element declarations, along with the attribute declaration, are local, and their scope is the type (`ProductType` or `NameType`) in which they are declared. If you're writing a schema with XQuery in mind, you should use a global declaration for any elements that you want to validate separately. That's because you can only validate against a global element declaration.

Types

Every element and attribute is associated with a type. Types are used to specify a class of elements (or attributes), including their allowed values, the structure of their content, and/or their attributes.

Simple and complex types

Types in XML Schema can be either simple or complex. Simple types are those that allow text content, but no child elements or attributes. In our `catalog.xml` document, the elements `number` and `colorChoices` have simple types because they have neither children nor attributes. Attributes themselves always have simple types because they always have simple values.

Complex types, by contrast, allow children and/or attributes. In `catalog.xml`, the elements `catalog`, `product`, and `desc` have complex types because they have children. The `name` element also has a complex type, even though it does not have children, because it can have an attribute.

Complex types are further divided into four different content types. The different content types vary in whether they allow child elements and text content. Table 13-1 lists the four content types and provides examples for each. The content type is not affected by the presence of attributes; all complex types allow attributes, regardless of content type.

Table 13-1. Content types for complex types

Content type	Allows children?	Allows text content?	Example
Simple	No	Yes	`<name lang="en">Shirt</name>`
Element-only	Yes	No	`<product dept="MEN">` ` <number>784</number>` `</product>`
Mixed	Yes	Yes	`<desc>Our <i>best</i> shirt!</desc>`
Empty	No	No	`<discounted value="true"/>`

User-defined types

XML Schema allows user-defined types to be created based on existing types. A new simple type can be defined that is a restriction of another type. Example 13-1 shows a simple type LangType that is derived from the built-in type xs:string. New complex types can also be derived from other complex types, either by restriction (further constraining the base type) or extension (adding new attributes or child elements). For example, based on the schema in Example 13-1 you could define a new complex type ShirtType that extends ProductType to add child elements that are relevant only to shirts, such as sleeve length, not to products in general.

As with the built-in types, these type derivations result in a type definition hierarchy that is in some ways analogous to an object-oriented hierarchy of sub- and superclasses.

List types

A list type is a different variety of atomic type that represents whitespace-separated lists of values. The type of each item in the list is known as the item type. In our example schema, the colorChoices element is declared to be of a type that is a list of xs:string values. Therefore, the element:

```
<colorChoices>navy black</colorChoices>
```

has content that is treated like two separate values, navy and black. An XQuery processor treats it somewhat differently than if it had an atomic type: it treats it like a sequence of two atomic values, in this case strings. If you test the value for equality, as follows:

```
doc("catalog.xml")//product[colorChoices = 'navy']
```

it will return that element (the first product in the catalog). If colorChoices were of type xs:string, or untyped, the product would not be selected because the value navy black would be treated as one string.

Namespaces and XML Schema

When a target namespace is indicated in a schema, all of the globally declared elements and attributes take on that target namespace as part of their name. Example 13-2 shows the beginning of the catalog schema, which specifies a target namespace, http://datypic.com/prod, using the targetNamespace attribute on the xs:schema element.

Example 13-2. Beginning of the catalog schema with target namespace

```
<xs:schema xmlns:xs="http://www.w3.org/2001/XMLSchema"
           elementFormDefault="qualified"
           targetNamespace="http://datypic.com/prod"
           xmlns:prod="http://datypic.com/prod">
  <xs:element name="catalog" type="prod:CatalogType"/>
  <xs:complexType name="CatalogType">
  <!-- ... -->
```

Using this schema, the catalog element would have to be associated with a namespace in an instance document (and in any queries on that instance document). In addition, named type definitions also have names that are qualified by the target namespace. To refer to CatalogType, you use its qualified name—for example, prod:CatalogType if the prefix prod is mapped to the namespace http://datypic.com/prod.

In-Scope Schema Definitions

In any module, there is a set of in-scope schema definitions (ISSDs) that can be referenced within the query. This includes type definitions, element declarations and attribute declarations. They can describe the input documents, the result XML, or both. You may want to reference schema definitions for a number of reasons, such as:

- To write functions that only accept values of a certain user-defined type. For example, a function that queries sleeve length might accept only elements of type ShirtType.

- To validate a node that you constructed in your query. For example, you used constructors to create a product element and its children, and you want to ensure that it is valid according to ProductType.

- To determine whether a value is an instance of a particular user-defined type in order to decide how to process it. For example, if the size value is an instance of ShirtSizeType, you want to call one function, whereas if it is a value of HatSizeType, you want to call a different function.

- You want to perform static type analysis and you want the schema definitions to be taken into account.

If you don't need to do any of these things, you are not required to include your schemas in the in-scope schema definitions. This is true even if your input document was validated against a schema.

Where Do In-Scope Schema Definitions Come from?

Definitions for the built-in types are automatically included in the ISSD. A processor may include additional schema declarations and definitions in the ISSD according to implementation-defined rules. For example, it may have a set of built-in schemas that are always present. Processors that support schema validation may add definitions from the schema with which an input document is validated. Additionally, some implementations will allow you to specify programmatically or as a parameter—outside the scope of the query—what schemas to import.

Schema Imports

A schema import is used in XQuery to add a schema to the ISSD for a module. When a schema is imported, all of its global element and attribute declarations and type definitions are added.

A schema import, which appears in the query prolog, specifies the target namespace and, optionally, the schema location. For example:

```
import schema "http://datypic.com/prod"
        at "http://datypic.com/prod.xsd";
```

imports the schema document at `http://datypic.com/prod.xsd` whose target namespace is `http://datypic.com/prod`.

The syntax of a schema import is shown in Figure 13-1. The schema location and namespace must be literal values in quotes (not evaluated expressions), and they should be syntactically valid absolute URIs.

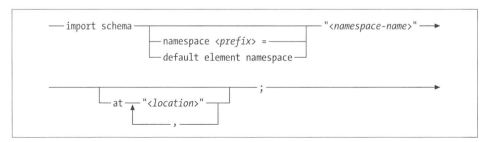

Figure 13-1. Syntax of a schema import

For convenience, it is also possible to include a namespace declaration as part of the schema import. For example:

```
import schema namespace prod = "http://datypic.com/prod"
        at "http://datypic.com/prod.xsd";
```

maps the `prod` prefix to the namespace, in addition to importing it. Additionally, a default namespace declaration can be included in a schema import, as in:

```
import schema default element namespace "http://datypic.com/prod"
        at "http://datypic.com/prod.xsd";
```

This has the effect of making `http://datypic.com/prod` the default element namespace, in addition to importing the schema with that target namespace.

If the at keyword and schema location are left off, it is assumed that the processor knows where to locate the schema for the specified namespace. It is also legal for the processor to ignore the location provided if it has another method of locating the schema.

Schema import is an optional feature that is not supported by all implementations.

Importing a schema with no target namespace

If the imported schema has no target namespace, a zero-length string should be used for the target namespace, as in:

```
import schema "" at "http://datypic.com/prod.xsd";
```

In order to reference any of the element or type names in that schema, you must make the default namespace the zero-length string (""). You can do this using the same syntax described in the previous section:

```
import schema default element namespace ""
              at "http://datypic.com/prod.xsd";
```

Importing multiple schemas with the same target namespace

Multiple schema imports can appear in the query prolog, but only one per namespace. To specify multiple schema documents with the same target namespace, use a single schema import with multiple schema locations separated by commas, as in:

```
import schema "http://datypic.com/prod"
              at "http://datypic.com/prod.xsd",
                 "http://datypic.com/prod2.xsd";
```

Schema imports and library modules

When importing a library module into your query, it is important to understand that a module import *only* imports the function and variable declarations of the library module. It does not automatically import the schemas that are imported in the prolog of the library module.

For example, suppose you have a library module called `strings.xq` that imports a schema named `stringtypes.xsd`. When the main module imports `strings.xq`, the `stringtypes.xsd` definitions are not automatically added to the in-scope schema definitions of the main module. If the main module needs to refer directly to any of the types or declarations of `stringtypes.xsd`, it must import that schema explicitly in its prolog.

In addition, the main module must import `stringtypes.xsd` if it uses any variables or functions from `strings.xq` that depend on a type definition from the schema. For example, suppose `strings.xq` contains the variable declaration:

```
declare variable $strings:LetterA as strings:smallString := "A";
```

where `smallString` is a user-defined type defined in `stringtypes.xsd`. The main module must import the `stringtypes.xsd` schema if it uses the `LetterA` variable. This does not apply to the built-in types, such as `xs:integer` or `xs:string`, whose definitions are always in scope.

Schema Validation and Type Assignment

Adding a schema to the ISSD does not automatically cause any input documents or result XML to be validated or annotated with types. There are two occasions during query evaluation when schema validation may occur:

The first is when an input document is opened, for example using the `doc` or `collection` function. Depending on the implementation, the processor *may* validate the input document at this time. However, a processor is not required to automatically validate input documents, even if it supports XML Schema. It can choose the way it finds and selects schemas for the input document. Additionally, the processor is not required to stop evaluating the query if an input document is found to be invalid but still well formed. You should consult the documentation for your XQuery implementation to determine how it handles these choices.

If you're relying on an input document being prevalidated in this way, it's a good idea to declare this. For example you can write:

```
declare variable $in as document-node(schema-element(catalog)) := doc("catalog.xml");
```

This causes the query to fail if the validation hasn't been done (or if validation failed). It also tells the query compiler what the expected type of `$in` is, which is useful information for optimization and error checking.

If an input document is validated, the definitions used must be consistent with any definitions added to the ISSD. For example, if your input document is a `catalog.xml` document that was validated using `catalog.xsd`, you cannot then import a different catalog schema that has conflicting definitions.

The second occasion is when a `validate` expression is used to explicitly validate documents and elements.

The Validate Expression

A validate expression can be used to validate a document or element node, which may come from an input document or be constructed in the query. It will validate the node according to a schema declaration if that declaration is in scope (i.e., if it is in the ISSD). For example:

```
validate strict { <product dept="ACC">
  <number>563</number>
  <name language="en">Floppy Sun Hat</name>
</product> }
```

validates the product element using a global product element declaration from the in-scope schema definitions, if one exists. This includes validating its attributes and descendants.

The syntax of a validate expression is shown in Figure 13-2.

Figure 13-2. Syntax of a validate expression

The expression to be validated must be either a single element node or a single document node that has exactly one element child.

The value of a validate expression is a new document or element node (with a new identity) annotated with the appropriate type indicated in the element declaration.

As with all schema validation, it also fills in default or fixed values and normalizes whitespace. When a document node is being validated, full schema validation is performed. When an element node is being validated, certain validation constraints are skipped. These omitted constraints include identity constraint (key) validation, checking xs:ID values for uniqueness, and ensuring that xs:ENTITY, xs:NOTATION, and xs:IDREF values have matching entities, notations, and IDs.

 Not all implementations support the validate expression; it is an optional feature.

Validation Mode

The validation mode controls how strictly an element or document is validated. There are two possible validation modes:

strict
> When it is strict, the processor requires that a declaration be present for the element in the validate expression and that it be valid according to those declarations. If the element is not valid or a declaration cannot be found for it, an error is raised.

lax
> When it is lax, the processor validates the element if it can find a declaration for it. It may not be able to find declarations if, for example, the schema was not imported or provided by the processor. If a declaration is found, the element or attribute must be valid according to it, or an error is raised. If no declaration is found, the processor will attempt to recursively validate the element's children and attributes, and the process repeats. If no declarations are found in the entire tree or no validation errors are encountered, no error is raised.

In a validate expression, the validation mode can be specified just after the `validate` keyword. For example:

```
validate lax {<number>563</number>}
```

results in lax validation on the `number` element. If it is not specified, the default mode `strict` is used.

Assigning Type Annotations to Nodes

It is worth taking a closer look at how the validation process assigns type annotations to elements and attributes. If the node is valid according to the type designated in its declaration, the node is usually quite straightforward. For example, the `product` element in the previous example would be assigned the type `ProductType`. However, there are some special cases.

An element or attribute is assigned a generic type (`xs:untyped` for elements, and `xs:untypedAtomic` for attributes) if:

- No schema validation was attempted.
- It was not validated because it was included as part of a wildcard (`xs:any` or `xs:anyAttribute`) that does not require validation.
- It is the result of an element constructor, and construction mode is set to `strip`. Construction mode is described in "Types and Newly Constructed Elements and Attributes," later in this chapter.
- It is the result of a validate expression, but it was not validated against an in-scope schema definition. This might happen if the validation mode is `lax` with no relevant declaration in scope.

Another generic type, `xs:anyType`, is used in a few other cases. The difference between `xs:anyType` and `xs:untyped` is that an element of type `xs:anyType` may contain other elements that have specific types. Elements of type `xs:untyped`, on the other hand, always have children that are untyped. An element is assigned the type `xs:anyType` if:

- When an input document was accessed, validation was attempted but the element was found to be invalid (or partially valid). Some implementations may allow the query evaluation to continue even if validation fails.
- It is the result of an element constructor, and construction mode is set to `preserve`.

A node that is declared to have a union type is assigned the specific member type for which it was validated (which is the first one to which it conforms). For example, if the `<a>12` element is validated using a union type whose member types are `xs:integer` and `xs:string`, in that order, it is assigned the type `xs:integer`, not the union type itself.

An element that uses the XML Schema attribute xsi:type for type substitution is assigned the type specified by xsi:type if it is valid according to that type definition.

Nodes and Typed Values

In most cases, you can retrieve the typed value of an element or attribute using the data function. Usually, it is simply the string value of the node, cast to the type of the element or attribute. For example, if the number element has the type xs:integer, the string value is 784 (type xs:string), while the typed value is 784 (type xs:integer). If the number element is untyped, its typed value is 784 (type xs:untypedAtomic).

There are two exceptions to this rule:

- Elements whose types have element-only content (that is, they allow only children) do not have typed values, even if that particular element does not have any children. For example, the product element does not have a typed value if it is annotated with a type other than xs:untyped.

- The typed value of an element or attribute whose type is a list type is a sequence of atomic values, one for each item in the list. For example, if the element <colorChoices>navy black</colorChoices> has a type that is a list of strings, the typed value is a sequence of two strings, navy and black.

An element's typed value will be the empty sequence in two cases:

- Its type is a complex type with an empty content model.
- It has been nilled, meaning that it has an attribute xsi:nil="true".

The typed value will not be the empty sequence just because the element has no content. For example, the typed value of <name></name> is the value "" (type xs:untypedAtomic) if name is untyped, and a zero-length string (type xs:string) if name has a complex type with mixed content but happens to be empty.

A summary of the rules for the typed values of elements and attributes appears in Table 13-2.

Table 13-2. Typed values of elements and attributes

Kind of node	Typed value	Type of typed value
An untyped element	The character data content of the element and all its descendants	xs:untypedAtomic
An element whose type is a simple type, or a complex type with simple content	The character data content of the element	The type of the element's content
An element whose type has mixed content	The character data content of the element and all its descendants	xs:untypedAtomic
An element whose type has element-only content	Error	N/A
An element whose type has empty content	()	N/A
An untyped attribute	The attribute value	xs:untypedAtomic

Table 13-2. Typed values of elements and attributes (continued)

Kind of node	Typed value	Type of typed value
A typed attribute	The attribute value	The type of the attribute
An element or attribute whose type is a list type	A sequence containing the values in the list	The list type's item type

Types and Newly Constructed Elements and Attributes

Newly constructed nodes don't automatically take on the type of their content. For example, the expression <abc>{2}</abc> does not create an abc element whose type annotation is xs:integer just because its content is of type xs:integer. In fact, element constructors that have simple content, as in this example, are always annotated with xs:untyped unless they are enclosed in a validate expression.

The type of a newly constructed element with complex content is also generic, but any children it copies from an input document may or may not retain their original types from the input document. This is determined by construction mode, which can have one of two values: strip or preserve. If construction mode is strip, the type of the newly constructed element, and all of its descendants, is xs:untyped. If the element is contained in a validate expression, it may then be annotated with a new schema type.

If construction mode is preserve, the type of the newly constructed element is xs:anyType, and all of its copied children retain their original types from the input document.

For example, suppose you construct a productList element with the following expression:

```
<productList>{doc("catalog.xml")//product}</productList>
```

Suppose also that the catalog.xml document has been validated with a schema, and the product elements from this document are annotated with the type ProductType. This query will result in a productList element that contains four product elements.

If construction mode is strip, both productList and all the product elements in the results will be annotated with xs:untyped. If construction mode is preserve, productList will be annotated with xs:anyType, and the product elements will be annotated with ProductType.

Construction mode is set using a construction declaration, which may appear in the query prolog. Its syntax is shown in Figure 13-3.

Figure 13-3. Syntax of a construction declaration

Sequence Types and Schemas

Chapter 11 showed how sequence types are used to match sequences in various expressions, including function calls. When schemas have been imported into a query, additional tests are available for sequence types, including testing for name and type. Their syntax is shown in Figure 13-4. These tests can be used not just in sequence types but also as kind tests in path expressions.

Figure 13-4. Element and attribute tests (for sequence types and kind tests)

Chapter 11 introduced the element() and attribute() tests. For example, you can use the test element(prod:product) to test for elements whose name is prod:product.

These tests can also be used with user-defined types. For example, the sequence type:

```
element(prod:product, prod:ProductType)
```

matches an element whose name is prod:product and that has the type prod:ProductType, or any type derived by restriction or extension from prod:ProductType. Yet another syntax is:

```
element(*, prod:ProductType)
```

which matches any element that has the type prod:productType (or a derived type), regardless of name. Note that the element must already have been validated and annotated with the type prod:ProductType. It is not enough that it *would* be a valid instance of that type if it *were* validated.

You can also match an element or attribute based on its name using the schema-element() and schema-attribute() tests. For example, you can use the sequence type schema-element(prod:product) to match only elements whose qualified name is prod:product. This differs from the element(prod:product) syntax in that the name must be among the globally declared element or attribute names in the ISSD. Also, in order to match, a node must have been validated according to that declaration.

Another difference is that schema-element(prod:product) will also match elements that are in the substitution group of product. Substitution groups are a feature of XML Schema that allows you to specify that certain elements are equivalent. For example, you might put elements shirt, hat, and suitcase in the substitution group headed by the product element. These three elements can then appear in content anywhere a product element may appear. The sequence type schema-element(prod:product) would then match shirt, hat, and suitcase elements in addition to product elements.

For attributes, you can specify schema-attribute and attribute and the same rules apply. However, these constructs are rarely used because attributes don't have substitution groups, and global attribute declarations are quite rare. Table 13-3 shows some examples.

Table 13-3. Examples of sequence types based on name and type

Example	Explanation
schema-element (product)+	One or more elements whose qualified name is product, that have been validated using a global element declaration in the ISSD
schema-element (prod:product)	One element whose qualified name is equal to prod:product, that has been validated using a global element declaration in the ISSD
schema-attribute (prod:dept)	One attribute whose qualified name is prod:dept, that has been validated using a global attribute declaration in the ISSD
element(*, prod:ProductType)	One element whose type annotation is prod:ProductType or a type derived from prod:ProductType
element (prod:product, prod:ProductType)	One element whose qualified name is equal to prod:product, whose type annotation is prod:ProductType or a type derived from prod:ProductType, that is in the ISSD

You can use a question mark at the end of the type name in an element sequence type. This means that if an element is nilled (i.e., it has the attribute xsi:nil set to true), it can match the sequence type even though it does not have any content. For example, element(product, ProductType?) matches both a regular product element and a nilled product element such as <product xsi:nil="true"/>. Note that this is different from a question mark at the very end of the sequence type, which indicates that the empty sequence should match.

Static Typing

Errors in a query can be reported in either the static analysis phase or the dynamic evaluation phase. These two phases are roughly analogous to compiling and running program code. Certain XQuery implementations take a more aggressive approach to finding type-related errors in the static analysis phase. These implementations are said to support static typing.

What Is Static Typing?

Static typing, as the term is used in XQuery, refers to reporting all possible type errors at analysis (compile) time rather than evaluation (run) time. This is sometimes referred to as *pessimistic static typing*, where the philosophy is to report any errors that could possibly happen, not just those that it knows will happen. The static typing feature of XQuery is optional; implementations are not required to support static typing and many do not fully support it.

The fact that a processor doesn't support this feature doesn't mean that it is doing no compile-time analysis. It might use the analysis transparently for optimization purposes, or it might report some errors at compile time; but in this case, it will report errors optimistically. It will only report errors when it can see that there is definitely something wrong, like in the expression "x" + 3, and not simply in cases of ambiguity, as in $x + 3, where the value of $x depends on some input data.

Static typing has the advantages of allowing type errors to be caught earlier and more reliably, and can help some implementations optimize queries. However, as you will see in this chapter, it can also be an irritation to query authors in that it reports many "false" errors.

As part of the static typing process, the processor checks all expressions in a query and assigns them a static type, which is the supplied type of the expression. For example, the expression "abc" is assigned the static type of xs:string. The expression count(doc("catalog.xml")//product) is assigned the static type of xs:integer, which is the return type of the count function.

A type error is reported when a function or operator expects a value of a certain type and a parameter or operand of an incompatible type is used.

Obvious Static Type Errors

A number of obvious type errors can be caught in the analysis phase, for example:

- Passing an integer to a function that expects a string, as in upper-case(2)
- Attempting a cast between two types that do not allow casting, as in current-date() cast as xs:integer
- Attempting to add two strings, as in "abc" + "def"
- Passing a sequence of multiple values to a function or operation that expects a single atomic value, as in substring(("a","b"),3)

All of these examples will raise a type error no matter what the input document contains. Many implementations that do not support the static typing feature will also report these errors at analysis time, since they will always result in an error.

Static Typing and Schemas

Static typing also takes into account any in-scope schema definitions. A schema can make static typing much more useful by providing the processor with extra information about the input documents, namely:

Specific types
> If the number element is declared to be of type xs:string, it is obviously an error to try to multiply it by 2.

Cardinalities
> If a product can have more than one name child, you don't want to use the expression product/name as an argument to the substring function, because the substring function only accepts a single string (or the empty sequence), not a sequence of multiple strings.

Allowed names
> If you refer to an element produt (misspelled) in your query, it must be an error, because no produt element is declared in the schema.

Allowed paths
> The path catalog/number contains an error because the schema does not allow number to be a child of catalog, even if both of those elements are declared in the schema.

None of the above errors could be caught during the static analysis phase if no schema were present. Sometimes this type of feedback can be extremely useful. For one thing, it can lead to queries that are more robust. You may not have envisioned a product with more than one name in your test data, but you would have found this

error the hard way later when querying some new input data that happened to have that characteristic.

Static typing can also make query debugging and testing much easier. If you get an error message saying that `catalog/number` will always return the empty sequence (and therefore is not a valid path), it is much more useful than getting no results from your entire query and wondering why. Coming up with test data that addresses every single possible combination of elements and values in an input document can relieve the burden on you.

Raising "False" Errors

The down side of static typing is that sometimes the errors raised are less useful. Sometimes you know that an error situation would never arise in your input document, even if the schema might allow it. Suppose you want to substring the name of a single product, based on its product number. You might use the expression:

```
substring(doc("catalog.xml")//product[number = 557]/name, 1, 10)
```

However, if static typing is in effect, this expression causes a static error. This is because, as far as the processor knows, there could be more than one `name` element that matches that criterion, but the `substring` function's signature requires that only zero or one item be provided as the first argument. You may know for sure that no two products will have the same product number (perhaps because you are familiar with the application that generates the XML documents), but the processor doesn't know that.

This particular error can be avoided by calling the `zero-or-one` function, described in "The zero-or-one, one-or-more, and exactly-one Functions," later in this chapter.

Static Typing Expressions and Constructs

It is useful to have expressions and functions that you can use in your query to get around these false static errors. These constructs include treat and typeswitch expressions, type declarations, and the `zero-or-one`, `one-or-more`, and `exactly-one` functions.

The Typeswitch Expression

The typeswitch expression provides a convenient syntax for performing special processing based on the type of an expression. An example is shown in Example 14-1.

Example 14-1. Binding variables to typeswitch expressions

```
typeswitch ($myProduct)
  case element(*,prod:HatType) return xs:string($myProduct/size)
  case element(*,prod:ShirtType)
```

Example 14-1. Binding variables to typeswitch expressions (continued)

```
    return xs:string(concat($myProduct/size/@system, ": ",
                            $myProduct/size))
  case element(*,prod:UmbrellaType) return "none"
  default return "n/a"
```

The example assumes that $myProduct is bound to a product element. In the schema, assume that product elements are declared to have type ProductType. However, in the input document, a product element may carry an xsi:type attribute that indicates another type that is derived by extension from ProductType, such as HatType, ShirtType, or UmbrellaType.

ProductType itself does not allow a size child. Depending on which subtype it has, it may or may not have a size child. The typeswitch expression will return a different value depending on the type annotation of the product element.

The syntax of a typeswitch expression is shown in Figure 14-1. The typeswitch keyword is followed by an expression in parentheses (called the operand expression), which evaluates to the sequence whose type is to be evaluated. This is followed by one or more case clauses, plus a required default clause that indicates the value if none of the case clauses applies.

Figure 14-1. Syntax of a typeswitch expression

The processor uses sequence type matching (described in Chapter 11) to determine whether a case clause applies. This means that if the type of the items in the sequence is the same as, *or is derived from*, the type identified by the case clause, it matches. If more than one case clause is applicable, the first one is used. Remember, with sequence type matching, it is not enough that the items are valid according to the specified type, they must actually have been validated and have that type (or a type derived from it) as their type annotation.

Each of the case and default clauses can have an optional variable name before the return keyword. That variable is bound to the value of the operand expression. This is useful if the return expression is dependent on the sequence being tested. In Example 14-2, the $h, $s, and $p variables are bound to the $myProduct value, and the return expression references the variable. This example uses user-defined schema types, which are explained in the previous chapter.

Example 14-2. Binding variables to typeswitch expressions

```
typeswitch ($myProduct)
  case $h as element(*,prod:HatType) return xs:string($h/size)
  case $s as element(*,prod:ShirtType)
      return xs:string(concat($s/size/@system, ": ", $s/size))
  case element(*,prod:UmbrellaType) return "none"
  default return "n/a"
```

The typeswitch expression can serve as shorthand for multiple if-then-else expressions that use instance of expressions to determine the type of the variable. Example 14-3 shows this alternative, which is similar to Example 14-2.

Example 14-3. Alternative to a typeswitch expression

```
if ($myProduct instance of element(*,prod:HatType))
then xs:string($myProduct/size)
else if ($myProduct instance of element(*,prod:ShirtType))
    then xs:string(concat($myProduct/size/@system, ": ", $myProduct/size))
    else if ($myProduct instance of element(*,prod:UmbrellaType))
        then "none"
        else "n/a"
```

However, there is an important difference between the two: an implementation that supports static typing will raise a type error with Example 14-3. This is because, as far as the processor knows, $myProduct is of type ProductType, which does not allow a size child. Even though the processor is aware that there are subtypes that allow a size child, the static typing feature does not extend to parsing out the if expressions to determine that you would never evaluate the expression $myProduct/size on anything that didn't allow a size child. The typeswitch expression in Example 14-2, on the other hand, assures the processor that the branch that contains $h/size will only ever be evaluated for elements of type HatType. Remember that static typing is *pessimistic*; it will give you an error if anything could go wrong, not only if it knows that things *will* go wrong.

The Treat Expression

The treat expression, like the typeswitch expression, is used to assure the processor that only values of a certain type will participate in a particular function or operation. The syntax of a treat expression is shown in Figure 14-2.

Figure 14-2. Syntax of a treat expression

Building on the ProductType/HatType example from the previous section, suppose you would like to display the size of a product, if it is a hat. Although ProductType doesn't allow a size child, HatType does. You could use the query shown in Example 14-4.

Example 14-4. A query without a treat expression

```
if ($myProduct instance of element(*,prod:HatType))
then <p>The size is: {data($myProduct/size)}</p>
else ()
```

It tests to see if the product is a hat, and if it is, constructs a p element that contains its size. Unfortunately, an implementation that supports static typing will raise a type error with this query. This is because, as far as the processor knows, $myProduct has type ProductType, which does not allow a size child. As discussed in the previous section, it does not matter that you check the type of $myProduct in the enclosing if expression.

Example 14-5 shows a revised query that uses a treat expression to assure the processor that $myProduct is indeed an element of type HatType.

Example 14-5. A query with a treat expression

```
if ($myProduct instance of element(*,prod:HatType))
then
  <p>The size is: {data(($myProduct treat as element(*,prod:HatType))/size)}</p>
else ()
```

Unlike a cast expression or a type constructor, the treat expression does not actually change the type of $myProduct. It doesn't need to, because the type of $myProduct should already be prod:HatType or some matching type. Like other static-typing-related expressions, it simply postpones any errors to runtime by saying, "I know that all the values are going to be valid HatType values, so don't raise an error during the analysis phase."

If it turns out later during the evaluation phase that there is a $myProduct value that does not match HatType, the error is raised at that time. The rules of sequence type matching are used to determine whether the value matches. In this particular example, it will never raise this error because it checks the type of $myProduct before evaluating the /size path.

If you're familiar with casts in Java or C#, you'll recognize that most casts in those languages are assertions (like treat as) rather than actual type conversions. XQuery uses cast as to mean a type conversion, and treat as to mean a type assertion.

Type Declarations

Some expressions, namely FLWORs, quantified expressions, and global variable declarations, allow the use of a type declaration to force the static type of an expression. A type declaration uses the keyword as, followed by a sequence type. The sequence types used in these expressions follow the syntax described in Chapter 11.

Type Declarations in FLWORs

Sequence types can be used in the `for` and `let` clauses of FLWORs to declare the type of variable being bound. In this case, the type declaration appears immediately after the variable name, as in Example 14-6.

Example 14-6. A FLWOR with a type declaration

```
for $prod as element(*,ProductType) in doc("catalog.xml")/catalog/*
order by $prod/name
return $prod/name
```

The sequence type `element(*,ProductType)` is specified as the type of the variable `$prod`. Without the type declaration, this query might raise a type error using a processor that implements static typing, if the schema allows the possibility of `catalog` having children that don't themselves have `name` children. The type declaration serves as a way of telling the processor, "I know that all the children of `catalog` will be valid elements of type `ProductType`, which all have `name` children, so don't raise a static error. If it turns out I'm wrong, you can raise a dynamic error later."

With the type declaration, this error checking is postponed to evaluation time. When the query is evaluated, if the value of `$prod` does not have the type `ProductType`, a type error is raised. Note that the purpose of the sequence type specification is not to filter out items that do not conform, but to raise type errors when nonconforming items are encountered.

Unlike type declarations in function signatures, no conversions take place. Untyped atomic data won't be converted to the required type, numeric type promotion won't happen—in fact, you won't even get atomization. The only difference allowed between the actual type of the value and the declared type is subtype substitution: if the required type is `xs:decimal`, for example, the supplied value can be `xs:integer`, but it can't be a node containing an `xs:integer`.

Type Declarations in Quantified Expressions

Quantified expressions also allow sequence types to be specified for variables, using a similar syntax, as in Example 14-7.

Example 14-7. A quantified expression with a type declaration

```
every $number as element(*,xs:integer) in
    doc("catalog.xml")//number satisfies ($number > 0)
```

In this case, the `$number` variable is given the sequence type `element(*,xs:integer)`. If any of the items returned by the expression `doc("catalog.xml")//number` do not match that sequence type, a type error is raised.

 Declaring sequence types for variables in quantified expressions, or for clauses, is not supported in XPath 2.0.

Type Declarations in Global Variable Declarations

An optional type declaration can be specified in a global variable declaration, as in:

```
declare variable $firstNum as xs:integer
   := data(doc("catalog.xml")//product[1]/number);
```

which associates $firstNum with the static type xs:integer. As with other type declarations, this type declaration does not change or cast the value in any way. It is simply used to reassure the processor that the typed value of $firstNum will always be an integer, so it can be used in arithmetic operations, for example. This is especially useful for external variables, since their static type cannot be determined any other way.

The zero-or-one, one-or-more, and exactly-one Functions

Three functions relate specifically to static typing: zero-or-one, one-or-more, and exactly-one. These functions are useful when static typing is in effect, to override apparent static type errors.

Each of the functions takes a single argument and either returns the argument as is or raises an error if the argument is a sequence containing the wrong number of items. For example, when calling the zero-or-one function, if the argument is a sequence of zero or one items, it is returned. If it is a sequence of more than one item, an error is raised.

Earlier in this chapter, we saw how the expression:

```
number(doc("prices.xml")//prod[@num = 557]/price)
```

will cause a static error when static typing is in effect. This is because, as far as the processor knows, there could be more than one price element that matches that criterion, while the number function's signature requires that only zero or one item be provided. A static error can be avoided by using the expression:

```
number (zero-or-one(doc("prices.xml")//prod[@num = 557]/price))
```

In this case, no static error is raised. Rather, a dynamic error is raised if more than one price element is returned by the path expression. This is useful if you know that there will only be one product with number 557 in the document, and wish to override the static error.

Principles of Query Design

Well-designed, robust queries have the advantages of running faster and with fewer errors, as well as being easier to debug and maintain. This chapter describes some of the goals of query design, with particular attention to handling errors and tuning for performance.

Query Design Goals

Some of the elements of good query design include:

Clarity
> Queries that clearly convey their meaning are much easier to understand and therefore to maintain.

Modularity
> Expressions should be reusable in many parts of a query and across multiple queries.

Robustness
> Queries should be able to handle all possible combinations of values of input data.

Error handling
> Queries should handle dynamic errors gracefully, with useful messages.

Performance
> Queries should be tuned for performance.

The rest of this chapter takes a closer look at these design goals.

Clarity

You can increase the clarity of your queries by improving the layout of the query, making appropriate use of names, and using comments liberally. In addition to the recommendations in this chapter, you can go to *http://www.xqdoc.org/xquery-style.html* for some more detailed XQuery style conventions.

Improving the Layout

To make the structure of a query more obvious, you should make appropriate use of whitespace and parentheses. Whitespace (line breaks, spaces, and tabs) is allowed anywhere between keywords to make it more readable.

It is helpful to split longer FLWOR and conditional expressions into multiple lines and indent each clause to line up, as shown in Example 15-1. FLWORs embedded within FLWORs should be further indented. When constructing XML results, you should indent the element constructors just as you would indent the elements in an XML document.

Example 15-1. Making use of whitespace

```
Less clear query
for $product in doc("catalog.xml")//product return
<product><number>{$product/number}</number>
<price>{for $price in doc("prices.xml")//prod
where $product/number = $price/@num
return $price/price}</price>
</product>
More clear query
for    $product in doc("catalog.xml")//product
return <product>
        <number>{$product/number}</number>
        <price>{for    $price in doc("prices.xml")//prod
                where  $product/number = $price/@num
                return $price/price}</price>
      </product>
```

Parentheses can be used around most expressions to group them together. If the beginning and end of an expression are not obvious, parentheses are highly recommended. For example, a complex where clause in a FLWOR, or a complex then clause in a conditional expression, are much clearer when wrapped in parentheses.

Choosing Names

Choosing meaningful names can also make a query much easier to understand. This includes the names of variables, functions, and function parameters. Names can also be used along with repeating let clauses to make an expression more clear. For example, in the expression:

```
let $substring := substring($myString,1,32)
let $substringNoQuotes := replace($substring,'"','')
let $substringUpperCase := upper-case($substringNoQuotes)
return $substringUpperCase
```

the names are bound to the string in various states of processing. This is more obvious than its equivalent:

```
upper-case(replace(substring($myString,1,32),'"',''))
```

Namespace prefixes should also be chosen carefully. When possible, use popular prefix conventions such as `xs` for XML Schema, `wsdl` for Web Services Description Language, and `html` for XHTML. If you are using several namespaces, assign prefixes to all of them rather than making one the default. This makes it more clear which namespace each name belongs to.

Using Comments for Documentation

An important part of writing understandable queries is documenting them. Comments delimited by (: and :) can appear anywhere that insignificant whitespace is allowed in a query. For example, they may appear at the end of a line to explain the expression on that line, as a separate line, or as a block on multiple lines, as in:

```
(:::::::::::::::::::::::::::::::::::
 : The following expression returns the price of a product
 : It assumes there is one price per product element
 :::::::::::::::::::::::::::::::::::)
```

A standard method of documenting XQuery modules and functions is by using xqdoc tags. These tags, listed in Table 15-1, appear in normal XQuery comments. All of them are optional and most are allowed to repeat.

Table 15-1. xqdoc tags

Tag	Meaning
@author	The author of the component
@version	The version number
@since	The first version (e.g., of a library) when a component is supported
@see	Where to go for additional information; it can be a URL or a textual description
@param	A description of a function parameter, in the form @param $name text
@return	A description of what a function returns
@deprecated	An indication that the component has been deprecated and should therefore no longer be used; text can follow the keyword for further explanation
@error	A description of a type of error the function might return

Once a module is documented using xqdoc tags, human-readable HTML documentation can be generated automatically. The process is very similar to that of Javadoc, which generates documentation for Java classes. For more information, or to download the scripts to generate the documentation, see *http://www.xqdoc.org*.

Example 15-2 shows a function that is documented using xqdoc comments. The documentation, which appears before the function declaration, contains a textual description of the function, followed by the @param and @return tags to describe the inputs and output of the function. HTML tags (the b elements) are used in the description to enhance the display of the description in the resulting HTML documentation.

Example 15-2. Documenting a function with xqdoc

```
(:~
 : The <b>functx:substring-after-last</b> function returns the part
 : of <b>$string</b> that appears after the last occurrence of
 : <b>$delim</b>. If <b>$string</b> does not contain
 : <b>$delim</b>, the entire string is returned.
 :
 : @param $string the string to substring
 : @param $delim the delimiter
 : @return the substring
 :)
declare function functx:substring-after-last
($string as xs:string?, $delim as xs:string) as xs:string?
 { ... };
```

Modularity

Expressions that are used more than once or twice should be separated into functions and shared. Functions make it clearer to the query reader what is going on. Having a function clearly named, with a set of named, typed parameters, serves as a form of documentation. It also physically separates it from the rest of the query, which makes it easier to decipher complex queries with many nested expressions.

In addition, function declarations encourage reuse. When reused, an expression needs to be written (and maintained) only once. If you want to change the algorithm later, for example to accept the empty sequence or to fix a bug, you can do it in one place only.

Functions can be made even more reusable by separating them into library modules. XQuery libraries can also be used to create standardized sets of functions for specific XML vocabularies. These libraries can serve as an API to an XML vocabulary, shielding query authors from some of the complexity of the vocabulary. They can then be distributed to a variety of query writers, allowing reuse among an entire community of users.

Robustness

Queries should be able to handle all possible combinations of values of input data. This includes handling any potential variations in the data, and considering the impact of missing or empty values.

Handling Data Variations

It is important to consider variations in the input documents that may cause incorrect results or dynamic errors. Some common problems occur when:

Sequences of multiple items appear where only one item was expected

For example, the expressions `$prod[name eq "Floppy Sun Hat"]` and `substring($prod/name, 1, 30)` raise an error if there is more than one `name` child. The expression `$prod/name != "Floppy Sun Hat"` evaluates to `true` if two `name` children exist and either one is not equal to `Floppy Sun Hat`.

Zero items appear where one was expected

For example, the expression `$prod/price - $prod/discount` returns the empty sequence if there is no `discount` element.

Values do not conform to the expected type

For example, the expression `max($prod/number)` raises a type error if the product number is `N/A` instead of an integer.

Values are outside the expected range

Especially zero and negative numbers where a positive number was expected.

You should not assume that because an input document is validated by a schema it must be exactly as you expect. A schema can validate, for example, that a required element is present, but other assumptions might be made that cannot be validated by a schema. For example, the constraint "if the `discounted` attribute is `true`, a discount child must appear" cannot be validated by XML Schema.

Handling Missing Values

Individual data values may be missing from an input document. Sometimes these missing values are in error, and sometimes they are not. In either case, they need to be handled gracefully.

Suppose you are calculating the sale price of an item by taking the regular price, and applying a discount. Some product prices have discounts, but others do not. The absence of a discount could be represented in (at least) four ways:

- A `discount` element or attribute that is entirely absent from the input document
- An empty element or an attribute whose value is a zero-length string—for example, `<discount></discount>`, `<discount/>`, or `discount=""`
- An element that is marked with the attribute `xsi:nil`—for example, `<discount xsi:nil="true"></discount>`
- An element or attribute that has a default "missing" value such as `N/A` or `0`—for example, `<discount>N/A</discount>`

Absent values

An expression used to calculate a sequence of prices might be:

```
for $prod in doc("prices.xml")//prod
return $prod/price - $prod/discount
```

In the case where the discount element is absent, the value of the discount expression is the empty sequence, and therefore the $prod/price - $prod/discount expression also returns the empty sequence. You probably intended instead for the discount to default to zero, and for your expression to return the price itself if no discount was available.

Another problem that might occur when the discount value is missing is in calculating an average. To find the average discount, you might be tempted to use an expression like avg(doc("prices.xml")//discount). However, that function gives the average of the discount values that exist, ignoring any prices that do not have discounts.

if-absent

The if-absent function shown below is useful for providing default values in case a data item is absent:

```
declare namespace functx = "http://www.functx.com";
declare function functx:if-absent (
  $node as node( )?, $value as xs:anyAtomicType) as xs:anyAtomicType*
{
  if ($node)
  then data($node)
  else $value
};
```

The function checks if the first argument (an optional node) is the empty sequence, and whether it is, it returns the second argument. Otherwise, it returns the typed value of the first argument. For example, if you use the expression;

```
for $prod in doc("prices.xml")//prod
return $prod/price - functx:if-absent($prod/discount, 0)
```

your missing discount problem is solved.

Empty and nil values

The second possible scenario is that the discount element appears, but it is empty (and it may or may not have an xsi:nil attribute). It may appear in the input document as either <discount></discount> or <discount/>, which are equivalent elements in XML. This scenario also poses problems for the $prod/price - $prod/discount expression. Assuming the discount element is untyped, the processor attempts to cast the empty value to xs:double for use of the arithmetic expression. This results in a type error because the value is not a valid number.

Default "missing" values

The final scenario is one where the discount element contains a value such as N/A to indicate that it is absent. A simple conditional expression can handle this scenario, as in:

```
for $prod in doc("prices.xml")//prod
return if ($prod/discount = "N/A")
        then $prod/price
        else $prod/price - $prod/discount
```

Alternatively, if N/A is used for a number of different elements, you could alter the if-absent or if-empty function to check for this value, too.

if-empty

The if-empty function shown below is similar to if-absent, except that it also checks for empty content of an element or for zero-length strings as attribute values.

```
declare namespace functx = "http://www.functx.com";
declare function functx:if-empty (
  $node as node( )?, $value as xs:anyAtomicType) as xs:anyAtomicType*
{
  if (string($node) != "")
  then data($node)
  else $value
};
```

Using the discount example, the expression:

```
for $prod in doc("prices.xml")//prod
return $prod/price - functx:if-empty($prod/discount, 0)
```

solves the empty discount problem.

Error Handling

Evaluating a query has two phases: the analysis phase, which catches static errors, and the evaluation phase, which catches dynamic errors. This section does not cover static errors, since they can be caught by the query processor and debugged as part of the development process. The dynamic errors are the unexpected errors that need to be considered carefully when writing queries.

Some programming languages have a try/catch feature that allows the processor to try to perform a series of instructions (specified in the "try" clause), but if there is an error, gracefully bow out and perform another series of instructions (specified in the "catch" clause). There is no concept of try/catch in XQuery, so it is up to the query author to anticipate the kinds of errors the processor will raise and avoid evaluating those expressions.

Avoiding Dynamic Errors

It is important to consider variations in the input documents that may cause dynamic errors. For example, if you are dividing a total amount by the number of items in an order, consider the possibility that there are no items in the order, which may result in a "division by zero" error. You can avoid this by checking the number of items first, as in:

```
if ($items) then $orderTotal div count($items) else 0
```

Dynamic type errors often occur when data cannot be cast to the required type. For example, to double the price discount, you might use the expression 2 * $discount. This expression raises a dynamic error if the value of discount is N/A or a zero-length string, which cannot be cast to a numeric type. You can avoid a dynamic error by checking whether a value is castable in advance, as in:

```
if ($discount castable as xs:decimal) then 2 * $discount else 0
```

If the input data is really in error (and you are not performing schema validation), it may be helpful to test for the error condition and raise a more meaningful error using the error function. If the input data is not in error, you should modify the query to allow for the variations in input documents.

If an input document is schema validated, you can be less concerned about some of these dynamic errors. For example, if the schema specifies that the number of items in an order must be more than zero, you may not have to worry about a "division by zero" error. If the schema validates that the type of a discount element is xs:decimal, there is no chance that it is N/A.

The error and trace Functions

The error function is used to explicitly raise an error when certain conditions arise. For example, if an important data item is missing or invalid, you may want to stop evaluation of the query with a specific error message. To do this, you can incorporate calls to the error function in your query. For example:

```
if (not($product/number))
then error(QName("http://datypic.com/err", "ProdNumReq"), "missing product number")
else $product/number
```

raises a ProdNumReq error (whose description is "missing product number") if $product has no number child.

During the query debugging process, the trace function can be used to track the value of an item. For example:

```
trace($var1, "The value of $var1 is: ")
```

might write the string The value of $var1 is: 4 to a logfile.

Performance

When querying large documents or databases, it is important to tune queries to optimize performance. Implementations vary significantly in their ability to take clues from the query in order to optimize its evaluation. This section provides some general tips for improving query performance. For more specific tuning information for your XQuery processor, consult the documentation.

Avoid Reevaluating the Same or Similar Expressions

A let clause can be used to evaluate an expression once and bind the value to a variable that can be referenced many times. This can be much more efficient than evaluating the expression many times. For example, suppose you want to add a bargain-bin element to your results, but only if there are products whose price is less than 30. You first need to check whether any bargain products exist, and if so, construct a bargain-bin element and list the products in it. Example 15-3 shows an example of this.

Example 15-3. Avoid re-evaluating the same expression

Less efficient query
```
if (doc("prices.xml")/prices/priceList/prod[price < 30])
then <bargain-bin>{
     doc("prices.xml")/*/priceList/prod[price < 30]
   }</bargain-bin>
else ()
```
More efficient query
```
let $bargains := doc("prices.xml")/prices/priceList/prod[price < 30]
return if ($bargains)
     then <bargain-bin>{$bargains}</bargain-bin>
     else ()
```

In the first query, similar path expressions appear in the if expression and in the bargain-bin element constructor. In the second query, the expression is evaluated once and bound to the variable $bargains, then referenced twice in the rest of the query. This is considerably more efficient, since the expensive expression need only be evaluated once. Using some XQuery implementations, the difference in performance can be dramatic, especially when the doc function is part of the expression.

Avoid Unnecessary Sorting

If you are not concerned about the order in which your results are returned, you can improve the performance of your query by not sorting. Some expressions, particularly path expressions and the union, intersect, and except expressions, always sort the results in document order unless they appear in an unordered expression or function. Example 15-4 shows two queries that select all the number and name elements from the catalog document.

Example 15-4. Avoid unnecessary sorting

Less efficient query
```
let $doc := doc("catalog.xml")
return $doc//number | $doc//name
```
More efficient query
```
unordered {
  let $doc := doc("catalog.xml")
  return $doc//(number|name)
}
```

The first query has two inefficiencies related to sorting:

- It selects the elements without using an unordered expression, so each of the two path expressions sorts the elements in document order.
- It performs a union of the two sequences, which causes them to be resorted in document order.

The more efficient query uses an unordered expression to indicate that the order of the elements does not matter. Even if you care about the order of the final results, there may be some steps along the way that can be unordered. More information on indicating that order is not significant can be found in the section "Indicating that Order Is Not Significant" in Chapter 7.

Avoid Expensive Path Expressions

The use of the descendant-or-self axis (abbreviated //) in path expressions can be very expensive, because every descendant node must be checked. If the path to the desired descendant is known and consistent, it is far more efficient to specify the exact path. Example 15-5 shows an example of this situation.

Example 15-5. Avoid expensive path expressions

Less efficient query
```
doc("catalog.xml")//number
```
More efficient query
```
doc("catalog.xml")/catalog/product/number
```

The first query uses the // abbreviation to indicate all number descendants of the input document, while the second specifies the exact path to the number descendants. Use of the parent, ancestor, or ancestor-or-self axis can also be costly when using some XQuery implementations based on databases.

Use Predicates Instead of where Clauses

Using some XQuery implementations that are based on databases, predicates are more efficient than where clauses of FLWORs. An example of this is shown in Example 15-6.

Example 15-6. Use predicates instead of where clauses

Less efficient query
```
for $prod in doc("catalog.xml")//product
where $prod/@dept = "ACC"
order by $prod/name
return $prod/name
```
More efficient query
```
for $prod in doc("catalog.xml")//product[@dept = "ACC"]
order by $prod/name
return $prod/name
```

The first query uses a where clause $prod/@dept = "ACC" to filter out elements, while the second query uses the predicate [@dept = "ACC"]. The predicate is more efficient in some implementations because it filters out the elements *before* they are selected from the database and stored in memory.

Working with Numbers

A variety of numerical calculations can be performed using XQuery. This chapter describes the four major numeric types, along with the operators and functions that act on numeric values. These include comparisons, arithmetic operations, and functions that operate on numeric values such as round and sum.

The Numeric Types

The four main numeric types supported in XQuery are xs:decimal, xs:integer, xs:float, and xs:double. All of the operations and functions that can be performed on these types of numeric values can also be performed on values whose types are restrictions of these types. This includes user-defined types that appear in a schema, as well as the built-in derived types such as xs:positiveInteger and xs:unsignedByte. For a complete list and explanation of these built-in derived types, see Appendix B.

The xs:decimal Type

The type xs:decimal represents a signed decimal number of implementation-defined precision. Numeric literals that contain only digits and a decimal point (no letter E or e) are considered decimal numbers, with the type xs:decimal. For example, 25.5 and 25.0 are xs:decimal values.

The xs:integer Type

The type xs:integer represents a signed integer. The limit on how large an xs:integer value can be is implementation-defined. Numeric literals that contain only digits (no decimal points or the letter E or e) are considered integers, with the type xs:integer. For example, 25 is an xs:integer value.

In the type hierarchy, xs:integer is derived by restriction from xs:decimal. Therefore, anywhere XQuery is expecting an xs:decimal value, an xs:integer value may be used in its place because of subtype substitution.

The xs:float and xs:double Types

The type xs:float is patterned after IEEE single-precision 32-bit floating-point numbers, and xs:double is patterned after IEEE double-precision 64-bit floating-point numbers. The representation of both xs:float and xs:double values is a mantissa (a decimal number) followed by the character E or e, followed by an exponent, which must be an integer. For example, 3E2 represents 3×10^2, or 300. Numeric literals that contain an E or e are considered to have the type xs:double.

In addition, the following values are represented: INF (infinity), -INF (negative infinity), and NaN (not a number).

Constructing Numeric Values

How does a value become "numeric"? As with any type, a value may be assigned one of the numeric types in a number of ways, for example:

- It may be selected from an input document that has a schema declaring it to have a numeric type.
- It may be a numeric literal value that appears in the query and is not surrounded by quotes. For example, $price > 25.5 compares $price to the xs:decimal value 25.5.
- It may be the result of a function that returns a number, such as count($products), which returns an xs:integer.
- It may be the result of one of the standard constructor functions, such as:
 — xs:float("25.5E3"), which constructs an xs:float value from a string
 — xs:decimal($prod/price), which constructs an xs:decimal value from an element
- It may be the result of an explicit cast, such as $prod/price cast as xs:decimal.
- It may be cast automatically when it is passed to a function, such as the sum function.

The number Function

In addition to the standard type constructors, the number function is useful for telling the processor to treat a node or atomic value as a number, regardless of its declared type (if any). It returns that argument cast as an xs:double. If no argument is provided, the number function uses the context node.

One difference between using the number function and the xs:double constructor is that the number function returns the xs:double value NaN in the case that the value cannot be cast to a numeric value, whereas the xs:double constructor throws an error. Table 16-1 shows some examples that use the number function.

Table 16-1. The number function

Example	Return value
number(doc("prices.xml")//prod[1]/price)	29.99
number(doc("prices.xml")//prod[1]/price/@currency)	NaN
number("29.99")	29.99
number(())	NaN

Numeric Type Promotion

If an operation, such as a comparison or arithmetic operation, is performed on values of two different primitive numeric types, one value is promoted to the type of the other value. Specifically, an xs:decimal value can be promoted to xs:float or xs:double, and an xs:float value to xs:double. For example, the expression 1.0 + 1.2E0 adds a decimal number to a floating-point number. The xs:decimal number (1.0) is promoted to xs:double before the expression is evaluated.

Numeric type promotion happens automatically in arithmetic expressions and comparison expressions. It is also used in calls to functions that expect numeric values. For example, if a function expects an xs:double value, you can pass it an xs:decimal value, and xs:decimal will be promoted to xs:double.

In addition to these specific promotion rules, any numeric value can be treated as if it has its type's base type or any ancestor type. This is known as subtype substitution. For example, if in your schema you define a type myDecimal that is derived by restriction from xs:decimal, a myDecimal value can be added to an xs:decimal value, returning an xs:decimal value. This rule also applies to built-in types. For example, since xs:integer is derived from xs:decimal, an xs:integer value can be used anywhere an xs:decimal value is expected.

Comparing Numeric Values

Two numeric values can be compared using the general comparison operators: =, !=, <, <=, >, and >=. Values of different numeric types can be compared; one is promoted to the other's type. Nodes that contain numeric values can also be compared using these operators; in that case, they are atomized to extract their typed values. Table 16-2 shows some examples of comparing numeric values.

Some caution should be used when comparing untyped values using the general comparison operators. When an untyped value is compared to a numeric value (for example, a numeric literal), it is cast to the numeric type. However, when two untyped values are compared, they are treated like strings. This means that, for example, the untyped value 100 would evaluate to less than the value 99. If you want to compare two untyped values, you must explicitly cast the value(s) to a numeric type, as shown in the fourth example in Table 16-2.

Table 16-2. *Comparing numeric values*[a]

Example	Value
doc("prices.xml")//prod[3]/discount > 10	false
doc("prices.xml")//prod[3]/discount gt 10	Type error
doc("prices.xml")//prod[3]/discount > doc("prices.xml")//prod[1]/discount	true (it is comparing the string 3.99 to the string 10.00)
doc("prices.xml")//prod[3]/number(discount) > doc("prices.xml")//prod[1]/number(discount)	false (it is comparing the number 3.99 to the number 10.00)
3 gt 2	true
1 = 1.0	true
xs:float("NaN") = xs:float("NaN")	false
xs:string(xs:float("NaN")) = "NaN"	true

[a] This table assumes that prices.xml is untyped, i.e., has not been validated with a schema.

Numeric values can also be compared using the value comparison operators: eq, ne, lt, le, gt, and ge. However, the value comparison operators treat *every* untyped operand like a string, even if the other operand is numeric. This means that if you want a numeric comparison, you have to say so, by using an explicit cast.

The value INF (positive infinity) is greater than all other values, and –INF (negative infinity) is less than all other values, but each equals itself. The value NaN cannot usefully be compared with any other value (including itself) using comparison operators, because the result of the comparison operation is always false (unless the operator is !=, in which case it's always true). To determine whether a value is NaN, you can compare its string value to the string NaN, as in string($myVal) = "NaN". In some functions, such as the distinct-values function, NaN *is* considered to be equal to itself.

Arithmetic Operations

The following typical arithmetic operations can be performed on numeric values:

- Addition and subtraction using the plus (+) and the minus (–) sign
- Negation of a single value using the minus sign (–)
- Multiplication using the * operator
- Division using the div operator
- Integer division (with results truncated) using the idiv operator
- Modulus (the remainder of a division) using the mod operator

Some of these arithmetic operators can be used on date and time types in addition to numeric types. Date/time arithmetic is described in Chapter 19.

If the value NaN is involved in an arithmetic operation (and the other operand is not the empty sequence), the result is always NaN. If the empty sequence is used in an arithmetic operation, the result is always the empty sequence. It is important to understand that the empty sequence is different from zero. For example, $product/price - $product/discount is equal to the empty sequence (not the value of $product/price) if there is no element that matches the $product/discount path.

Arithmetic Operations on Multiple Values

Arithmetic operators cannot accept a sequence of more than one value as one of their operands. For example:

```
doc("prices.xml")//price * 2
```

will raise a type error because more than one price element is returned by the path expression. To perform an arithmetic operation on a sequence of values, you can put parentheses around the arithmetic operation, as in:

```
doc("prices.xml")//(price * 2)
```

which will perform the operation on each price element individually and return a sequence of doubled price values. You could get the same results using a FLWOR, as in:

```
for $aPrice in doc("prices.xml")//price
return $aPrice * 2
```

Arithmetic Operations and Types

When an operation is performed on two values that are the same type, the result is also a value of that type. For example, adding two xs:integer values results in an xs:integer. However, if an operation is performed on values of two different numeric types, one value is promoted to the type of the other value. For example, adding an xs:decimal to an xs:float results in an xs:float. This is true for all arithmetic operations except division of two xs:integer values, which results in an xs:decimal, and integer division, which always results in an xs:integer.

If an untyped value is used in an arithmetic operation, it is automatically cast to xs:double. For example, when adding the xs:integer 2 to the untyped value 3, the untyped value is cast to xs:double, and the result is the xs:double value 5. All non-numeric types must be explicitly cast to a numeric type before being used in an arithmetic operation.

Atomization occurs on the operands of arithmetic expressions. This means that the operations can be performed on nodes that contain numeric values as well as numeric atomic values themselves. For example, an arithmetic expression might be ($price * 2) if $price represents the path to a single node that contains a numeric value. For more information on atomization, see "Atomization" in Chapter 11.

 XQuery 1.0 and XPath 2.0 have three differences from XPath 1.0 regarding the way arithmetic operations are handled:

- In XPath 1.0, the result of an arithmetic operation on the empty sequence is NaN, not the empty sequence.
- In XPath 1.0, if an arithmetic operation is attempted on a sequence of more than one value, the first value is used and the rest are discarded. In XQuery 1.0/XPath 2.0, this raises a type error.
- In XPath 1.0, operands of all types are automatically converted to numbers. In XQuery 1.0/XPath 2.0, the operands must be untyped or numeric.

Precedence of Arithmetic Operators

Multiplication and division take precedence over addition and subtraction, as is customary in mathematical expressions. For example, 2 + 3 * 5 is equal to 2 + (3 * 5), or 17, rather than (2 + 3) * 5, or 25. The unary minus operator has precedence over all others. For example, - 3 + 5 is equal to 2, *not* - (3 + 5), or –8.

Multiplication and division operators (*, div, idiv, and mod) have equal precedence and are evaluated from left to right. Likewise, addition and subtraction operators have equal precedence and are evaluated from left to right. When in doubt, it is a good practice to use parentheses to delimit expressions for the sake of clarity.

Addition, Subtraction, and Multiplication

Addition, subtraction, and multiplication are straightforward. Table 16-3 shows some examples.

Table 16-3. Examples of arithmetic expressions

Example	Value	Value type
5 + 3	8	xs:integer
5 + 3.0	8	xs:decimal
5 + 3.0E0	8	xs:double
5 * 3	15	xs:integer
2 + 3 * 5	17	xs:integer
(2 + 3) * 5	25	xs:integer
- 3 + 5	2	xs:integer
() + 3	()	N/A
doc("prices.xml")//prod[1]/price+5	34.99	xs:decimal
doc("prices.xml")//prod[1]/price-5	()	N/A
doc("prices.xml")//prod[1]/price - 5	24.99	xs:decimal

Generally, you are not required to put whitespace before or after arithmetic operators. For example, price+5, with no spaces, is a valid expression meaning "the value of the price child plus 5." However, there is a special rule for subtraction. Because the dash (-) is a valid character in XML names, it is necessary to put whitespace after any valid XML name that precedes it. For example, price-5 is interpreted as a single name, so to subtract, you should use price - 5 instead.[*]

Division

There are two division operators: div and idiv. A slash (/) *cannot* be used to indicate division because the / operator is used to delimit steps in a path expression. The div operator is used to perform division of the first operand (the dividend) by the second operand (the divisor). If both numbers being divided are xs:integer-based values, the result is an xs:decimal. Otherwise, normal type promotion rules apply, and the type of the result is the same as the type of the operands.

The idiv operator is used to divide two numbers and obtain the integer portion of the division result. The operands can have any numeric type. If the result of the division is not an even integer, the decimal portion of the number is truncated rather than rounded. For example, (14 div 4) is equal to 3.5, but (14 idiv 4) is equal to 3.

Table 16-4 shows examples of the div and idiv operators.

Table 16-4. Examples of the div and idiv operators

Example	Value	Value type
14 div 4	3.5	xs:double
14 idiv 4	3	xs:integer
-14 idiv 4	-3	xs:integer
14.0 div 3.5	4.0	xs:decimal
14.0 idiv 3.5	4	xs:integer
() div 3	()	N/A
14 div 0	Error (division by zero)	N/A
xs:float("14") div 0	INF	xs:float
xs:double("INF") div 2	INF	xs:double
xs:float("NaN") div 2	NaN	xs:float

Attempting to divide by zero will raise an error when using the idiv operator or when using the div operator with values of type xs:integer or xs:decimal. Using the div operator on values of type xs:float or xs:double will not raise an error; it will return NaN (if the dividend is 0), or INF or –INF.

[*] The space after the dash is technically unnecessary since a name cannot start with a hyphen, but it looks cleaner.

Modulus (Remainder)

The mod operator is used to obtain the remainder after dividing the first operand (the dividend) by the second operand (the divisor). For example, (14 mod 4) equals 2. The sign of the result is the same as the sign of the first operand. Table 16-5 shows examples of the mod operator.

Table 16-5. Examples of the mod operator

Example	Value	Value type
14 mod 4	2	xs:integer
-14 mod 4	-2	xs:integer
14 mod -4	2	xs:integer
14.9 mod 2.1	0.2	xs:decimal
14.5E1 mod 2E1	5	xs:double
xs:float("14") mod 0	NaN	xs:float
xs:double("INF") mod 2	NaN	xs:double
14 mod ()	()	N/A
14 mod xs:double("INF")	14	xs:double

Special rules, depicted in Table 16-6, apply when one of the operands is INF, –INF, or 0.

Table 16-6. Results for the mod operator

Divisor	Dividend		
	INF or –INF	Finite number	0 or –0
INF or –INF	NaN	The dividend	The dividend
Finite number	NaN	The remainder	0
0 or –0	NaN	NaN[a]	NaN[a]

[a] Or, if the operands are of type xs:decimal or xs:integer, a "division by zero" error is raised.

Functions on Numbers

XQuery provides a number of functions that operate on numeric values. Some operate on single numeric values. They are summarized in Table 16-7 and covered in more detail in Appendix A. Each of these functions returns a numeric value whose type is the same as its argument, or the empty sequence if the argument is the empty sequence.

Table 16-7. Functions on single numbers

Function name	Description
round	The argument rounded to the nearest whole number
round-half-to-even	The argument rounded to a specified precision, with half values rounded to the nearest even number
floor	The largest whole number that is not greater than the argument
ceiling	The smallest whole number that is not smaller than the argument
abs	The absolute value of the argument

Table 16-8 lists some additional functions that can be used to aggregate or summarize numeric data. These functions accept a sequence of numeric values and return a single numeric result. All of these functions will automatically cast untyped values to xs:double, so it is not necessary to perform any explicit casting to have the values treated like numbers.

Table 16-8. Functions on sequences of numbers

Function name	Description
avg	The average of a sequence of numbers
sum	The sum of a sequence of numbers
min	The minimum value of a sequence of numbers
max	The maximum value of a sequence of numbers

Working with Strings

Strings are probably the most used type of atomic values in queries. This chapter discusses constructing and comparing strings and provides an overview of the many built-in functions that manipulate strings. It also explains string- and text-related features such as whitespace handling and internationalization.

The xs:string Type

The basic string type that is intended to represent generic character data is called, appropriately, xs:string. The xs:string type is not the default type for untyped values. If a value is selected from an input document with no schema, the value is given the type xs:untypedAtomic, not xs:string. However, it is easy enough to cast an untyped value to xs:string. In fact, you can cast a value of any type to xs:string and cast an xs:string value to any type.

The xs:string type is a primitive type from which a number of other types are derived. All of the operations and functions that can be performed on xs:string values can also be performed on values whose types are restrictions of xs:string. This includes user-defined types that appear in a schema, as well as built-in derived types such as xs:token, xs:language, and xs:ID. For a complete explanation of the built-in types, see Appendix B.

Constructing Strings

There are three common ways to construct strings: using string literals, the xs:string constructor, and the string function.

String Literals

Strings can be included in queries as literals, using double or single quotes. For example, ($name = "Priscilla") and string-length('query') are valid expressions

that contain string literals. If a literal value is enclosed in quotes, it is automatically assumed to be a string as opposed to a number.

Between quotes, you can escape the surrounding quote character by including it twice. For example, the literal expression `"inner ""quotes""!"` evaluates to the string `inner "quotes"!`. This is true for both single and double quotes.

In string literals, you can use single character references that use XML syntax. For example, ` ` can be used to include a space. You can also use the predefined entity references. For example, you can specify the string literal `"PB&J"` to represent the string PB&J. In fact, ampersands *must* be escaped with `&` in string literals.

The xs:string Constructor and the string Function

There is a standard constructor for strings named `xs:string`. The `xs:string` constructor, like all constructors, accepts either an atomic value or a single node. If it is an atomic value, it simply returns that value cast as an `xs:string`.

Some types have special rules about how their values are formatted when they are cast to `xs:string`. For example, integers have their leading zeros stripped, and `xs:hexBinary` values have their letters converted to uppercase. In addition, when values of most nonstring types are cast to `xs:string`, their whitespace is collapsed. This means that consecutive whitespace characters are replaced by a single space, and leading and trailing whitespace is removed. The rules (if any) for each type are described in Appendix B.

If the `xs:string` constructor is passed a node, it uses atomization to extract the typed value of the node, and then casts it to `xs:string`. For an attribute, this is simply its value. For an element, it is the character data of the element itself and all its descendants, concatenated together in document order.

In addition, there is a built-in function named `string` that has almost identical behavior. One difference is that if you use the `string` function with no arguments, it will use the current context item.

Comparing Strings

Several functions, summarized in Table 17-1, are available for comparing and matching strings.

Table 17-1. Functions that compare strings

Name	Description
compare	Compares two strings, optionally based on a collation
starts-with	Determines whether a string starts with another string
ends-with	Determines whether a string ends with another string

Name	Description
contains	Determines whether a string contains another string
matches	Determines whether a string matches a regular expression

Comparing Entire Strings

Strings can be compared using the comparison operators: =, !=, >, <, >=, and <=. For example, "abc" < "def" evaluates to true.

The comparison operators use the default collation, as described in "Collations," later in this chapter. You can also use the compare function, which fulfills the same role as the comparison operators but allows you to explicitly specify a collation. The compare function accepts two string arguments and returns one of the values –1, 0, or 1 depending on which argument is greater.

Determining Whether a String Contains Another String

Three functions test whether a string contains the characters of another string. They are the contains, starts-with, and ends-with functions. Each of them returns a Boolean value and takes two strings as arguments: the first is the containing string being tested, and the second is the contained string. Table 17-2 shows some examples of these functions.

USEFUL FUNCTION

contains-word

You may be interested to know whether a string contains another string, but only as a separate word. The contains-word function, shown here, accomplishes this:

```
declare namespace functx = "http://www.functx.com";
declare function functx:contains-word
($string as xs:string?, $word as xs:string) as xs:boolean
 {
   let $upString := upper-case($string)
   let $upWord := upper-case($word)
   return matches($upString, concat("^(.*\W)?", $upWord, "(\W.*)?$"))
 };
```

The function takes as arguments the string to search and the word to find. Making use of the matches function described in the next section, it finds the word if it is contained in the string, separated by nonword characters or the beginning or end of the string. It is case-insensitive; it matches a word even if the case is different.

This function is good enough for English and some European languages, but the concept of a word in Asian languages is much more subtle.

Table 17-2. Examples of contains, starts-with, and ends-with

Example	Return value
contains("query", "ery")	true
contains("query", "query")	true
contains("query", "x")	false
starts-with("query", "que")	true
starts-with("query", "u")	false
ends-with("query", "y")	true
ends-with("query ", "y")	false

Matching a String to a Pattern

The matches function determines whether a string matches a pattern. It accepts two string arguments: the string being tested and the pattern itself. The pattern is a regular expression, whose syntax is covered in Chapter 18. There is also an optional third argument, which can be used to set additional options in the interpretation of the regular expression, such as multi-line processing and case sensitivity. These options are described in detail in the section "Using Flags" in Chapter 18.

Table 17-3 shows examples of the matches function.

Table 17-3. Examples of the matches function

Example	Return value
matches("query", "q")	true
matches("query", "qu")	true
matches("query", "xyz")	false
matches("query", "q.*")	true
matches("query", "[a-z]{5}")	true

Substrings

Three functions are available to return part of a string. The substring function returns a substring based on a starting position (starting at 1 not 0) and optionally a length. For example:

 substring("query", 2, 3)

returns the string uer. If no length is specified, the function returns the rest of the string. For example:

 substring("query", 2)

returns uery.

The substring-before function returns all the characters of a string that occur before the first occurrence of another specified string. The substring-after function returns all the characters of a string that occur after the *first* occurrence of another specified string. Table 17-4 shows examples of the substring functions.

USEFUL FUNCTION

substring-after-last

If you want the substring that appears after the *last* occurrence of the specified string, you can use the substring-after-last function, shown here:

```
declare namespace functx = "http://www.functx.com";
declare function functx:substring-after-last
($string as xs:string?, $delim as xs:string) as xs:string?
  {
    if (contains ($string, $delim))
    then functx:substring-after-last(substring-after($string, $delim), $delim)
    else $string
  };
```

For example, calling this function with:

```
functx:substring-after-last("2006-05-03", "-")
```

will return 03. This function uses recursion to call the substring-after function repeatedly until the string no longer contains the search characters.

Table 17-4. Examples of the substring functions

Example	Return value
substring("query", 2, 3)	uer
substring("query", 2)	uery
substring-before("query", "er")	qu
substring-before("queryquery", "er")	qu
substring-after("query", "er")	y
substring-after("queryquery", "er")	yquery

Finding the Length of a String

The length of a string can be determined using the string-length function. It accepts a single string and returns its length as an integer. Whitespace is significant, so leading and trailing whitespace characters are counted. Table 17-5 shows some examples.

set-string-to-length

The set-string-to-length function, shown here, pads a string to a desired length:

```
declare namespace functx = "http://www.functx.com";
declare function functx:set-string-to-length
($stringToPad as xs:string?, $padChar as xs:string,
 $length as xs:integer) as xs:string
 {
   substring(
     string-join (($stringToPad, for $i in (1 to $length) return $padChar),"")
   ,1,$length)
 };
```

The function accepts as arguments a string, a character to pad the string with, and the desired length of the string. For example, you might call this function with:

```
functx:set-string-to-length("abc", "*", 7)
```

which returns abc****. This function truncates $stringToPad if it is longer than $length.

Table 17-5. Examples of the string-length function

Example	Return value
string-length("query")	5
string-length(" query ")	9
string-length(normalize-space(" query "))	5
string-length("")	0
string-length(" ")	1

Concatenating and Splitting Strings

Five functions, summarized in Table 17-6, concatenate and split apart strings.

Table 17-6. Functions that concatenate and split apart strings

Name	Description
concat	Concatenates two or more strings
string-join	Concatenates a sequence of strings, optionally using a separator
tokenize	Breaks a single string into a sequence of strings, using a specified separator
codepoints-to-string	Converts a sequence of Unicode code-point values to a string
string-to-codepoints	Converts a string to a sequence of Unicode code-point values

Concatenating Strings

Strings can be concatenated together using one of two functions: concat or string-join. XQuery does not allow use of concat operators such as +, &, or || to concatenate strings. The concat function accepts individual string arguments and concatenates them together. This function is unique in that it accepts a variable number of arguments. For example:

```
concat("a", "b", "c")
```

returns the string abc. The string-join function, on the other hand, accepts a *sequence* of strings. For example:

```
string-join( ("a", "b", "c"), "")
```

also returns the string abc. In addition, string-join allows a separator to be passed as the second argument. For example:

```
string-join( ("a", "b", "c"), "/")
```

returns the string a/b/c.

Splitting Strings Apart

Strings can be split apart, or tokenized, using the tokenize function. This function breaks a string into a sequence of strings, using a regular expression to designate the separator character(s). For example:

```
tokenize("a/b/c", "/")
```

returns a sequence of three strings: a, b, and c. Regular expressions such as \s, which represents a whitespace character (space, line feed, carriage return, or tab), and \W, which represents a nonword character (anything other than a letter or digit) are often used with this function. A list of useful regular expressions for tokenization can be found in Appendix A in the discussion of the tokenize function. Table 17-7 shows some examples of the tokenize function.

Table 17-7. Examples of the tokenize function

Example	Return value
tokenize("a b c", "\s")	("a", "b", "c")
tokenize("a b c", "\s+")	("a", "b", "c")
tokenize("a-b--c", "-")	("a", "b", "", "c")
tokenize("-a-b-", "-")	("", "a", "b", "")
tokenize("a/ b/ c", "[/\s]+")	("a", "b", "c")
tokenize("2006-12-25T12:15:00", "[\-T:]")	("2006","12","25","12","15","00")
tokenize("Hello, there.", "\W+")	("Hello", "there")

Converting Between Code Points and Strings

Strings can be constructed from a sequence of Unicode code-point values (expressed as integers) using the codepoints-to-string function. For example:

```
codepoints-to-string((97, 98, 99))
```

returns the string abc. The string-to-codepoints function performs the opposite; it converts a string to a sequence of code points. For example:

```
string-to-codepoints("abc")
```

returns a sequence of three integers 97, 98, and 99.

Manipulating Strings

Four functions can be used to manipulate the characters of a string. They are listed in Table 17-8.

Table 17-8. Functions that manipulate strings

Name	Description
upper-case	Translates a string into uppercase equivalents
lower-case	Translates a string into lowercase equivalents
translate	Replaces individual characters with other individual characters
replace	Replaces characters that match a regular expression with a specified string

Converting Between Uppercase and Lowercase

The upper-case and lower-case functions are used to convert a string to all uppercase or lowercase. For example, upper-case("Query") returns QUERY. The mappings between lowercase and uppercase characters are determined by Unicode case mappings. If a character does not have a corresponding uppercase or lowercase character, it is included in the result string unchanged. Table 17-9 shows some examples.

Table 17-9. Examples of the uppercase and lowercase functions

Example	Return value
upper-case("query")	QUERY
upper-case("Query")	QUERY
lower-case("QUERY-123")	query-123
lower-case("Query")	query

Replacing Individual Characters in Strings

The translate function is used to replace individual characters in a string with other individual characters. It takes three arguments:

- The string to be translated
- The list of characters to be replaced (as a string)
- The list of replacement characters (as a string)

Each character in the second argument is replaced by the character in the same position in the third argument. For example:

```
translate("**test**321", "*123", "-abc")
```

returns the string `--test--cba.` If the second argument is longer than the third argument, the extra characters in the second argument are simply omitted from the result. For example:

```
translate("**test**321", "*123", "-")
```

returns the string `--test--.`

Replacing Substrings That Match a Pattern

The `replace` function is used to replace nonoverlapping substrings that match a regular expression with a specified replacement string. It takes three arguments:

- The string to be manipulated
- The pattern, which uses the regular expression syntax described in Chapter 18
- The replacement string

While it is nice to have the power of regular expressions, you don't have to be familiar with regular expressions to replace a particular sequence of characters; you can simply specify the string you want replaced for the `$pattern` argument, as long as it doesn't contain any special characters.

An optional fourth argument allows for additional options in the interpretation of the regular expression, such as multi-line processing and case sensitivity. Table 17-10 shows some examples.

Table 17-10. Examples of the replace function

Example	Return value
`replace("query", "r", "as")`	queasy
`replace("query", "qu", "quack")`	quackery
`replace("query", "[ry]", "l")`	quell
`replace("query", "[ry]+", "l")`	quel
`replace("query", "z", "a")`	query
`replace("query", "query", "")`	A zero-length string

XQuery also supports variables in the replacement text, which allow parenthesized subexpressions to be referenced by number. You can use the variables $1 through $9

to represent the first nine parenthesized expressions in the pattern. This is very useful when replacing strings, on the condition that they come directly before or after another string. For example, if you want to change instances of the word *Chap* to the word *Sec*, but only those that are followed by a space and a digit, you can use the function call:

```
replace("Chap 2...Chap 3...Chap 4...", "Chap (\d)", "Sec $1.0")
```

which returns Sec 2.0...Sec 3.0...Sec 4.0.... Subexpressions are discussed in more detail in "Using Sub-Expressions with Replacement Variables" in Chapter 18.

USEFUL FUNCTION

replace-first

If you want to replace the first instance that matches a pattern, you can use the replace-first function, shown here:

```
declare namespace functx = "http://www.functx.com";
declare function functx:replace-first
($string as xs:string?, $pattern as xs:string,
 $replacement as xs:string) as xs:string
 {
   replace($string, concat("(^.*?)", $pattern), concat("$1",$replacement))
 };
```

This function uses an anchor (^) to tie the pattern to the beginning of the string only. It then uses a subexpression variable ($1) to include the beginning of the string (before the first matched occurrence) in the results. For example, calling it with functx:replace-first("this is a string", "is", "xx") will return thxx is a string (where the second is is not replaced).

Whitespace and Strings

Whitespace handling varies by implementation and depends on whether the implementation uses schema validation, and how it chooses to handle whitespace in element content. Every XML parser normalizes the whitespace in attribute values, replacing carriage returns, line feeds, and tabs with spaces. XML Schema processors may further normalize whitespace of an attribute or element value based on its type. During XML Schema validation, whitespace is preserved in values of type xs:string (and some of its descendants), but collapsed in all others.

Within string literals in queries, whitespace is always significant. For example, the expression string-length(" x ") evaluates to 3, not 1.

Normalizing Whitespace

The `normalize-space` function collapses whitespace in a string. Specifically, it performs the following steps:

1. Replaces each carriage return (#xD), line feed (#xA), and tab (#x9) character with a single space (#x20)

2. Collapses all consecutive spaces into a single space

3. Removes all leading and trailing spaces

Table 17-11 shows some examples.

Table 17-11. Examples of the normalize-space function

Example	Return value
normalize-space("query")	query
normalize-space(" query ")	query
normalize-space("xml query")	xml query
normalize-space("xml query")	xml query
normalize-space(" ")	A zero-length string

Internationalization Considerations

XML, through its support for Unicode, is designed to allow for many natural languages. XQuery provides several functions and mechanisms that support multiple natural languages: collations, the `normalize-unicode` function, and the `lang` function.

Collations

Collations are used to specify the order in which characters should be compared and sorted. Characters can be sorted simply based on their code points, but this has a number of limitations. Different languages and locales alphabetize the same set of characters differently. In addition, an uppercase letter and its lowercase equivalent may need to be sorted together. For example, if you sort on code points alone, an uppercase A comes *after* a lowercase z.

Collations are not just for sorting. They can be used to equate two strings that contain equivalent values. Some languages and locales may consider two different characters or sequences of characters to be equivalent. For example, a collation may equate the German character β with the two letters ss. This type of comparison comes into play when using, for example, the `contains` function, which determines whether one string contains the characters of another string.

Collations in XQuery are identified by a URI. The URI serves only as a name and does not necessarily point to a resource on the Web, although it might. All XQuery implementations support at least one collation, whose name is `http://www.w3.org/` `2005/xpath-functions/collation/codepoint`. This is a simple collation that compares strings based only on Unicode code points. Although it is based on Unicode code points, it should not be confused with the Unicode collation algorithm, which is a far more sophisticated collation algorithm.

There are several ways to specify a collation. Some XQuery functions, such as `compare` and `distinct-values`, accept a `$collation` argument that allows you to specify the collation URI. In addition, you can specify a collation in the `order by` clause of a FLWOR. These expressions accept either an absolute or a relative URI. If a relative URI is provided, it is relative to the base URI of the static context, which is described in Chapter 20.

You can also specify a default collation in the query prolog. This default is used by some functions as well as `order by` clauses when no `$collation` is specified. The default collation is also used in operations that do not allow you to specify collation, such as those using the comparison operators =, !=, <, <=, >, and >=. The syntax of a default collation declaration is shown in Figure 17-1.

```
──declare default collation "<collation-name>" ;──▶
```

Figure 17-1. Syntax of a default collation declaration

An example is:

```
declare default collation "http://datypic.com/collation/custom";
```

The collation URI must be a literal value in quotes (not an evaluated expression), and it should be a syntactically valid absolute URI.

Alternatively, the implementation may have a built-in default collation, or allow a user to specify one, through means other than the query prolog.

As a last resort, if no `$collation` argument is provided, no default collation is specified, and the implementation does not provide a default collation, the simple code-point collation named `http://www.w3.org/2005/xpath-functions/collation/codepoint` is used.

The default collation can be obtained using the `default-collation` function, which takes no arguments.

You should consult the documentation of your XQuery implementation to determine which collations are supported. Some collations may expect the strings to be Unicode-normalized already. For these collations, consider using the `normalize-unicode` function on strings before comparing them. Other collations perform implicit normalization on the strings.

Although it is possible in XML to use an `xml:lang` attribute to indicate the natural language of character data, use of this attribute has no effect on the collation algorithm used in XQuery. Unlike SQL, the choice of collation depends entirely on the user writing the query, and not on any properties of the data.

Unicode Normalization

Unicode normalization allows text to be compared without regard to subtle variations in character representation. It replaces certain characters with equivalent representations. Two normalized values can then be compared to determine whether they are the same. Unicode normalization is also useful for allowing character strings to be sorted appropriately.

The `normalize-unicode` function performs Unicode normalization on a string. It takes two arguments: the string to be normalized and the normalization form to use. The normalization form controls which characters are replaced. Some characters may be replaced by equivalent characters, while others may be decomposed to an equivalent representation that has two or more code points.

Determining the Language of an Element

It is possible to test the language of an element based on the existence of an `xml:lang` attribute among its ancestors. This is accomplished using the `lang` function.

The `lang` function accepts as arguments the language to test and, optionally, the node to be tested. The function returns `true` if the relevant `xml:lang` attribute of the node (or the context node if no second argument is specified) has a value that matches the argument. The function returns `false` if the relevant `xml:lang` attribute does not match the argument, or if there is no relevant `xml:lang` attribute.

Regular Expressions

Regular expressions are patterns that describe strings. They can be used as arguments to three XQuery built-in functions to determine whether a string value matches a particular pattern (`matches`), to replace parts of string that match a pattern (`replace`), and to tokenize strings based on a delimiter pattern (`tokenize`). This chapter explains the regular expression syntax used by XQuery.

The Structure of a Regular Expression

The regular expression syntax of XQuery is based on that of XML Schema, with some additions. Regular expressions, also known as regexes, can be composed of a number of different parts: atoms, quantifiers, and branches.

Atoms

An atom is the most basic unit of a regular expression. It might describe a single character, such as d, or an escape sequence that represents one or more characters, like \s or \p{Lu}. It could also be a character class expression that represents a range or choice of several characters, such as [a-z]. These kinds of atoms are described later in this chapter.

Quantifiers

Atoms may indicate required, optional, or repeating strings. The number of times a matching string may appear is indicated by a quantifier, which appears directly after an atom. For example, to indicate that the letter d must appear one or more times, you can use the expression d+, where the + means "one or more." The different quantifiers are listed in Table 18-1.

Table 18-1. Kinds of quantifiers

Quantifier	Number of occurrences
none	1
?	0 or 1
*	0, 1, or many
+	1 or many
{n}	n
{n,}	n to many
{n,m}	n to m

Examples of the use of these quantifiers are shown in Table 18-2. Note that in these cases, the quantifier applies only to the letter o, not to the preceding f.

Table 18-2. Quantifier examples

Regular expression	Strings that match	Strings that do not match
fo	fo	f, foo
fo?	f, fo	foo
fo*	f, fo, foo, fooo, ...	fx
fo+	fo, foo, fooo, ...	f
fo{2}	foo	fo, fooo
fo{2,}	foo, fooo, foooo, ...	f, fo
fo{2,3}	foo, fooo	f, fo, foooo

Parenthesized Sub-Expressions and Branches

A parenthesized sub-expression can be used as an atom in a larger regular expression. Parentheses are useful for repeating certain sequences of characters. For example, suppose you want to indicate a repetition of the string fo. The expression fo* matches fooo, but not fofo, because the quantifier applies to the final atom, not the entire string. To allow fofo, you can parenthesize fo, resulting in the regular expression (fo)*.

Parenthesized sub-expressions are also useful for specifying a choice between several different patterns. For example, to allow either the string fo or the string xy to come before z, you can use the expression (fo|xy)z. The two expressions on either side of the vertical bar character (|), in this case fo and xy, are known as branches.

The | character does not act on the atom immediately preceding it, but on the entire expression that precedes it (back to the previous | or corresponding opening parenthesis). For example, the regular expression (yes|no) indicates a choice between yes and no, not "ye, followed by s or n, followed by o." Branches at the top level can also be used without parentheses, as in yes|no.

Placing parentheses around a sub-expression also allows it to be referenced, which is useful for two purposes: back-references, and variable references when using the replace function. These features are covered in "Back-References" and "Using Sub-Expressions with Replacement Variables," respectively.

Table 18-3 shows some examples that exhibit the interaction between branches, atoms, and parentheses.

Table 18-3. Examples of parentheses in regular expressions

Regular expression	Strings that match	Strings that do not match
(fo)+z	foz, fofoz	z, fz, fooz, ffooz
(fo\|xy)z	foz, xyz	z
(fo\|xy)+z	fofoz, foxyz, xyfoz	z
(f+o)+z	foz, ffoz, foffoz	z, fz, fooz
yes\|no	yes, no	

Representing Individual Characters

A single character can be used to represent itself in a regular expression. In this case, it is known as a normal character. For example, the regular expression d matches the letter d, and def matches the string def, as you might expect. Each of the three single characters (d, e, and f) is its own atom, and it can have a quantifier associated with it. For example, the regular expression d+ef matches the strings def, ddef, dddef, etc.

Certain characters, in order to be taken literally, must be escaped because they have another meaning in a regular expression. For example, the asterisk (*) will be treated like a quantifier unless it is escaped. These characters, called metacharacters, must be escaped (except when they are within square brackets): ., \, ?, *, +, |, ^, $, {, }, (,), [, and].

These characters are escaped by preceding them with a backslash. This is referred to as a single-character escape because there is only one matching character. For convenience, there are three additional single-character escapes for the whitespace characters tab, line feed, and carriage return. Table 18-4 lists the single-character escapes.

Table 18-4. Single-character escapes

Escape sequence	Character
\\	\
\|	\|
\.	.
\-	-
\^	^
\$[a]	$
\?	?

Table 18-4. Single-character escapes (continued)

Escape sequence	Character
*	*
\+	+
\{	{
\}	}
\((
\))
\[[
\]]
\n	Line feed (#xA)
\r	Carriage return (#xD)
\t	Tab (#x9)

a This single-character escape can be used in XQuery,
 but not in XML Schema regular expressions.

You can also use the standard XML syntax for character references and predefined entity references in regular expressions, as long as they are in quoted strings. For example, a space can be represented as , and a less-than symbol (<) can be represented as <. This can be useful for special characters. It is described further in "XML Entity and Character References" in Chapter 21.

Table 18-5 shows some examples of representing individual characters in regular expressions.

Table 18-5. Representing individual characters

Regular expression	Strings that match	Strings that do not match
d	d	g
d+efg+	defg, ddefgg	defgefg, deffgg
defg	defg	d, efg
d\|e\|f	d, e, f	g
f*o	fo, ffo, fffo	f*o
f*o	f*o	fo, ffo, fffo
déf	déf	def, df

Representing Any Character

The period (.) has special significance in regular expressions; it matches any character *except* the line feed character (#xA). The period character represents only one matching character, but a quantifier (such as *) can be applied to it to represent multiple characters. Table 18-6 shows some examples of the wildcard escape character in use.

Table 18-6. The wildcard escape character

Regular expression	Strings that match	Strings that do not match
f.o	fao, fbo, f2o	fo, fbbo
f..o	faao, fbco, f12o	fo, fao
f.*o	fo, fao, fbcde23o	f o[a]
f\.o	f.o	fao

[a] Assume a line feed character between f and o. This string does not match unless you are in dot-all mode.

It is important to note that the period loses its wildcard power when placed in a character class expression (within square brackets).

Some XQuery functions (namely matches, replace, and tokenize) allow you to indicate that the processor should operate in dot-all mode. This is specified using the letter s in the $flags argument. In dot-all mode, the period matches any character whatsoever, including the line feed character (#xA). See "Using Flags," later in this chapter, for more information.

Representing Groups of Characters

Sometimes characters fall into convenient groups, such as decimal digits or punctuation characters. Three different kinds of escapes can be used to represent a group of characters: multi-character escapes, category escapes, and block escapes. Like single-character escapes, they all start with a backslash.

Multi-Character Escapes

Multi-character escapes, listed in Table 18-7, represent groups of related characters. They are called multi-character escapes because they allow a choice of multiple characters. However, each escape represents only one character in a matching string. To allow several replacement characters, you should use a quantifier such as +.

Table 18-7. Multi-character escapes

Escape	Meaning
\s	A whitespace character, as defined by XML (space, tab, carriage return, or line feed)
\S	A character that is not a whitespace character
\d	A decimal digit (0 to 9), or a digit in another style, for example, an Indic Arabic digit
\D	A character that is not a decimal digit
\w	A "word" character, that is, any character *not* in one of the Unicode categories Punctuation, Separators, and Other
\W	A nonword character, that is, any character in one of the Unicode categories Punctuation, Separators, and Other
\i	A character that is allowed as the first character of an XML name, i.e., a letter, an underscore (_), or a colon (:); the "i" stands for "initial"

Table 18-7. Multi-character escapes (continued)

Escape	Meaning
\I	A character that cannot be the first character of an XML name
\c	A character that can be part of an XML name, i.e., a letter, a digit, an underscore (_), a hyphen (-), a colon (:), or a period (.)
\C	A character that cannot be part of an XML name

Category Escapes

The Unicode standard defines categories of characters based on their purpose. For example, there are categories for punctuation, uppercase letters, and currency symbols. These categories, listed in Table 18-8, can be referenced in regular expressions using category escapes.

Table 18-8. Unicode categories

Category	Property	Meaning
Letters	L	All letters
	Lu	Uppercase
	Ll	Lowercase
	Lt	Titlecase
	Lm	Modifier
	Lo	Other
Marks	M	All marks
	Mn	Nonspacing
	Mc	Spacing combining
	Me	Enclosing
Numbers	N	All numbers
	Nd	Decimal digit
	Nl	Letter
	No	Other
Punctuation	P	All punctuation
	Pc	Connector
	Pd	Dash
	Ps	Open
	Pe	Close
	Pi	Initial quote
	Pf	Final quote
	Po	Other

Table 18-8. Unicode categories (continued)

Category	Property	Meaning
Separators	Z	All separators
	Zs	Space
	Zl	Line
	Zp	Paragraph
Symbols	S	All symbols
	Sm	Math
	Sc	Currency
	Sk	Modifier
	So	Other
Other	C	All others
	Cc	Control
	Cf	Format
	Co	Private use
	Cn	Not assigned

Category escapes take the form \p{XX}, with XX representing the property listed in Table 18-8. For example, \p{Lu} matches any uppercase letter. Category escapes that use an uppercase P, as in \P{XX}, match all characters that are *not* in the category. For example, \P{Lu} matches any character that is not an uppercase letter.

Note that the category escapes include all alphabets. If you intend for an expression to match only the capital letters A through Z, it is better to use [A-Z] than \p{Lu}, because \p{Lu} allows uppercase letters of all character sets. Likewise, if your intention is to allow only the decimal digits 0 through 9, use [0-9] rather than \p{Nd} or \d, because there are decimal digits other than 0 through 9 in other character sets.

Block Escapes

Unicode defines a numeric code point for each character. Each range of characters is represented by a block name, also defined by Unicode. For example, characters 0000 through 007F are known as *basic latin*. Table 18-9 lists the first five block escape ranges as an example. For a complete, updated list, see the blocks file of the Unicode standard at *http://www.unicode.org/Public/UNIDATA/Blocks.txt*.

Table 18-9. Partial list of Unicode block names

Start code	End code	Block name (with spaces removed)
#x0000	#x007F	BasicLatin
#x0080	#x00FF	Latin-1Supplement
#x0100	#x017F	LatinExtended-A

Table 18-9. Partial list of Unicode block names (continued)

Start code	End code	Block name (with spaces removed)
#x0180	#x024F	LatinExtended-B
#x0250	#x02AF	IPAExtensions
...

Block escapes can be used to refer to these character ranges in regular expressions. They take the form \p{IsXX}, with XX representing the Unicode block name with all spaces removed. For example, \p{IsLatin-1Supplement} matches any one character in the range #x0080 to #x00FF. As with category escapes, you can use an uppercase P to match characters *not* in the block. For example, \P{IsLatin-1Supplement} matches any character outside of that range.

Table 18-10 provides examples of representing groups of characters in regular expressions.

Table 18-10. Representing groups of characters

Regular expression	Strings that match	Strings that do not match	Comment
f\d	f0, f1	f, f01	multi-character escape
f\d*	f, f0, f012	ff	multi-character escape
f\s*o	fo, f o	foo	multi-character escape
\p{Ll}	a, b	A, B, 1, 2	category escape
\P{Ll}	A, B, 1, 2	a, b	category escape
\p{L}	a, b, A, B	1, 2	category escape
\P{L}	1, 2	a, b, A, B	category escape
\p{IsBasicLatin}	a, b	â, ß	block escape
\P{IsBasicLatin}	â, ß	a, b	block escape

Character Class Expressions

Character class expressions, which are enclosed in square brackets, indicate a choice among several characters. These characters can be listed singly, expressed as a range of characters, or expressed as a combination of the two.

Single Characters and Ranges

To specify a choice of several characters, you can simply list them inside square brackets. For example, [def] matches d or e or f. To match multiple occurrences of these letters, you can use a quantifier with a character class expression, as in [def]*, which will match not only defdef, but eddfefd as well. The characters listed can also be any of the escapes described earlier in this chapter. The expression [\p{Ll}\d] matches either a lowercase letter or a digit.

It is also possible to specify a range of characters, by separating the starting and ending characters with a hyphen. For example, [a-z] matches any letter from a to z. The endpoints of the range must be single characters or single character escapes (not a multi-character escapes such as \d).

You can specify more than one range in the same character class expression, which means that it matches a character in any of the ranges. The expression [a-zA-Z0-9] matches one character that is either between a and z, or between A and Z, or a digit from 0 to 9. Unicode code points are used to determine whether a character is in the range.

Ranges and single characters can be combined in any order. For example, [abc0-9] matches either a letter a, b, or c or a digit from 0 to 9. This regular expression could also be expressed as [0-9abc] or [a0-9bc].

Subtraction from a Range

Subtraction allows you to express that you want to match a range of characters but leave a few out. For example, [a-z-[jkl]] matches any character from a to z except j, k, or l. A hyphen (-) precedes the character group to be subtracted, which is itself enclosed in square brackets. Like any character class expression, the subtracted group can be a list of single characters or ranges, or both. The expression [a-z-[j-l]] has the same meaning as the previous example. You can also subtract from a multi-character escape, for example [\p{Lu}-[ABC]].

Negative Character Class Expressions

It is also possible to specify a negative character class expression, meaning that a string should *not* match any of the characters specified. This is accomplished using the ^ character after the left square bracket. For example, [^a-z] matches any character that is *not* a letter from a to z. Any character class expression can be negated, including those that specify single characters, ranges, or a combination of the two. The negation applies to the entire character class expression, so [^a-z0-9] will match anything that is not a letter from a to z and also not a digit from 0 to 9.

Some examples of character class expressions are shown in Table 18-11.

Table 18-11. Character class expression examples

Regular expression	Strings that match	Strings that do not match	Comment
[def]	d, e, f	def	Single characters
[def]*	d, eee, dfed	a, b	Single characters, repeating
[\p{Ll}\d]	a, b, 1	A, B	Single characters with escapes
[d-f]	d, e, f	a, D	Range of characters
[0-9d-fD-F]	3, d, F	a, 3dF	Multiple ranges

Table 18-11. Character class expression examples (continued)

Regular expression	Strings that match	Strings that do not match	Comment
[0-9stu]	4, 9, t	a, 4t	Range plus single characters
[s-u\d]	4, 9, t	a, t4	Range plus single-character escape
[a-x-[f]]	a, d, x	f, 2	Subtracting from a range
[a-x-[fg]]	a, d, x	f, g, 2	Subtracting from a range
[a-x-[e-g]]	a, d, x	e, g, 2	Subtracting from a range with a range
[^def]	a, g, 2	d, e, f	Negating single characters
[^\[]	a, b, c	[Negating a single-character escape
[^\d]	d, E	1, 2, 3	Negating a multi-character escape
[^a-cj-l]	d, 4	b, j, l	Negating a range

Escaping Rules for Character Class Expressions

Special escaping rules apply to character class expressions. They are:

- The characters [,], \, and - must be escaped when included as single characters.[*]
- The character \ must be escaped if it is the lower bound of the range.
- The characters [and \ must be escaped if one of them is the upper bound of the range.
- The character ^ must be escaped only if it appears first in the character class expression, directly after the opening bracket ([).

The other metacharacters do not need to be escaped when used in a character class expression, because they have no special meaning in that context. This includes the period character, which does not serve as a wildcard escape character when it appears inside a character class expression. However, it is never an error to escape any of the metacharacters, and getting into the habit of always escaping them eliminates the need to remember these rules.

Reluctant Quantifiers

XQuery supports reluctant quantifiers, which allow part of a regular expression to match the shortest possible string. Reluctant quantifiers are indicated by adding a question mark (?) to the end of any of the kinds of quantifiers identified in Table 18-1.

For example, given the string reluctant and the regular expression r.*t, the regular expression could match reluct or reluctant. Since a standard quantifier (*) is used,

[*] There has been a lot of confusion about the rules for escaping "-" in successive corrections to the XML Schema recommendation, so there are variations between products, but it's always safe to escape it.

the match is on the longest possible string, `reluctant`. If the regular expression were `r.*?t` instead, which uses a reluctant quantifier, it would match `reluct`, the shorter of the two strings.

Reluctant quantifiers come into play when replacing matching values in a string. Table 18-12 shows some examples of calls to the `replace` function that use reluctant and nonreluctant quantifiers.

Table 18-12. Reluctant versus nonreluctant quantifiers

Example	Return value
`replace("reluctant", "r.*t", "X")`	X
`replace("reluctant", "r.*?t", "X")`	Xant
`replace("aaah", "a{2,3}", "X")`	Xh
`replace("aaah", "a{2,3}?", "X")`	Xah
`replace("aaaah", "a{2,3}", "X")`	Xah
`replace("aaaah", "a{2,3}?", "X")`	XXh

Reluctant quantifiers have no effect on simply determining whether a string matches a regular expression, which explains why they are not supported in XML Schema. It may seem that the regular expression `r.*?tly` would not match the string `reluctantly` because `r.*?t` would match the shorter string `reluct`, leaving an extra `antly` which does not match the pattern `ly`. However, this is not the way it works. Reluctant quantifiers do not indicate that *only* the shorter string matches, just that the processor uses the shorter of the two matches if called on to perform a replacement or some other operation. Any of the quantifiers in the examples in Table 18-2 could be replaced by reluctant quantifiers, and the list of matching and nonmatching strings would be the same.

Anchors

XQuery adds the concept of anchors to XML Schema regular expressions. In XML Schema validation, the regular expression is expected to match the entire string, not a part of it. For example, the regular expression `str` matches only the string `str` and not other strings that contain `str`, like `5str5`. In XQuery, however, the expression `str` matches all strings that *contain* `str`, including `5str5`.

Because of this looser interpretation, it is sometimes useful to explicitly say that the expression should match the beginning or end of the string (or both). Anchors can be used for this purpose. The `^` character is used to match the beginning of the string, and the `$` character is used to match the end of the string. For example, the regular expression `^str` specifies that a matching string must start with `str`. Table 18-13 shows some examples that use anchors.

Table 18-13. Anchors

Regular expression	Strings that match	Strings that do not match
str	str, str5, 5str, 5str5	st, sttr
^str$	str	5str5, str5, 5str
^str	str, str5	5str5, 5str
str$	str, 5str	5str5, str5

Anchors and Multi-Line Mode

Some XQuery functions (namely matches, replace, and tokenize) allow you to indicate that the processor should operate in multi-line mode. This is specified using the letter m in the $flags argument. In multi-line mode, anchors match not just the beginning and end of the entire string, but also the beginning and end of any line within the string, as indicated by a line feed character (#xA). Table 18-14 shows some examples of using anchors in multi-line mode.

Table 18-14. Anchors in multi-line mode[a]

Regular expression	Strings that match	Strings that do not match
str	str	st
^str$	str, 555 str 555	555str 555
^str	str555, 555 str555	555str 555
str$	555str, 555str 555	555 str555

[a] Some of the examples span several lines; individual examples are separated by commas.

Back-References

XQuery supports the use of back-references.[*] Back-references allow you to ensure that certain characters in a string match each other. For example, suppose you want to ensure that a string is a product number delimited by either single or double quotes. The product number must be three digits, followed by a dash, followed by two uppercase letters. You could write the expression:

```
('|")\d{3}-[A-Z]{2}('|")
```

[*] Back-references are not supported in XML Schema regular expressions.

However, this would allow a string that starts with a single quote and ends with a double quote. You want to be sure the quotes match. You could write the expression:

```
'\d{3}-[A-Z]{2}'|"\d{3}-[A-Z]{2}"
```

but this requires repeating the entire pattern for the product number. Instead, you can parenthesize the expression representing the quotes and refer back to it using an escaped digit. For example, the expression:

```
('|")\d{3}-[A-Z]{2}\1
```

is equivalent to the prior example, but it is shorter and simpler. The atom \1 indicates that you want to repeat the first parenthesized expression, namely ('|"). The characters that match the first parenthesized expression must be the same characters that match the back-reference. This means that the regular expression does not match a string that starts with a single quote and ends with a double quote.

The parenthesized sub-expressions are numbered in order from left to right based on the position of the opening parenthesis, starting with 1 (not 0). You can reference any of them by number. You can use as many digits as you want, provided that the number does not exceed the number of sub-expressions preceding it.

Using Flags

Three XQuery functions use regular expressions: matches, replace, and tokenize. Each of these functions accepts a $flags argument that allows for additional options in the interpretation of the regular expression, such as multi-line processing and case insensitivity. Options are indicated by single letters; the $flags argument is a string that can include any of the valid letters in any order, and duplicates are allowed.

The $flags argument allows four options:

s The letter s indicates dot-all mode, which affects the period wildcard (.). (This is known as single-line mode in Perl.) This means that the period wildcard matches any character whatsoever, including the line feed (#xA) character. If the letter s is not specified, the period wildcard matches any character except the line feed (#xA) character.

m The letter m indicates multi-line mode, which affects anchors. In multi-line mode, the ^ and $ characters match the beginning and end of a line, as well as the beginning and end of the whole string.

i The letter i indicates case-insensitive mode. This means that matching does not distinguish between normal characters that are case variants of each other, as defined by Unicode. For example, in case-insensitive mode, [a-z] matches the lowercase letters a through z, uppercase letters A through Z, and a few other characters such as a Kelvin sign. The meaning of category escapes such as \p{Lu} is not affected.

x The letter x indicates that whitespace characters within regular expressions should be ignored. This is useful for making long regexes readable by splitting over many lines. If x is not specified, whitespace characters are considered to be significant and to match those in the string. If you want to represent significant whitespace when using the x flag, you can use the multi-character escape \s.

If no flag options are desired, you should either pass a zero-length string, or omit the $flags argument entirely. Table 18-15 shows some examples that use the $flags argument, which is the third argument of the matches function. They assume that the variable $address is bound to the following string (the line break is significant):

```
123 Main Street
Traverse City, MI 49684
```

Table 18-15. Examples of the $flags argument

Example	Return value
matches($address, "Street.*City")	false
matches($address, "Street.*City", "s")	true
matches($address, "Street$")	false
matches($address, "Street$", "m")	true
matches($address, "street")	false
matches($address, "street", "i")	true
matches($address, "Main Street")	true
matches($address, "Main Street", "x")	false
matches($address, "Main \s Street", "x")	true
matches($address, "street$", "im")	true

Using Sub-Expressions with Replacement Variables

The replace function allows parenthesized sub-expressions (also known as groups) to be referenced by number in the replacement string. In the $replacement string, you can use the variables $1, $2, $3, etc. to represent (in order) the parenthesized expressions in $pattern. This is very useful when replacing strings on the condition that they come directly before or after another string—for example, if you want to change instances of the word *Chap* to the word *Sec*, but only those that are followed by a space and a digit. This technique can also be used to reformat data for presentation. Table 18-16 shows some examples.

get-matches-and-non-matches

The regular expression capabilities of XQuery allow you to determine whether a string matches a regular expression and to replace matches in a string. However, one feature it does not directly provide is the ability to retrieve the parts of a string that do match a pattern. In XSLT 2.0, this can be achieved using the xsl:analyze-string instruction that has no equivalent in XQuery. However, this can be accomplished using the get-matches-and-non-matches function below, which returns a sequence of alternating match and non-match elements containing the strings that do and do not match a pattern. It starts with the entire string, constructs an element depending on whether it begins with a match or nonmatch, and recursively calls itself with the rest of the string.

This function depends on two other functions, also listed here:

index-of-match-first

> This function determines where the first match (if any) occurs in the string. It does this by tokenizing the string and determining the length of the first token.

replace-first

> This function replaces the first match in the string by concatenating an anchor and reluctant wildcard to the beginning of the pattern. It is used by the get-matches-and-non-matches to help determine the length of any particular match.

```
declare namespace functx = "http://www.functx.com";
declare function functx:get-matches-and-non-matches
  ($string as xs:string?, $regex as xs:string) as element()* {

   let $iomf := functx:index-of-match-first($string, $regex)
   return
   if (empty($iomf))
   then <non-match>{$string}</non-match>
   else if ($iomf > 1)
   then (<non-match>{substring($string,1,$iomf - 1)}</non-match>,
         functx:get-matches-and-non-matches(
            substring($string,$iomf),$regex))
   else
   let $length :=
      string-length($string) -
      string-length(functx:replace-first($string, $regex,''))
   return (<match>{substring($string,1,$length)}</match>,
           if (string-length($string) > $length)
           then functx:get-matches-and-non-matches(
              substring($string,$length + 1),$regex)
           else ())
  } ;

declare function functx:index-of-match-first
  ($arg as xs:string?, $pattern as xs:string) as xs:integer? {
```

—*continued*—

```
                    if (matches($arg,$pattern))
          then string-length(tokenize($arg, $pattern)[1]) + 1
          else ()
          } ;

      declare function functx:replace-first
        ($arg as xs:string?, $pattern as xs:string,
          $replacement as xs:string ) as xs:string {

        replace($arg, concat('(^.*?)', $pattern),
                concat('$1',$replacement))
        } ;
```

For example, calling this function with:

```
functx:get-matches-and-non-matches('abc123def', '\d+')
```

returns a sequence of three elements:

```
<non-match>abc</non-match>
<match>123</match>
<non-match>def</non-match>
```

Table 18-16. Examples of using replacement variables

Example	Return value
replace("Chap 2...Chap 3...Chap 4...", "Chap (\d)", "Sec $1.0")	Sec 2.0...Sec 3.0...Sec 4.0...
replace("abc123", "([a-z])", "$1x")	axbxcx123
replace("2315551212", "(\d{3})(\d{3})(\d{4})", "($1) $2-$3")	(231) 555-1212
replace("2006-10-18", "\d{2}(\d{2})-(\d{2})-(\ d{2})", "$2/$3/$1")	10/18/06
replace("25", "(\d+)", "\$$1.00")	$25.00

The variables are bound in order from left to right based on the position of the opening parenthesis. The variable $0 can be used to represent the string matched by the entire regular expression. If the variable number exceeds the number of parenthesized sub-expressions in the regular expression, it is replaced with a zero-length string.

If you wish to include the character $ in your replacement string, you must escape it with a backslash (i.e., \$), as shown in the fifth example. Backslashes must also be escaped in the $replacement string, as in \\.

Working with Dates, Times, and Durations

XQuery provides advanced capabilities for querying, creating, and manipulating date-related values. There are eleven date-related types built into XQuery. They fall into three categories:

- The date and time types, which represent a point in time—for example, a specific date or time
- The duration types, which represent periods of time, such as a number of years or minutes
- The date component types, which represent parts of dates, such as the year 2006, the month of May, or the 10th day of each month

This chapter explains the date-related types used in XQuery and the functions and operators that act on them.

The Date and Time Types

Three types represent specific dates and/or times: `xs:date`, `xs:time`, and `xs:dateTime`. These XML Schema built-in types are based on the ISO 8601 standard. They are summarized in Table 19-1.

Table 19-1. Summary of date and time types

Type name	Description	Format	Examples
xs:date	Date	YYYY-MM-DD	2006-05-03
xs:dateTime	Date and time	YYYY-MM-DDThh:mm:ss.sss	2006-05-03T10:32:15 2006-05-03T10:32:15.55
xs:time	Time	hh:mm:ss.sss	10:32:15

The `xs:date` type has year, month, and day components, while `xs:time` has hour, minute, and seconds components. The `xs:dateTime` type is a concatenation of the `xs:date` and `xs:time` types, with the letter `T` in between them. Times (in both the `xs:time` and `xs:dateTime` types) are based on a 24-hour time period, so hours are

represented as 00 through 23 (midnight can also be represented as 24:00:00). Additional digits can be used to increase the precision of fractional seconds if desired.

Constructing and Casting Dates and Times

There are several ways to construct date and time values:

- You can obtain the current date and/or time using one of the functions current-dateTime, current-date, or current-time. For example, the function call current-dateTime() might return the xs:dateTime value 2006-08-15T12:15:00-05:00.

- You can create them from strings using type constructors, whose names are identical to the type name. For example, xs:dateTime("2006-04-30T12:30:00") creates an xs:dateTime value.

- The built-in function dateTime (not to be confused with the xs:dateTime constructor) can be used to construct an xs:dateTime value from an xs:date and an xs:time. For example, dateTime(xs:date("2006-04-30"),xs:time("12:30:00")) also creates an xs:dateTime value.

- You can also cast values among the xs:date, xs:time, and xs:dateTime types.

Time Zones

The date and time types allow an optional time zone to be specified. The time zone indicator appears at the end of the date or time value. Coordinated Universal Time (UTC) can be represented using the letter Z. For example, the time 11:03:05Z is in the UTC time zone.

Other time zones are specified by their offset from UTC in the format +hh:mm or –hh:mm. These values can range from –14:00 to +14:00. For example, US Pacific Time is indicated as –08:00 because it is eight hours behind UTC. The time value 11:03:05-08:00 is in that time zone.

For the purposes of some XQuery functions, time zone values are treated as durations of hours and minutes. For example, the time zone -05:00 is considered a negative xs:dayTimeDuration value –PT5H for the purposes of the functions that adjust time zones. Duration types are discussed in detail in the section "The Duration Types," later in this chapter.

Explicit versus implicit time zones

Because the time zone component of a date or time is optional, some values have time zones and others do not. A value that does have a time zone specified is said to have an explicit time zone. A value that does not have any particular time zone associated with it is assumed to have an implicit time zone that is defined by the implementation. For example, if the implicit time zone is –05:00, any value that does not have

MMDDYYYY-to-date

Sometimes, dates are included in XML in some other format than that required by the xs:date type. For example, they may use different separators, or put the components in a different order. However, you may still want to create xs:date values from them because you want to use date-related functions.

It is easy enough to write a function that reformats a date and casts it to xs:date. The function shown below converts a date that is in MMDDYYYY format (with any separators between the MM, DD and YYYY) to an xs:date value. It assumes that months and days are always two digits, and years are always four digits.

```
declare namespace functx = "http://www.functx.com";
declare function functx:MMDDYYYY-to-date
  ($dateString as xs:string?) as xs:date
  {
    xs:date(
      let $dateWithoutSeps := replace($dateString,"[^\d]", "")
      return concat( substring($dateWithoutSeps, 5,4), "-",
                     substring($dateWithoutSeps, 1,2), "-",
                     substring($dateWithoutSeps, 3,2))
    )
  };
```

For example, calling this function with:

```
functx:MMDDYYYY-to-date("09/15/2006")
```

returns the xs:date value 2006-09-15.

an explicit time zone is treated as if it is in the − −05:00 time zone. If the implementation does not define an implicit time zone, it is assumed to be UTC. Without implicit time zones, it would be impossible to compare values that have time zones with values that don't.

The implicit-timezone function can be used to determine the implicit time zone. It takes no arguments and returns the implicit time zone as an xs:dayTimeDuration value. For example, implicit-timezone() returns the value −PT5H if the time zone is UTC minus 5 hours (also represented as −05:00). If no implicit time zone is defined, the function returns the empty sequence (not UTC).

Adjusting time zones

Three functions are available to adjust the time zone of a date or time value. The idea is to return the equivalent time in a different time zone—for example, 14:00 in New York is equivalent to 19:00 in London. The function names take the form adjust-xxx-to-timezone, where xxx is one of date, dateTime, or time, depending on the type of the first argument.

Each of these functions takes as arguments the value to be adjusted, followed by the desired time zone, expressed as an `xs:dayTimeDuration` between `-PT14H` and `PT14H`. If the date or time value to be adjusted does not already have a time zone associated with it, the time zone is applied to it. For example:

```
adjust-time-to-timezone(xs:time("17:00:00"), xs:dayTimeDuration("-PT5H"))
```

returns the `xs:time` value `17:00:00-05:00`. If the date or time value already has a time zone associated with it, its value is changed to the new time zone. Note that the time zone argument is treated as the new time zone rather than an adjustment to the existing time zone. For example:

```
adjust-time-to-timezone(xs:time("17:00:00-03:00"), xs:dayTimeDuration("-PT5H"))
```

returns the value `15:00:00-05:00` (not `15:00:00-08:00`). If the second argument is the empty sequence, the time zone is removed from the value. For example:

```
adjust-time-to-timezone(xs:time("17:00:00-03:00"), ( ) )
```

returns the value `17:00:00` (with no time zone).

You can omit the second argument (the time zone) with each of these functions. (Remember, ommitting an argument is different from passing the empty sequence.) In this case, the function uses the implicit time zone defined by the implementation. For example, if the implicit time zone is `-08:00`, the function call:

```
adjust-time-to-timezone(xs:time("17:00:00-03:00"))
```

returns the value `12:00:00-08:00`.

Finding the time zone of a value

You can determine the time zone of an `xs:date`, `xs:time`, or `xs:dateTime` value using one of the functions named `timezone-from-xxx`, where `xxx` is `date`, `time`, or `dateTime`. The result is expressed as an `xs:dayTimeDuration` value that represents the deviation of the time zone from UTC. For example:

```
timezone-from-time(xs:time("09:54:00-05:00"))
```

returns the value `-PT5H`. If there is no time zone in the argument, the empty sequence is returned. These functions do not take into account the implicit time zone. For example:

```
timezone-from-time(xs:time("09:54:00"))
```

returns the empty sequence, regardless of the implicit time zone.

Comparing Dates and Times

A value of type `xs:date`, `xs:dateTime`, or `xs:time` can be compared with another value of the same type using any of the comparison operators. You cannot compare values of different date/time types without explicitly casting one of the values to the other's

type. For example, if you want to determine whether the xs:date value 2006-05-06 is greater than the xs:dateTime value 2006-05-03T13:20:00, you have to cast the xs:dateTime value to the xs:date type first, as in:

```
xs:date("2006-05-06") >
        xs:dateTime("2006-05-03T13:20:00") cast as xs:date
```

Time zones are taken into consideration when comparing dates and times. If a time zone is not present on any of the values, the implicit time zone is assumed for those values. The values are then compared based on their relationship to UTC. For example, 2006-05-03T14:25:00-08:00 (2:25 P.M. Pacific Time) is greater than 2006-05-03T16:25:00-05:00 (4:25 P.M. U.S. Eastern Standard Time) because the former is actually equivalent to 5:25 P.M. U.S. Eastern Standard Time.

Table 19-2 shows some examples of comparing dates and times.

Table 19-2. Examples of comparing dates and times[a]

Example	Value
xs:time("17:15:20-00:00") = xs:time("12:15:20-05:00")	true
xs:time("12:15:20-05:00") > xs:time("12:15:20-04:00")	true
xs:time("12:15:20-05:00") = xs:time("12:15:20")	true
xs:dateTime("2006-05-03T05:00:00") = xs:dateTime("2006-05-03T07:00:00")	false
xs:date("2006-12-25") < xs:date("2005-01-06")	false
xs:time("12:15:20") > xs:time("12:15:30")	false
xs:date("2006-05-06") > xs:dateTime("2006-05-03T13:20:00")	Type error

[a] The third example assumes that the implicit time zone (implementation-defined) is -05:00.

The Duration Types

XQuery uses three types to represent durations of time: xs:duration, xs:yearMonthDuration, and xs:dayTimeDuration.

The xs:duration type represents a duration of time expressed as a number of years, months, days, hours, minutes, and seconds. Its format is PnYnMnDTnHnMnS, where P is a literal value that starts the expression, nY is the number of years followed by a literal Y, and so on where M refers to months, D refers to days, H refers to hours, the second M refers to minutes, and S refers to seconds. T is a literal value that separates the date and time. The numbers are all integers, except the number of seconds, which may be a decimal number. It is also possible to have a negative duration by preceding the P with a minus sign (-).

The xs:duration type is not totally ordered, meaning that values of this type cannot always be compared. For example, if you try to determine whether the xs:duration value P1M is greater than or less than the xs:duration value P30D, it is ambiguous. Months may have 28, 29, 30, or 31 days. So, is 30 days less than a month, or not?

The yearMonthDuration and dayTimeDuration Types

Because xs:duration is not ordered, XQuery defines two types that are derived from duration: xs:yearMonthDuration and xs:dayTimeDuration. By ensuring that month and day components never appear in the same duration, the ambiguity is eliminated.

Values of type xs:yearMonthDuration can only specify years and months, and they are represented as PnYnM. Values of type xs:dayTimeDuration can only specify days, hours, minutes, and seconds, and are represented as PnDTnHnMnS.

 In previous versions of XQuery (including the Candidate Recommendation), the names of the types yearMonthDuration and dayTimeDuration were prefixed with xdt: instead of xs: because they were in the now defunct XPath Datatypes Namespace rather than the XML Schema Namespace. Some processors still support the old names for these types instead.

Table 19-3 summarizes the three duration types and provides some examples.

Table 19-3. Summary of duration types

Type name	Description	Format	Examples
xs:duration	Duration of time	PnYnMnDTnHnMnS.SS	P5Y4M5DT3H5M15.5S, P5Y, PT3H
xs:yearMonthDuration	Duration in years and months	PnYnM	P5Y4M, P15M
xs:dayTimeDuration	Duration in days, hours, minutes, and seconds	PnDTnHnMnS.SS	P5DT3H5M15.5S, PT125S

Comparing Durations

Two values of xs:duration can be tested for equality (or inequality), but you cannot compare them using the operators <, <=, >, or >= because attempting to do so results in a type error. However, values of one of the two derived types, xs:yearMonthDuration and xs:dayTimeDuration *can* be compared because they are totally ordered. They are compared based on the number of months and the number of seconds, respectively.

For example, the xs:yearMonthDuration value P1Y is equal to the xs:yearMonthDuration value P12M. Even though they have different components, they represent an equal number of months. However, xs:yearMonthDuration values cannot be compared with xs:dayTimeDuration values, or with xs:duration values.

Table 19-4 shows some examples of comparing duration values.

Table 19-4. Examples of comparing durations

Example	Value
xs:yearMonthDuration("P1Y") = xs:yearMonthDuration("P1Y")	true
xs:yearMonthDuration("P1Y") = xs:yearMonthDuration("P12M")	true

Table 19-4. Examples of comparing durations (continued)

Example	Value
xs:yearMonthDuration("P1Y2M") > xs:yearMonthDuration("P1Y3M")	false
xs:dayTimeDuration("P1DT12H") = xs:dayTimeDuration("PT36H")	true
xs:dayTimeDuration("P1DT12H") < xs:dayTimeDuration("PT37H")	true
xs:yearMonthDuration("P1Y") < xs:dayTimeDuration("P366D")	Type error
xs:duration("P11M") < xs:duration("P12M")	Type error

Extracting Components of Dates, Times, and Durations

A number of functions allow you to extract specific parts of dates, times, and durations. For example, to retrieve the year part of a date, you can use the year-from-date function. Table 19-5 lists all the component extraction functions for date, time, and duration values.

Table 19-5. Component extraction functions

year-from-dateTime	day-from-dateTime	minutes-from-dateTime
year-from-date	day-from-date	minutes-from-time
years-from-duration	days-from-duration	minutes-from-duration
month-from-dateTime	hours-from-dateTime	seconds-from-dateTime
month-from-date	hours-from-time	seconds-from-time
months-from-duration	hours-from-duration	seconds-from-duration

When working with duration values, these functions calculate the result based on the canonical representation of the values. For example, the function years-from-duration does not necessarily return the integer that appears before the Y in the original value. Rather, it returns the number of whole years in the duration, taking into account that the number of months might be more than 12. If the xs:duration value is P1Y15M, the function returns 2, not 1. This is because the canonical representation of P1Y15M (1 year and 15 months) is actually P2Y3M (2 years and 3 months). To extract the number of years as a decimal number, you could instead divide the value by the duration P1Y, which would return 2.25. This is described in "Dividing Durations by Durations," later in this chapter.

Table 19-6 shows some examples of calls to the component extraction functions.

Table 19-6. Examples of the component extraction functions

Example	Return value
month-from-date(xs:date("1999-05-31"))	5
hours-from-time(xs:time("09:54:00"))	9
seconds-from-duration (xs:duration("P5DT1H13.6S"))	13.6
seconds-from-duration(xs:duration("-P5DT1H13.6S"))	-13.6
years-from-duration (xs:duration("P5Y3M"))	5
years-from-duration (xs:duration("P1Y15M"))	2

If you want to extract the entire date or time from an xs:dateTime value, you can cast that value to the desired type (either xs:date or xs:time).

Using Arithmetic Operators on Dates, Times, and Durations

The arithmetic operations performed on date and time types fall into five categories, described in the following sections:

1. Subtracting a date or time from another date or time to determine, for example, the elapsed time between 1:32 P.M. and 4:53 P.M.

2. Adding or subtracting durations from dates to determine, for example, what date is 30 days prior to April 15.

3. Adding or subtracting two durations to obtain a third duration, which might be used to extend a time period by 30 days.

4. Multiplying or dividing a duration by decimal numbers to obtain a third duration, which might be used to double a time period or to convert a numeric value to a duration.

5. Dividing a duration by another duration, which might be used to calculate the ratio of two durations or to convert a duration value to a number.

In addition to these operations, it is also possible to use the aggregation functions (max, min, avg, and sum) on sequences of duration values. You can also use the max and min functions on dates, times, and date/time values.

Subtracting Dates and Times

A value of type xs:date, xs:time, or xs:dateTime can be subtracted from another value of the same type. This is useful for determining the elapsed duration between two points in time. For example, if you want to calculate the response time on a customer order, you can subtract the order date from the delivery date.

The result is negative if the second date or time occurs later in time than the first date or time.

The resulting value, in all cases, is an xs:dayTimeDuration value. There is no way to determine the difference between two dates measured in months, because it's not clear that everyone would agree what the answer is if the dates are, for example, 2004-02-29 and 2005-02-28.

Time zones are taken into consideration during subtraction. If either of the values does not have a time zone, it is assumed to have the implicit time zone.

Table 19-7 shows some examples. The last example assumes that the implicit time zone is -05:00.

Table 19-7. Examples of subtracting dates and times

Example	Value
xs:dateTime("2006-04-11T09:23:30.5") - xs:dateTime("2006-04-04T02:15:10.2")	P7DT7H8M20.3S
xs:dateTime("2006-05-03T12:15:30.5") - xs:dateTime("2006-05-03T12:15:10.2")	PT20.3S
xs:date("2006-05-06") - xs:date("2006-05-03")	P3D
xs:date("2006-04-02") - xs:date("2005-03-11")	P387D
xs:date("2006-05-03") - xs:date("2006-05-03")	PT0S
xs:date("2006-05-03") - xs:date("2006-05-06")	-P3D
xs:time("13:12:02.001") - xs:time("13:12:00")	PT2.001S
xs:time("13:12:00-03:00") - xs:time("13:12:00-05:00")	-PT2H
xs:time("08:00:00-05:00") - xs:time("09:00:00-02:00")	PT2H
xs:time("13:12:00-03:00") - xs:time("13:12:00")	-PT2H

Adding and Subtracting Durations from Dates and Times

You can add or subtract durations from dates and times. This is useful for determining, for example, what date occurs 30 days after a specified date, or what time it will be when some process of fixed duration is completed.

Note that you can't add or subtract an xs:yearMonthDuration from an xs:time; attempting to do so raises a type error. This makes sense, since an xs:yearMonthDuration would not affect an xs:time anyway. Another restriction is that, when subtracting, the date/time operand must appear first (before the operator), and the duration operand second.

If the original xs:date, xs:time, or xs:dateTime has a time zone, the result has that same time zone. If it does not, the result does not. Table 19-8 shows some examples of adding and subtracting durations from dates and times.

Table 19-8. Examples of adding durations to dates and times

Example	Value
xs:dateTime("2006-05-03T09:12:35") + xs:yearMonthDuration("P1Y2M")	2007-07-03T09:12:35
xs:dateTime("2006-04-29T09:12:35") + xs:dayTimeDuration("P5DT2H12M")	2006-05-04T11:24:35
xs:dateTime("2006-04-29T09:12:35") + xs:dayTimeDuration("P5DT17H12M")	2006-05-05T02:24:35
xs:dateTime("2006-04-29T09:12:35") - xs:yearMonthDuration("P1Y")	2005-04-29T09:12:35
xs:yearMonthDuration("P1Y5M") + xs:date("2006-10-02")	2008-03-02
xs:date("2006-10-02") - xs:dayTimeDuration("PT48H")	2006-09-30
xs:date("2006-03-31") - xs:yearMonthDuration("P1M")	2006-02-28

Table 19-8. Examples of adding durations to dates and times (continued)

Example	Value
xs:time("09:12:35") + xs:dayTimeDuration("P5DT2H12M")	11:24:35
xs:time("09:12:35") + xs:yearMonthDuration("P1Y2M")	Type error

If adding a number of months to a date would result in a day value being out of range—for example, if you attempt to add P1M to 2006-05-31, the result has the last possible day of that month, e.g., 2006-06-30. This can cause surprises: if you add six months to a date and then subtract six months, you might not get the date you started with.

Adding and Subtracting Two Durations

You can add and subtract values of type xs:yearMonthDuration or xs:dayTimeDuration (but not xs:duration). This is useful for extending time periods or adding up the durations of various fixed-length processes.

The result of the operation has the same type as both the operands. The result will be negative if a larger duration is subtracted from a smaller duration. Table 19-9 shows some examples of adding and subtracting durations. The two operands must have the same type. If you attempt to add an xs:yearMonthDuration to an xs:dayTimeDuration, a type error is raised.

Table 19-9. Examples of adding and subtracting durations

Example	Value
xs:yearMonthDuration("P3Y10M") + xs:yearMonthDuration("P5Y5M")	P9Y3M
xs:dayTimeDuration("P2DT14H55.3S") - xs:dayTimeDuration("P1DT12H51.2S")	P1DT2H4.1S
xs:dayTimeDuration("P1DT12H51.2S") - xs:dayTimeDuration("P2DT14H55.3S")	-P1DT2H4.1S
xs:yearMonthDuration("P3Y10M") + xs:dayTimeDuration("P1DT12H")	Type error

Multiplying and Dividing Durations by Numbers

Multiplying and dividing durations by decimal numbers is useful, for example, to double a time period or reduce it by half. Another common use case is to convert a value from a number to a duration. For example, if the $numMonths variable has the integer value 10 that represents a number of months, and you want to convert it to a duration, you can use the expression:

```
$numMonths * xs:yearMonthDuration("P1M")
```

This would result in a duration value of 10 months (P10M).

Table 19-10 shows some examples of multiplying and dividing durations by numbers.

Table 19-10. Examples of multiplying and dividing durations

Example	Value	Value type
xs:yearMonthDuration("P1Y6M") * 3.5	P5Y3M	xs:yearMonthDuration
3 * xs:dayTimeDuration("PT50M")	PT2H30M	xs:dayTimeDuration
xs:yearMonthDuration("P2Y6M") div 2	P1Y3M	xs:yearMonthDuration
10 * xs:yearMonthDuration("P1M")	P10M	xs:yearMonthDuration

When working with an xs:yearMonthDuration value, the result is rounded to the nearest month.

Dividing Durations by Durations

Dividing a duration by another duration will calculate the ratio of two durations. This is useful if you need to convert a value from a duration to a number. For example, if the $showLength variable has the xs:dayTimeDuration value PT2H, and you want the equivalent number of minutes as a decimal number, you can use the expression:

```
$showLength div xs:dayTimeDuration("PT1M")
```

This would result in the number 120, representing 120 minutes.

As with addition and subtraction, the two operands must have the same type. The result of the operation has the type xs:decimal. Table 19-11 shows some examples of dividing durations by other durations.

Table 19-11. Examples of multiplying and dividing durations

Example	Value
xs:yearMonthDuration("P1Y") div xs:yearMonthDuration("P6M")	2
xs:dayTimeDuration("PT25M") div xs:dayTimeDuration("PT50M")	0.5
xs:dayTimeDuration("PT2H") div xs:dayTimeDuration("PT1M")	120

The Date Component Types

In addition to the date and time types already discussed, there are several other date-related types that represent components of dates. Specifically, they are: xs:gYear, xs:gYearMonth, xs:gMonth, xs:gMonthDay, and xs:gDay. The letter g at the beginning of these type names signifies "Gregorian," the name of the calendar used in most of the world. They are summarized in Table 19-12 and covered in detail in Appendix B.

Table 19-12. The date component types

Type name	Description	Format	Example
xs:gYear	Year	YYYY	2006
xs:gYearMonth	Year and month	YYYY-MM	2006-05
xs:gMonth	Recurring month	--MM	--05
xs:gMonthDay	Recurring month and day	--MM-DD	--05-30
xs:gDay	Recurring day	---DD	---30

Values of these types can be tested for equality (or inequality) with other values of the same type. However, you cannot compare them using the operators <, <=, >, or >=. For example, attempting to check if one xs:gMonth value is less than another xs:gMonth value raises a type error.

Working with Qualified Names, URIs, and IDs

This chapter describes the functions and constructors that act on namespace-qualified names, Uniform Resource Identifiers (URIs), and IDs. Each of these types has unique properties and complexities that sets it apart from simple strings.

Working with Qualified Names

The type xs:QName is used to represent qualified names in XQuery. An xs:QName value has three parts: a namespace, a local part, and an associated prefix. The namespace and the prefix are optional. If a QName does not have a namespace associated with it, it is considered to be in "no namespace."

A prefix may be used to represent a namespace in a qualified name, for example in an XML document. The prefix is mapped to a namespace using a namespace declaration. The prefix itself has no meaning; it is just a placeholder. Two QNames that have the same local part and namespace are equivalent, regardless of prefix. However, the XQuery processor does keep track of a QName's prefix. This simplifies certain processes like serializing QNames and casting them to strings.

Most query writers who are working with qualified names are working with the names of elements and attributes. (It is also possible for a qualified name to appear as element content or as an attribute value, but this is less common.) You may want to *retrieve* all or part of a name if, for example, you want to test to see if it is a particular value, or you want to include the name in the query results. You may want to *construct* a qualified name for a node if you are dynamically creating the name of a node using a computed element constructor. These two use cases are discussed in this section.

Retrieving Node Names

Four functions retrieve node names or parts of node names: node-name, name, local-name, and namespace-uri from element and attribute nodes. They are summarized in Table 20-1.

Table 20-1. Functions that return node names

Function	Return value
node-name	The qualified name of the node as an xs:QName
name	The qualified name of the node as an xs:string that may be prefixed
local-name	The local part of the node name as an xs:string
namespace-uri	The namespace part of a node name (a full namespace name, not a prefix) as an xs:anyURI

Each of these functions takes as an argument a single (optional) node. Table 20-2 shows examples of all four functions. They use the input document names.xml shown in Example 20-1.

Example 20-1. Namespaces in XML (names.xml)

```
<noNamespace>
  <pre:prefixed xmlns="http://datypic.com/unpre"
          xmlns:pre="http://datypic.com/pre">
    <unprefixed pre:prefAttr="a" noNSAttr="b">123</unprefixed>
  </pre:prefixed>
</noNamespace>
```

Note that the original prefixes from the input document (or lack thereof) are taken into account when retrieving the names. For example, calling the name function with the unprefixed element results in the unprefixed string unprefixed. This does not mean that the unprefixed element is not in a namespace; it is in the http://datypic.com/unpre namespace. It simply indicates that the unprefixed element was not prefixed in the input document, because its namespace was the default, and therefore had no prefix as part of its QName. Therefore, if you are testing the name or manipulating it in some way, it is best to use node-name rather than name, because node-name provides a result that includes the namespace.

Table 20-2. Examples of the name functions

Node	node-name returns an xs:QName with:	name returns	local-name returns	namespace-uri returns
noNamespace	Namespace: empty Prefix: empty Local part:noNamespace	noNamespace	noNamespace	A zero-length string
pre:prefixed	Namespace: http://datypic.com/pre Prefix: pre Local part: prefixed	pre:prefixed	prefixed	http://datypic.com/pre
unprefixed	Namespace: http://datypic.com/unpre Prefix: empty Local part: unprefixed	unprefixed	unprefixed	http://datypic.com/unpre

Table 20-2. Examples of the name functions (continued)

Node	node-name returns an xs:QName with:	name returns	local-name returns	namespace-uri returns
@pre:prefAttr	Namespace: http:// datypic.com/pre Prefix: pre Local part: prefAttr	pre:prefAttr	prefAttr	http://datypic. com/pre
@noNSAttr	Namespace: empty Prefix: empty Local part: noNSAttr	noNSAttr	noNSAttr	A zero-length string

Suppose you want to create a report on the product catalog. You want to list all the properties of each product element in an XHTML list. You could accomplish this using the query shown in Example 20-2. It uses the local-name function to return the names like name, colorChoices, and desc, allowing them to appear as part of the report.

Example 20-2. Using names as result data

Query
```
<html>{
  for $prod in doc("catalog.xml")//product
  return (<p>Product # {string($prod/number)}</p>,
          <ul>{
            for $child in $prod/(* except number)
            return <li>{local-name($child)}: {string($child)}</li>
          }</ul>)
}</html>
```
Results
```
<html>
  <p>Product # 557</p>
  <ul>
    <li>name: Fleece Pullover</li>
    <li>colorChoices: navy black</li>
  </ul>
  <p>Product # 563</p>
  <ul>
    <li>name: Floppy Sun Hat</li>
  </ul>
  <p>Product # 443</p>
  <ul>
    <li>name: Deluxe Travel Bag</li>
  </ul>
  <p>Product # 784</p>
  <ul>
    <li>name: Cotton Dress Shirt</li>
    <li>colorChoices: white gray</li>
    <li>desc: Our favorite shirt!</li>
  </ul>
</html>
```

Constructing Qualified Names

There are several ways to construct qualified names. Qualified names are constructed automatically when using direct element and attribute constructors. They can also be constructed directly from strings in certain expressions such as computed element constructors. In addition, three functions are available to construct QNames: the xs:QName constructor, the QName function, and the resolve-QName function.

The xs:QName type has a constructor just like all other atomic types. The argument may be prefixed (e.g., prod:number) or unprefixed (e.g., number). However, it has a special constraint that it can only accept a literal xs:string value (not an evaluated expression). This limits its usefulness, since names cannot be dynamically generated.

A function called QName can also be used to construct QNames. Unlike the xs:QName constructor, it can be used to generate names dynamically. It accepts a namespace URI and name (optionally prefixed), and returns a QName. For example:

```
QName("http://datypic.com/p", "pre:child")
```

returns a QName with the namespace http://datypic.com/p, the local part child, and the prefix pre. As with any function call, the arguments are not required to be literal strings. You could just as easily use an expression such as concat("pre:",$myElName) to express the local part of the name.

A third option is the resolve-QName function, which accepts two arguments: a string and an element. The string represents the name, which may have a prefix. The element is used to determine the appropriate namespace URI for that prefix. Typically, this function is used to resolve a QName appearing in the content of a document against the namespace context of the element where the QName appears. For example, to retrieve all products that carry the attribute xsi:type="prod:ProductType", you can use a path such as:

```
declare namespace prod = "http://datypic.com/prod";

doc("catalog.xml"//product[resolve-QName(@xsi:type, .) = xs:QName("prod:ProductType")]
```

This test allows the value of xsi:type in the input document to use any prefix (not just prod) as long as it is bound to the http://datypic.com/prod namespace.

Other Name-Related Functions

Three functions exist to extract parts of an xs:QName:

local-name-from-QName
> Returns the local part of the name as a string

prefix-from-QName
> Returns the prefix as a string

namespace-uri-from-QName
> Returns the namespace URI

change-element-ns and change-element-ns-deep

Suppose you wish to copy an element from the input document, but you wish to put the result element in a different namespace. This function accomplishes this:

```
declare namespace functx = "http://www.functx.com";
declare function functx:change-element-ns
($element as element(), $newns as xs:string) as element()
 {
   let $newName := QName($newns, local-name($element))
   return (element {$newName} {$element/@*, $element/node()})
 };
```

It accepts as arguments an element, and the new namespace as a string. It calculates the new name of the element using the QName function and binds it to the variable $newName. It then uses a computed element constructor to create an element with the new name, and copies all of its attributes and children. Note that no prefix is associated with the new name.

The function above only changes the namespace of the node that is passed to it, not its children. To modify the namespaces of the element descendants as well, you need to use a recursive function such as this one:

```
declare namespace functx = "http://www.functx.com";
declare function functx:change-element-ns-deep
($element as element(), $newns as xs:string) as element() {
  let $newName := QName ($newns, local-name($element))
  return (element {$newName}
   {$element/@*,
    for $child in $element/node()
    return if ($child instance of element())
           then functx:change-element-ns-deep($child, $newns)
           else $child
   }
  )
};
```

For example, calling this function with:

```
<test xmlns:pre="pre">{
  functx:change-element-ns-deep(
    <pre:x><pre:y>123</pre:y></pre:x>, "http://new")
}</test>
```

returns:

```
<test xmlns:pre="pre">
  <x xmlns="http://new">
    <y>123</y>
  </x>
</test>
```

The `local-name-from-QName` and `namespace-uri-from-QName` functions are similar to the `local-name` and `namespace-uri` functions, respectively, except that they take an atomic `xs:QName` rather than a node as an argument. If you are working with element or attribute names, it is easier to use the functions for retrieving node names, such as `local-name` and `name`.

XQuery also has two other prefix-related functions: `in-scope-prefixes` and `namespace-uri-for-prefix`. The `in-scope-prefixes` function returns a list of all the prefixes that are in scope for a given element, as a sequence of strings. The `namespace-uri-for-prefix` function retrieves the namespace URI associated with a particular prefix, in the scope of a specified element. Because most processing is based on namespaces rather than prefixes (which are technically irrelevant), these functions are not especially useful to the average query writer.

Working with URIs

Uniform Resource Identifiers (URIs) are used to uniquely identify resources, and they may be absolute or relative. Absolute URIs provide the entire context for identifying the resources, such as `http://datypic.com/prod.html`. Relative URI references are specified as the difference from a base URI, such as `../prod.html`. A URI reference may also contain a fragment identifier following the # character, such as `../prod.html#shirt`.

The three previous examples happen to be HTTP Uniform Resource Locators (URLs), but URIs also encompass URLs of other schemes (e.g., FTP, gopher, telnet), as well as Uniform Resource Names (URNs). URIs are not required to be dereferenceable; that is, it is not necessary for there to be a web page or other resource at `http://datypic.com/prod.html` in order for this to be a valid URI. Sometimes URIs just serve as names. For example, in XQuery, URIs are used as the names of namespaces and collations.

The built-in type `xs:anyURI` represents a URI reference. Most XQuery functions that accept URIs as arguments call for `xs:string` values instead, but an `xs:anyURI` value is acceptable also. This is because of a special type-promotion rule that allows `xs:anyURI` values to be automatically promoted to `xs:string` when a string is expected. Most of the URI-related functions return `xs:anyURI` values, following the philosophy of being liberal in what they accept and specific in what they produce.

Base and Relative URIs

Relative URIs are interpreted relative to an absolute URI, known as a base URI. For example, the relative URI `prod.html` is useless unless interpreted in the context of an absolute URI. In HTML documents, the base URI is often the URI of the document

itself. If an HTML document is located at `http://datypic.com/order.html`, and it contains a link to `prod.html`, that `prod.html` relative URI is resolved in the context of the `http://datypic.com/order.html`, and the link points to `http://datypic.com/prod.html`.

Using the xml:base attribute

In XML documents, you can also explicitly specify a base URI using the `xml:base` attribute. The scope of each `xml:base` attribute is the element on which it appears and all its content.

Example 20-3 shows an XML document that uses the `xml:base` attribute on the catalog elements, with relative URI references (the `href` attributes) for each `product`. The `href="prod443.html"` attribute of the first product element, for example, is resolved relative to the `xml:base` attribute of the first catalog element, namely `http://example.org/ACC/`.

Example 20-3. Document using xml:base (http://datypic.com/cats.xml)

```
<catalogs>
  <catalog name="ACC" xml:base="http://example.org/ACC/">
    <product number="443" href="prod443.html"/>
    <product number="563" href="prod563.html"/>
  </catalog>
  <catalog name="WMN" xml:base="http://example.org/WMN/">
    <product number="557" href="prod557.html"/>
  </catalog>
</catalogs>
```

Finding the base URI of a node

The base-uri function can be used to retrieve the base URI of a node. For document nodes, the base URI is the URI from which the document was retrieved. For example:

```
base-uri(doc("http://datypic.com/cats.xml"))
```

returns `http://datypic.com/cats.xml`.

For element nodes, the base URI is the value of its `xml:base` attribute, if any, or the `xml:base` attribute of its nearest ancestor. For example, if $prod is bound to the first product element in `cats.xml`, the function call:

```
base-uri($prod)
```

returns `http://example.org/ACC/`, because that is the `xml:base` value of its nearest ancestor.

If no `xml:base` attributes appear among its ancestors, it defaults to the base URI of the document node, if one exists.

Resolving URIs

The `resolve-uri` function takes a relative URI and a base URI as arguments, and constructs an absolute URI. For example, the function call:

```
resolve-uri("prod.html", "http://datypic.com/order.html")
```

returns `http://datypic.com/prod.html`.

The base URI of the static context

The base URI of an individual node is set by the `xml:base` attribute or by the document URI. There is also a separate base URI, known as the base URI of the static context. The base URI of the static context is used in several cases:

- When an element is constructed in a query, its base URI is set to the base URI of the static context, if one is defined. Otherwise, its base URI is the empty sequence.
- When relative URI references are used as arguments to the `doc` and `collection` functions, or to functions that accept collations as arguments, they are resolved relative to the base URI of the static context.
- When a base URI argument is not provided to the `resolve-uri` function, it resolves the URI relative to the base URI of the static context.

The base URI of the static context can be set in the query prolog, using a base URI declaration. Its syntax is shown in Figure 20-1.

```
——declare base-uri "<base-uri>" ;——▶
```

Figure 20-1. Syntax of a base URI declaration

Here's an example of a base URI declaration:

```
declare base-uri "http://datypic.com";
```

The base URI must be a literal value in quotes (not an evaluated expression), and it should be a syntactically valid absolute URI.

It is also possible for the processor to set the base URI of the static context outside the scope of the query. Although it is implementation-defined, it's reasonable to expect that if the query itself is read from a file, the base URI of the static context will default to the location of that file. The value of the base URI of the static context can be retrieved using the `static-base-uri` function.

Documents and URIs

When accessing an input document using the doc function, a URI is used to specify the document of interest. Processors interpret the URI passed to the doc function in different ways. Some, like Saxon, will dereference the URI, that is, go out to the URL and retrieve the resource at that location. Other implementations, such as those embedded in XML databases, consider the URIs to be just names. The processor might take the name and look it up in an internal catalog to find the document associated with that name.

Finding the URI of a document

You can find the absolute URI from which a document node was retrieved using the document-uri function. This function is basically the inverse of the doc function. Where the doc function accepts a URI and returns a document node, the document-uri function accepts a document node and returns a URI.

For example, if the variable $orderDoc is bound to the result of doc("http://datypic.com/order.xml"), then document-uri($orderDoc) returns "http://datypic.com/order.xml".

In most cases, this has the same effect as calling the base-uri function on the document node.

Opening a document from a dynamic value

Most of the examples of the doc function in this book use a hardcoded URI, as in doc("order.xml"). However, suppose you wanted to open the documents referenced in Example 20-3. For example, you want to open the product information page for product number 443. Its relative URI is prod443.html, and its base URI is http://example.org/ACC/. To do this, you could use:

```
let $prod := doc("cats.xml")/catalogs/catalog[1]/product[1]/@href
let $absoluteURI := resolve-uri($prod, base-uri($prod))
return doc($absoluteURI)
```

which would open the document at http://example.org/ACC/prod443.html.

Escaping URIs

URIs require that some characters be escaped with their hexadecimal Unicode code point preceded by the % character. This includes non-ASCII characters and some ASCII characters, namely control characters, spaces, and several others. In addition, certain characters in URIs are separators that are intended to delimit parts of URIs, namely the characters ; , / ? : @ & = + $ [] and %. If these delimiter characters must be used in a URI, having a meaning other than as a delimiter, they too must be escaped.

open-ref-document

It may be useful to use a general-purpose function to resolve URIs and dereference them, returning a document node. This function accomplishes this:

```
declare namespace functx = "http://www.functx.com";
declare function functx:open-ref-document
  ($refNode as node()) as document-node( )
  {
    let $absoluteURI := resolve-uri($refNode, base-uri($refNode))
    return doc($absoluteURI)
  };
```

open-ref-document accepts a node (either attribute or element) whose value is a relative URI reference. For example, this function call opens the document named in the href attribute:

```
let $ref := doc("cats.xml")/catalogs/catalog[1]/product[1]/@href
return functx:open-ref-document($ref)
```

Three functions are available for escaping URI values: iri-to-uri, escape-html-uri, and encode-for-uri. All three replace each special character with an escape sequence in the form %xx (possibly repeating), where xx is two hexadecimal digits (in upper-case) that represent the character in UTF-8. For example, ../édition.html is changed to ../%C3%A9dition.html, with the é escaped as %C3%A9.

They vary in which characters they escape:

iri-to-uri

Escapes only those characters that are not allowed in URIs, but not the delimiters ; , / ? : @ & = + $ [] or %. It is appropriate for escaping entire URIs.

escape-html-uri

Escapes characters as required by HTML agents. Specifically, it escapes everything except ASCII characters 32 to 126. It is appropriate for URIs that are to be handled by browsers.

encode-for-uri

Is the most aggressive of the three. It escapes all the characters that are required to be escaped in URIs, plus all the delimiter characters. It is appropriate for escaping pieces of URIs, such as filenames, that cannot contain delimiter characters.

Note that none of these functions check whether the argument provided is a valid URI; they simply act on the argument as if it were any string.

Working with IDs

IDs and IDREFs are used in XML to uniquely identify elements within a document and to create references to those elements. This is useful, for example, to create footnotes and references to them, or to create hyperlinks to specific sections of XHTML documents.

Typically, an attribute is used as an ID to uniquely represent the element that carries it.[*] The value of that ID attribute must be a valid NCName (an XML name with no colon).

Attributes named `xml:id` (in the `http://www.w3.org/XML/1998/namespace` namespace) are always considered to be IDs. Attributes with other names can also be considered IDs if they are declared to have the built-in type `xs:ID` in a schema or DTD.

Example 20-4 shows an XML document that contains some ID attributes, namely the `id` attribute of the `section` element, and the `fnid` attribute of the `fn` element. Each `section` and `fn` element is uniquely identified by an ID value, such as `fn1`, `preface`, or `context`.

The example assumes that this document was validated with a schema that declares these attributes to be of type `xs:ID`. The `id` attributes are not automatically considered to be IDs because they are not in the appropriate namespace. In fact, the name is irrelevant if it is not `xml:id`; an attribute named `foo` can have the type `xs:ID`, and an attribute named `id` can have the type `xs:integer`.

Example 20-4. XML document with IDs and IDREFs (book.xml)

```
<book>
  <section id="preface">This book introduces XQuery...
    The examples are downloadable<fnref ref="fn1"/>...
  </section>
  <section id="context">...</section>
  <section id="language">...Expressions, introduced
   in <secRef refs="context"/>, are...
  </section>
  <section id="types">...As described in
    <secRef refs="context language"/>, you can...
  </section>
  <fn fnid="fn1">See http://datypic.com.</fn>
</book>
```

The type `xs:IDREF` is used for an attribute that references an `xs:ID`. All attributes of type `xs:IDREF` must reference an ID in the same XML document. A common use case for `xs:IDREF` is to create a cross-reference to a particular section of a document. The

[*] It is technically possible to use a child element as an ID, but it is discouraged for reasons of compatibility with XML 1.0 DTDs.

ref attribute of the fnref element in Example 20-4 contains an xs:IDREF value (again, assuming it is validated with a schema or DTD). Its value, fn1, matches the value of the fnid attribute of the fn element.

The type xs:IDREFS represents a whitespace-separated list of one or more xs:IDREF values. In Example 20-4, the refs attribute of secRef is assumed to be of type xs: IDREFS. The first refs attribute contains only one xs:IDREF (context), while the second contains two xs:IDREF values (context and language).

Joining IDs and IDREFs

Two functions allow you to reference elements based on the ID/IDREF relationship: id and idref.

The id function returns elements that have specified IDs, for example, all elements whose ID is either preface or context (in this case, the first two section elements). Given a sequence of IDs, the id function returns the elements whose xs:ID attributes match them. For example, the function call:

```
doc("book.xml")/id( ("preface", "context") )
```

returns the first two section elements, because their ID attributes have the values preface and context, respectively.

The idref function returns elements that *refer* to specified IDs, using either an xs: IDREF or xs:IDREFS attribute. For example, the function call:

```
doc("book.xml")/idref( ("context", "language") )
```

returns the refs attributes of the two secRef elements, because each of these attributes is of type xs:IDREFS and contains either context or language or both.

The previous examples used literal strings for the second argument. These two functions become even more useful when they are used to link referring elements to referred elements. For example, the expression:

```
for $child in (doc("book.xml")//section[1]/node( ))
return if (name($child) = "fnref")
       then concat ("[", string(doc("book.xml")/id($child/@ref)), "]")
       else string($child)
```

uses the id function to resolve the footnote reference in the first section. It returns:

```
This book introduces XQuery...
The examples are downloadable [See http://datypic.com.]...
```

The text that was contained in the fn element now appears where it was referenced using fnref.

get-ID

No built-in function exists to retrieve the ID of an element, but it is simple enough to define a function for this purpose. It might look like this:

```
declare namespace functx = "http://www.functx.com";
declare function functx:get-ID($element as element( )?) as xs:ID?
{ data($element/@*[id(.)is ..])};
```

This function takes an element and returns all the attributes (of which there can only be one) whose parent element has that value as its ID. If no such attribute exists, or if the argument is the empty sequence, the function returns the empty sequence. The attribute must have been declared to be of type xs:ID in a schema or DTD, and validated by that schema or DTD, for this function to work. For example, the function call:

```
functx:get-ID(doc("book.xml")//section[1])
```

returns the xs:ID value preface.

Constructing IDs

You can create result elements with IDs by using the xml:id attribute in your element constructors. For example, the constructor:

```
<prod xml:id="{concat('P', $prodNum)}"/>
```

will create a prod element with an ID attribute that is equal to the letter P concatenated with the value of the $prodNum variable. The value assigned to an attribute named xml:id must be a valid XML name. Any whitespace in its value will be normalized automatically.

Working with Other XML Components

So far, this book has focused on elements and attributes. This chapter discusses the other kinds of nodes, namely comments, processing instructions, documents, and text nodes. CDATA sections and XML character and entity references are also covered in this chapter.

XML Comments

XML comments, delimited by `<!--` and `-->`, can be both queried and constructed in XQuery. Some implementations will discard comments when parsing input documents or loading them into a database, so you should consult the documentation for your implementation to see what is supported.

XML Comments and the Data Model

Comments may appear at the beginning or end of an input document, or within element content. Example 21-1 shows a small XML document with two comments, on the second and fifth lines.

Example 21-1. XML document with comments (comment.xml)

```
<?xml version="1.0" encoding="UTF-8"?>
<!-- This is a business document -->
<b:businessDocument xmlns:b="http://datypic.com/b">
  <b:header>
    <!-- date created --><b:date>2006-10-15</b:date>
  </b:header>
</b:businessDocument>
```

Comment nodes do not have any children, and their parent is either a document node or an element node. In this example, the comment on the second line is a child of the document node, and the comment on the fifth line is a child of the `b:header` element.

Comment nodes do not have names, so calling any of the name-related functions with a comment node will result in the empty sequence or a zero-length string, depending on the function. The string value (and typed value) of a comment node is its content, as an instance of xs:string.

Querying Comments

Comments can be queried using path expressions. The comment() kind test can be used to specifically ask for comments. For example:

```
doc("comment.xml")//comment( )
```

will return both comments in the document, while:

```
doc("comment.xml")/b:businessDocument/b:header/comment( )
```

will return only the second comment.

The node() kind test will return comments as well as all other node kinds. For example:

```
doc("comment.xml")/b:businessDocument/b:header/node( )
```

will return a sequence consisting of the second comment, followed by the b:date element. This is in contrast to *, which selects child *element* nodes only.

You can take the string value of a comment node (e.g., using the string function) and use that string in various operations.

Comments and Sequence Types

The comment() keyword can also be used in sequence types to match comment nodes. For example, if you wanted to write a function that places the content of a comment in a constructed comment element, you could use the function shown in Example 21-2. The use of the comment() sequence type in the function signature ensures that only comment nodes are passed to this function.

Example 21-2. Function that processes comments

```
declare function local:createCommentElement
  ($commentToAdd as comment()) as element() {
  <comment>{string($commentToAdd)}</comment>
};
```

A comment node will also match the node() and item() sequence types.

Constructing Comments

XML comment constructors can be used in queries to specify XML comments. Unlike XQuery comments, which are delimited by (: and :), XML comments are intended to appear in the results of the query.

XML comments can be constructed using either direct or computed constructors. A direct XML comment constructor is delimited as it would be in an XML document, by `<!--` and `-->`. It is included character by character in the results of the query; no expressions that appear in direct comment constructors are evaluated.

Computed comment constructors are useful when you want to calculate the value of a comment. A computed comment constructor consists of an expression surrounded by `comment{` and `}`, as shown in Figure 21-1. The expression within the constructor is evaluated and cast to `xs:string`.

Figure 21-1. Syntax of a computed comment constructor

As in XML syntax, neither direct nor computed comment constructors can result in a comment that contains two consecutive hyphens (`--`) or ends in a hyphen.

Example 21-3 shows examples of XML comment constructors. As you can see, the enclosed expression in the direct constructor is not evaluated, while the expression in the computed constructor *is* evaluated. In either case, a comment constructor results in a standard XML comment appearing in the query results.

Example 21-3. XML comment constructors

```
Query
let $count := count(doc("catalog.xml")//product)
(: unordered list :)
return <ul>
        <!-- {concat(" List of ", $count, " products ")} -->
        {comment{concat(" List of ", $count, " products ")}}
      </ul>
Results
<ul>
  <!-- {concat(" List of ", $count, " products ")} -->
  <!-- List of 4 products -->
</ul>
```

Note that the XQuery comment (`: unordered list :`) is not included in the results. XQuery comments, described in Chapter 3, are used to comment on the query itself.

Processing Instructions

Processing instructions are generally used in XML documents to tell the XML application to perform some particular action. For example, a processing instruction similar to:

```
<?xml-stylesheet type="text/xsl" href="formatter.xsl"?>
```

appears in some XML documents to associate them with an XSLT stylesheet. When opened in some browsers, the XML document will be displayed using that stylesheet. This processing instruction has a target, which consists of the characters after the <?, up to the first space, namely xml-stylesheet. The rest of the characters are referred to as its content, namely type="text/xsl" href="formatter.xsl". Although the content of this particular processing instruction looks like a pair of attributes, it is simply considered a string.

Processing instructions can be both queried and constructed using XQuery.

Processing Instructions and the Data Model

Although processing instructions often appear at the beginning of an XML document, they can actually appear within element content or at the end of the document as well. Example 21-4 shows a small XML document with two processing instructions. The xml-stylesheet processing instruction appears on the second line, whereas doc-processor appears within the content of the b:header element. The first line is the XML declaration, which, although it looks like a processing instruction, is not considered to be one.

Example 21-4. XML document with processing instructions (pi.xml)

```
<?xml version="1.0" encoding="UTF-8"?>
<?xml-stylesheet type="text/xsl" href="formatter.xsl"?>
<b:businessDocument xmlns:b="http://datypic.com/b">
  <b:header>
    <?doc-processor appl="BDS" version="4.3"?>
    <b:date>2006-10-15</b:date>
  </b:header>
</b:businessDocument>
```

Processing instruction nodes do not have any children, and their parent is either a document node or an element node. In this example, the xml-stylesheet processing instruction is a child of the document node, and doc-processor is a child of the b:header element.

The node name of a processing instruction node is its target. It is never in a namespace, so the namespace portion of the name will be a zero-length string. The string value (and typed value) is its content, minus any leading spaces, as an instance of xs:string. For example, the node name of the first processing instruction in the example is xml-stylesheet, and its string value is type="text/xsl" href="formatter.xsl".

Querying Processing Instructions

Processing instructions can be queried in path expressions using the processing-instruction() kind test. For example:

```
doc("pi.xml")//processing-instruction( )
```

will return the both processing instructions in the document, whereas:

```
doc("pi.xml")/b:businessDocument/b:header/processing-instruction()
```

will return only the doc-processor processing instruction. You can also specify a target between the parentheses. For example, specifying processing-instruction(doc-processor) returns only processing instructions whose target is doc-processor. Quotes can optionally be used around the target for compatibility with XPath 1.0.

The node() kind test will return processing instructions as well as all other node kinds. For example, the expression:

```
doc("pi.xml")/b:businessDocument/b:header/node()
```

will return a sequence consisting of the doc-processor processing instruction node, followed by the b:date element. This is in contrast to *, which selects child *element* nodes only.

Processing Instructions and Sequence Types

The processing-instruction() keyword can also be used in sequence types to match processing-instruction nodes. For example, to display the target and content of a processing instruction as a string, you could use the function shown in Example 21-5. The use of the processing-instruction() sequence type in the function signature ensures that only processing-instruction nodes are passed to this function.

Example 21-5. Function that displays processing instructions

```
declare function local:displayPIValue
  ($pi as processing-instruction())as xs:string {

  concat("Target is ", name($pi),
        " and content is ", string($pi))
};
```

As with node kind tests, a specific target may be specified in the sequence type. If the sequence type for the argument had been processing-instruction("xml-stylesheet"), the function would only accept only processing-instruction nodes with that target, or a type error would be raised.

A processing-instruction node will also match the node() and item() sequence types.

Constructing Processing Instructions

Processing instructions can be constructed in queries, using either direct or computed constructors. A direct processing-instruction constructor uses the XML syntax, namely target, followed by the optional content, enclosed in <? and ?>.

A computed processing-instruction constructor allows you to use an expression for its target and/or content. Its syntax, shown in Figure 21-2, has three parts:

1. The keyword processing-instruction

2. The target, which can be either a literal name or an enclosed expression (in braces) that evaluates to a name

3. The content as an enclosed expression (in braces), that is evaluated and cast to xs:string

Figure 21-2. Syntax of a computed processing-instruction constructor

Example 21-6 shows three different processing-instruction constructors. The first is a direct constructor, the second is a computed constructor with a literal name, and the third is a computed constructor with a calculated name.

Example 21-6. Processing-instruction constructors

Query
```
<ul>{
  <?doc-processor version="4.3"?>,
  processing-instruction doc-processor2 {'version="4.3"'},
  processing-instruction {concat("doc-processor", "3")}
      {concat('version="', '4.3', '"')}
}</ul>
```
Results
```
<ul>
  <?doc-processor version="4.3"?>
  <?doc-processor2 version="4.3"?>
  <?doc-processor3 version="4.3"?>
</ul>
```

Whether it's a direct or computed constructor, the target specified must be a valid NCName, which means that it must follow the rules for XML names and not contain a colon.

Documents

Document nodes represent entire XML documents in the XQuery data model. When an input document is opened using the doc function, a document node is returned. The document node should not be confused with the outermost element node, which is its child.

Not all XML data selected or constructed by queries has a document node at its root. Some implementations will allow you to query XML fragments, such as an element or a sequence of elements that are not part of a document. When XML is stored in a

relational database, it often holds elements without any containing document. It is also possible, using element constructors, to create result elements that are not part of a document.

The root function can be used to determine whether a node is part of a document. It will return the root of the hierarchy, whether it is a document node or simply a standalone element.

Document Nodes and the Data Model

A document node is the root of a node hierarchy, and therefore has no parent. The children of a document node are the comments and processing instructions that appear outside of any element, and the outermost element node. For example, the document shown in Example 21-4 would be represented by a single document node that has two children: the xml-stylesheet processing-instruction node and the businessDocument element node.

The string value of a document node is the string value of all its text node descendants, concatenated together. In Example 21-4, that would simply be 2006-10-15. Its typed value is the same as its string value, but with the type xs:untypedAtomic.

Document nodes do not have names. In particular, the base URI of a document node is not its name. Therefore, calling any of the name-related functions with a document node will result in the empty sequence or a zero-length string, depending on the function.

Document Nodes and Sequence Types

The document-node() keyword can be used in sequence types to match document nodes. Used with nothing in between the parentheses, it will match any document node. It is also possible to include an element test in between the parentheses. For example:

```
document-node(element(product))
```

tests for a document whose only element child (the outermost element) is named product. The document-node() keyword can also be used with a schema element test, as in:

```
document-node(schema-element(product))
```

Schema element tests are described in "Sequence Types and Schemas" in Chapter 13.

Constructing Document Nodes

Documents can be explicitly constructed using XQuery. This is generally not necessary, because the results of a query do not have to be an XML document node; they can be a single element, or a sequence of multiple elements, or even any combination of nodes and atomic values. If the results of a query are serialized, they become

an XML "document" automatically, regardless of whether a document node was constructed in the query.

However, being able to construct a document node is useful if the application that processes the results of the query expects a complete XML document, with a document node. It's also useful when you are doing schema validation. Validation of a document node gives a more thorough check than validation of the outermost element, because it checks schema-defined identity constraints and ID/IDREF integrity.

A computed document constructor is used to construct a complete XML document. Its syntax, shown in Figure 21-3, consists of an expression enclosed in document{ and }. An example of a computed document constructor is shown in Example 21-7.

Figure 21-3. Syntax of a computed document constructor

The enclosed expression must evaluate to a sequence of nodes. If it contains (directly) any attribute nodes, a type error is raised.

Example 21-7. Computed document constructor

Query
```
document {
  element product {
    attribute dept { "ACC" },
    element number { 563 },
    element name { attribute language {"en"}, "Floppy Sun Hat"}
  }
}
```
Results
```
<product dept="ACC">
  <number>563</number>
  <name language="en">Floppy Sun Hat</name>
</product>
```

No validation is performed on the document node, unless it is enclosed in a validate expression. XQuery does not require that a document node only contains one single element node, although XML syntax does require a document to have only one outermost element. If you want a result document that is well-formed XML, you should ensure that the enclosed expression evaluates to only one element node.

Text Nodes

Text nodes represent the character data content within elements. Every adjacent string of characters within element content makes up a single text node. Text nodes can be both queried and constructed in XQuery, although these expressions have limited usefulness.

Text Nodes and the Data Model

A text node does not have any children, and its parent is an element. In Example 21-8, the desc element has three children:

- A text node whose content is Our (ending with a space)
- A child element i
- A text node whose content is shirt! (starting with a space)

The i element itself has one child: a text node whose content is favorite.

Example 21-8. Text nodes in XML (desc.xml)

```
<desc>Our <i>favorite</i> shirt!</desc>
```

The string value of a text node is its content, as an instance of xs:string. Its typed value is the same as the string value, except that it is of type xs:untypedAtomic rather than xs:string.

Text nodes do not have names, so calling any of the name-related functions with a text node will result in the empty sequence or a zero-length string, depending on the function.

If your document has no DTD or schema, any whitespace appearing between the tags in your source XML will be translated into text nodes. This is true even if it is just there to indent the document. For example, the following b:header element node:

```
<b:header>
    <b:date>2006-10-15</b:date>
</b:header>
```

has three children. The first and third children are text nodes that contain only whitespace, and the second child is, of course, the b:date element node. If a DTD or schema *is* used, and the element's type allows only child elements (no character data content), then the whitespace will be discarded and b:header will not have text node children.

In the data model, there are never two adjacent text nodes with the same parent; all adjacent text is merged into a single text node. This means that if you construct a new element using:

```
<example>{1}{2}{3}</example>
```

the resulting example element will have only one text node child, whose value is 123. There is also no such thing as an empty text node, so the element constructor:

```
<example>{""}</example>
```

will result in an element with no children at all.

Querying Text Nodes

Text nodes can be queried using path expressions. The text() kind test can be used to specifically ask for text nodes. For example:

```
doc("desc.xml")//text( )
```

will return all of the three text nodes in the document, while:

```
doc("desc.xml")/desc/text( )
```

will return only the two text nodes that are children of desc.

The node() kind test will return text nodes as well as all other node kinds. For example:

```
doc("desc.xml")/desc/node( )
```

will return a sequence consisting of the first text node, the i element node, and the second text node. This is in contrast to *, which selects child *element* nodes only.

Text Nodes and Sequence Types

The text() keyword can also be used in sequence types to match text nodes. For example, to display the content of a text node as a string, you could use the function shown in Example 21-9. The use of the text() sequence type in the function signature ensures that only text nodes are passed to this function.

Example 21-9. Function that displays text nodes

```
declare function local:displayTextNodeContent
  ($textNode as text()) as xs:string {
  concat("Content of the text node is ", $textNode)
};
```

A text node will also match the node() and item() sequence types.

Why Work with Text Nodes?

Because text nodes contain all the data content of elements, it may seem that the text() kind test would be used frequently and would be covered earlier in this book. However, because of atomization and casting, it is often unnecessary to ask explicitly for the text nodes. For example, the expression:

```
doc("catalog.xml")//product[name/text( )="Floppy Sun Hat"]
```

has basically the same effect as:

```
doc("catalog.xml")//product[name="Floppy Sun Hat"]
```

because the name element is atomized before being compared to the string Floppy Sun Hat. Likewise, the expression:

```
distinct-values(doc("catalog.xml")//product/number/text( ))
```

is very similar to:

```
distinct-values(doc("catalog.xml")//product/number)
```

because the function conversion rules call for atomization of the number elements.

One difference is that text nodes, when atomized, result in untyped values, while element nodes will take on the type specified in the schema. Therefore, if your number element is of type xs:integer, the second distinct-values expression above will compare the numbers as integers. The first expression will compare them as untyped values, which, according to the rules of the distinct-values function, means that they are treated like strings.

 Not only is it almost always unnecessary to use the node test text(), it sometimes yields surprising results. For example, the expression:

```
doc("catalog.xml")//product[4]/desc/text( )
```

has a string value of Our shirt! instead of Our favorite shirt! because only the text nodes that are direct children of the desc element are included. If /text() is left out of the expression, its string value is Our favorite shirt!.

There are some cases where the text() sequence type does come in handy, though. One case is when you are working with mixed content and want to work with each text node specifically. For example, suppose you wanted to modify the product catalog to change all the i elements to em elements (without knowing in advance where i elements appear). You could use the recursive function shown in Example 21-10.

Example 21-10. Testing for text nodes

```
declare function local:change-i-to-em
  ($node as element()) as node( ) {
  element {node-name($node)} {
    $node/@*,
    for $child in $node/node( )
    return if ($child instance of text( ))
          then $child
          else if ($child instance of element(i))
               then <em>{$child/@*,$child/node( )}</em>
               else if ($child instance of element( ))
                    then local:change-i-to-em($child)
                    else ()
  }
};
```

The function checks all the children of an element node. If it encounters a text node, it copies it as is. If it encounters an element child, it recursively calls itself to process that child element's children. When it encounters an i element, it constructs an em and includes the original children of i.

It is important in this case to test for text nodes because the desc element has mixed content; it contains both text nodes and child element nodes. If you throw away the text nodes, it changes the content of the document.

Constructing Text Nodes

You can also construct text nodes, using a text node constructor. The syntax of a text node constructor, shown in Figure 21-4, consists of an expression enclosed by text{ and }. For example, the expression:

```
text{concat("Sequence number: ", $seq)}
```

will construct a text node whose content is Sequence number: 1.

——text { <expr> }——▶

Figure 21-4. Syntax of a text node constructor

The value of the expression used in the constructor is atomized (if necessary) and cast to xs:string. Text node constructors have limited usefulness in XQuery because they are created automatically in element constructors using literal text or expressions that return atomic values. For example, the expression:

```
<example>{concat("Sequence number: ", $seq)}</example>
```

will automatically create a text node as a child of the example element node. No explicit text node constructor is needed.

XML Entity and Character References

Like XML, the XQuery syntax allows for the escaping of individual characters using two mechanisms: character references and predefined entity references. These escapes can be used in string literals, as well as in the content of direct element and attribute constructors.

Character references are useful for representing characters that are not easily typed on a keyboard. They take two forms:

- &# plus a sequence of decimal digits representing the character's code point, followed by a semicolon (;).

- &#x plus a sequence of hexadecimal digits representing the character's code point, followed by a semicolon (;).

For example, a space can be represented as or . The number always refers to the Unicode code point; it doesn't depend on the query encoding. Table 21-1 lists a few common XML character references.

Table 21-1. XML character reference examples

Character reference	Meaning
 	Space

	Line feed
	Carriage return
		Tab

Predefined entity references are useful for escaping characters that have special meaning in XML syntax. They are listed in Table 21-2.

Table 21-2. Predefined entity references

Entity reference	Meaning
&	Ampersand (&)
<	Less than (<)
>	Greater than (>)
'	Apostrophe/single quote (')
"	Double quote (")

Certain of these characters must be escaped, namely:

- In literal strings, ampersands, as well as single or double quotes (depending on which was used to surround the literal)
- In the content of direct element constructors (but not inside curly braces), both ampersands and less-than characters
- In attribute values of direct element constructors (but not inside curly braces), single or double quotes (depending on which was used to surround the attribute value)

The set of predefined entities does not include certain entities that are predefined for HTML, such as and é. If these characters are needed as literals in queries, they should be represented using character references. For example, if your query is generating HTML output and you want to generate a nonbreaking space character, which is often written as in HTML, you can represent it in your query as . If you want to be less cryptic, you can use a variable, as in:

```
declare variable $nbsp := " ";
<h1>aaa{$nbsp}bbb</h1>
```

Example 21-11 shows a query that uses character and entity references in both a literal string and in the content of an element constructor. The first line of the query uses A in place of the letter A in a quoted string. The second line uses various predefined entity references, as well as the character reference #x20;, which represents the space character inside a direct element constructor.

Example 21-11. Query with XML entities

Query
```
if (doc("catalog.xml")//product[@dept='&#65;CC'])
then <h1>Accessories & Misc&#x20;List from &lt;catalog&gt;</h1>
else ()
```
Results
```
<h1>Accessories & Misc List from &lt;catalog&gt;</h1>
```

In element constructors, references must appear directly in the literal content, outside of any enclosed expression. For example, the constructor:

```
<quoted>'{"abc"}'</quoted>
```

returns the result `<quoted>'abc'</quoted>`, while the constructor:

```
<quoted>{'"abc"'}</quoted>
```

raises a syntax error, because `'` is within the curly braces of the enclosed expression.

Including an entity or character reference in a query does *not* necessarily result in a reference in the query results. As you can see from Example 21-11, the results of the query (when serialized) contain a space character rather than a character reference.

CDATA Sections

A CDATA section is a convenience used in XML documents that allows you to include literal text in element content without having to use `<` and `&` entity references to escape less-than and ampersand symbols, respectively. CDATA sections are not a separate kind of node; they are not represented in the XQuery data model at all.

CDATA sections are delimited by `<![CDATA[` and `]]>`. Example 21-12 shows two `h1` elements. The first element has a CDATA section that contains some literal text, including an unescaped ampersand character. It also contains a reference to a `<catalog>` element that is intended to be taken as a string, not as an XML element in the document. If this text were not enclosed in a CDATA section, the XML element would not be well formed. The second `h1` element shown in the example is equivalent, using predefined entities to escape the ampersand and less-than characters.

Example 21-12. Two equivalent h1 elements, one with a CDATA section

```
<h1><![CDATA[Catalog & Price List from <catalog>]]></h1>
<h1>Catalog & Price List from &lt;catalog></h1>
```

When your query accesses an XML document that contains a CDATA section, the CDATA section is not retained. If the `h1` element in Example 21-12 is queried, its content is `Product Catalog & Price List from <catalog>`. There is no way for the query processor to know that a CDATA section was used in the input document.

For convenience, CDATA sections can also be specified in a query, in the character data content of an element constructor. Example 21-13 shows a query that uses a CDATA section. All of the text in a CDATA section is taken literally; it is not possible to include enclosed expressions in a CDATA section.

Just as in an XML document, a CDATA section in a query serves as a convenient way to avoid having to escape characters. Including a CDATA section in a query does *not* result in a CDATA section in the query results. As you can see from Example 21-13, the results of the query (when serialized) contain an escaped ampersand and less-than sign in the element content.

Example 21-13. Query with CDATA section

Query
```
if (doc("catalog.xml")//product)
then <h1><![CDATA[Catalog & Price List from <catalog>]]></h1>
else <h1>No catalog items to display</h1>
```
Results
```
<h1>Catalog & Price List from &lt;catalog></h1>
```

CHAPTER 22

Additional XQuery-Related Standards

This book describes the core features of the XQuery 1.0 language and its associated built-in functions and data model. There are several peripheral standards that complement, but are not central to, the XQuery 1.0 language. These standards, which are in varying stages of completion, include Serialization, XQueryX, XQuery Updates, Full-Text search, and XQJ.

Serialization

Serialization is the process of writing the results of a query out to XML syntax. (Implementations are not required to support serialization at all, but most do.) In your query, you construct (or select) a number of XML elements and attributes to include in the results. These results conform to the data model described in Chapter 2. However, the data model does not define the details of the XML syntax and format to be used. Certain syntactic differences may appear when working with different implementations, such as the encoding used, whether an XML declaration is included at the beginning of a document, or whether the results are indented.

Some of these syntactic differences can be controlled using serialization parameters, which are listed in Table 22-1. Some implementations will allow you to specify values for some of the serialization parameters; this is covered further in the section entitled "Specifying Serialization Parameters" in Chapter 23.

For more information on serialization, including a detailed description of the effect of each serialization parameter, see *XSLT 2.0 and XQuery 1.0 Serialization* at *http://www.w3.org/TR/xslt-xquery-serialization*.

Table 22-1. Serialization parameters

Parameter name	Description
method	The type of output, namely xml, xhtml, html, or text.
byte-order-mark	yes/no; default is implementation-defined. Use yes if you would like a byte order mark to precede the serialized results.

Table 22-1. Serialization parameters (continued)

Parameter name	Description
cdata-section-elements	An optional list of qualified element names; the default is a zero-item list. Add an element name to the list if you would like its contents to be enclosed in a CDATA section in the output.
doctype-public	A public identifier to be included in a document type declaration.
doctype-system	A system identifier to be included in a document type declaration.
encoding	The encoding to be used for the results. The default is either UTF-8 or UTF-16 (whichever one is implementation-defined). Implementations are required to support at least these two values.
escape-uri-attributes	yes/no; default is implementation-defined. Applies only to html and xhtml output types. Use yes if you want to perform URI escaping on attributes that are defined in (X)HTML to be URIs, such as href and src.
include-content-type	yes/no; default is implementation-defined. Applies only to html and xhtml output types. Use yes if you want to include a meta element that specifies the content type, as in: `<meta http-equiv="Content-Type" content="text/html; charset=EUC-JP" />`.
indent	yes/no; default is no. Use yes if you want to pretty-print the results, i.e., put line breaks and indenting spaces between elements.
media-type	The media type (MIME type); default is implementation-defined.
normalization-form	One of NFC, NFD, NFKC, NFKD, fully-normalized, or an implementation-defined value. Default is implementation-defined. Unicode normalization is discussed in Chapter 17.
omit-xml-declaration	yes/no; default is implementation-defined. Use yes if you do *not* want an XML declaration in your results.
standalone	yes, no or omit; default is implementation-defined. The value of the standalone parameter of the XML declaration. Use omit to not include the standalone parameter.
undeclare-prefixes	yes/no; default is no. When using XML 1.1, use yes to instruct the processor to insert namespace "undeclarations," e.g., xmlns:dty="", to indicate that a namespace declaration is no longer in scope. This is rarely, if ever, necessary.
use-character-maps	Default is an empty list. A list of character maps that can be used to perform character substitution on the results.
version	Default is implementation-defined, generally 1.0 or 1.1 for XML—the version of XML (or HTML if the output method is html).

Errors occasionally occur during serialization. They may be the result of conflicting serialization parameters or a query that returns results that cannot be serialized. For example:

```
doc("catalog.xml")//@dept
```

is a perfectly valid query, but it will return a sequence of attribute nodes. This cannot be serialized and will raise an error. Serialization errors all start with the letters SE and are listed in Appendix C.

XQueryX

XQueryX is an alternate, XML syntax to represent XQuery queries. It is not covered in detail in this book because it is unlikely that most query authors will want to write XQueryX by hand. However, it may be useful as a syntax used by processors for storing and/or transferring queries because XML is easier to parse and/or transform than a non-XML syntax. It can also be useful for embedding queries in XML documents.

A simple FLWOR is shown in Example 22-1.

Example 22-1. Simple FLWOR

```
for $product in doc("catalog.xml")//product
order by $product/name
return $product/number
```

The equivalent XQueryX is shown in Example 22-2. As you can see, the XQueryX syntax is far more verbose, and breaks the query down to a very granular level, with at least one element for every expression.

Example 22-2. Partial XQueryX equivalent of Example 22-1

```
<?xml version="1.0"?>
<xqx:module xmlns:xqx="http://www.w3.org/2005/XQueryX"
            xmlns:xsi="http://www.w3.org/2001/XMLSchema-instance"
            xsi:schemaLocation="http://www.w3.org/2005/XQueryX
                                http://www.w3.org/2005/XQueryX/xqueryx.xsd">
  <xqx:mainModule>
    <xqx:queryBody>
      <xqx:flworExpr>
        <xqx:forClause>
          <xqx:forClauseItem>
            <xqx:typedVariableBinding>
              <xqx:varName>product</xqx:varName>
            </xqx:typedVariableBinding>
            <xqx:forExpr>
              <xqx:pathExpr>
                <xqx:argExpr>
                  <xqx:functionCallExpr>
                    <xqx:functionName>doc</xqx:functionName>
                    <xqx:arguments>
                      <xqx:stringConstantExpr>
                        <xqx:value>catalog.xml</xqx:value>
                      </xqx:stringConstantExpr>
                    </xqx:arguments>
                  </xqx:functionCallExpr>
                </xqx:argExpr>
                <xqx:stepExpr>
                  <xqx:xpathAxis>descendant-or-self</xqx:xpathAxis>
                  <xqx:anyKindTest/>
                </xqx:stepExpr>
                <xqx:stepExpr>
```

Example 22-2. Partial XQueryX equivalent of Example 22-1 (continued)

```
                <xqx:xpathAxis>child</xqx:xpathAxis>
                <xqx:nameTest>product</xqx:nameTest>
            </xqx:stepExpr>
          </xqx:pathExpr>
        </xqx:forExpr>
      </xqx:forClauseItem>
    </xqx:forClause>  <!-- ... --->
```

For more information on XQueryX, see the recommendation at *http://www.w3.org/TR/ xqueryx*. If you do use XQueryX, the W3C provides a handy converter to convert XQuery to XQueryX, found at *http://www.w3.org/2005/qt-applets/xqueryApplet.html.*

XQuery Update Facility

The XQuery 1.0 language provides expressions for querying input documents and adding to the results. However, it does not have any specific expressions for inserting, updating, or deleting XML data. As we saw in Chapter 9, it is possible to modify input elements and attributes using user-defined functions, but this is somewhat cumbersome. In addition, this only transforms input documents to be returned as the query results; it offers no ability to specify that XML data should be permanently changed in a database.

To address this need, the W3C XQuery Working Group is working on an XQuery Update Facility that will provide specialized operators and/or built-in functions for updates. At the time of this writing, only a draft requirements document has been publicly released. It specifies that the XQuery Update Facility will have functionality that allows for:

- Deleting nodes
- Inserting nodes in specified positions
- Replacing nodes
- Moving nodes
- Changing the typed value of nodes
- Modifying properties of a node, such as name, type, content, base URI, etc.

For more information on the XQuery Update Facility requirements, see *http://www. w3.org/TR/xquery-update-requirements.*

Full-Text Search

Search facilities have become an increasingly important (and complex) tool to locate relevant information in the vast amount of data that is now structured as XML, whether it is in large text databases or on the Web itself. Searching is a natural use

case for XQuery because of its built-in knowledge of XML structures and its syntax, which can be written by reasonably nontechnical users.

XQuery 1.0 contains some limited functionality for searching text. For example, you can use the `contains` or `matches` function to search for specific strings inside element content. However, the current features are quite limited, especially for textual XML documents.

The W3C XQuery Working Group is working on a separate recommendation entitled *XQuery 1.0 and XPath 2.0 Full-Text* that provides specialized operators for full-text searching. These operators will be additions to the XQuery 1.0 syntax, and they will not be supported by all XQuery implementations.

The Full-Text recommendation, currently a working draft, supports the following search functionality:

Boolean operators
 Combining search terms using && (and), || (or), ! (not), and `not in` (mild not)

Stemming
 Finding words with the same linguistic stem, for example, finding both "mouse" and "mice" when the search term is "mouse"

Weighting
 Specifying weights (priorities) for different search terms

Proximity and order
 Specifying how far apart the search terms may be, and in what order

Scope
 Searching for multiple terms within the same sentence or paragraph

Score and relevance
 Determining how relevant the results are to the terms searched

Occurrences
 Restricting results to search terms that appear a specific number of times

Thesaurus
 Specifying synonyms for search terms

Case-(in)sensitivity
 Considering uppercase versus lowercase letters either relevant or irrelevant

Diacritics-(in)sensitivity
 Considering, for example, accents on characters either relevant or irrelevant

Wildcards
 Specifying wildcards in search terms, such as `run.*` to match all words that start with "run"

Stopwords
 Specifying common words to exclude from searches, such as "a" and "the"

An example of a full-text query, taken from the Full-Text recommendation, is shown in Example 22-3.

Example 22-3. Full-text query example

```
for $b score $s in /books/book[content ftcontains ("web site" weight 0.2)
                                        && ("usability" weight 0.8)]
where $s > 0.5
order by $s descending
return <result>
          <title> {$b//title} </title>
          <score> {$s} </score>
      </result>
```

This example uses a familiar FLWOR syntax, but with some additional operators and clauses:

- The `score $s` in the for clause is used to specify that the variable `$s` should contain the relevance score of the results. This variable is then used to constrain the results to those where the score is greater than 0.5, and also to sort the results, with the most relevant appearing first.

- The `ftcontains` operator is used to find text containing the specific search terms "web site" and "usability."

- The `&&` operator is used to find a union of the two search terms, returning only documents that contain both terms.

- The `weight` keyword is used to weight the individual search terms.

Some XQuery implementations, such as Mark Logic and eXist, provide special built-in functions and operators to address some of these full-text requirements. These implementations generally do not follow the W3C recommendation because they were implemented before it was a publicly available document.

For more information on the XQuery Full-Text recommendation, see *http://www.w3.org/TR/xquery-full-text*.

XQuery API for Java (XQJ)

XQJ is a standard for calling XQuery from Java. XQJ is to XML data sources what JDBC is to relational data sources. It provides a standard set of classes for connecting to a data source, executing a query, and traversing through the result set. It is being developed using the Java Community Process as JSR 225 and is currently in the Early Draft Review 2 stage.

Example 22-4 shows an example of Java code that connects to an XML data source and iterates through the results.

Example 22-4. XQJ example

```
// connect to the data source
XQConnection conn = xqds.getConnection( );

// create a new expression object
XQExpression expr = conn.createExpression( );

// execute the query
XQResultSequence result = expr.executeQuery(
    "for $prod in doc('catalog.xml')//product" +
    "order by $prod/number" +
    "return $prod/name");

// iterate through the result sequence
while (result.next( )) {

    // retrieve the atomic value of the current item
    String prodName = result.getAtomicValue( );
    System.out.println("Product name: " + prodName);
}
```

For more information on XQJ, see the specification at *http://jcp.org/en/jsr/detail?id=225*.

Implementation-Specific Features

XQuery can be used for a wide variety of XML processing needs. As such, different XQuery implementations provide customized functions and settings for specific use cases. This chapter looks at some of the implementation-specific aspects of XQuery.

Conformance

The XQuery specification consists of a core set of features that all implementations are required to support. Supporting these features is known as minimal conformance. In addition, there are a handful of optional features that are clearly defined and scoped. These optional features are listed in Table 23-1.

Table 23-1. Features

Feature	Description	Chapter
Full Axis	Support for the axes `ancestor`, `ancestor-or-self`, `following`, `following-sibling`, `preceding`, `preceding-sibling`	4
Module	Support for library modules and module imports	12
Schema Import	Support for schema imports in the prolog	13
Schema Validation	Support for `validate` expressions	13
Static Typing	Detection of all static type errors in the analysis phase	14
Serialization	Ability to serialize query results to an XML document	22

In addition to these six features, some aspects of the core language are either implementation-dependent or implementation-defined. Implementation-*defined* features are those where the implementer is required to document the choices she has made. For example, the list of supported collations or additional built-in functions is implementation-defined. Implementation-*dependent* behavior may vary by implementation but does not have to be explicitly stated in the documentation and cannot necessarily be predicted. For example, when an unordered expression is used, the order of the results is implementation-dependent.

XML Version Support

An XQuery 1.0 implementation may choose to support either XML 1.0 and Namespaces 1.0, *or* XML 1.1 and Namespaces 1.1. This is an implementation-defined choice that should be clearly documented. XML 1.1 allows a much wider set of characters in XML names, and adds two line-end characters to the set of characters that are considered to be whitespace. The main changes in Namespaces 1.1 are the ability to undeclare prefixes, and support for Internationalized Resources Identifiers (IRIs) rather than just URIs.

In addition, an XQuery implementation can choose what version of Unicode to support for the functions that rely on Unicode definitions, such as normalization and case mapping.

Setting the Query Context

Every query is analyzed and evaluated within a context that is defined by the implementation. This context includes settings like implicit time zone, context node, and default collation. In some cases, the settings of the context can be overridden by prolog declarations in the query, but sometimes they cannot. It is useful to know what defaults and choices your implementation supports for these settings.

Your implementation may do any of the following to augment the built-in functions and features of the XQuery language:

- Add built-in functions
- Add predeclared namespaces (including a default element and function namespace)
- Add built-in schemas, whose type names can be used in queries and whose element and attribute declarations can be used in validation
- Add built-in global variables and their values
- Specify a list of supported collations

In addition, your implementation may set default values for any of the prolog "setters," namely:

- Boundary-space policy
- Ordering mode
- Empty-order specification
- Copy-namespaces mode
- Construction mode
- Default collation
- Base-URI of the static context

The implementation may or may not allow you the option of overriding these settings outside the scope of the query. For example, you may be allowed to enter them into a dialog box in a user interface, specify them at a command-line prompt, or set them programmatically. However, any settings specified in the query prolog take priority.

Option Declarations and Extension Expressions

Two methods are available for specifying the values of implementation-specific settings in the query itself: option declarations and extension expressions. This section describes how these settings are defined and used. The documentation for your XQuery implementation should provide information on what specific options and extensions it supports.

The Option Declaration

An option declaration can be used to specify an implementation-defined setting in the query prolog. This is useful for settings that affect the entire query, or other settings in the prolog. The syntax of an option declaration is shown in Figure 23-1.

```
──── declare option <option-name> "<option-contents>" ; ───▶
```

Figure 23-1. Syntax of an option declaration

The Saxon implementation allows for several different types of options. Example 23-1 shows two of them.

Example 23-1. Option declarations

```
declare namespace saxon="http://saxon.sf.net/";

declare option saxon:default "25";
declare variable $maxRowsToReturn external;

declare option saxon:output "method=xhtml";
```

The first option declaration, for `saxon:default`, is used to specify a default value for the global variable whose declaration follows it. If no value is supplied for `$maxRowsToReturn` outside the scope of the query, the value 25 is used. The second option declaration, for `saxon:output`, is used to specify values for serialization parameters, in this case, the output method when serializing the results. Serialization parameters are discussed in Chapter 22.

An option declaration may apply to the whole query, or just the subsequent prolog declaration, or any other scope defined by the implementation.

Options have namespace-qualified names, which means that the prefixes used must be declared, and processors recognize them by their namespace. If an option belongs to a namespace that is not supported by the implementation, it is ignored. If a processor recognizes the option but determines that the content is invalid, the behavior is implementation-dependent. It may raise an error, or it may ignore it.

Extension Expressions

Queries can also contain implementation-specific extension expressions that may be used to specify additional parameters to a query. Extensions are similar to options, except that they can appear anywhere that an expression is allowed in the query (not just the prolog) and they apply to an individual expression.

For example, the extension:

```
(# datypic:timeOut 200 #)
  { count($doc//author) }
```

might be used to tell the processor to time out after 200 seconds. The syntax of an extension is shown in Figure 23-2.

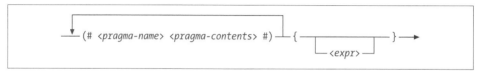

Figure 23-2. Syntax of an extension

Extension expressions consist of one or more pragmas, each delimited by (# and #), followed by the affected expression in curly braces. A pragma has two parts: a qualified name, and optional content, which can be any string of characters (except for #)).

Extensions can be used in a number of ways. Examples include:

- Providing hints to the processor regarding how best to evaluate the expression, such as what index to use or how long to wait before timing out.

- Allowing nonstandard interpretation of XQuery syntax, for example, allowing the comparison of xs:gDay values using the < operator, which is normally not permitted. However, the expression in curly braces still must use valid XQuery syntax.

- Specifying an alternate proprietary syntax in the pragma content that may be more efficient or otherwise preferable to the expression in curly braces.

 Use of options and pragmas that affect the result of the expression make for queries that are not interoperable across implementations. Use such extensions only when absolutely necessary.

Like options, pragmas are recognized by their namespace, and a processor will ignore any pragmas in namespaces it doesn't recognize. If all the pragmas associated with an expression are ignored, the expression is evaluated normally, as if no pragmas were specified.

If a processor recognizes the namespace used in a pragma, but not the local name, it may either raise an error or ignore it.

Specifying Serialization Parameters

Serialization, described in Chapter 22, is the process of writing your query results out to an XML document. Certain syntactic differences may appear when working with different implementations, such as the encoding used, whether an XML declaration is included at the beginning of a document, or whether the results are indented.

The default values for many serialization parameters are implementation-defined. Some implementations will let you specify values for the serialization parameters in a user interface, programmatically, or even as custom option declarations in the query. However, they are not required to provide this capability. As such, there is no XQuery syntax to specify these parameters. Example 23-1 shows how Saxon allows for an implementation-specific option, named output, which allows a query author to set values for serialization parameters in the query itself.

CHAPTER 24

XQuery for SQL Users

This chapter is designed to provide some background material for readers who are already using SQL and relational databases. It compares SQL and XQuery at both the data model and syntax levels. It also provides pointers for using SQL and XQuery together, and describes the role of SQL/XML.

Relational Versus XML Data Models

As you know, relational databases represent data in terms of tables, rows, and columns. Some XML documents, such as our product catalog document, map fairly cleanly onto a relational model. Example 24-1 shows catalog2.xml, a slightly simplified version of the product catalog document used throughout this book.

Example 24-1. Product catalog document (catalog2.xml)

```
<catalog>
  <product dept="WMN">
    <number>557</number>
    <name>Fleece Pullover</name>
  </product>
  <product dept="ACC">
    <number>563</number>
    <name>Floppy Sun Hat</name>
  </product>
  <product dept="ACC">
    <number>443</number>
    <name>Deluxe Travel Bag</name>
  </product>
  <product dept="MEN">
    <number>784</number>
    <name>Cotton Dress Shirt</name>
    <desc>Our favorite shirt!</desc>
  </product>
</catalog>
```

Because the product catalog document is relatively uniform and does not contain any repeating relationships between objects, the product catalog can be represented as a single relational table, shown in Table 24-1. Each product is a row, and each possible property of the product is a column.

Table 24-1. The catalog table

number	dept	name	desc
557	WMN	Fleece Pullover	
563	ACC	Floppy Sun Hat	
443	ACC	Deluxe Travel Bag	
784	MEN	Cotton Dress Shirt	Our favorite shirt!

Some of the products do not have descriptions, which means that nulls (or zero-length strings) are stored in the desc column for these rows. XML does not have a direct equivalent of null values in the relational model. In XML, a "missing" value could be represented as an element or attribute that is simply omitted, as in our example, where the desc element does not appear when it does not apply. It could also be represented as an empty element (<desc></desc> or <desc/>). Yet another representation uses the XML Schema concept of "nilled" elements, as in <desc xsi: nil="true"/>.

Some XML documents encompass multiple "entities" with repeating relationships between them. The order document (order.xml) is such a document, since it describes a hierarchical relationship between an order and the items it contains. There are properties of the order itself, as well as properties of each item, so each needs to be represented by a table (see Tables 24-2 and 24-3).

Table 24-2. The orders table

num	date	cust
00299432	2006-09-15	0221A

Table 24-3. The order_item table

ordnum	dept	num	quantity	color
00299432	WMN	557	1	navy
00299432	ACC	563	1	
00299432	ACC	443	2	
00299432	MEN	784	1	white
00299432	MEN	784	1	gray
00299432	WMN	557	1	black

Comparing SQL Syntax with XQuery Syntax

This section compares SQL syntax with XQuery syntax in order to give readers already familiar with SQL a jumpstart on learning XQuery. If you notice similarities between SQL and XQuery, it is not a coincidence; some of the key developers of the SQL standard also worked on the XQuery standard. Not all SQL syntax is covered in this chapter, only the most commonly used constructs.

A Simple Query

To compare SQL and XQuery queries, will we first start with our simple product catalog document. A basic SQL query might select all the values from the table that meet some specific criteria, for example those in the ACC department. The SQL statement that accomplishes this is:

```
select * from catalog
where dept='ACC'
```

In XQuery, we can use a straight path expression for such a simple query, as in:

```
doc("catalog2.xml")//product[@dept='ACC']
```

If you don't want to sort your results or construct new elements, it is often simpler (and possibly faster) to just use a path expression. However, we could also use a full FLWOR expression that uses a where clause similar to SQL, as in:

```
for $prod in doc("catalog2.xml")//product
where $prod/@dept='ACC'
return $prod
```

In the where clause, we need to start the reference to the dept attribute with $prod/ in order to give it some context. This is different from SQL, where if there is only one dept column in the table(s) in the query, it is assumed to be that one column. In XQuery, you must be explicit about where the dept attribute appears, because it could appear on any level of the document.

Now, suppose we want to sort the values by the product number. In SQL, we would simply add an order by clause, as in:

```
select * from catalog
where dept='ACC'
order by number
```

We would also add an order by clause to the FLWOR, again giving it the context, as in:

```
for $prod in doc("catalog2.xml")//product
where $prod/@dept='ACC'
order by $prod/number
return $prod
```

Conditions and Operators

Conditions and operators are used to filter query results. Many of the conditions and operators available in SQL can also be used in XQuery, although sometimes with a slightly modified syntax.

Comparisons

The example in the previous section used the equals sign (=) to compare the value of the department to ACC. XQuery has the same comparison operators as SQL, namely =, !=, <, <=, >, and >=. The BETWEEN condition in SQL is not directly supported, but you can always use two comparisons, as in:

```
for $prod in doc("catalog2.xml")//product
where $prod/number > 500 and $prod/number < 700
return $prod
```

Like SQL, quotes are used to surround string values, whereas they are not used to surround numeric values.

Strings in SQL can also be matched to wildcards using a LIKE condition. For example, the query:

```
select * from catalog
where name LIKE 'F%'
```

will return products whose names start with the letter F. XQuery provides a starts-with function that would be useful in this particular case. For example:

```
for $prod in doc("catalog2.xml")//product
where starts-with($prod/name,'F')
return $prod
```

For the more general case, the matches function allows you to match a string against any regular expression. In regular expressions, a single period (.) represents any one character, much like the underscore character (_) in LIKE conditions. Adding an asterisk after the period (.*) allows any number of any characters, similar to the % character in LIKE conditions. Anchors (^ and $) can be used indicate the start and end of a string. Another way of expressing the previous query is:

```
for $prod in doc("catalog2.xml")//product
where matches($prod/name,'^F.*')
return $prod
```

Regular expressions are much more powerful than LIKE conditions, though (see Table 24-4). They are discussed in detail in Chapter 18.

Table 24-4. LIKE condition values versus regular expressions

Like clause	Equivalent regular expression	Examples of matching values
xyz	^xyz$	xyz
xyz_	^xyz.$	xyza

Table 24-4. LIKE condition values versus regular expressions (continued)

Like clause	Equivalent regular expression	Examples of matching values
xyz%	^xyz.*$	xyz, xyza, xyzaaa
_xyz	^.xyz$	axyz
xyz%	^xyz	xyz, xyza, xyzaa
%xyz	xyz$	xyz, axyz, aaxyz
x_yz	^x.yz$	xayz
x%yz	^x.*yz$	xyz, xayz, xaayz

The IN condition in SQL is useful for comparing a value with a list of specified values. For example, to find all the products that are in either the ACC or WMN departments, you could use the query:

```
select * from catalog
where dept in ('ACC', 'WMN')
```

In XQuery, no special "in" operator is needed because the equals operator (=) allows multiple values on either side of the comparison, as in:

```
for $prod in doc("catalog2.xml")//product
where $prod/@dept = ('ACC', 'WMN')
return $prod
```

The meaning of the = operator in this case is that the product department must be equal to *at least one* of the values ACC or WMN.

Arithmetic and string operators

For arithmetic operations, XQuery uses +, −, and * for addition, subtraction, and multiplication, just like SQL. For division, XQuery does not support the / operator (because that's needed in path expressions), but instead uses div and idiv operators. These are covered in detail in "Arithmetic Operations" in Chapter 16.

Boolean operators

In SQL, multiple conditions are often combined with and and or operators, and sometimes parentheses are used to group conditions together. For example, the following query selects the products that are in the ACC department whose names start with either F or G:

```
select * from catalog
where dept='ACC' and
      (name like 'F%' or name like 'G%')
```

Parentheses are used around the name-related conditions to prevent the and operator from taking precedence. If the parentheses were not there, the first two conditions would be "and-ed" together, with different results.

The and and or operators, and the parentheses, work identically in XQuery. An equivalent XQuery query is:

```
for $prod in doc("catalog2.xml")//product
where $prod/@dept='ACC' and
      (matches($prod/name,'F.*') or matches($prod/name,'G.*'))
return $prod
```

To negate a condition in SQL, you can use a not operator, which is sometimes applied to a parenthesized group, and is sometimes part of the comparison syntax, as in name **not** like 'F%'. In XQuery, you use a not *function*, so it is always followed by an expression in parentheses. For example, the SQL query:

```
select * from catalog
where not(dept='ACC') and
      (name not like 'F%')
```

is equivalent to the following XQuery query:

```
for $prod in doc("catalog2.xml")//product
where not($prod/@dept='ACC') and
      not(matches($prod/name,'F.*'))
return $prod
```

Functions

SQL has a number of built-in functions, many of which have equivalent XQuery functions, often with the same name. Some of the commonly used SQL functions and their XQuery equivalents are listed in Table 24-5. The syntax to call functions is the same in both languages: the arguments are enclosed in parentheses and separated by commas.

Table 24-5. Equivalent functions

SQL function	XQuery function
Numeric functions	
sum	sum
avg	avg
count	count
max	max
min	min
round	round
ceil	ceiling
floor	floor
String functions	
substr	substring
concat	concat

Table 24-5. Equivalent functions (continued)

SQL function	XQuery function
upper	upper-case
lower	lower-case
trim	normalize-space
replace	replace
length	string-length
Date-related functions	
current_date	current-date
current_timestamp	current-dateTime

Selecting Distinct Values

SQL has a DISTINCT keyword that allows only distinct values to be selected. For example, to get a list of the unique departments in the catalog, you would use the query:

```
select distinct dept from catalog
```

In XQuery, you would make a call to the distinct-values function, as in:

```
distinct-values(doc("catalog2.xml")//product/@dept)
```

or, if you prefer a FLWOR:

```
for $value in distinct-values(doc("catalog2.xml")//product/@dept)
return $value
```

Often you are interested in a combination of distinct values. In SQL, this is quite straightforward; you simply add more columns to the query. To get the distinct combinations of department and product number, you could use:

```
select distinct dept, number from catalog
```

However, the XQuery distinct-values function only accepts one set of values. This means that you must use a FLWOR expression with multiple for clauses to achieve the same result. This is shown in Example 24-2 and described further in "Selecting Distinct Values" in Chapter 6.

Example 24-2. Distinctness on a combination of values

Query
```
for $d in distinct-values(doc("catalog2.xml")//product/@dept),
    $n in distinct-values(doc("catalog2.xml")//product[@dept = $d]/number)
return <result dept="{$d}" number="{$n}"/>
```
Results
```
<result dept="WMN" number="557"/>
<result dept="ACC" number="563"/>
<result dept="ACC" number="443"/>
<result dept="MEN" number="784"/>
```

Working with Multiple Tables and Subqueries

Many SQL queries join multiple tables together. For example, suppose you want to join the order and product tables to retrieve results that contain values from both tables. In SQL, you might write a query such as:

```
select order_item.num, catalog.name, order_item.quantity
from order_item, catalog
where order_item.num = catalog.number
```

In XQuery, joins are not needed so frequently because the data will often be stored in a single hierarchy rather than being split across multiple tables. However, joins still arise and the mechanism is similar. In XQuery, the join in the where clause might look like Example 24-3.

Example 24-3. Two-way join in XQuery

Query
```
for $item in doc("order.xml")//item,
    $product in doc("catalog2.xml")//product
where $item/@num = $product/number
return <item num="{$item/@num}"
             name="{$product/name}"
             quan="{$item/@quantity}"/>
```
Results
```
<item num="557" name="Fleece Pullover" quan="1"/>
<item num="563" name="Floppy Sun Hat" quan="1"/>
<item num="443" name="Deluxe Travel Bag" quan="2"/>
<item num="784" name="Cotton Dress Shirt" quan="1"/>
<item num="784" name="Cotton Dress Shirt" quan="1"/>
<item num="557" name="Fleece Pullover" quan="1"/>
```

The XQuery example constructs an item element to hold each set of three values. This is because XQuery by default does not return the result of each evaluation of the return clause in a "row" or any other container. If you simply returned the three values for each product, as in:

```
return ($item/@num, $product/name,$item/@quantity)
```

the result would be 18 sequential values (557, Fleece Pullover, 1, 563, Floppy Sun Hat, etc.), with no relationship among them. The item element serves as a container to group the related three values together—the same purpose a row would serve in an SQL result.

As an alternative to a where clause, you can use one or more predicates in your for clause, as in:

```
for $item in doc("order.xml")//item,
    $product in doc("catalog2.xml")//product[number = $item/@num]
return <item num="{$item/@num}"
             name="{$product/name}"
             quan="{$item/@quantity}"/>
```

More information on joins in XQuery can be found in"Joins" in Chapter 6, including examples of three-way joins and outer joins.

Subselects

Another way to use multiple tables in SQL (or, indeed, multiple queries on the same table) is using subselects. Suppose we wanted to return all products from the catalog that are included in a particular order. We might use the following query:

```
select *
from catalog
where number in (select num from order_item
                 where ordnum = '00299432')
```

Like SQL select statements, XQuery FLWOR expressions can also be contained within each other. The following query uses a FLWOR embedded in the where clause.

```
for $product in doc("catalog2.xml")//product
where $product/number =
    (for $item in doc("order.xml")/order[@num='00299432']/item
    return $item/@num)
return $product
```

In fact, XQuery allows expressions to be nested more freely than SQL does. For example, you can use a nested FLWOR expression in the in clause, or in the return clause.

Combining queries using set operators

SQL supports the use of set operators such as UNION to combine the rows from multiple select statements. These set operators have equivalents in XQuery, as shown in Table 24-6.

Table 24-6. Set operators

SQL Syntax	XQuery Syntax
query1 UNION query2	query1 union query2 or query1 \| query2
query1 UNION ALL query2	(query1, query2)
query1 INTERSECT query2	query1 intersect query2
query1 MINUS query2	query1 except query2

Grouping

In SQL, it is straightforward to group data by certain values. For example, if you want to count the number of products in each department, you can use the query:

```
select dept, count(*)
from catalog
group by dept
```

XQuery does not have an explicit grouping syntax, but grouping can be achieved using FLWOR expressions and the distinct-values function. Example 24-4 is comparable to the SQL example.

Example 24-4. Grouping in XQuery

Query
```
for $d in distinct-values(doc("catalog2.xml")//product/@dept)
return
  <result dept="{$d}"
          count="{count(doc("catalog2.xml")//product[@dept = $d])}"/>
```
Results
```
<result code="ACC" count="2"/>
<result code="MEN" count="1"/>
<result code="WMN" count="1"/>
```

As you can see, in order to construct a "table" of return values, we construct result elements with two attributes representing the "columns." Grouping is covered in more detail in Chapter 7.

Combining SQL and XQuery

Most major relational database vendors now allow you to store XML in your databases. The examples in this section use Microsoft SQL Server 2005 syntax, but there is similar functionality available in Oracle and IBM DB2.

Combining Structured and Semistructured Data

One use case is to combine narrative text with more highly structured data. An example is when each of the products has a textual description that can span multiple paragraphs and can be marked up with HTML-like tags to indicate sections of text that need to be in bold or italic. This is shown in Table 24-7.

Table 24-7. The prod_desc table

number	desc
557	`<p>This pullover is made from recycled polyester.</p>`
563	`<p>Enjoy the sun in this <i>gorgeous</i> hat!</p>`
443	`<p>You'll never be disorganized with this bag.</p>`
784	`<p>Our <i>favorite</i> shirt!</p>` `<p>Can be monogrammed upon request.</p>`

When you create the table, you declare the desc column to be of type XML, as in:

```
CREATE TABLE prod_desc (
  number INTEGER NOT NULL,
  desc XML
  );
```

If desired, you can specify the location of a schema for the desc column, which will ensure that any values inserted into desc conform to that schema. It will also provide all the other benefits of using a schema, such as query debugging.

Flexible Data Structures

Another use case for storing XML in a relational table is to take advantage of the flexibility of XML. Suppose each product has a set of custom properties that needs to change flexibly over time. It is possible to create columns on the catalog table for each property, but that is inflexible because a new column needs to be added when a new property is added, also necessitating changes in the application that reads and writes to the table.

Another approach might be to create generic columns named property1, property2, etc., but this is problematic because you don't know how many columns to create, and you need some sort of mapping scheme to figure out what each column means for each product. A more flexible approach might be to store the properties as XML, as shown in Table 24-8. This allows them to be queried and even indexed, but does not force a rigid database structure.

Table 24-8. The prod_properties table

number	properties
557	`<properties>` ` <sleeveLength>24</sleeveLength>` `</properties>`
563	`<properties/>`
443	`<properties>` ` <capacity>80</capacity>` `</properties>`
784	`<properties>` ` <sleeveLength>25</sleeveLength>` ` <extraButtons>2</extraButtons>` `</properties>`

To constrain the query based on the contents of the desc column, you can use an XQuery expression embedded in your SQL statement. In the case of SQL Server, one way to do this is through the use of an exist function. For example:

```
select number, properties
from prod_properties
where properties.exist('/properties/sleeveLength[. > 20]') = 1
```

The SQL Server exist function returns true (which equals 1) if there are any nodes that match the criteria. The expression in parentheses passed to the exist function is in XQuery syntax, and it is evaluated relative to the root of the document in the properties column, for each row. The results are shown in Table 24-9.

Table 24-9. Results containing the properties element

number	properties
557	```<properties>``` ```<sleeveLength>24</sleeveLength>``` ```</properties>```
784	```<properties>``` ```<sleeveLength>25</sleeveLength>``` ```<extraButtons>2</extraButtons>``` ```</properties>```

To return only the sleeveLength element, I could use another SQL Server function called query in my select clause, as in:

```
select number,
       properties.query('//sleeveLength') slength
from prod_properties
where properties.exist('/properties/sleeveLength[. > 20]') = 1
```

Like the exist function, the query function accepts an XQuery query as a parameter. The string slength is used to provide a name for the column in the results. This will return a sleeveLength element for each row, as shown in Table 24-10.

Table 24-10. Results containing the sleeveLength element

number	slength
557	`<sleeveLength>24</sleeveLength>`
784	`<sleeveLength>25</sleeveLength>`

If I want to further reduce my result set to the contents of the sleeveLength element, I can call the XQuery data function in my query, as in:

```
select number,
       properties.query('data(//sleeveLength)') slength
from prod_properties
where properties.exist('/properties/sleeveLength[. > 20]') = 1
```

The results are shown in Table 24-11.

Table 24-11. Results containing the sleeveLength value

number	slength
557	24
784	25

Alternatively, I can use the SQL Server value function, which requires me to specify a type for the value, as in:

```
select properties.value('(/properties/sleeveLength)[1]','integer') slength
from prod_properties
where properties.exist('/properties/sleeveLength[. > 20]') = 1
```

The value function forces the use of the [1] predicate to ensure that only a single node is returned. If a schema were in use, and it specified that there could only ever be one sleeveLength child of properties, this would not be necessary.

SQL/XML

We've seen how you can query XML data stored in a table, but how do you select relational data and return it as XML? This is where SQL/XML comes in. SQL/XML is an extension to SQL that is part of the ISO SQL 2003 standard. It adds an XML datatype, and allows XML elements to be constructed within the SQL query. Example 24-5 shows an SQL/XML query that might be used on our catalog table (Table 24-1).

Example 24-5. SQL/XML query

```
SELECT c.number,
       XMLELEMENT ( NAME "product",
                    XMLATTRIBUTES (
                      c.dept AS "dept",
                      c.name AS "prodname",
                    ) AS "product_as_xml"
FROM catalog c;
```

Table 24-12 shows the results, which consist of two columns. The product_as_xml column, whose type is XML, contains a newly constructed product element for each row.

Table 24-12. Results of SQL/XML query

number	product_as_xml
557	<product dept="WMN" prodname="Fleece Pullover"/>
563	<product dept="ACC" prodname="Floppy Sun Hat"/>
443	<product dept="ACC" prodname="Deluxe Travel Bag"/>
784	<product dept="MEN" prodname="Cotton Dress Shirt"/>

SQL/XML is not used to query XML documents, only relational data. As you can see, it can turn relational data into XML elements. For more information on SQL/XML, please see *http://www.sqlx.org*.

XQuery for XSLT Users

XQuery 1.0 and XSLT 2.0 have a lot in common: a data model, a set of built-in functions and operators, and the use of path expressions. This chapter delves further into the details of the similarities and differences between XQuery and XSLT. It also alerts XSLT 1.0/XPath 1.0 users to differences and potential compatibility issues when moving to XQuery/XPath 2.0.

XQuery and XPath

XPath started out as a language for selecting elements and attributes from an XML document while traversing its hierarchy and filtering out unwanted content. XPath 1.0 is a fairly simple yet useful recommendation that specifies path expressions and a limited set of functions. XPath 2.0 has become much more than that, encompassing a wide variety of expressions and functions, not just path expressions.

XQuery 1.0 and XPath 2.0 overlap to a very large degree. They have the same data model and the same set of built-in functions and operators. XPath 2.0 is essentially a subset of XQuery 1.0. XQuery has a number of features that are not included in XPath, such as FLWORs and XML constructors. This is because these features are not relevant to selecting, but instead have to do with structuring or sorting, query results. The two languages are consistent in that any expression that is valid in both languages evaluates to the same value using both languages.

Figure 25-1 depicts the relationship among XQuery, XPath, and XSLT.

XQuery Versus XSLT

XQuery and XSLT are both languages designed to query and manipulate XML documents. There is an enormous amount of overlap among the features and capabilities of these two languages. In fact, the line between querying and transformation is somewhat blurred. For example, suppose someone wants a list of all the product names from the catalog, but wants to call them product_name in the results. On the

one hand, this could be considered a query: "Retrieve all the name elements from the catalog, but give them the alias product_name." On the other hand, it could be considered a transformation: "Transform all the name elements to product_name elements, and ignore everything else in the document."

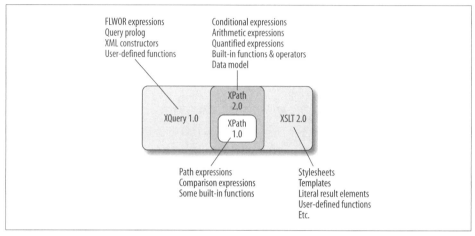

Figure 25-1. XQuery, XPath, and XSLT

Shared Components

The good news is that if you've learned one of these two languages, you're well on your way toward learning the other. XQuery 1.0 and XSLT 2.0 were developed together, with compatibility between them in mind. Among the components they share are:

The data model
> Both languages use the data model described in Chapter 2. They have the same concepts of sequences, atomic values, nodes, and items. Namespaces are handled identically. In addition, they share the same type system and relationship to XML Schema.

XPath 2.0
> XQuery 1.0 is essentially a superset of XPath 2.0. XSLT 2.0 makes use of XPath 2.0 expressions in many areas, from the expressions used to match templates to the instructions that copy nodes from input documents.

Built-in functions and operators
> All of the built-in functions described in Appendix A can be used in both XQuery and XSLT 2.0, with the same results. All of the operators, such as comparison and arithmetic operators, yield identical values in both languages.

Equivalent Components

In addition to the components they directly share, XQuery 1.0 and XSLT 2.0 also have some features that are highly analogous in the two languages; they just use a different syntax. XSLT instructions relating to flow control (e.g., `xsl:if` and `xsl:for-each`) have direct equivalents in XQuery (conditional and FLWOR expressions). Literal result elements in XSLT are analogous to direct XML constructors in XQuery, while the use of `xsl:element` and `xsl:attribute` in XSLT is like using computed constructors in XQuery. Some of these commonly used features are listed in Table 25-1.

Table 25-1. Comparison of XSLT and XQuery features

XSLT feature	Present in 1.0?	XQuery equivalent	Chapter
`xsl:for-each`	yes	for clause in a FLWOR expression	6
XPath for expression	no	for clause in a FLWOR expression	6
`xsl:variable`	yes	let clause in a FLWOR expression or global variable declaration	6, 12
`xsl:sort`	yes	order by clause in a FLWOR expression	7
`xsl:if`, `xsl:choose`	yes	Conditional expressions (if-then-else)	3
Literal result elements	yes	Direct constructors	5
`xsl:element`	yes	Computed constructors	5
`xsl:attribute`	yes	Computed constructors	
`xsl:function`	no	User-defined functions	8
Named templates	yes	User-defined functions	8
`xsl:value-of`	yes	An enclosed expression in curly braces inside an element constructor	4
`xsl:copy-of`	yes	The path or other expression that would appear in the `select` attribute	4
`xsl:sequence`	no	The path or other expression that would appear in the `select` attribute	4
`xsl:include`	yes	Module import	12
`xsl:template`	yes	No direct equivalent; can be simulated with user-defined functions	25

Differences

The most obvious difference between XQuery and XSLT is the syntax. A simple XQuery query might take the form:

```
<ul type="square">{
  for $product in doc("catalog.xml")/catalog/product[@dept = 'ACC']
  order by $product/name
  return <li>{data($product/name)}</li>
}</ul>
```

The XSLT equivalent of this query is:

```
<xsl:stylesheet version="1.0" xmlns:xsl="http://www.w3.org/1999/XSL/Transform">
  <xsl:template match="/">
    <ul type="square">
      <xsl:for-each select="catalog/product[@dept = 'ACC']">
        <xsl:sort select="name"/>
        <li><xsl:value-of select="name"/></li>
      </xsl:for-each>
    </ul>
  </xsl:template>
</xsl:stylesheet>
```

XQuery is somewhat less verbose, and many people find it less cumbersome than using the XML syntax of XSLT. Users who know SQL find XQuery familiar and intuitive. Its terseness also makes it more convenient to embed in program code than XSLT.

On the other hand, XSLT stylesheets use XML syntax, which means that they can be easily parsed and/or created by standard XML tools. This is convenient for the dynamic generation of stylesheets.

Paradigm differences: push versus pull

The most significant difference between XQuery and XSLT lies in their ability to react to unpredictable content. To understand this difference, we must digress briefly into the two different paradigms for developing XSLT stylesheets, which are sometimes called pull and push. *Pull* stylesheets, also known as program-driven stylesheets, tend to be used for highly structured, predictable documents. They use xsl:for-each and xsl:value-of elements to specifically request the information that is desired. An example of a pull stylesheet is shown in Example 25-1.

Example 25-1. A pull stylesheet

```
<xsl:stylesheet version="1.0" xmlns:xsl="http://www.w3.org/1999/XSL/Transform">
  <xsl:template match="catalog">
    <ul>
      <xsl:for-each select="product">
        <li>Product #: <xsl:value-of select="number"/></li>
        <li>Product name: <xsl:value-of select="name"/></li>
      </xsl:for-each>
    </ul>
  </xsl:template>
</xsl:stylesheet>
```

The stylesheet is counting on the fact that the product elements appear as children of catalog and that each product element has a single name and a single number child. The template states exactly what to do with the descendants of the catalog element, and where they can be found.

By contrast, *push* stylesheets use multiple templates that specify what to do for each element type, and then pass processing off to other templates using xsl:apply-templates.

Which templates are used depends on the type of children of the current node. This is sometimes called a content-driven approach, because the stylesheet is simply reacting to child elements found in the input content by matching them to templates. Example 25-2 shows a push stylesheet that is equivalent to Example 25-1.

Example 25-2. A push stylesheet

```
<xsl:stylesheet version="1.0" xmlns:xsl="http://www.w3.org/1999/XSL/Transform">
  <xsl:template match="catalog">
    <ul>
      <xsl:apply-templates/>
    </ul>
  </xsl:template>
  <xsl:template match="product">
    <xsl:apply-templates/>
  </xsl:template>
  <xsl:template match="number">
    <li>Product #: <xsl:value-of select="."/></li>
  </xsl:template>
  <xsl:template match="name">
    <li>Product name: <xsl:value-of select="."/></li>
  </xsl:template>
  <xsl:template match="node()"/>
</xsl:stylesheet>
```

This may not seem like a particularly useful approach for a predictable document like the product catalog. However, consider a narrative document structure, such as an HTML paragraph. The p (paragraph) element has mixed content and may contain various inline elements such as b (bold) and i (italic) to style the text in the paragraph, as in:

```
<p>It was a <b>dark</b> and <i>stormy</i> night.</p>
```

This input is less predictable because there is no predefined number or order of the b or i children in any given paragraph. A push stylesheet on this paragraph is shown in Example 25-3.

Example 25-3. A push stylesheet on narrative content

```
<xsl:stylesheet version="1.0" xmlns:xsl="http://www.w3.org/1999/XSL/Transform">
  <xsl:template match="p">
    <para>
      <xsl:apply-templates/>
    </para>
  </xsl:template>
  <xsl:template match="b">
    <Strong><xsl:apply-templates/></Strong>
  </xsl:template>
  <xsl:template match="i">
    <Italics><xsl:apply-templates/></Italics>
  </xsl:template>
</xsl:stylesheet>
```

It would be difficult to write a good pull stylesheet on the narrative paragraph. Example 25-4 shows an attempt.

Example 25-4. An attempt at a pull stylesheet on narrative content

```
<xsl:stylesheet version="1.0" xmlns:xsl="http://www.w3.org/1999/XSL/Transform">
  <xsl:template match="p">
    <para>
        <xsl:for-each select="node()">
          <xsl:choose>
            <xsl:when test="self::text()">
                <xsl:value-of select="."/>
            </xsl:when>
            <xsl:when test="self::b">
              <Strong><xsl:value-of select="."/></Strong>
            </xsl:when>
            <xsl:when test="self::i">
              <Italics><xsl:value-of select="."/></Italics>
            </xsl:when>
          </xsl:choose>
        </xsl:for-each>
    </para>
  </xsl:template>
</xsl:stylesheet>
```

However, this stylesheet is not very robust, because it does not handle the case where a b element is embedded within an i element. It is cumbersome to maintain because the code would have to be repeated if b and i can also appear in some other parent element besides p. If a change is made, or a new type of inline element is added, it has to be changed in multiple places.

The distinction between push and pull XSLT stylesheets is relevant to the comparison with XQuery. XQuery can easily handle the scenarios supported by pull stylesheets. The equivalent of Example 25-1 in XQuery is:

```
for $catalog in doc("catalog.xml")/catalog
return <ul>{for $prod in $catalog/product
          return (<li>Product #: {data($prod/number)}</li>,
                  <li>Product name: {data($prod/name)}</li> )
      }</ul>
```

XQuery has a much harder time emulating the push stylesheet model, due to its lack of templates. In order to write a query that modifies the HTML paragraph, you could use a brittle pull model analogous to the one shown in Example 25-4. Alternatively, you could emulate templates using user-defined functions, as shown in Example 25-5. This is somewhat better in that it supports b elements within i elements and vice versa, and it specifies in one place what to do with each element type. However, it is still more cumbersome than its XSLT equivalent and does not support features of XSLT like modes, priorities, or imports that override templates.

Example 25-5. Emulating templates with user-defined functions

```
declare function local:apply-templates($nodes as node()*) as node()* {
  for $node in $nodes
  return typeswitch ($node)
        case element(p) return local:p-template($node)
        case element(b) return local:b-template($node)
        case element(i) return local:i-template($node)
        case element() return local:apply-templates($node/(@*|node()))
        default return $node
};
declare function local:p-template($node as node()) as node()* {
   <para>{local:apply-templates($node/(@*|node()))}</para>
};
declare function local:b-template($node as node()) as node()* {
   <Strong>{local:apply-templates($node/(@*|node()))}</Strong>
};
declare function local:i-template($node as node()) as node()* {
   <Italics>{local:apply-templates($node/(@*|node()))}</Italics>
};
local:apply-templates(doc("p.xml")/p)
```

It is very important to note that this does *not* mean that XQuery is not good for query-ing narrative content. On the contrary, XQuery is an easy and fast method of search-ing within large bodies of narrative content. However, it is not ideal for taking that retrieved narrative content and significantly transforming or restructuring it. If this is your objective, you may want to consider pipelining two processes together: an XQuery query to retrieve the appropriate content from the database, and an XSLT stylesheet to transform it for presentation or other uses.

Optimization for particular use cases

Implementations of XSLT and XQuery tend to be optimized for particular use cases. XSLT implementations are generally built for transforming one whole document. They load the entire input document into memory and take one or more complete passes through the document. This is appropriate behavior when an entire docu-ment is being transformed, since the entire document needs to be accessed anyway. Additional input documents can be accessed using the doc or document functions, in which case they too are loaded into memory.

XQuery implementations, on the other hand, are generally optimized for selecting fragments of data—possibly across many documents—for example, from a data-base. When content is loaded into the database, it is broken into chunks that are usually smaller than the entire documents. Those chunks are indexed so that they can be retrieved quickly. XQuery queries can access these chunks without being forced to load the entire documents that contain them. This makes selecting a sub-set of information from a large body of XML documents much faster using the aver-age XQuery implementation.

Convenient features of XSLT

XSLT 2.0 has several convenient features that are absent from XQuery. They include:

`xsl:analyze-string`
> This instruction breaks a string into parts that match and do not match a regular expression and allows manipulation of them.

`xsl:result-document`
> This instruction allows the creation of multiple output files directly in a stylesheet.

`xsl:for-each-group`
> This instruction allows grouping by position in addition to grouping by value.

`xsl:import`
> This instruction allows you to override templates and functions in an imported stylesheet.

The `xsl:import` instruction of XSLT gives you some of the capabilities of inheritance and polymorphism from object languages, which is particularly useful when writing large application suites designed to handle a variety of related and overlapping tasks. This is quite hard to organize in XQuery, which has neither the polymorphism of object-oriented languages nor the function pointers of a language like C. The modules of XQuery also have significant limitations when writing large applications, such as the rule banning cyclic imports.

Differences Between XQuery 1.0/XPath 2.0 and XPath 1.0

XPath 1.0 is a subset of XPath 2.0, which is essentially a subset of XQuery 1.0. If you already know XPath 1.0 from using it in XSLT 1.0, you will probably find parts of XQuery very familiar.

Backward- and cross-compatibility are mostly maintained among the three languages, so that an expression in any of the three languages will usually yield the same results. However, there are a few important differences, which are described in this section. All of these differences between XPath 1.0 and XPath 2.0 are also relevant if you plan to use XSLT 2.0.

The few areas of backward incompatibility between XPath 1.0 and XPath 2.0 are discussed in greater detail in Appendix I of the XPath 2.0 specification, which is at *http:// www.w3.org/TR/xpath20*. In XSLT, you can choose to process 2.0 stylesheets while setting an XPath 1.0 Compatibility Mode to treat XPath expressions just like XPath 1.0 expressions. This helps to avoid unexpected changes in the behavior of stylesheets when they are upgraded from 1.0 to 2.0. The mode is not available in XQuery 1.0, since there is no previous version of XQuery.

Data Model

The XPath 1.0 data model has the concept of a *node-set*, which is a set of nodes that are always in document order. In XQuery 1.0/XPath 2.0, there is the similar concept of a sequence. However, sequences differ in that they are ordered (not necessarily in document order), and they can contain duplicates. Another difference is that sequences can contain atomic values as well as nodes.

Root nodes in XPath 1.0 have been renamed *document nodes* in XQuery 1.0/XPath 2.0. Namespaces nodes are now deprecated in XPath 2.0, and not at all accessible in XQuery 1.0. They have been replaced by two functions that provide information about the namespaces in scope: `in-scope-prefixes` and `namespace-uri-for-prefix`.

New Expressions

XPath 2.0 encompasses a lot more than just paths. Some of the new kinds of expressions include:

- Conditional expressions (if-then-else)
- `for` expressions, which are a subset of XQuery FLWORs that have only two clauses: one `for` and one `return`
- Quantified expressions (`some`/`every-satisfies`)
- Ordered sequence constructors (`(($x, $y)`)
- Additional operators to combine sequences (`intersect`, `except`)
- Node comparison operators (`is`, `<<`, `>>`)

These new expressions are all part of XPath 2.0 itself, not just XQuery.

Path Expressions

If you already use XPath 1.0, the path expressions in XQuery should be familiar. The basic syntax and meaning of node tests and predicates is the same. The set of axes is almost the same, except that the `namespace::` axis is not available.

There are some additional enhancements to path expressions. One is the ability to have the last step in a path return atomic values rather than nodes. So, for example,

```
doc("catalog.xml")//product/name/substring(.,1,5)
```

will return the first five characters of each product name, resulting in a sequence of four string atomic values. This makes it really easy to do things that were tough in XPath 1.0; for example, summing over the product of price and quantity becomes:

```
sum(//item/(@price * @qty))
```

Another improvement is that it is now possible to have any expression as a step. You can take advantage of all the newly added kinds of expressions described in the previous section. It also allows you to create navigational functions that are very useful as steps, for example:

```
customer/orders-for-customer(.)/product-code
```

Function Conversion Rules

In XPath 1.0, if you call a function that is expecting a single value, and pass it a sequence of multiple values, it simply takes the first value and discards the others. For example:

```
substring(doc("catalog.xml")//product/name,1,5)
```

In this case, there are four product nodes. XPath 1.0 just takes the name of the first one and returns Fleec. In XQuery 1.0/XPath 2.0, a type error is raised.

XQuery 1.0/XPath 2.0 is strongly typed, while XPath 1.0 is not. In XPath 1.0, if you pass a value to a function that is of a different type—for example, a number to a function expecting a string, or vice versa—the value is cast automatically. In XQuery 1.0/XPath 2.0, a type error is raised. For example:

```
substring(12345678,1,4)
```

attempts to take the substring of a number. It will return 1234 in XPath 1.0, and raise an error in XQuery 1.0/XPath 2.0. Instead, you would need to explicitly convert the value into a string, as in:

```
substring(string(12345678),1,4)
```

Arithmetic and Comparison Expressions

In XPath 1.0, performing an arithmetic operation on a "missing" value results in the value NaN. In XQuery 1.0/XPath 2.0, it returns the empty sequence—for example, the expression:

```
catalog/foo * 2
```

Similar to the function conversion rules, in XPath 1.0 an arithmetic expression will take the first value of a sequence and discard the rest. In XQuery 1.0/XPath 2.0, it raises a type error.

It is possible in XQuery 1.0/XPath 2.0 to compare non-numeric values such as strings using the operators <, <=, >, and >=. In XPath 1.0, this was not supported. By default, XQuery 1.0/XPath 2.0 treats untyped operands of a comparison like strings, whereas they were treated as numbers in XPath 1.0. This is a significant compatibility risk, because the results of the comparison will be different if, for example, you

are comparing `<price>29.99</price>` to `<price>100.00</price>`. XPath 1.0 would say that the first price is less than the second, while XQuery 1.0/XPath 2.0 (in the absence of a schema that says they are numeric) would say that the second price is less, because its string value is lower.

Built-in Functions

There are approximately 80 new built-in functions in XPath 2.0. All of the built-in functions from XPath 1.0 are also supported in XQuery 1.0/XPath 2.0, with a couple of minor differences:

- Some XQuery 1.0/XPath 2.0 function calls return the empty sequence where in XPath 1.0 they would have returned a zero-length string. This is the case if the empty sequence is passed as the first argument to `substring`, `substring-before`, or `substring-after`.

- Some XQuery 1.0/XPath 2.0 function calls return the empty sequence where in XPath 1.0 they would have returned the value `NaN`. This is the case if the empty sequence is passed to `round`, `floor`, or `ceiling`.

Built-in Function Reference

This appendix describes the functions that are built into XQuery. Table A-1 lists all of the built-in functions by subject for easy reference. They are all in the XPath Functions Namespace, `http://www.w3.org/2005/xpath-functions`.

In addition to a brief sentence explaining the purpose of the function, each function is described by the following characteristics:

- "Signature" lists the parameters and their types, and the return type of the function.
- "Usage Notes" covers the function in more detail.
- "Special Cases" lists error conditions and other unusual situations.
- "Example(s)" provides one or more example function calls with their return values.
- "Related Functions" lists names of related functions.

 XSLT 2.0 has some additional built-in functions, namely current, current-group, current-grouping-key, document, element-available, format-date, format-dateTime, format-number, format-time, function-available, generate-id, key, regex-group, system-property, type-available, unparsed-entity-uri, unparsed-entity-public-id, unparsed-text, unparsed-text-available. These functions are part of XSLT 2.0 only, not XQuery 1.0 and XPath 2.0, and are therefore not covered in this appendix.

Many of the built-in functions have more than one signature. For example, adjust-date-to-timezone has a signature with just $arg, and another with two arguments—$arg and $timezone:

```
adjust-date-to-timezone($arg as xs:date?) as xs:date?
adjust-date-to-timezone($arg as xs:date?,
                        $timezone as xs:dayTimeDuration?) as xs:date?
```

For simplicity, in this appendix, only one signature is shown, with the "required" arguments in **constant width bold**, and the "optional" ones in *constant width italic*. For example:

```
adjust-date-to-timezone($arg as xs:date?,
                        $timezone as xs:dayTimeDuration?) as xs:date?
```

This convention indicates that the function can be called with or without the $timezone argument. Don't forget that passing the empty sequence or a zero-length string for an argument is not the same as omitting an argument.

It is possible to use this convention because the built-in functions (shown in Table A-1) have been designed so that in cases where there are several versions of a function with different numbers of arguments, the common arguments have the same type and meaning in each case. User-defined functions don't have to follow this design pattern, but it's good practice.

Table A-1. Function finder

Numeric functions

abs, avg, ceiling, floor, max, min, number, round, round-half-to-even, sum

String functions

codepoint-equal, codepoints-to-string, compare, concat, contains, default-collation, ends-with, lang, lower-case, matches, normalize-space, normalize-unicode, replace, starts-with, string-join, string-length, string-to-codepoints, substring, substring-after, substring-before, tokenize, translate, upper-case

Date functions

adjust-date-to-timezone, adjust-dateTime-to-timezone, adjust-time-to-timezone, current-date, current-dateTime, current-time, implicit-timezone, dateTime

Date functions (component extraction)

day-from-date, day-from-dateTime, days-from-duration, hours-from-dateTime, hours-from-duration, hours-from-time, minutes-from-dateTime, minutes-from-duration, minutes-from-time, month-from-date, month-from-dateTime, months-from-duration, seconds-from-dateTime, seconds-from-duration, seconds-from-time, timezone-from-date, timezone-from-dateTime, timezone-from-time, year-from-date, year-from-dateTime, years-from-duration

Boolean functions

boolean, false, true, not

Document and URI functions

base-uri, collection, doc, doc-available, document-uri, encode-for-uri, escape-html-uri, iri-to-uri, resolve-uri, root, static-base-uri

Name and namespace functions

QName, in-scope-prefixes, local-name, local-name-from-QName, name, namespace-uri, namespace-uri-for-prefix, namespace-uri-from-QName, node-name, prefix-from-QName, resolve-QName

Node-related functions

data, deep-equal, empty, exists, id, idref, nilled, string

Sequence-related functions

count, distinct-values, index-of, insert-before, last, position, remove, reverse, subsequence, unordered

Error handling and trapping functions

error, exactly-one, one-or-more, trace, zero-or-one

abs

Signature

```
abs($arg as numeric?) as numeric?
```

Usage Notes

This function accepts any numeric value and returns its absolute value. It returns a numeric value of type xs:float, xs:double, xs:decimal, or xs:integer, depending on which type the argument is derived from. If $arg is untyped, it is cast to xs:double.

Special Cases

- If $arg is the empty sequence, the function returns the empty sequence.
- If $arg is INF or -INF, the function returns INF.
- If $arg is NaN, the function returns NaN.

Examples

Example	Return value
abs(3.5)	3.5
abs(-4)	4
abs(xs:float("-INF"))	INF

adjust-date-to-timezone

Signature

```
adjust-date-to-timezone($arg as xs:date?,
                $timezone as xs:dayTimeDuration?) as xs:date?
```

Usage Notes

The behavior of this function depends on whether the $arg date value already has a time zone and on the value of the time zone provided. Table A-2 shows the possible combinations.

The $timezone argument is expressed as an xs:dayTimeDuration, for example, -PT5H for U.S. Eastern Standard Time. If $timezone is the empty sequence, it is assumed that the desired result is a date value that is in no time zone. If $timezone is omitted from the function call,[*] it is assumed to be the implicit time zone.

The $arg date is assumed for the sake of time zone calculation to be just like an xs:dateTime value whose time is midnight (00:00:00). If $arg does not already have a time zone, its date part stays the same, but it is now associated with the specified time zone.

[*] Remember, omitting an argument is different from passing the empty sequence for that argument.

If $arg already has a time zone, its value is adjusted to that time zone. This may change the actual date in some cases. For example, if $arg is 2006-02-15-05:00, and $timezone is –PT8H, the resulting date is 2006-02-14-08:00, which is the day before. This is because $arg is considered to be 2006-02-15T00:00:00-05:00, which is equivalent to 2006-02-14T21:00:00-08:00. In other words, midnight in the U.S. Eastern time zone is equal to 9 P.M. the day before in the U.S. Pacific time zone.

For more information on time zones in XQuery, see "Time Zones" in Chapter 19.

Special Cases

- If $arg is the empty sequence, the function returns the empty sequence.
- If the value of $timezone is not between –PT14H and PT14H, inclusive, or if it does not have an integral number of minutes (i.e., the number of seconds is not 0), the error "Invalid timezone value" (FODT0003) is raised.

Table A-2. Behavior of the adjust--to-timezone functions*

Does $arg have a time zone?	Value of $timezone argument	Explanation of result
No	An xs:dayTimeDuration	$arg, now associated with the time zone $timezone (but has the same date)
Yes	An xs:dayTimeDuration	$arg, adjusted to the time zone $timezone
No	The empty sequence	$arg, unchanged
Yes	The empty sequence	$arg with no associated time zone (but has the same date)
No	Not provided	$arg, now associated with the implicit time zone (but has the same date)
Yes	Not provided	$arg, adjusted to the implicit time zone

Examples

These six examples represent the six scenarios described in Table A-2.

Example[a]	Return value
adjust-date-to-timezone(xs:date("2006-02-15"), xs:dayTimeDuration("-PT8H"))	2006-02-15-08:00
adjust-date-to-timezone(xs:date("2006-02-15-03:00"), xs:dayTimeDuration("-PT8H"))	2006-02-14-08:00
adjust-date-to-timezone(xs:date("2006-02-15"), ())	2006-02-15
adjust-date-to-timezone(xs:date("2006-02-15-03:00"), ())	2006-02-15
adjust-date-to-timezone(xs:date("2006-02-15"))	2006-02-15-05:00
adjust-date-to-timezone(xs:date("2006-02-15-03:00"))	2006-02-14-05:00

[a] This table assumes an implicit time zone of –05:00.

adjust-dateTime-to-timezone

Adjusts the time zone of a date/time

Signature

```
adjust-dateTime-to-timezone($arg as xs:dateTime?,
                            $timezone as xs:dayTimeDuration?) as xs:dateTime?
```

Usage Notes

The behavior of this function is identical to that of `adjust-date-to-timezone`, described in Table A-2, except that the actual time, not midnight, is used.

Special Cases

- If $arg is the empty sequence, the function returns the empty sequence.
- If the value of $timezone is not between –PT14H and PT14H, inclusive, or if it does not have an integral number of minutes (i.e., the number of seconds is not 0), the error "Invalid timezone value" (FODT0003) is raised.

Examples

These examples represent the scenarios described in Table A-2.

Example[a]	Return value
adjust-dateTime-to-timezone (xs:dateTime("2006-02-15T17:00:00"), xs:dayTimeDuration("-PT7H"))	2006-02-15T17:00:00-07:00
adjust-dateTime-to-timezone (xs:dateTime("2006-02-15T17:00:00-03:00"), xs:dayTimeDuration("-PT7H"))	2006-02-15T13:00:00-07:00
adjust-dateTime-to-timezone (xs:dateTime("2006-02-15T17:00:00"), ())	2006-02-15T17:00:00
adjust-dateTime-to-timezone (xs:dateTime("2006-02-15T17:00:00-03:00"), ())	2006-02-15T17:00:00
adjust-dateTime-to-timezone (xs:dateTime("2006-02-15T17:00:00"))	2006-02-15T17:00:00-05:00
adjust-dateTime-to-timezone (xs:dateTime("2006-02-15T17:00:00-03:00"))	2006-02-15T15:00:00-05:00
adjust-dateTime-to-timezone (xs:dateTime("2006-02-15T01:00:00-03:00"), xs:dayTimeDuration("-PT7H"))	2006-02-14T21:00:00-07:00

[a] This table assumes an implicit time zone of -05:00.

adjust-time-to-timezone

Adjusts the time zone of a time

Signature

```
adjust-time-to-timezone($arg as xs:time?,
                        $timezone as xs:dayTimeDuration?) as xs:time?
```

Usage Notes

The behavior of this function is identical to that of adjust-date-to-timezone, described in Table A-2, except that the actual time, not midnight, is used.

Special Cases

- If $arg is the empty sequence, the function returns the empty sequence.
- If the value of $timezone is not between – –PT14H and PT14H, inclusive, or if it does not have an integral number of minutes (i.e., the number of seconds is not 0), the error "Invalid timezone value" (FODT0003) is raised.

Examples

Some examples are shown here. See Table A-2 for a description of the scenarios these examples represent.

Example[a]	Return value
adjust-time-to-timezone(xs:time("17:00:00"), xs:dayTimeDuration("-PT7H"))	17:00:00-07:00
adjust-time-to-timezone(xs:time("17:00:00-03:00"), xs:dayTimeDuration("-PT7H"))	13:00:00-07:00
adjust-time-to-timezone(xs:time("17:00:00"), ())	17:00:00
adjust-time-to-timezone(xs:time("17:00:00-03:00"), ())	17:00:00
adjust-time-to-timezone(xs:time("17:00:00"))	17:00:00-05:00
adjust-time-to-timezone(xs:time("17:00:00-03:00"))	15:00:00-05:00
adjust-time-to-timezone(xs:time("22:00:00-08:00"))	01:00:00-05:00
adjust-time-to-timezone(xs:time("01:00:00-02:00"))	22:00:00-05:00
adjust-time-to-timezone(xs:time("17:00:00"), xs:dayTimeDuration("-PT20H"))	Error FODT0003

a This table assumes an implicit time zone of –05:00.

avg

Finds the average value of the items in a sequence

Signature

```
avg($arg as xs:anyAtomicType*) as xs:anyAtomicType?
```

Usage Notes

The $arg sequence can contain a mixture of numeric and untyped values. Numeric values are promoted as necessary to make them all the same type. Untyped values are cast as numeric xs:double values.

The function can also be used on duration values, so the $arg sequence can contain all xs:yearMonthDuration values or all xs:dayTimeDuration values (but not a mixture of the two). The $arg sequence cannot contain a mixture of duration and numeric values.

Special care should be taken with any "missing" values when using the avg function. This is described further in "Counting "Missing" Values" in Chapter 7.

Special Cases

- If $arg is the empty sequence, the function returns the empty sequence.
- If $arg contains untyped values that cannot be cast to numbers, the error "Invalid value for cast/constructor" (FORG0001) is raised.
- If $arg contains typed values that are not numeric or duration values, or values that have a variety of types, the error "Invalid argument type" (FORG0006) is raised.
- If $arg contains values that are NaN, the function returns NaN.

Examples

Example	Return value
avg((1, 2, 3, 4, 5))	3
avg((1, 2, 3, (), 4, 5))	3
avg((xs:yearMonthDuration("P4M"), xs:yearMonthDuration("P6M")))	P5M
avg(doc("order.xml")//item/@quantity)	1.166667 (with implementation-defined precision)
avg(())	()
avg(doc("order.xml")//item/@dept)	Error FORG0001

Related Functions

sum, count

base-uri

Gets the base URI of a node

Signature

 base-uri($arg as node()?) as xs:anyURI?

Usage Notes

The essential purpose of a base URI is to establish a baseline for resolving any relative URIs in the content.

The $arg argument may be any kind of node. If $arg is a document node, this function usually returns the URI from which the document was retrieved,* if it is known. This can also be achieved by using the document-uri function. An example where the base URI might not be known is where the document is created by parsing an anonymous input stream. Check your processor's documentation for details of how to supply a base URI in such cases.

If $arg is an element, the function returns the value of its xml:base attribute, if any, or the xml:base attribute of its nearest ancestor. If no xml:base attributes appear among its ancestors, it defaults to the base URI of the document node. If the original document consisted of multiple external entities (files), the base URI would be the URI of the containing entity.

* Some documents, such as those contained in a multipart MIME message, may have a base URI that is different from the URI that can be used to retrieve it.

If $arg is any other kind of node, the function returns the same value as if the argument were its parent element or document.

For more information on URIs, see "Working with URIs" in Chapter 20.

Special Cases

- If $arg is the empty sequence, the function returns the empty sequence.
- If $arg is not provided, the function returns the base URI of the current context node. Note that this is not the same as the base URI from the static context, which is retrieved using the static-base-uri function.
- If $arg is not provided, and the context item is not a node, the error XPTY0004 is raised.
- If $arg is not provided, and the context item is undefined, the error XPDY0002 is raised.
- If no base URI can be found, for example because the element node has no base URI and does not have a document node as its root, the function returns the empty sequence.

Examples

These examples assume that the variable $cats is bound to the input document http://datypic.com/cats.xml shown in Example A-1.

Example	Return value
base-uri($cats//catalog[1])	http://example.org/ACC/
base-uri($cats//catalog[2]/product)	http://example.org/WMN/
base-uri ($cats//catalog[2]/product/@href)	http://example.org/WMN/
base-uri($cats)	http://datypic.com/cats.xml
base-uri($cats/catalogs)	http://datypic.com/cats.xml

Example A-1. Using xml:base (http://datypic.com/cats.xml)

```
<catalogs>
  <catalog name="ACC" xml:base="http://example.org/ACC/">
    <product number="443" href="prod443.html"/>
    <product number="563" href="prod563.html"/>
  </catalog>
  <catalog name="WMN" xml:base="http://example.org/WMN/">
    <product number="557" href="prod557.html"/>
  </catalog>
</catalogs>
```

Related Functions

static-base-uri, resolve-uri, document-uri

boolean

Signature

```
boolean($arg as item()*) as xs:boolean
```

Usage Notes

This function calculates the effective Boolean value of a sequence (that is, any value). For more information, see "Effective Boolean Value" in Chapter 11.

In most cases, it is unnecessary to call this function because the effective Boolean value is calculated automatically in many expressions, including conditional and logical expressions, where clauses, and predicates.

This boolean function, which can also be written as fn:boolean, should not be confused with the xs:boolean constructor, which casts a value to xs:boolean. In some cases, they return different results, namely when the argument is:

- A single node that contains the value false (xs:boolean returns false because it atomizes the node, while fn:boolean returns true)
- The string value false (xs:boolean returns false, fn:boolean returns true)
- A zero-length string, or any string other than true, false, 0, or 1 (xs:boolean raises an error, fn:boolean returns false if it's a zero-length string; otherwise, true)
- A sequence of more than one node (xs:boolean raises an error, fn:boolean returns true)

Special Cases

- If the effective Boolean value of $arg is undefined, for example because $arg is a sequence of multiple atomic values, the error "Invalid argument type" (FORG0006) is raised.

Examples

Example	Return value
boolean(())	false
boolean("")	false
boolean(0)	false
boolean("0")	true
boolean(false())	false
boolean("false")	true
boolean(xs:float("NaN"))	false
boolean((false(), false(), false()))	Error FORG0006
boolean(doc("order.xml")/order[1])	true
boolean(doc("order.xml")/noSuchChild)	false
boolean(<a>false)	true

ceiling

Rounds a number up to the next integer

Signature

```
ceiling($arg as numeric?) as numeric?
```

Usage Notes

This function returns the smallest integer that is not less than $arg. It returns a numeric value of type xs:float, xs:double, xs:decimal, or xs:integer, depending on which type the argument is derived from. If $arg is untyped, it is cast to xs:double.

Special Cases

- If $arg is the empty sequence, the function returns the empty sequence.
- If $arg is between −0.5 and −0 (inclusive), the function may return 0 or -0 (it is implementation-dependent).
- If $arg is one of the values 0, -0, NaN, INF, or -INF, the function returns this same value.

Examples

Example	Return value
ceiling(5)	5
ceiling(5.1)	6
ceiling(5.5)	6
ceiling(-5.5)	-5
ceiling(-5.51)	-5
ceiling(())	()

Related Functions

floor, round, round-half-to-even

codepoint-equal

Determines whether two strings contain the same code points

Signature

```
codepoint-equal($comparand1 as xs:string?,
                $comparand2 as xs:string?) as xs:boolean?
```

Usage Notes

The function determines whether the two string arguments have the same Unicode code points, in the same order. This is similar to calling the compare function with the simple collation http://www.w3.org/2005/xpath-functions/collation/codepoint, except that the result is a Boolean value.

Special Cases

- If either argument is the empty sequence, the function returns the empty sequence.

Examples

Example	Return value
codepoint-equal("abc", "abc")	true
codepoint-equal("abc", "ab c")	false
codepoint-equal("abc", ())	()

codepoints-to-string

Constructs a string from Unicode code-point values

Signature

```
codepoints-to-string($arg as xs:integer*) as xs:string
```

Usage Notes

The $arg argument is a sequence of integers representing Unicode code-point values.

Special Cases

- If one or more of the $arg integers does not refer to a valid XML character, the error "Code point not valid" (FOCH0001) is raised.
- If $arg is the empty sequence, the function returns a zero-length string.

Examples

Example	Return value
codepoints-to-string((97, 32, 98, 32, 99))	a b c
codepoints-to-string(97)	a
codepoints-to-string(())	A zero-length string

collection

Gets the nodes that make up a collection

Signature

```
collection($arg as xs:string?) as node( )*
```

Usage Notes

A collection may be any sequence of nodes, identified by a URI. Often, they are sequences of documents that are organized into collections so that they can be queried or managed together.

Exactly how the collection URI ($arg) is associated with the nodes is defined by the implementation. Most XML database implementations allow you to define collections (and add documents to them) using the product's user interface or implementation-specific

functions. Saxon, on the other hand, dereferences the URI to retrieve an XML collection document that lists all of the documents in the collection.

If $arg is a relative URI, it is resolved based on the base URI of the static context. The base URI of the static context may be set by the processor outside the scope of the query, or it may be declared in the query prolog.

The collection function is stable. This means that if you call the collection function more than once with the exact same argument, within the same query, the result is the same, even if somehow the resources associated with the URI have changed.

Special Cases

- If $arg is not lexically a valid URI or it cannot be resolved, the error "Error retrieving resource" (FODC0004) is raised.
- If $arg is not the URI of a collection supported by the implementation, the error "Invalid argument to fn:collection()" (FODC0004) is raised.
- If no argument is provided, or if $arg is the empty sequence, the function returns the default collection as defined by the implementation. If no default collection is defined, the error "Error retrieving resource" (FODC0002) is raised.

Example

The expression collection("myXMLdocs") will return all the document nodes of the XML documents associated with the collection myXMLdocs.

Related Functions

doc

compare

Compares strings, optionally with an explicit collation

Signature

```
compare($comparand1 as xs:string?, $comparand2 as xs:string?,
        $collation as xs:string) as xs:integer?
```

Usage Notes

This function returns one of the values:

- −1 if $comparand1 is less than $comparand2
- 0 if $comparand1 is equal to $comparand2
- 1 if $comparand1 is greater than $comparand2

A comparand is greater than the other comparand if it starts with the other comparand and has additional characters. For example, abc is greater than ab.

Comparison operators (=, !=, <, <=, >, >=) can also be used to compare strings, and you may find the syntax more convenient. However, compare is also useful if you want to take different action in each of the three result cases. Also, if you need to use a specific collation other than the default, you must use the compare function. More information can be found in "Collations" in Chapter 17.

Special Cases

- If either comparand is the empty sequence, the function returns the empty sequence.
- If $collation is provided, the comparison uses that collation; otherwise, it uses the default collation.

Examples

Example[a]	Return value
compare("a", "b")	-1
compare("a", "a")	0
compare("b", "a")	1
compare("ab", "abc")	-1
compare("a", "B")	1
compare(upper-case("a"), upper-case("B"))	-1
compare("a", ())	()
compare('Strasse', 'Straße', 'http://datypic.com/german')	0 if the collation equates the ß character with two s's.
compare("a", "b", "FOO")	Error FOCH0002

[a] The examples in this table assume that no default collation is specified.

The fifth example in the table shows that when using the simple code-point collation, a lowercase a comes after an uppercase B. If you do not want case to be taken into account when comparing strings, convert the strings to uppercase first, as shown in the sixth example. Alternatively, you could use a case-insensitive collation.

concat

Concatenates two or more strings together

Signature

```
concat($arg1 as xs:anyAtomicType?,
       $arg2 as xs:anyAtomicType?, ...) as xs:string
```

Usage Notes

The concat function requires at least two arguments (which can be the empty sequence) and accepts an unlimited number of additional arguments. This is the only XQuery function that has a flexible number of arguments, for compatibility with XPath 1.0. The function is also unusual in that arguments that are not of type xs:string will be cast to xs:string.

The function does not accept a *sequence* of multiple values, just individual atomic values (or nodes) passed as separate arguments. To concatenate a sequence of multiple values, use the string-join function instead.

Special Cases

- If an argument is the empty sequence, it is treated as a zero-length string.

Examples

Example	Return value
concat("a")	Error XPST0017
concat("a", "b")	ab
concat("a", "b", "c")	abc
concat("a", (), "b", "", "c")	abc
concat(("a", "b", "c"))	Error XPST0017 (use string-join instead)
concat(doc("catalog.xml")//name)	Error XPST0017 (use string-join instead)
concat("a", <x>b</x>, <x>c</x>)	abc

Related Functions

string-join

contains Determines whether one string contains another

Signature

contains(**$arg1 as xs:string?**, **$arg2 as xs:string?**,
 $collation as xs:string) as xs:boolean

Usage Notes

This function returns true if $arg1 contains the characters of $arg2 anywhere in its contents, including at the beginning or end. Note that contains does *not* test whether a sequence of multiple strings contains a given value. For that, use the = operator.

Special Cases

- If $arg2 is a zero-length string or the empty sequence, the function returns true.
- If $arg1 is a zero-length string or the empty sequence, but $arg2 is not, the function returns false.
- If $collation is provided, the comparison uses that collation; otherwise, it uses the default collation. Collations are described in Chapter 17.

Examples

Example	Return value
contains("query", "e")	true
contains("query", "ery")	true
contains("query", "query")	true
contains("query", "x")	false
contains("query", "")	true
contains("query", ())	true

Example	Return value
contains((), "q")	false
contains("","")	true
contains("", "query")	false

Related Functions

starts-with, ends-with, matches

count

Counts the number of items in a sequence

Signature

 count($arg as item()*) as xs:integer

Usage Notes

This function returns the number of items in a sequence as an xs:integer.

To test whether or not the number of items in a sequence is zero, use the exists or empty function instead. Depending on your processor's optimizer, exists($x) may be more efficient than count($x) = 0.

Special Cases

• If $arg is the empty sequence, the function returns 0.

Examples

Example	Return value
count((1, 2, 3))	3
count(doc("order.xml")//item)	6
count(distinct-values(doc("order.xml")//item/@num))	4
count((1, 2, 3, ()))	3
count(())	0

As shown in the third example, the count function can be combined with the distinct-values function to count only distinct values.

current-date

Gets the current date

Signature

 current-date() as xs:date

Usage Notes

This function takes no parameters and returns the current date with time zone. The time zone is implementation-dependent. To eliminate the time zone from the value, you can call adjust-date-to-timezone with the empty sequence as the second argument, as in:

```
adjust-date-to-timezone(current-date(), ())
```

Example

current-date() might return the xs:date value 2006-04-10-05:00, which is April 10, 2006 in the –05:00 time zone.

Related Functions

current-dateTime, current-time

current-dateTime Gets the current date and time

Signature

```
current-dateTime( ) as xs:dateTime
```

Usage Notes

This function takes no parameters and returns the current date and time with time zone. If the function is called multiple times within the same query, it returns the same value every time. The time zone and the precision of the seconds part are implementation-dependent. To eliminate the time zone from the value, you can call adjust-dateTime-to-timezone with the empty sequence as the second argument, as in:

```
adjust-dateTime-to-timezone(current-dateTime(), ())
```

Example

current-dateTime() might return the xs:dateTime value 2006-04-10T13:40:23.83-05:00.

Related Functions

current-date, current-time

current-time Gets the current time

Signature

```
current-time( ) as xs:time
```

Usage Notes

This function takes no parameters and returns the current time with time zone. If the function is called multiple times within the same query, it returns the same value every time. The time zone and the precision of the seconds part are implementation-dependent. To

eliminate the time zone from the value, you can call `adjust-time-to-timezone` with the empty sequence as the second argument, as in:

```
adjust-time-to-timezone(current-time(), ())
```

Example

current-time() might return the xs:time value 13:40:23.83-05:00.

Related Functions

current-dateTime, current-date

data Extracts the typed value of one or more items

Signature

```
data($arg as item( )*) as xs:anyAtomicType*
```

Usage Notes

This function accepts a sequence of items and returns their typed values. For atomic values, this simply means returning the value itself, unchanged. For nodes, this means extracting the typed value of the node.

Calling this function is usually unnecessary because the typed value of a node is extracted automatically (in a process known as atomization) for many XQuery expressions, including comparisons, arithmetic operations, function calls, and sorting in FLWORs. The most common use case for the data function is in element constructors. For example, the expression:

```
for $prod in doc("catalog.xml")//product
return <newEl>{data($prod/name)}</newEl>
```

uses the data function to extract the typed value of the name element, in order to put it in the content of newEl. If it had not used the data function, the resulting newEl elements would each have a name child instead of just character data content.

In most cases, the typed value of an element or attribute is simply its string value, cast to the type of the element or attribute. For example, if the number element has the type xs:integer, the string value of the element is 784 (type xs:string), while the typed value is 784 (type xs:integer). If the number element is untyped, its typed value is 784 (type xs:untypedAtomic).

The typed value of an element will not be the empty sequence just because the element has no content. For example, the typed value of <name></name> is the value "" (type xs:untypedAtomic) if name is untyped, not the empty sequence.

There are some additional subtleties for schema-validated elements that are described in "Nodes and Typed Values" in Chapter 13.

Other kinds of nodes have typed values as well, but they are less useful; they are described in the appropriate sections of Chapter 21.

Special Cases

- If $arg is the empty sequence, the function returns the empty sequence.
- If $arg is an element whose type has element-only content, the error "Argument node does not have a typed value" (FOTY0012) is raised.

Examples

Table A-3 shows some examples of the data function applied to untyped nodes. They assume that the variable $cat is bound to the document node of catalog.xml, which has *not* been validated with a schema.

Table A-3. Examples of the data function on untyped nodes

Example	Return value	Return type
data($cat//product[1]/number)	557	xs:untypedAtomic
data($cat//number)	(557, 563, 443, 784)	xs:untypedAtomic*
data($cat//product[1]/@dept)	WMN	xs:untypedAtomic
data($cat//product[1]/ colorChoices)	navy black	xs:untypedAtomic
data($cat//product[1])	557 Fleece Pullover navy black	xs:untypedAtomic
data($cat//product[4]/desc)	Our favorite shirt!	xs:untypedAtomic

Now suppose you have the schema shown in Example 13-1 in Chapter 13, and catalog.xml was validated using this schema. The typed values of the nodes would then change, as shown in Table A-4.

Table A-4. Examples of the data function on typed nodes

Example	Return value	Return type
data($cat//product[1]/number)	557	xs:integer
data($cat//number)	(557, 563, 443, 784)	xs:integer*
data($cat//product[1]/@dept)	WMN	xs:string
data($cat//product[1]/ colorChoices)	(navy, black)	xs:string*
data($cat//product[1])	Error FOTY0012	N/A
data($cat//product[4]/desc)	Our favorite shirt!	xs:untypedAtomic

Related Functions

string

dateTime

Constructs a date/time value from separate date and time values

Signature

```
dateTime($arg1 as xs:date?, $arg2 as xs:time?) as xs:dateTime?
```

Usage Notes

This function constructs an xs:dateTime value from an xs:date value and an xs:time value. It should not be confused with the xs:dateTime constructor, which accepts a single argument that includes the date and time.

Time zone is taken into account when constructing the date/time. If neither the date nor the time has a time zone, the result has no time zone. If only one of the arguments has a time zone, or they both have the same time zone, the result has that time zone.

Special Cases

- If the two arguments have different time zones, the error "Both arguments to fn: dateTime have a specified timezone" (FORG0008) is raised.
- If either of the two arguments is the empty sequence, the function returns the empty sequence.

Example

dateTime(xs:date("2006-08-15"),xs:time("12:30:45-05:00")) returns the xs:dateTime value 2006-08-15T12:30:45-05:00.

day-from-date

Gets the day portion of a date

Signature

day-from-date(**$arg as xs:date?**) as xs:integer?

Usage Notes

This function returns the day portion from an xs:date value as an integer between 1 and 31 inclusive.

Special Cases

- If $arg is the empty sequence, the function returns the empty sequence.

Example

day-from-date(xs:date("2006-08-15")) returns 15.

Related Functions

day-from-dateTime

day-from-dateTime

Gets the day portion of a date/time

Signature

day-from-dateTime(**$arg as xs:dateTime?**) as xs:integer?

Usage Notes

This function returns the day portion from an xs:dateTime value as an integer between 1 and 31 inclusive.

Special Cases

- If $arg is the empty sequence, the function returns the empty sequence.

Example

day-from-dateTime(xs:dateTime("2006-08-15T10:30:23")) returns 15.

Related Functions

day-from-date

days-from-duration

Gets the normalized number of days in a duration

Signature

days-from-duration(**$arg as xs:duration?**) as xs:integer?

Usage Notes

This function calculates the total number of whole days in an xs:duration value. This is not necessarily the same as the integer that appears before the D in the value. For example, if the duration is P1DT36H, the function returns 2 rather than 1. This is because 36 hours is equal to 1.5 days, and the normalized value is therefore P2DT12H.

The days-from-duration function does not round the number of days; if the duration is 2 days and 23 hours, it returns the integer 2.

Special Cases

- If $arg is a negative duration, the function returns a negative value.
- If $arg is the empty sequence, the function returns the empty sequence.

Examples

Example	Return value
days-from-duration(xs:duration("P5D"))	5
days-from-duration(xs:duration("-PT24H"))	-1
days-from-duration(xs:duration("PT23H"))	0
days-from-duration(xs:duration("P1DT36H"))	2
days-from-duration(xs:duration("PT1440M"))	1
days-from-duration(xs:duration("P1Y"))	0

deep-equal Determines whether the values of two sequences of items are equal (contain the same data)

Signature

```
deep-equal($parameter1 as item()*, $parameter2 as item()*,
           $collation as xs:string) as xs:boolean
```

Usage Notes

This function returns true if the $parameter1 and $parameter2 sequences contain the same values, in the same order.

Atomic values are compared based on their typed values, using the eq operator. If two atomic values cannot be compared (e.g., because one is a number and the other is a string), the function returns false rather than raising an error.

The comparison of nodes takes into account the descendants and attributes. In order to be considered deep-equal, two nodes must:

- Have the same qualified name.
- Have the same node kind.
- If they are elements, have the exact same attributes with the same qualified names and the same values (possibly in a different order).
- If they are attributes or elements with simple content (no children), their typed values must be equal. For example, 2 is considered the same as 02 if they are both typed as integers, but not if they are both strings.
- If they are elements with children, have element children and text nodes in the same order, that are themselves deep-equal.
- If they are document nodes, have element and text children in the same order, that are themselves deep-equal.
- If they are processing-instruction nodes, have the same name (target) and the exact same string value.
- If they are text or comment nodes, have the exact same string value.

The two nodes do *not* have to have the same type, parent, or base URI. Namespace declarations are considered only to the extent that they affect element and attribute names or values typed as QNames; "unused" namespaces are ignored.

When comparing two element or document nodes, child comments and processing instructions are ignored. However, the presence of a comment that splits a text node in two will cause the text nodes to be unequal. Whitespace-only text nodes are considered significant.

Special Cases

- If both $parameter1 and $parameter2 are the empty sequence, the function returns true.
- If only one of $parameter1 or $parameter2 is the empty sequence, the function returns false.
- If $collation is provided, values of type xs:string are compared using that collation; otherwise, the default collation is used.
- In the context of this function, NaN is considered equal to itself. This is to ensure that a node is always deep-equal to itself, even if some descendant has a typed value of NaN.

Examples

The following two product elements are considered deep-equal:

```
<product dept="MEN" id="P123">
  <number>784</number>
</product>
<product id="P123" dept="MEN"><!--comment-->
  <number>784</number>
</product>
```

The examples below assume that the variables $prod1 and $prod2 are bound to the two product elements above.

Example	Return value
deep-equal(1, 1)	true
deep-equal((1, 1), (1, 1))	true
deep-equal((1, 2), (1.0, 2.0))	true
deep-equal((1, 2), (2, 1))	false
deep-equal($prod1, $prod2)	true
deep-equal($prod1/number, $prod2/number)	true
deep-equal($prod1/node(), $prod2/node())	false because of the extra comment node

default-collation

Gets the default collation

Signature

```
default-collation( ) as xs:string
```

Usage Notes

This function returns the default collation that is used in most operations where a collation is not explicitly specified. If no default collation is specified in the query prolog, the function returns the system default collation. If no system default collation is defined, the function returns a value representing the Unicode code-point collation, http://www.w3.org/2005/xpath-functions/collation/codepoint. See "Collations" in Chapter 17 for more information.

Example

default-collation() might return http://datypic.com/collations/custom if that is the name of the default collation declared in the query prolog.

distinct-values

Selects distinct atomic values from a sequence

Signature

```
distinct-values($arg as xs:anyAtomicType*,
                $collation as xs:string) as xs:anyAtomicType*
```

Usage Notes

This function returns a sequence of unique atomic values from $arg. Values are compared based on their typed value. Values of different numeric types may be equal—for example, the xs:integer value 1 is equal to the xs:decimal value 1.0, so the function only returns one of these values. If two values have incomparable types, e.g., xs:string and xs:integer, they are considered distinct, and no error is raised. Untyped values are treated like strings.

The $arg sequence can contain atomic values or nodes, or a combination of the two. The nodes in the sequence have their typed values extracted using the usual function conversion rules. This means that only the *contents* of the nodes are compared, not any other properties of the nodes (for example, their names or identities). To eliminate nodes by identity instead, you can simply use the expression $seq/., which resorts the nodes and removes duplicates.

Because XQuery does not specify which of the duplicates to exclude, there may be some variation among implementations in the order and type of items in the result sequence.

Special Cases

- If $arg is the empty sequence, the function returns the empty sequence.
- If $arg contains more than one NaN value, only one of them is returned (even though one NaN value is technically not equal to other NaN values).
- Dates and times with no time zone component are assumed to be in the implicit time zone.
- If $collation is provided, values of type string are compared using that collation; otherwise, it uses the default collation.
- If $arg contains an element whose schema type has element-only content, the type error XPTY0004 is raised, because such nodes do not have typed values.

Examples

Example	Return value
distinct-values(("a", "b", "a"))	("a", "b")
distinct-values((1, 2, 3))	(1, 2, 3)
distinct-values(("a", 2, 3))	("a", 2, 3)
distinct-values((xs:integer("1"), xs:decimal("1.0"), xs:float("1.0E0")))	(1)
distinct-values((<a>3, 5))	(3, 5)
distinct-values((<a>3, 3))	(3)
distinct-values(())	()

doc

Signature

```
doc($uri as xs:string?) as document-node()?
```

Usage Notes

This function returns the document node of the resource associated with the specified URI. For example:

```
doc("http://datypic.com/order.xml")
```

returns the document node of the document whose URI is http://datypic.com/order.xml. Relative URI references are also allowed, as in:

```
doc("order.xml")
```

If $uri is a relative URI, it is resolved based on the base URI of the static context. The base URI of the static context may be set by the processor outside the scope of the query, typically to the URI of the file from which the query was read. Alternatively, it may be declared in the query prolog.

If you are accessing documents on a filesystem, your implementation may require you to precede the filename with file:///, use forward slashes to separate directory names, and/or escape each space in the filename with %20. For example,

```
doc("file:///C:/Documents%20and%20Settings/my%20order.xml")
```

The doc function is often combined with a path expression to retrieve specific children, as in:

```
doc("catalog.xml")/catalog/product
```

Note that the doc function returns the document node, not the outermost element node. Therefore, you need to include the outermost element node in your path (catalog in the previous example).

Processors interpret the URI passed to the doc function in different ways. Some, like Saxon, will dereference the URI, that is, go out to the URL and retrieve the resource at that location. Other implementations, such as those embedded in XML databases, consider the URIs to be just names. The processor might take the name and look it up in an internal catalog to find the document associated with that name. Many processors provide user hooks or configuration options allowing the behavior to be controlled by the application, and the result may also depend on the configuration of the underlying environment (for example, HTTP proxy settings).

Implementations also have some leeway in how they handle errors when retrieving documents, how they handle different MIME types, and whether they validate the documents against a schema or DTD.

The doc function is stable, meaning that it returns the same results each time it is called within a query. If you call the doc function more than once with the exact same argument, within the same query, the result is the same, even if somehow the resource at $uri has changed. Furthermore, the document nodes retrieved from each of these calls are identical to each other.

 The doc function should not be confused with the XSLT document function, which is not available in XQuery. The document function has different behavior, in that it will accept multiple URIs, allows the specification of a base URI, and has specific processing defined for handling fragment identifiers. These effects can be achieved in XQuery by combining use of doc with other functions such as resolve-uri and base-uri or by using it in a FLWOR expression.

Special Cases

- If $uri is the empty sequence, the function returns the empty sequence.
- If $uri is not a lexically valid URI, the error "Invalid argument to fn:doc" (FODC0005) is raised.
- If $uri refers to a resource that is not supported by the implementation, the error "Invalid argument to fn:doc" (FODC0005) is raised.
- If the resource cannot be retrieved or parsed, for example, because it does not reference a resource, or the resource is not well-formed XML, the behavior is implementation-defined. It may result in the error "Error retrieving resource" (FODC0002) being raised, or in some other error handling behavior (such as a default document being opened).

Example

doc("http://datypic.com/order.xml") returns the document node of the document associated with the URI http://datypic.com/order.xml.

Related Functions

collection, doc-available

doc-available

Determines whether a document is available

Signature

 doc-available($uri as xs:string?) as xs:boolean

Usage Notes

The doc-available function is a way to avoid the errors returned by the doc function if a document is not available. This function will return true if calling the doc function on the same URI will result in a document node. It will return false if the doc function will not return a document node.

Special Cases

- If $uri is not a valid lexical value of xs:anyURI, the error "Invalid argument to fn:doc" (FODC0005) is raised.
- If $arg is the empty sequence, the function returns false.

Example

This query will check if an XML document named `http://datypic.com/new_order.xml` is available:

```
if (doc-available("http://datypic.com/new_order.xml"))
then doc("http://datypic.com/new_order.xml")
else ()
```

If a document is available, it will return its document node. Otherwise, it will return the empty sequence. If the doc function had been called without verifying the existence of the document first, an error might have been raised.

Related Functions

doc

document-uri

Gets the URI of a document node

Signature

```
document-uri($arg as node()?) as xs:anyURI?
```

Usage Notes

This function is basically the inverse of the doc function. Where the doc function accepts a URI and returns a document node, the document-uri function accepts a document node and returns the absolute URI associated with it. The URI may represent the location from which it was retrieved, or simply the URI that serves as its name in an XML database.

In most cases, calling this function has the same result as calling the base-uri function with the document node.

Special Cases

- If $arg is not a document node, the function returns the empty sequence.
- If $arg does not have a document URI (for example, because it is constructed), the function returns the empty sequence.
- If the $arg node's document URI is a relative URI that cannot be resolved, the function returns the empty sequence.
- If $arg is the empty sequence, the function returns the empty sequence.

Example

If the variable $orderDoc is bound to the result of doc("http://datypic.com/order.xml"), then document-uri($orderDoc) returns "http://datypic.com/order.xml".

Related Functions

doc, base-uri

empty

Determines whether a sequence is empty

Signature

```
empty($arg as item( )*) as xs:boolean
```

Usage Notes

A sequence is empty if it contains zero items. A sequence is *not* considered empty just because it only contains a zero-length string, the value 0, or an element with empty content. To test whether an element has empty content, use the expression:

```
string($node1) = ""
```

It is often unnecessary to call the empty function because sequences are automatically converted to their effective Boolean value where a Boolean value is expected. For example, if you want to test whether there are any item children of items, you can use the if clause:

```
if not($input//catalog/product) then ....
```

In this case, the sequence of selected item elements is converted to the Boolean value true if the sequence is not empty, and false if the sequence is empty. There is no need to call the empty function to determine this. But beware: this only works for node sequences, not for atomic values.

Examples

Example	Return value
empty(("a", "b", "c"))	false
empty(())	true
empty(0)	false
empty(<desc/>)	false
empty(<desc></desc>)	false
empty(doc("order.xml")/order)	false
empty(doc("order.xml")/foo)	true

Related Functions

exists, boolean

encode-for-uri

Applies URI escaping rules to a string that is to be used as a path segment of a URI

Signature

```
encode-for-uri($uri-part as xs:string?) as xs:string
```

Usage Notes

URIs require that some characters be escaped with their hexadecimal Unicode code point preceded by the % character. This includes non-ASCII characters and some ASCII characters, namely control characters, spaces, and several others.

In addition, certain characters in URIs are separators that are intended to delimit parts of URIs, namely the characters ; , / ? : @ & = + $ [] %. If the intended use of a string is as a segment of a URI path, where such separators have special meaning, the encode-for-uri function allows you to escape these separator characters, while also escaping the other necessary special characters.

Like the escape-html-uri and iri-to-uri functions, the encode-for-uri function replaces each special character with an escape sequence in the form %xx (possible repeating), where xx is two hexadecimal digits (in uppercase) that represent the character in UTF-8. For example, édition.html is changed to %C3%A9dition.html, with the é escaped as %C3%A9.

The encode-for-URI function is the most aggressive of the three encoding functions. All characters *except* the following are escaped:

- Letters a through z and A through Z
- Digits 0 through 9
- Hyphen (-), underscore (_), period (.), and tilde (~)

Because the function escapes delimiter characters, it's unsuitable for escaping a complete URI. Instead, it's useful for escaping strings before they are assembled into a URI—for example, the values of query parameters.

Special Cases

- If $uri-part is the empty sequence, the function returns a zero-length string.

Examples

The first example below shows a typical use case, where a filename contains the separator % character and some spaces that need to be escaped. The second example shows the escaping of an entire URL using this function, which can have undesired results. The escape-html-uri function would have been a better choice.

Example	Return value
encode-for-uri("Sales % Numbers.pdf")	Sales%20%25%20Numbers.pdf
encode-for-uri("http://datypic.com/a%20URI#frag")	http%3A%2F%2Fdatypic.com%2Fa%2520URI%23frag

Related Functions

escape-html-uri, iri-to-uri

ends-with

Determines whether one string ends with another

Signature

```
ends-with($arg1 as xs:string?, $arg2 as xs:string?,
        $collation as xs:string) as xs:boolean
```

Usage Notes

This function returns an xs:boolean value indicating whether one string ($arg1) ends with the characters of a second string ($arg2). Trailing whitespace is significant, so you may want to use the normalize-space function to trim the strings before using this function.

Special Cases

- If $arg2 is a zero-length string or the empty sequence, the function returns true.
- If $arg1 is a zero-length string or the empty sequence, but $arg2 is not, the function returns false.
- If $collation is provided, the comparison uses that collation; otherwise, it uses the default collation.

Examples

Example	Return value
ends-with("query", "y")	true
ends-with("query", "query")	true
ends-with("query", "")	true
ends-with("query ", "y")	false
ends-with("", "y")	false

Related Functions

starts-with, contains, matches

error

Explicitly raise an error

Signature

```
error($error as xs:QName?, $description as xs:string,
      $error-object as item( )*) as none
```

Usage Notes

This function allows you to stop execution of the query, with a specific error message. This is useful if an unexpected or invalid condition exists, such as a missing or invalid data item. You can incorporate calls to the error function in your query to signal such problems to the query user. For example:

```
if (not ($product/number))
then error(QName("http://datypic.com/err", "ProdNumReq"),
          "Missing product number.")
else $product/number
```

results in a ProdNumReq error if $product has no number child.

How a processor will use the optional $description and $error-object arguments is implementation-dependent. Most processors will report the $description as part of the error message to the user.

Some processors may report the error name as a URI, where the local part is a fragment identifier, as in `http://datypic.com/err#ProdNumReq`.

The error function is the same function that the processor calls implicitly whenever there is an error during query evaluation. The return type of `none` is only used for the error function and is not available to query authors. It simply means that the error function never returns any value; evaluation of the query stops once the error function is called.

Remember that order of execution in XQuery is undefined. You can't always rely on the fact that your error test will be evaluated before some other expression that it is designed to guard. In fact, you can't always rely on the error expression being evaluated at all if, for example, it appears as part of a larger expression (perhaps a variable assignment) whose result is never used. However, simple cases such as `if ($condition) then $value else error()` should be safe.

Special Cases

- If no `$error` argument is provided, the error name defaults to `FOER0000` ("Unidentified error"), in the `http://www.w3.org/2005/xqt-errors` namespace.

Examples

Example
`error()`
`error (xs:QName("dty:ProdNumReq"))`[a]
`error(QName("http://datypic.com/err", "ProdNumReq"), "Missing number.")`
`error(QName("http://datypic.com/err", "ProdNumReq"), "Missing number.", $prod)`

[a] Assumes the `dty` prefix has been declared

Related Functions

trace

escape-html-uri

Escapes all non-ASCII characters in a string

Signature

escape-html-uri(**$uri as xs:string?**) as xs:string

Usage Notes

HTML agents require that some URI characters be escaped with their hexadecimal Unicode code point preceded by the % character. This includes non-ASCII characters and some ASCII characters, namely control characters, spaces, and several others.

The `escape-html-uri` function replaces each of these special characters with an escape sequence in the form %xx (possible repeating), where xx is two hexadecimal digits (in uppercase) that represent the character in UTF-8. For example, `édition.html` is changed to `%C3%A9dition.html`, with the é escaped as `%C3%A9`. Specifically, it escapes everything except

those ASCII characters whose decimal code point is between 32 and 126 inclusive. This allows these URIs to be appropriately handled by HTML agents such as web browsers, for example in HTML href attributes.

The way this function is specified is a pragmatic compromise. HTTP requires special characters such as spaces to be escaped. However, HTML documents often contain URIs designed for local use within the browser—for example, JavaScript function calls—and these local URIs (which are never sent over HTTP) will often fail if spaces and other ASCII characters are escaped. This function therefore only escapes non-ASCII characters.

Special Cases

- If $uri is the empty sequence, the function returns a zero-length string.

Examples

Example	Return value
escape-html-uri ("http://datypic.com/")	http://datypic.com/
escape-html-uri("édition.html")	%C3%A9dition.html
escape-html-uri ("/datypic.com/a URI#frag")	/datypic.com/a URI#frag

Related Functions

encode-for-uri, iri-to-uri

exactly-one

Verifies that a sequence contains exactly one item

Signature

```
exactly-one($arg as item( )*) as item( )
```

Usage Notes

If $arg contains one item, $arg is returned. Otherwise, the error "fn:exactly-one called with a sequence containing zero or more than one item" (FORG0005) is raised.

This function is useful when static typing is in effect, to avoid apparent static type errors. For example, to use a computed element constructor, you might be tempted to write the expression:

```
element {node-name($prod)}  { 563 }
```

However, if static typing is used, this expression causes a static error. This is because the node-name function returns 0 or 1 xs:QName values, while the computed element constructor requires that one and only one xs:QName value be provided. A static error can be avoided by using the expression:

```
element {exactly-one(node-name($prod))}  { 563 }
```

In this case, no static error is raised. Rather, a dynamic error is raised if node-name returns the empty sequence. For more information on static typing, see Chapter 14.

If static typing is NOT in effect, calling exactly-one is not usually necessary, but it does no harm. The effect is usually to make explicit a runtime type check that would otherwise have been done automatically.

Examples

Example	Return value
exactly-one(())	Error FORG0005
exactly-one("a")	a
exactly-one(("a", "b"))	Error FORG0005

Related Functions

one-or-more, zero-or-one

exists

Determines whether a sequence is *not* empty

Signature

exists(**$arg as item()***) as xs:boolean

Usage Notes

This function returns true if the sequence contains one or more items; it is the opposite of the empty function. It is often unnecessary to call the exists function because sequences are automatically converted to the effective Boolean value where a Boolean value is expected. For example, if you want to test whether there are any product elements in catalog.xml, you can use the if clause:

```
if (doc("catalog.xml")//product)  then ....
```

In this case, the sequence of selected product elements is converted to the Boolean value true if the sequence is not empty, and false if the sequence is empty. There is no need to call the exists function to determine this. But beware: this only works for node sequences, not for atomic values.

Examples

Example	Return value
exists(("a", "b", "c"))	true
exists("")	true
exists(())	false
exists(false())	true

Related Functions

empty, one-or-more

false

Constructs a Boolean `false` value

Signature

```
false() as xs:boolean
```

Usage Notes

This function, which takes no arguments, is useful for constructing the Boolean value false. XQuery uses the false() and true() functions instead of keywords false and true. This is most commonly used to supply a value in a function call where a Boolean value is required.

Example

The expression false() returns the xs:boolean value false.

Related Functions

true

floor

Rounds a number down to the next lowest integer

Signature

```
floor($arg as numeric?) as numeric?
```

Usage Notes

This function returns the largest integer that is not greater than $arg. It returns a numeric value of type xs:float, xs:double, xs:decimal, or xs:integer, depending on which type the argument is derived from. If $arg is untyped, it is cast to xs:double.

Special Cases

- If $arg is the empty sequence, the function returns the empty sequence.
- If $arg is one of the values 0, -0, NaN, INF, or -INF, the function returns this same value.

Examples

Example	Return value
floor(5)	5
floor(5.1)	5
floor(5.7)	5
floor(-5.1)	-6
floor(-5.7)	-6
floor(())	()

Related Functions

ceiling, round, round-half-to-even

hours-from-dateTime

Gets the hour portion of a date/time

Signature

 hours-from-dateTime($arg as xs:dateTime?) as xs:integer?

Usage Notes

This function returns the hour portion of an xs:dateTime value, as an integer between 0 and 23 inclusive.

Special Cases

- If $arg is the empty sequence, the function returns the empty sequence.
- If the time portion of $arg is 24:00:00, the function will return 0.

Examples

Example	Return value
hours-from-dateTime(xs:dateTime("2006-08-15T10:30:23"))	10
hours-from-dateTime(xs:dateTime("2006-08-15T10:30:23-05:00"))	10

Related Functions

hours-from-time

hours-from-duration

Gets the normalized number of hours in a duration

Signature

 hours-from-duration($arg as xs:duration?) as xs:integer?

Usage Notes

This function calculates the hours component of a normalized xs:duration value, as an integer between −23 and 23 (inclusive). This is not necessarily the same as the integer that appears before the H in the value. For example, if the duration is PT1H90M, the function returns 2 rather than 1. This is because 90 minutes is equal to 1.5 hours, and the normalized value is therefore PT2H30M. Likewise, if the duration is PT36H, the result is 12, because the normalized value is P1DT12H.

Special Cases

- If $arg is a negative duration, the function returns a negative value.
- If $arg is the empty sequence, the function returns the empty sequence.

Examples

Example	Return value
hours-from-duration(xs:duration("P1DT5H"))	5
hours-from-duration(xs:duration("-PT36H"))	-12
hours-from-duration(xs:duration("PT1H90M"))	2
hours-from-duration(xs:duration("PT2H59M"))	2
hours-from-duration(xs:duration("PT3600S"))	1
hours-from-duration(xs:duration("P1Y"))	0

hours-from-time
Gets the hour portion of a time

Signature

hours-from-time(**$arg as xs:time?**) as xs:integer?

Usage Notes

This function returns the hour portion of an xs:time value, as an integer between 0 and 23 inclusive.

Special Cases

- If $arg is the empty sequence, the function returns the empty sequence.
- If $arg is 24:00:00, the function returns 0.

Examples

Example	Return value
hours-from-time(xs:time("10:30:23"))	10
hours-from-time(xs:time("10:30:23-05:00"))	10

Related Functions

hours-from-dateTime

id
Returns elements by their IDs

Signature

id(**$arg as xs:string***, *$node as node()*) as element()*

Usage Notes

Given a sequence of IDs, this function returns the elements with those IDs. If $node is not provided, the function looks for elements in the same document as the current context item. If $node is provided, the function looks for elements in the same document as $node.

The strings in the $arg sequence can either be individual ID values or space-separated lists of ID values. Although $arg is a sequence of xs:string values, you can also pass values of type xs:IDREF or xs:IDREFS, since these types are derived from xs:string.

An element is considered to have a particular ID if either:

- It has an attribute, that is marked as an ID, that has that ID value.
- The type of the element itself is marked as an ID and its content is that particular ID value.

An element or attribute node can become "marked as an ID" by being validated by a schema where it is declared as having type xs:ID, or (for an attribute) being described in a DTD as being of type ID. Also, if it's name is xml:id, it is automatically considered to be an ID.

The default collation is not used to match ID values; a simple comparison of Unicode code points is used.

The function returns the nodes in document order, not the order designated by the sequence of $arg values. The result sequence contains no duplicate elements, even if an ID value was included twice in $arg.

Working with IDs and IDREFs is discussed in further detail in "Working with IDs" in Chapter 20.

Special Cases

- Any values in $arg that are not lexically valid IDs (i.e., XML NCNames) are ignored, even if there is an element with that invalid ID.
- If there is no element with the specified ID, an error is not raised, but no element is returned for that ID value.
- In the case of an invalid (but well-formed) document where more than one element has the same ID, the function returns the first element with that ID.
- If $arg is the empty sequence, the function returns the empty sequence.
- If no matching elements were found, the function returns the empty sequence.
- The error "No context document" (FODC0001) is raised if:
 — $node is not part of a document (its root is not a document node).
 — $node is not provided and the context node is not part of a document.
- If $node is not provided and no context item is defined, the error XPDY0002 is raised.
- If $node is not provided and the context item is an atomic value rather than a node, the error XPTY0004 is raised.

Examples

These examples use the input document book.xml shown in Example A-2. It is assumed that the input document has been validated and that the type of the id attribute is xs:ID.

Example	Return value
doc("book.xml")/id("preface")	The first section element
doc("book.xml")/id(("context", "preface"))	The first two section elements, in document order
doc("book.xml")/id("context preface")	The first two section elements, in document order

Example	Return value
doc("book.xml")//section[3]/secRef/id(@refs)	The second section element
doc("book.xml")//section[4]/secRef/id(@refs)	The second and third section elements
doc("book.xml")//secRef/id(@refs)	The second and third section elements
doc("book.xml")/ id(("preface", "noMatch", "in!valid"))	The first section element

Example A-2. XML document with IDs and IDREFs (book.xml)

```
<book>
  <section id="preface">This book introduces XQuery...
    The examples are downloadable<fnref ref="fn1"/>...
  </section>
  <section id="context">...</section>
  <section id="language">...Expressions, introduced
   in <secRef refs="context"/>, are...
  </section>
  <section id="types">...As described in
    <secRef refs="context language"/>, you can...
  </section>
  <fn fnid="fn1">See http://datypic.com.</fn>
</book>
```

Related Functions

idref

idref

Finds references to a specified set of IDs

Signature

idref(**$arg as xs:string***, *$node as node()*) as node()*

Usage Notes

This function returns the nodes (elements or attributes) that reference one of a specified sequence of IDs. If $node is not provided, the function looks for elements and attributes in the same document as the current context item. If $node is provided, the function looks for elements and attributes in the same document as $node.

In order to be considered to reference an ID, the node must be marked as an IDREF or IDREFS type, and it must contain that ID value. Generally, this means that it was declared to be of type xs:IDREF or xs:IDREFS in an in-scope schema definition (or the equivalent in a DTD). If it is an IDREFS value, only one of the values in the list need match the ID. The default collation is not used to match ID values; a simple comparison of Unicode code points is used.

The function returns the nodes in document order, not the order designated by the sequence of $arg values. The result sequence contains no duplicate elements, even if an ID value was included twice in $arg. However, there may be several elements or attributes in the results that reference the same ID.

Note that if the IDREF value is contained in an attribute, the function returns the attribute node, not the containing element. This is designed to handle cases where an element has more than one IDREF attribute and you need to know which one matched.

Special Cases

- Any values in $arg that are not lexically valid IDs (i.e., XML NCNames) are ignored, even if there is an element with a matching invalid IDREF.
- If $arg is the empty sequence, the function returns the empty sequence.
- If no matching nodes were found, the function returns the empty sequence.
- If $node is not part of a document (its root is not a document node), or if $node is not provided and the context node is not part of a document, the error "No context document" (FODC0001) is raised.
- If $node is not provided and no context item is defined, the error XPDY0002 is raised.
- If $node is not provided and the context item is an atomic value rather than a node, the error XPTY0004 is raised.

Working with IDs and IDREFs is discussed in further detail in "Working with IDs" in Chapter 20.

Examples

These examples use the input document book.xml shown in Example A-2. It is assumed that the input document has been validated, that the type of the id and fnid attributes is xs:ID, the type of the ref attribute is xs:IDREF, and the type of the refs attribute is xs:IDREFS.

Example	Return value
doc("book.xml")/idref("language")	The refs attribute of the second secRef element
doc("book.xml")/idref("context")	The refs attributes of both secRef elements
doc("book.xml")/idref(("context", "language"))	The refs attributes of both secRef elements
doc("book.xml")//fn[1]/idref(@fnid)	The ref attribute of the fnRef element
doc("book.xml")/idref(("language", "noMatch", "in!valid"))	The refs attribute of the second secRef element

Related Functions

id

implicit-timezone

Gets the implicit time zone used by the processor

Signature

```
implicit-timezone( ) as xs:dayTimeDuration
```

Usage Notes

This function returns the implicit time zone as an `xs:dayTimeDuration` value. The implicit time zone is used in comparisons and calculations involving date and time values that do not have explicitly defined time zones.

The implicit time zone is implementation-defined. In practice it will often default to the time zone used by the system clock in the operating system, or perhaps it will depend on the locale of the individual user.

Example

`implicit-timezone()` returns `-PT5H` if the implicit time zone is UTC minus five hours (also represented as `-05:00`).

in-scope-prefixes

Gets a list of all namespace prefixes that are in the scope of a specified element

Signature

 in-scope-prefixes($element as element()) as xs:string*

Usage Notes

This function returns a sequence of prefixes (as strings) that are used in the in-scope namespaces for the `$element` element. The results include a zero-length string if there is a default namespace declaration. It also always includes the `xml` prefix, which is built into the XML recommendation.

Note that the function uses *in-scope namespaces*, as opposed to *statically known namespaces*. That is, it returns information about the namespaces declared in the source document, not the namespaces declared in the query. The difference between in-scope and statically known namespaces is described further in "In-Scope Versus Statically Known Namespaces" in Chapter 10. More on working with namespaces and qualified names can be found in "Working with Qualified Names" in Chapter 20.

Example

The query:

 in-scope-prefixes(<prefList xmlns="http://datypic.com/prod"
 xmlns:prod2="http://datypic.com/prod2">xyz</prefList>)

returns the sequence (`""`, `"prod2"`, `"xml"`) in some arbitrary order.

Related Functions

`namespace-uri-for-prefix`

index-of

Determines where (and whether) an atomic value appears in a sequence

Signature

```
index-of($seqParam as xs:anyAtomicType*, $srchParam as xs:anyAtomicType,
        $collation as xs:string) as xs:integer*
```

Usage Notes

The $seqParam argument is the sequence to be searched, while $srchParam is the value to search for. This function returns a sequence of integers representing the position(s) of the value within the sequence, in order, starting with 1 (not 0).

The items in $seqParam are compared to those in $srchParam by their typed value, not their name or node identity. If either sequence contains nodes, those nodes are atomized to extract their atomic values. Untyped values are treated like strings.

Special Cases

- If $srchParam cannot be compared with a value in $seqParam, for example because $srchParam is a string and $seqParam contains an integer, it will not match that value, but it will not raise an error.
- If the $srchParam value does not appear in $seqParam, the function returns the empty sequence.
- If $seqParam is the empty sequence, the function returns the empty sequence.
- If $collation is provided, values of type xs:string are compared using that collation; otherwise, the default collation is used.

Examples

Example	Return value
index-of(("a", "b", "c"), "a")	1
index-of(("a", "b", "c"), "d")	()
index-of((4, 5, 6, 4), 4)	(1, 4)
index-of((4, 5, 6, 4), 04.0)	(1, 4)
index-of(("a", 5, 6), "a")	1
index-of((), "a")	()
index-of((<a>1, 1), <c>1</c>)	(1, 2)

Related Functions

position

insert-before

Inserts items into a sequence

Signature

```
insert-before($target as item( )*, $position as xs:integer,
            $inserts as item( )*) as item( )*
```

Usage Notes

This function returns a copy of the $target sequence with the item(s) in $inserts inserted at the position indicated by $position. Position numbers start at 1, not 0.

Special Cases

- If $inserts is the empty sequence, the function returns the $target sequence.
- If $target is the empty sequence, the function returns the $inserts sequence.
- If $position is greater than the number of items in $target, the $inserts items are appended to the end.
- If $position is less than 1, the $inserts items are inserted at the beginning.

Examples

Example	Return value
insert-before(("a", "b", "c"), 1, ("x", "y"))	("x", "y", "a", "b", "c")
insert-before(("a", "b", "c"), 2, ("x", "y"))	("a", "x", "y", "b", "c")
insert-before(("a", "b", "c"), 10, ("x", "y"))	("a", "b", "c", "x", "y")
insert-before(("a", "b", "c"), 0, ("x", "y"))	("x", "y", "a", "b", "c")
insert-before(("a", "b", "c"), 2, ())	("a", "b", "c")
insert-before((), 3, ("a", "b", "c"))	("a", "b", "c")

Related Functions

remove

iri-to-uri

Applies URI escaping rules to a string

Signature

iri-to-uri(**$uri-part as xs:string?**) as xs:string

Usage Notes

URIs require that some characters be escaped with their hexadecimal Unicode code point preceded by the % character. This includes non-ASCII characters and some ASCII characters, namely control characters, spaces, and several others.

The iri-to-uri function replaces each special character with an escape sequence in the form %xx (possible repeating), where xx is two hexadecimal digits (in uppercase) that represent the character in UTF-8. For example, édition.html is changed to %C3%A9dition.html, with the é escaped as %C3%A9.

All characters *except* the following are escaped:

- Letters a through z and A through Z
- Digits 0 through 9

- Hyphen (-), underscore (_), period (.), exclamation point (!), tilde (~), asterisk (*), apostrophe ('), parentheses ("(" and ")"), and hash mark (#)
- Semicolon (;), forward slash (/), question mark (?), colon (:), at sign (@), ampersand (&), equals sign (=), plus sign (+), dollar sign ($), comma (,), square brackets ([and]), and percent sign (%)

The last set of characters specified in the preceding list is generally used to delimit parts of URIs. If you are escaping a single step of a URI path (as opposed to an entire URI), it is better to use the encode-for-uri function, which does escape these characters.

Special Cases

- If $uri-part is the empty sequence, the function returns a zero-length string.

Examples

Example	Return value
iri-to-uri ("http://datypic.com/édition 2.html")	http://datypic.com/%C3%A9dition%202.html
iri-to-uri ("http://datypic.com/Sales Numbers.pdf")	http://datypic.com/Sales%20Numbers.pdf
iri-to-uri ("http://datypic.com/Sales % Numbers.pdf")	http://datypic.com/Sales%20%%20Numbers.pdf

Related Functions

encode-for-uri, escape-html-uri

lang
Tests whether the language of a node matches a specified language

Signature

lang(**$testlang as xs:string?**, *$node as node()*) as xs:boolean

Usage Notes

The language of a node is determined by the existence of an xml:lang attribute on the node itself or among its ancestors. The lang function can be used on any node, not just one containing string values. It is often used in the predicates of path expressions to filter data for a particular language.

The $testlang argument specifies the language to test. The function returns true if the relevant xml:lang attribute of the $node has a value that matches the $testlang value. The function returns false if the relevant xml:lang attribute does not match $testlang, or if there is no relevant xml:lang attribute.

The relevant xml:lang attribute is the one that appears as an attribute of the context node itself, or of one of its ancestors. If more than one xml:lang attribute can be found among the node and its ancestors, the nearest one applies.

The matching process is case-insensitive. If $testlang is en, it matches the xml:lang value EN, and vice versa. Also, the value of the xml:lang attribute can be a sublanguage of the $testlang value. For example, en-US, en-UK, and en-US-UK are all sublanguages of en. Therefore, if $testlang is en, and xml:lang is en-US, the node will be matched. This does not work in reverse; if $testlang is en-US, and xml:lang is en, it will *not* match.

More information on the format of languages can be found with the description of the xs:language type in Appendix B.

Special Cases

- If $testlang is the empty sequence, it is treated like a zero-length string.
- If $node is not provided, the context item is used.
- If no xml:lang attributes exist on the ancestors of a node, the function will return false.
- If $node is not provided, and the context item is undefined, the error XPDY0002 is raised.
- If $node is not provided, and the context item is not a node, the error XPTY0004 is raised.

Examples

These examples make use of the input document shown in Example A-3.

Example	Return value
doc("descs.xml")//desc[lang("en")]	The first desc element
doc("descs.xml")//desc[lang("en-US")]	The first desc element
doc("descs.xml")//desc[lang("fr")]	The second desc element
doc("descs.xml")//desc/line[lang("en")]	The first line element
doc("descs.xml")/desclist[lang("en-US")]	()
doc("descs.xml")//desc[lang("FR")]	The second desc element

Example A-3. Document with xml:lang attributes specified (descs.xml)

```
<desclist xml:lang="en">
  <desc xml:lang="en-US">
    <line>The first line of the description.</line>
  </desc>
  <desc xml:lang="fr">
    <line>La premi&#232;re ligne de la déscription.</line>
  </desc>
</desclist>
```

last

Gets the number of items in the current context

Signature

```
last() as xs:integer
```

Usage Notes

The last function returns an integer representing the number of items in the current context. It is most often used in the predicate of path expressions, to retrieve the last item. For example, catalog/product[last()] returns the last product child of catalog. That is because the last function returns 4, which serves as a positional predicate to retrieve the fourth product. The last function is also useful for testing whether an item is the last one in the sequence.

Special Cases

- If the context item is undefined, the error XPDY0002 is raised.

Examples

doc("catalog.xml")/catalog/product[last()] returns the last product child of catalog. Example A-4 demonstrates how you might test whether an item is the last one in the sequence. It shows a query that returns a list of all the product numbers, separated by commas. However, after the last product number, it includes a period rather than a comma. It uses the last function and an is expression to compare each product element to the last one in the catalog.

Example A-4. Example of the last function

Query
```
let $catalog := doc("catalog.xml")/catalog
for $prod in $catalog/product
return concat($prod/number,
          (if ($prod is $catalog/product[last( )]) then (".") else (", ")))
```
Results
```
557, 563, 443, 784.
```

Related Functions

position

local-name

Gets the local part of a node name, as a string

Signature

local-name(*$arg as node()?*) as xs:string

Usage Notes

This function is useful only for element, attribute, and processing instruction nodes. For an element or attribute, this is simply its name, stripped of any prefix it might have.

To find elements with a particular local name, instead of writing a/*[local-name()='nnn'], you can write a/*:nnn. However, the predicate test is useful if the name you are looking for is variable.

Special Cases

- If $arg is not provided, the context node is used.
- The function returns a zero-length string if:
 - — $arg is the empty sequence.
 - — $arg is a node that does not have a name (i.e., a comment, document, or text node).
- If $arg is a processing instruction node, the function returns its target.
- If $arg is not provided, and the context item is undefined, the error XPDY0002 is raised.
- If $arg is not provided, and the context item is not a node, the error XPTY0004 is raised.

Examples

These examples use the input document names.xml shown in Example A-5. They also assume that the prefixes pre and unpre have been mapped to the namespaces http://datypic.com/pre and http://datypic.com/unpre, respectively, in the query prolog.

Example	Return value
local-name(doc("names.xml")//noNamespace)	noNamespace
local-name(doc("names.xml")//pre:prefixed)	prefixed
local-name(doc("names.xml")//unpre:unprefixed)	unprefixed
local-name(doc("names.xml")//@pre:prefAttr)	prefAttr
local-name(doc("names.xml")//@noNSAttr)	noNSAttr

Example A-5. Namespaces in XML (names.xml)

```
<noNamespace>
  <pre:prefixed xmlns="http://datypic.com/unpre"
         xmlns:pre="http://datypic.com/pre">
    <unprefixed pre:prefAttr="a" noNSAttr="b">123</unprefixed>
  </pre:prefixed>
</noNamespace>
```

Related Functions

name, node-name, namespace-uri

local-name-from-QName

Gets the local part of a QName

Signature

```
local-name-from-QName($arg as xs:QName?) as xs:NCName?
```

Usage Notes

This function returns the local part of an xs:QName. If you want to retrieve the local part of an element or attribute name, you should consider using the local-name function instead; it requires one less step.

Special Cases

- If $arg is the empty sequence, the function returns the empty sequence.

Examples

Example	Return value
local-name-from-QName(QName("http://datypic.com/prod", "number"))	number
local-name-from-QName(QName ("", "number"))	number
local-name-from-QName(())	()

Related Functions

local-name, namespace-uri-from-QName, resolve-QName, QName

lower-case

Converts a string to lowercase

Signature

 lower-case(**$arg as xs:string?**) as xs:string

Usage Notes

The mappings between lowercase and uppercase characters are determined by Unicode case mappings. If a character in $arg does not have a corresponding lowercase character, it is included in the result string unchanged.

For English, you can do a case-blind comparison by writing lower-case($A)=lower-case($B) (or use upper-case instead). However this doesn't always work well for other languages. It's better to use a case-insensitive collation.

Special Cases

- If $arg is the empty sequence, the function returns a zero-length string.

Examples

Example	Return value
lower-case("QUERY")	query
lower-case("Query")	query
lower-case("QUERY123")	query123

Related Functions

upper-case

matches

Determines whether a string matches a particular pattern

Signature

```
matches($input as xs:string?, $pattern as xs:string,
        $flags as xs:string) as xs:boolean
```

Usage Notes

The $pattern argument is a regular expression, whose syntax is covered in Chapter 18. Unlike many of the string-related functions, the matches function does not use collations at all. Regular expression matching is solely based on Unicode code points. Unless the anchors ^ or $ are used, the function returns true if any substring of $input matches the regular expression.

The $flags parameter allows for additional options in the interpretation of the regular expression. It is discussed in detail in "Using Flags" in Chapter 18.

Special Cases

- If $input is the empty sequence, it is treated like a zero-length string.
- If $pattern is a zero-length string, the function will return true.
- If $pattern is not a valid regular expression, the error "Invalid regular expression" (FORX0002) is raised.
- If $flags contains unsupported options, the error "Invalid regular expression flags" (FORX0001) is raised.

Examples

Example	Return value
matches("query", "q")	true
matches("query", "ue")	true
matches("query", "^qu")	true
matches("query", "qu$")	false
matches("query", "[ux]")	true
matches("query", "q.*")	true
matches("query", "[a-z]{5}")	true
matches((), "q")	false
matches("query", "[qu")	Error FORX0002

The additional examples shown in the following table use the $flags argument. They assume that the variable $address is bound to the following string (the line break is significant):

```
123 Main Street
Traverse City, MI 49684
```

Example	Return value
matches($address, "Street.*City")	false
matches($address, "Street.*City", "s")	true
matches($address, "Street$")	false
matches($address, "Street$", "m")	true
matches($address, "street")	false
matches($address, "street", "i")	true
matches($address, "Main Street")	true
matches($address, "Main Street", "x")	false
matches($address, "Main \s Street", "x")	true
matches($address, "street$", "im")	true
matches($address, "Street$", "q")	Error FORX0001

Related Functions

contains

max

<div align="right">Returns the maximum of the values in a sequence</div>

Signature

max(**$arg as xs:anyAtomicType***, *$collation as xs:string*) as xs:anyAtomicType?

Usage Notes

The $arg sequence can only contain values of one type, or of types derived from it. The one exception is that they can be all numeric (of different numeric types), in which case numeric promotion rules apply. That type must be ordered; it must be possible to compare the values using the < and > operators.

This function assumes untyped values are numeric unless they are explicitly cast to xs:string. To treat untyped data as strings, use the string function as shown in the last example.

The max function returns an atomic value, not the node that contains that value. For example, the expression:

max(doc("catalog.xml")//number)

will return the number 784, not the number element that contains 784.

Special Cases

- If $arg is the empty sequence, the function returns the empty sequence.
- If $arg contains the value NaN, the function returns NaN.
- If $arg contains untyped values that cannot be cast to xs:double, the error "Invalid value for cast/constructor" (FORG0001) is raised.
- If $arg contains values of a type that does not support the < and > operators, the error "Invalid argument type" (FORG0006) is raised.

- If $arg contains values of various types, the error "Invalid argument type" (FORG0006) is raised.
- If $arg contains a date or time with no time zone, it is given the implicit time zone.
- If $collation is provided, values of type xs:string are compared using that collation; otherwise, the default collation is used.

Examples

Example	Return value
max((2, 1, 5, 4, 3))	5
max(("a", "b", "c"))	c
max((xs:date("1999-04-15"), current-date()))	The current date
max(("a", "b", 1))	Error FORG0006
max(2)	2
max(doc("order.xml")//item/@dept)	Type error, if dept is untyped
max(doc("order.xml")//item/string(@dept))	WMN

Related Functions

min

min

Returns the minimum of the values in a sequence

Signature

min(**$arg as xs:anyAtomicType***, *$collation as xs:string*) as xs:anyAtomicType?

Usage Notes

The $arg sequence can only contain values of one type, or a type derived from it. The one exception is that they can be all numeric, in which case numeric promotion rules apply. That type must be ordered; it must be possible to compare the values using the ⟨ and ⟩ operators.

This function assumes untyped values are numeric unless they are explicitly cast to xs:string. To treat untyped data as strings, use the string function as shown in the last example.

The min function returns an atomic value, not the node that contains that value. For example, the expression:

 min(doc("catalog.xml")//number)

will return the number 443, not the number element that contains 443.

Special Cases

- If $arg is the empty sequence, the function returns the empty sequence.
- If $arg contains untyped values that cannot be cast to xs:double, the error "Invalid value for cast/constructor" (FORG0001) is raised.

- If $arg contains values of a type that does not support the < and > operators, the error "Invalid argument type" (FORG0006) is raised.
- If $arg contains values of various types, the error "Invalid argument type" (FORG0006) is raised.
- If $arg contains a date or time with no time zone, it is assumed to be in the implicit time zone.
- If $collation is provided, values of type xs:string are compared using that collation; otherwise, the default collation is used. Collations are described in Chapter 17.

Examples

Example	Return value
min((2.0, 1, 3.5, 4))	1
min(("a", "b", "c"))	a
min(doc("order.xml")//item/@color)	Error FORG0006, if color is untyped
min(doc("order.xml")//item//string(@color))	""
min(doc("order.xml")//item/@color/string(.))	black

Note that the last example evaluates to black because the string function is only called for existing color attributes. The second-to-last example returns a zero-length string because it finds the string value of *every* item's color attribute, whether it has one or not.

Related Functions

max

minutes-from-dateTime

Gets the minutes portion of a date/time

Signature

minutes-from-dateTime(**$arg as xs:dateTime?**) as xs:integer?

Usage Notes

This function returns the minutes portion of an xs:dateTime value, as an integer between 0 and 59 inclusive.

Special Cases

- If $arg is the empty sequence, the function returns the empty sequence.

Example

minutes-from-dateTime(xs:dateTime("2006-08-15T10:30:23")) returns 30.

Related Functions

minutes-from-time

minutes-from-duration

Gets the normalized number of minutes in a duration

Signature

```
minutes-from-duration($arg as xs:duration?) as xs:integer?
```

Usage Notes

This function calculates the minutes component of a normalized xs:duration value, as an integer between –59 and 59 inclusive. This is not necessarily the same as the integer that appears before the M in the value. For example, if the duration is PT1M90S, the function returns 2 rather than 1. This is because 90 seconds is equal to 1.5 minutes, and the normalized value is therefore PT2M30S. Likewise, if the duration is PT90M, the result is 30, because the normalized value is PT1H30M.

Special Cases

- If $arg is a negative duration, the function returns a negative value.
- If $arg is the empty sequence, the function returns the empty sequence.

Examples

Example	Return value
minutes-from-duration(xs:duration("PT30M"))	30
minutes-from-duration(xs:duration("-PT90M"))	-30
minutes-from-duration(xs:duration("PT1M90S"))	2
minutes-from-duration(xs:duration("PT3H"))	0
minutes-from-duration(xs:duration("PT60M"))	0

minutes-from-time

Gets the minutes portion of a time

Signature

```
minutes-from-time($arg as xs:time?) as xs:integer?
```

Usage Notes

This function returns the minutes portion of an xs:time value, as an integer between 0 and 59 inclusive.

Special Cases

- If $arg is the empty sequence, the function returns the empty sequence.

Example

minutes-from-time(xs:time("10:30:23")) returns 30.

Related Functions

minutes-from-dateTime

month-from-date
Gets the month portion of a date

Signature

month-from-date(**$arg as xs:date?**) as xs:integer?

Usage Notes

This function returns the month portion of an xs:date value, as an integer between 1 and 12 inclusive.

Special Cases

- If $arg is the empty sequence, the function returns the empty sequence.

Example

month-from-date(xs:date("2006-08-15")) returns 8.

Related Functions

month-from-dateTime

month-from-dateTime
Gets the month portion of a date/time

Signature

month-from-dateTime(**$arg as xs:dateTime?**) as xs:integer?

Usage Notes

This function returns the month portion of an xs:dateTime value, as an integer between 1 and 12 inclusive.

Special Cases

- If $arg is the empty sequence, the function returns the empty sequence.

Example

month-from-dateTime(xs:dateTime("2006-08-15T10:30:23")) returns 8.

Related Functions

month-from-date

months-from-duration

Gets the normalized number of months in a duration

Signature

```
months-from-duration($arg as xs:duration?) as xs:integer?
```

Usage Notes

This function calculates the months component of a normalized xs:duration value, as an integer between –11 and 11 inclusive. This is not necessarily the same as the integer that appears before the M in the value. For example, if the duration is P18M, the function returns 6 rather than 18. This is because 12 of those months are considered to be one year, and the normalized value is therefore P1Y6M.

Special Cases

- If $arg is a negative duration, the function returns a negative value.
- If $arg is the empty sequence, the function returns the empty sequence.

Examples

Example	Return value
months-from-duration(xs:duration("P3M"))	3
months-from-duration(xs:duration("-P18M"))	-6
months-from-duration(xs:duration("P1Y"))	0
months-from-duration(xs:duration("P12M"))	0
months-from-duration(xs:duration("P31D"))	0

name

Gets the qualified name of a node as a string

Signature

```
name($arg as node( )?) as xs:string
```

Usage Notes

This function returns a string that consists of the namespace prefix and colon (:), concatenated with the local part of the name. If the $arg node's name is not in a namespace, the function returns the local part of the name, with no prefix. If the name is associated with the default namespace, the resulting name will not be prefixed.

The name function returns a value that depends on the choice of prefixes in the source document. This makes it well suited for displaying the name, for example in error messages, but it should never be used to test the name, because choice of prefixes shouldn't affect the result. For this purpose, use node-name instead.

Special Cases

- If $arg is not provided, the context node is used.
- The function returns a zero-length string if:
 - — $arg is the empty sequence.
 - — $arg is a node that does not have a name (i.e., a document, comment, or text node).
- If $arg is a processing instruction node, the function returns its target.
- If $arg is not provided, and the context item is undefined, the error XPDY0002 is raised.
- If $arg is not provided, and the context item is not a node, the error XPTY0004 is raised.

Examples

These examples use the input document `names.xml` shown in Example A-5, in the section "local-name." They also assume that the prefixes `pre2` and `unpre2` have been mapped to the namespaces `http://datypic.com/pre` and `http://datypic.com/unpre`, respectively, in the query prolog.

The prefixes `pre2` and `unpre2` are used rather than `pre` and `unpre` to demonstrate that when selecting nodes from an instance document, the prefix used in the instance document is returned (not the query).

Example	Return value
`name(doc("names.xml")//noNamespace)`	`noNamespace`
`name(doc("names.xml")//pre2:prefixed)`	`pre:prefixed`
`name(doc("names.xml")//unpre2:unprefixed)`	`unprefixed`
`name(doc("names.xml")//@pre2:prefAttr)`	`pre:prefAttr`
`name(doc("names.xml")//@noNSAttr)`	`noNSAttr`

Related Functions

`local-name, node-name, namespace-uri`

namespace-uri

Gets the namespace part of an element or attribute node name

Signature

`namespace-uri($arg as node()?) as xs:anyURI`

Usage Notes

This function returns the namespace part of the element or attribute name. This is the namespace that is mapped to its prefix, or the default namespace if it is unprefixed. If the element or attribute name is not in a namespace, a zero-length value is returned.

Special Cases

- If $arg is not provided, the context node is used.
- The function returns a zero-length xs:anyURI value if:
 - $arg is the empty sequence.
 - $arg is a kind of node that does not have a namespace (i.e., a document, comment, processing instruction or text node).
 - $arg is an element or attribute whose name is not in a namespace.
- If $arg is not provided, and the context item is undefined, the error XPDY0002 is raised.
- If $arg is not provided, and the context item is not a node, the error XPTY0004 is raised.

Examples

These examples use the input document names.xml shown in Example A-5, in the section "local-name." They also assume that the prefixes pre and unpre have been mapped to the namespaces http://datypic.com/pre and http://datypic.com/unpre, respectively, in the query prolog.

Example	Return value
namespace-uri(doc("names.xml")//noNamespace)	A zero-length URI value
namespace-uri(doc("names.xml")//pre:prefixed)	http://datypic.com/pre
namespace-uri (doc("names.xml")//unpre:unprefixed)	http://datypic.com/unpre
namespace-uri(doc("names.xml")//@pre:prefAttr)	http://datypic.com/pre
namespace-uri(doc("names.xml")//@noNSAttr)	A zero-length URI value

Related Functions

local-name, name, node-name

namespace-uri-for-prefix

Gets the namespace mapped to a particular prefix, within the scope of a particular element

Signature

```
namespace-uri-for-prefix($prefix as xs:string?,
                         $element as element()) as xs:anyURI?
```

Usage Notes

This function returns the namespace mapped to $prefix using the in-scope namespaces of $element. If $prefix is a zero-length string or the empty sequence, the function returns the default namespace, if any.

The function is most often used in conjunction with the in-scope-prefixes function to determine all the namespaces that are declared on a particular element, including any namespaces that appear to be unused.

Special Cases

- If $prefix is not mapped to a namespace in scope, the function returns the empty sequence.
- If $prefix is a zero-length string or the empty sequence, and there is no default namespace, the function returns the empty sequence.

Examples

These examples use the input document names.xml shown in Example A-5, in the section "local-name." They also assume that the prefixes pre and unpre have been mapped to the namespaces http://datypic.com/pre and http://datypic.com/unpre, respectively, in the query prolog.

Example	Return value
namespace-uri-for-prefix("", doc("names.xml")//noNamespace)	()
namespace-uri-for-prefix("pre", doc("names.xml")//noNamespace)	()
namespace-uri-for-prefix("pre", doc("names.xml")//pre:prefixed)	http://datypic.com/pre
namespace-uri-for-prefix("", doc("names.xml")//unpre:unprefixed)	http://datypic.com/unpre
namespace-uri-for-prefix("pre", doc("names.xml")//unpre:unprefixed)	http://datypic.com/pre

Related Functions

in-scope-prefixes, resolve-QName, QName

namespace-uri-from-QName

Gets the namespace URI part of a QName

Signature

namespace-uri-from-QName(**$arg as xs:QName?**) as xs:anyURI?

Usage Notes

This function returns the namespace part of an xs:QName. If you want to retrieve the namespace of an element or attribute name, you should consider using the namespace-uri function instead; it saves a step.

Special Cases

- If $arg is in no namespace, the function returns a zero-length string.
- If $arg is the empty sequence, the function returns the empty sequence.

Examples

Example	Return value
namespace-uri-from-QName(QName ("http://datypic.com/pre", "prefixed"))	http://datypic.com/pre
namespace-uri-from-QName(QName ("", "unprefixed"))	A zero-length URI value
namespace-uri-from-QName(())	()

Related Functions

local-name-from-QName, resolve-QName, QName, namespace-uri, namespace-uri-for-prefix

nilled

Determines whether an element is nilled

Signature

nilled(**$arg as node()?**) as xs:boolean?

Usage Notes

In a schema, element declarations can designate elements as nillable. This allows them to appear in an instance document empty, even if their type would otherwise require them to have some content (character data or children or both).

An element is not considered to be nilled just because it is empty. For an element to be nilled, it must have an attribute xsi:nil whose value is true. Nilled elements are always empty; it is not valid for an element to have content and also have the xsi:nil attribute set to true.

On the other hand, some elements may be validly empty, but not be nilled. This may occur if an element has a complex type that specifies all optional children, or a simple type that allows blank values, such as xs:string. To test for an empty (but not necessarily nilled) element, you can use the expression string($node) = "".

It is useful to be able to check for a nilled element using the nilled function to avoid unexpected results. For example, suppose you want to subtract the value of a discount element from the value of a price element. If the discount element is nilled, its typed value will be the empty sequence, and the result of the expression price - discount will be the empty sequence. You can avoid this using the expression price - (if nilled(discount) then 0 else discount).

Special Cases

- If $arg is not an element, the function returns the empty sequence.
- If $arg is the empty sequence, the function returns the empty sequence.

Examples

These examples use the input document `nils.xml` shown in Example A-6.

Example	Return value
`nilled(doc("nils.xml")//child[1])`	false
`nilled(doc("nils.xml")//child[2])`	true
`nilled(doc("nils.xml")//child[3])`	false
`nilled(doc("nils.xml")//child[4])`	false
`nilled(doc("nils.xml")//child[5])`	false

Example A-6. Nilled elements (nils.xml)

```
<root xmlns:xsi="http://www.w3.org/2001/XMLSchema-instance">
  <child>12</child>
  <child xsi:nil="true"></child>
  <child></child>
  <child/>
  <child xsi:nil="false"></child>
</root>
```

Related Functions

empty, exists

node-name Gets the qualified name of a node

Signature

> `node-name($arg as node()?)` as `xs:QName?`

Usage Notes

This function returns the qualified name of a node as an `xs:QName`. It is useful only for element, attribute, and processing instruction nodes. For elements and attributes, it is simply the names used in XML documents. If the node's name is not in any namespace, the namespace portion of the QName is empty, while the local part is the appropriate name.

Special Cases

- If $arg does not have a name (because it is a text, comment, or document node), the function returns the empty sequence.
- If $arg is a processing instruction node, the function returns its target.
- If $arg is the empty sequence, the function returns the empty sequence.

Examples

These examples use the input document `names.xml` shown in Example A-5, in the section "local-name." They also assume that the prefixes `pre2` and `unpre2` have been mapped to the namespaces `http://datypic.com/pre` and `http://datypic.com/unpre`, respectively, in the query prolog.

The prefix pre2 is used rather than pre to demonstrate that when selecting nodes from an instance document, it is the prefix used in the instance document is returned (not the query). Although prefixes are technically irrelevant, they are saved in QName values by XQuery processors.

Example	Return value (xs:QName)
node-name(doc("names.xml")//noNamespace)	Namespace: empty Prefix: empty Local part: noNamespace
node-name (doc("names.xml")//pre2:prefixed)	Namespace: http://datypic.com/pre Prefix: pre Local part: prefixed
node-name (doc("names.xml")//unpre2: unprefixed)	Namespace: http://datypic.com/unpre Prefix: empty Local part: unprefixed
node-name (doc("names.xml")//@pre2:prefAttr)	Namespace: http://datypic.com/pre Prefix: pre Local part: prefAttr
node-name(doc("names.xml")//@noNSAttr)	Namespace: empty Prefix: empty Local part: noNSAttr

Related Functions

local-name, name, namespace-uri

normalize-space

Normalize the whitespace in a string

Signature

normalize-space($arg as xs:string?) as xs:string

Usage Notes

This function collapses whitespace in a string. Specifically, it performs three steps:

1. Replaces each carriage return (#xD), line feed (#xA), and tab (#x9) character with a single space (#x20)
2. Collapses all consecutive spaces into a single space
3. Removes all leading and trailing spaces

Special Cases

- If $arg is the empty sequence, the function returns a zero-length string.
- If $arg is not provided, the function uses the value of the context item.
- If $arg is not provided and the context item is undefined, the error XPDY0002 is raised.

Examples

Example	Return value
normalize-space("query")	query
normalize-space(" query ")	query
normalize-space("xml query")	xml query
normalize-space("xml query")	xml query
normalize-space("xml query")[a]	xml query
normalize-space("")	A zero-length string
normalize-space(" ")	A zero-length string
normalize-space(())	A zero-length string
normalize-space(<element> query </element>)	query

[a] The line break in this example is significant.

normalize-unicode
Performs Unicode normalization on a string

Signature

```
normalize-unicode($arg as xs:string?,
                $normalizationForm as xs:string) as xs:string
```

Usage Notes

Unicode normalization allows text to be compared without regard to subtle variations in character representation. It replaces certain characters with equivalent representations. Two normalized values can then be compared to determine whether they are the same. Unicode normalization is also useful for allowing character strings to be sorted appropriately.

The $normalizationForm argument controls which normalization form is used, and hence which characters are replaced. Examples of replacements that might be made include:

- Some characters may be replaced by equivalent characters. The symbol £ (U+FFE1) is converted to an equivalent symbol, £ (U+00A3) using the form NFKC.

- Some characters with accents or other marks represented by one code point may be decomposed to an equivalent representation that has two or more code points. The ç character (U+00E7) is changed to a representation that uses two code points (U+0063, which is "c", and U+0327, which is the cedilla) using form NFKD. Other normalization forms may combine the two code points into a single code point.

- Some characters that represent symbols may be replaced by letters or other characters. The symbol dℓ (U+3397) is replaced by the two letters dl (U+0064 + U+006C) using the form NFKC. This change is not made when using the form NFC.

Valid values for $normalizationForm are listed in Table A-5. The value may be specified with leading or trailing spaces, in upper-, lower-, or mixed case. All implementations support the value NFC; some implementations may support the other values listed, as well as additional normalization forms.

Table A-5. Valid values for the $normalizationForm argument

Value	Meaning
NFC	Unicode Normalization Form C (NFC).
NFD	Unicode Normalization Form D (NFD).
NFKC	Unicode Normalization Form KC (NFKC).
NFKD	Unicode Normalization Form KD (NFKD).
FULLY-NORMALIZED	The fully normalized form, according to the W3C definition. This form takes into account XML constructs such as entity references and CDATA sections in text. [a]
Zero-length string	No normalization is performed.

[a] Essentially, "fully normalized" is NFC with the additional rule that "combining characters" (such as free-standing accents) may not appear on their own at the start of a string. The advantage of this form is that concatenating two fully normalized strings will always give a fully normalized string. For more information, see *Character Model for the World Wide Web* at *http://www.w3.org/TR/charmod*.

Special Cases

- If $normalizationForm is not provided, NFC is used as a default.
- If $normalizationForm is a form that is not supported by the implementation, the error "Unsupported normalization form" (FOCH0003) is raised.
- If $normalizationForm is a zero-length string, no normalization is performed.
- If $arg is the empty sequence, the function returns a zero-length string.

Examples

Example	Return value
normalize-unicode("query")	query
normalize-unicode("query", "")	query
normalize-unicode("£", "NFKC")	£
normalize-unicode("leçon", "NFKD")	lec̦on
normalize-unicode("15 dℓ")	15 dℓ
normalize-unicode("15 dℓ", "NFKC")	15 dl

For more information on Unicode normalization forms, see *http://www.unicode.org/unicode/reports/tr15*. The normalization charts, which identify the replacements for each character, for each form, can be found at *http://www.unicode.org/charts/normalization*.

not

Negates any Boolean value, turning false to true and true to false

Signature

```
not($arg as item( )*) as xs:boolean
```

Usage Notes

This function accepts a sequence of items, from which it calculates the effective Boolean value of the sequence as a whole before negating it. This means that when $arg is either a single Boolean value false, a zero-length string, the number 0 or NaN, or the empty

sequence, it returns true. Otherwise, it usually returns false. The detailed rules for evaluating the effective Boolean value of a sequence are described in "Effective Boolean Value" in Chapter 11.

Special Cases

- If the effective Boolean value of $arg is undefined, for example because $arg is a sequence of multiple atomic values, the error "Invalid argument type" (FORG0006) is raised.

Examples

Example	Return value
not($price > 20)	false if $price is greater than 20
not(doc("catalog.xml")//product)	false if there is at least one product element in catalog.xml
not(true())	false
not(())	true
not("")	true
not(0)	true
not(<e>false</e>)	false

number

Constructs an xs:double value

Signature

 number($arg as xs:anyAtomicType?) as xs:double

Usage Notes

This function constructs an xs:double value either from a node that contains a number, or from an atomic value. This function is useful for telling the processor to treat a node or value as a number, regardless of its declared type (if any). It returns the argument cast as an xs:double.

The difference between using the number function and the xs:double constructor is that the number function returns the value NaN in the case that the argument cannot be cast to a numeric value, whereas the xs:double constructor will raise an error.

Special Cases

- If $arg is not provided, the number function uses the context item.
- If $arg is not provided, and the context item is undefined, the error XPDY0002 is raised.
- The function returns the value NaN in the case that the argument cannot be cast to a numeric value, in any of the following situations:
 - No argument is passed to it and the context item is undefined, or the context item is not a node.
 - $arg is the empty sequence.
 - $arg is a value that cannot be cast to xs:double.

Examples

Example	Return value
number(doc("prices.xml")//prod[1]/price)	29.99
number(doc("prices.xml")//prod/price)	Error XPTY0004
number(doc("prices.xml")//prod[1]/@currency)	NaN
number("29.99")	29.99
number("ABC")	NaN
number(())	NaN
doc("prices.xml")//prod/price[number() > 35]	The two price elements with values over 35

one-or-more

Verifies that a sequence contains one or more items

Signature

```
one-or-more($arg as item( )*) as item( )+
```

Usage Notes

If $arg contains one or more items, $arg is returned. Otherwise, the error "fn:one-or-more called with a sequence containing zero items" (FORG0004) is raised.

This function is useful when static typing is in effect, to avoid apparent static type errors. For example, suppose you wanted to call a user-defined concatNames function that takes as an argument one or more strings (but not the empty sequence). To use the function, you might be tempted to write the expression:

```
local:concatNames (doc("catalog.xml")//name)
```

However, if static typing is used, this expression causes a static error if the name element is optional in the schema. This is because the path expression might return the empty sequence, while the concatNames function requires that at least one string be provided. A static error can be avoided by using the expression:

```
local:concatNames (one-or-more(doc("catalog.xml")//name))
```

In this case, no static error is raised. Rather, a dynamic error is raised if the path expression returns the empty sequence. For more information on static typing, see Chapter 14.

If static typing is *not* in effect, calling one-or-more is not usually necessary, but it does no harm. The effect is usually to make explicit a runtime type check that would otherwise have been done automatically.

Examples

Example	Return value
one-or-more(())	Error FORG0004
one-or-more("a")	a
one-or-more(("a", "b"))	("a", "b")

Related Functions

zero-or-one, exactly-one

position
Gets the position of the context item within the context sequence

Signature

```
position() as xs:integer
```

Usage Notes

This function returns an integer representing the position (starting with 1, not 0) of the current context item within the context sequence (the current sequence of items being processed). In XQuery, the position function is almost invariably used in predicates (in square brackets) to test the relative position of a node.

Special Cases

- If the context item is undefined, the error XPDY0002 is raised.

Examples

The expression:

```
doc("catalog.xml")/catalog/product[position() < 3]
```

returns the first two product children of catalog. You could also select the first two children of product, with any name, using a wildcard, as in:

```
doc("catalog.xml")/catalog/product/*[position() < 3]
```

Note that the expression product[position() = 3] is equal to the expression product[3], so the position function is not very useful in this case. However, you might use the expression:

```
doc("catalog.xml")/catalog/product[position() = (1 to 3)]
```

to get the first three products.

Related Functions

last

prefix-from-QName
Gets the prefix associated with a particular qualified name

Signature

```
prefix-from-QName($arg as xs:QName?) as xs:NCName?
```

Usage Notes

This function returns the prefix associated with a particular qualified name. Note that the prefix associated with a qualified name selected from an input document will be the prefix that is used in that input document, not a prefix used in the query.

Special Cases

- If $arg is the empty sequence, the function returns the empty sequence.
- If $arg has no prefix (e.g., because it is associated with the default namespace, or it is not in a namespace), the function returns the empty sequence.

Examples

These examples use the input document names.xml shown in Example A-5, in the section "local-name." They also assume that the prefixes pre2 and unpre have been mapped to the namespaces http://datypic.com/pre and http://datypic.com/unpre, respectively, in the query prolog.

The prefix pre2 is used rather than pre to demonstrate that when selecting nodes from an instance document, it is the prefix used in the instance document (not the query) that matters. However, when constructing a new element, the prefix used in the query itself is the one associated with the name, as shown in the last example.

Example	Return value
prefix-from-QName(node-name(doc("names.xml")//noNamespace))	()
prefix-from-QName(node-name(doc("names.xml")//pre2:prefixed))	pre
prefix-from-QName(node-name(doc("names.xml")//unpre:unprefixed))	()
prefix-from-QName(node-name(doc("names.xml")//@pre2:prefAttr))	pre
prefix-from-QName(node-name(doc("names.xml")//@noNSAttr))	()
prefix-from-QName(node-name(<pre2:new>xyz</pre2:new>))	pre2

Related Functions

local-name-from-QName, namespace-uri-from-QName, namespace-uri-for-prefix, in-scope-prefixes

QName

Constructs a QName from a URI and a local part

Signature

QName(**$paramURI as xs:string?, $paramQName as xs:string**) as xs:QName

Usage Notes

This function takes a namespace URI and a qualified (optionally prefixed) name as arguments and constructs a QName value from them. If $paramQName is prefixed, that prefix is retained in the resulting xs:QName value.

Unlike the xs:QName constructor, the QName function does not require a literal argument. Therefore, the name could be the result of a dynamically evaluated expression. Because this function supplies all three components of the QName (local name, prefix, and URI) the effect does not depend on the context. There is no requirement that the prefix and namespace are bound in an outer expression.

Special Cases

- If $paramURI is a zero-length string or the empty sequence, and $paramQName has a prefix, the error "Invalid lexical value" (FOCA0002) is raised.
- If $paramURI is a zero-length string or the empty sequence, and $paramQName does not have a prefix, the resulting name is considered to be in no namespace.
- If $paramQName does not follow the lexical rules for an XML qualified name (e.g., because it starts with a number or it contains two colons), the error "Invalid lexical value" (FOCA0002) is raised.

Examples

Example	Return value (xs:QName)
QName("http://datypic.com/prod", "product")	Namespace: http://datypic.com/prod
	Prefix: empty
	Local part: product
QName("http://datypic.com/prod", "pre:product")	Namespace: http://datypic.com/prod
	Prefix: pre
	Local part: product
QName("", "product")	Namespace: empty
	Prefix: empty
	Local part: product
QName("", "pre:product")	Error FOCA0002

Related Functions

resolve-QName, local-name-from-QName, namespace-uri-from-QName, namespace-uri-for-prefix

remove

Removes an item from a sequence based on its position

Signature

```
remove($target as item( )*, $position as xs:integer) as item( )*
```

Usage Notes

This function returns a copy of $target with the item at position $position removed. Position numbers start at 1, not 0.

A common usage is to get the "tail" of a sequence (all items except the first). This can be written as remove($seq, 1).

Special Cases

- If $position is less than 1 or greater than the number of items in $target, no items are removed.
- If $target is the empty sequence, the function returns the empty sequence.

Examples

Example	Return value
remove(("a", "b", "c"), 1)	("b", "c")
remove(("a", "b", "c"), 2)	("a", "c")
remove(("a", "b", "c"), 10)	("a", "b", "c")
remove(("a", "b", "c"), 0)	("a", "b", "c")

replace

Replaces substrings that match a pattern with a specified replacement string

Signature

```
replace($input as xs:string?, $pattern as xs:string,
        $replacement as xs:string, $flags as xs:string) as xs:string
```

Usage Notes

The $pattern argument is a regular expression; its syntax is covered in Chapter 18.

While it is nice to have the power of regular expressions, you don't have to be familiar with regular expressions to replace a particular sequence of characters; you can just specify the string you want replaced for $pattern, as long as it doesn't contain any special characters.

The $replacement argument specifies a string (not a pattern) that is to be used as a replacement. The $flags argument allows for additional options in the interpretation of the regular expression, such as multi-line processing and case insensitivity. It is discussed in detail in "Using Flags" in Chapter 18.

Reluctant quantifiers and sub-expressions are two extremely useful features that can be used in conjunction with the replace function. They are described in Chapter 18 in the sections entitled "Reluctant Quantifiers" and "Using Sub-Expressions with Replacement Variables," respectively.

Special Cases

- If $input is the empty sequence, it is treated like a zero-length string.
- If $pattern is not a valid regular expression, the error "Invalid regular expression" (FORX0002) is raised.
- If the entire $pattern matches a zero-length string, for example q?, the error "Regular expression matches zero-length string" (FORX0003) is raised.
- If $replacement contains an unescaped dollar sign ($) that is not followed by a digit, the error "Invalid replacement string" (FORX0004) is raised. (\$ is used to escape a dollar sign.)
- If $replacement contains an unescaped backslash (\) that is not followed by a dollar sign ($), the error "Invalid replacement string" (FORX0004) is raised. (\\ is used to escape a backslash.)
- If $flags contains unsupported options, the error "Invalid regular expression flags" (FORX0001) is raised.
- If two overlapping strings match $pattern, only the first is replaced.

Examples

Example	Return value	
replace("query", "r", "as")	queasy	
replace("query", "qu", "quack")	quackery	
replace("query", "[ry]", "l")	quell	
replace("query", "[ry]+", "l")	quel	
replace("query", "z", "a")	query	
replace("query", "query", "")	A zero-length string	
replace((), "r", "as")	A zero-length string	
replace("query", "r?", "as")	Error FORX0003	
replace("query", "(r", "as")	Error FORX0002	
replace("Chapter", "(Chap)	(Chapter)", "x")	xter
replace("elementary", "e.*?e", "*")	*mentary	

If more than one sub-expression matches, starting at the same position, the first alternative is chosen. This is exhibited by the second-to-last example, where Chap is replaced instead of Chapter.

The last example illustrates the meaning of *non-overlapping*. There are actually two substrings in the original string that match the pattern: ele and eme. Only the first of these is replaced, because the second overlaps the first. Note that this example uses a reluctant quantifier; otherwise, the whole eleme would be replaced.

Related Functions

translate, tokenize

resolve-QName

Constructs a QName from a string using the in-scope namespaces of an element

Signature

resolve-QName(**$qname as xs:string?**, **$element as element()**) as xs:QName?

Usage Notes

The $qname argument is a string representing a qualified name. It may be prefixed (for example, prod:number), or unprefixed (for example, number). The $element argument is the element whose in-scope namespaces are to be used to determine which namespace URI is mapped to the prefix. If $qname is unprefixed, the default namespace declaration of $element is used. If there is no default namespace declaration in scope, the constructed QName has no namespace.

Note that when using the function, the prefix is never resolved using the context of the query. For example, if you map the prefix pre to the namespace http://datypic.com/pre in the query prolog, that is irrelevant when you call the resolve-QName function with the first argument pre:myName. It is only relevant how that prefix is mapped in $element. If you want

to use the context of the query, you can simply use the xs:QName constructor, as in xs:QName("pre:myName").

Typically, this function is used (in the absence of a schema) to resolve a QName appearing in the content of a document against the namespace context of the element where the QName appears. For example, to retrieve all products that carry the attribute xsi:type="prod:ProductType", you can use a path such as:

```
declare namespace prod = "http://datypic.com/prod";

doc("catalog.xml"//product[resolve-QName(@xsi:type, .) = xs:QName("prod:ProductType")]
```

This test allows the value of xsi:type in the input document to use any prefix (not just prod), as long as it is bound to the http://datypic.com/prod namespace.

Special Cases

- If $qname is prefixed, and that prefix is not mapped to a namespace in scope, the error "No namespace found for prefix" (FONS0004) is raised.
- If $qname is not a lexically correct QName (for example, if it is not a valid XML name, or if it contains more than one colon), the error "Invalid lexical value" (FOCA0002) is raised.
- If $qname is the empty sequence, the function returns the empty sequence.

Examples

These examples assume that the variable $root is bound to the root element, and $order is bound to the order element in the following input document:

```
<root>
  <order xmlns:ord="http://datypic.com/ord"
         xmlns="http://datypic.com">
    <!-- ... -->
  </order>
</root>
```

Example	Return value (xs:QName)
resolve-QName("myName", $root)	Namespace: empty
	Prefix: empty
	Local part: myName
resolve-QName("myName", $order)	Namespace: http://datypic.com
	Prefix: empty
	Local part: myName
resolve-QName("ord:myName", $root)	Error FONS0004
resolve-QName("ord:myName", $order)	Namespace: http://datypic.com/ord
	Prefix: ord
	Local part: myName
declare namespace dty = "dty_ns"; resolve-QName("dty:myName", $order)	Error FONS0004

Related Functions

QName, local-name-from-QName, namespace-uri-from-QName, namespace-uri-for-prefix

resolve-uri

Resolves a relative URI reference, based on a base URI

Signature

resolve-uri(**$relative as xs:string?**, *$base as xs:string*) as xs:anyURI?

Usage Notes

This function takes a base URI ($base) and a relative URI ($relative) as arguments and constructs an absolute URI.

If $base is not provided, the base URI of the static context is used. This may have been set by the processor outside the scope of the query, or it may have been declared in the query prolog.

Special Cases

- If $relative is already an absolute URI, the function returns $relative unchanged.
- If $relative cannot be resolved relative to $base (e.g., because $base itself is a relative URI), the error "Error in resolving a relative URI against a base URI in fn:resolve-uri" (FORG0009) is raised.
- If $base is not provided and the base URI of the static context is undefined, the error "Base-uri not defined in the static context" (FONS0005) is raised.
- If $relative or $base is not a syntactically valid URI, the error "Invalid argument to fn:resolve-uri" (FORG0002) is raised.
- If $relative is the empty sequence, the function returns the empty sequence.

Examples

Example[a]	Return value
resolve-uri("prod", "http://datypic.com/")	http://datypic.com/prod
resolve-uri("prod2", "http://datypic.com/prod1")	http://datypic.com/prod2
resolve-uri("http://example.org", "http://datypic.com")	http://example.org
resolve-uri("http://datypic.com", "../base")	http://datypic.com
resolve-uri("prod")	http://datypic.com/prod
resolve-uri("", "http://datypic.com")	http://datypic.com
resolve-uri("")	http://datypic.com

a This table assumes that the base URI of the static context is http://datypic.com.

Related Functions

base-uri, encode-for-uri

reverse

Reverses the order of the items in a sequence

Signature

```
reverse($arg as item( )*) as item( )*
```

Usage Notes

This function returns the items in $arg in reverse order. These items may be nodes, or atomic values, or both.

Special Cases

- If $arg is the empty sequence, the function returns the empty sequence.

Examples

Example	Return value
reverse ((1, 2, 3, 4, 5))	(5, 4, 3, 2, 1)
reverse ((6, 2, 4))	(4, 2, 6)
reverse (())	()

root

Gets the root of the tree containing a node

Signature

```
root($arg as node( )?) as node( )?
```

Usage Notes

This function returns a document node if the $arg node is part of a document, but it may also return an element if the $arg node is not part of a document. The root function can be used in conjunction with path expressions to find siblings and other elements that are in the same document. For example:

```
root($myNode)/descendant-or-self::product
```

retrieves all product elements that are in the same document (or document fragment) as $myNode.

Calling the root function is similar to starting a path with / or //. It is more flexible in that it can appear anywhere in a path or other expression. Also, unlike starting a path with /, the root function does not require the root to be a document node; it could be an element in the case of a document fragment.

Special Cases

- If $arg is the empty sequence, the function returns the empty sequence.
- If $arg is the root node, the function simply returns $arg.
- If $arg is not provided, the function uses the context item.
- If $arg is not provided, and the context item is undefined, the error XPDY0002 is raised.
- If $arg is not provided, and the context item is not a node, the error XPTY0004 is raised.

Examples

Example	Return value
root($myNode)/descendant-or-self::product	All product elements that are in the same document (or document fragment) as $myNode
root()	The root of the current context node
root(.)	The root of the current context node
root(doc("order.xml")//item[1])	The document node of order.xml
let $a := <a><x></x> let $x := $a/x return root($x)	The a element

round

Rounds a number to the nearest whole number

Signature

round(**$arg as numeric?**) as numeric?

Usage Notes

The round function is used to round a numeric value to the nearest integer. If the decimal portion of the number is .5 or greater, it is rounded up to the greater whole number (even if it is negative); otherwise, it is rounded down.

The function returns a numeric value of type xs:float, xs:double, xs:decimal, or xs:integer, depending on which type the argument is derived from. If $arg is untyped, it is cast to xs:double.

Special Cases

- If $arg is the empty sequence, the function returns the empty sequence.
- If $arg is between −0.5 and −0 (inclusive), the function may return 0 or -0 (it is implementation-dependent).
- If $arg is one of the values 0, -0, NaN, INF, or -INF, the function returns this same value.

Examples

Example	Return value
round(5)	5
round(5.1)	5
round(5.5)	6
round(-5.5)	-5
round(-5.51)	-6

Related Functions

round-half-to-even, floor, ceiling

round-half-to-even
Rounds a number using a specified precision

Signature

round-half-to-even(**$arg as numeric?**, *$precision as xs:integer*) as numeric?

Usage Notes

This type of rounding is used in financial and statistical applications so that the sum of a column of rounded numbers comes closer to the sum of the same unrounded numbers.

The returned value is rounded to the number of decimal places indicated by $precision. For example, if the precision specified is 2, the function rounds 594.3271 to 594.33. If the precision is 0, the number is rounded to an integer. Specifying a negative precision results in the number being rounded to the left of the decimal point. For example, if $precision is –2, the function rounds 594.3271 to 600. If $precision is omitted, it defaults to 0.

If the argument is exactly half way between two values, it is rounded to whichever adjacent value is an even number.

The function returns a numeric value of type xs:float, xs:double, xs:decimal, or xs:integer, depending on the type from which the argument is derived. If $arg is untyped, it is cast to xs:double.

The function works best with xs:decimal values. With xs:double and xs:float values, the rounding may not work exactly as expected. This is because an xs:double value written as 0.005, being only an approximation to a decimal number, is often not precisely midway between 0.01 and 0.02.

Special Cases

- If $arg is the empty sequence, the function returns the empty sequence.
- If $arg is between –0.5 and –0 (inclusive), the function may return 0 or –0 (it is implementation-dependent).
- If $arg is one of the values 0, -0, NaN, INF, or –INF, the function returns this same value.

Examples

Example	Return value
round-half-to-even(5.5)	6
round-half-to-even(6.5)	6
round-half-to-even(9372.253, 2)	9372.25
round-half-to-even(9372.253, 0)	9372
round-half-to-even(9372.253, -3)	9000

Related Functions

round, floor, ceiling

seconds-from-dateTime

Gets the seconds portion of a date/time

Signature

```
seconds-from-dateTime($arg as xs:dateTime?) as xs:decimal?
```

Usage Notes

This function returns the seconds portion of an xs:dateTime value, as a decimal number.

Special Cases

- If $arg is the empty sequence, the function returns the empty sequence.

Example

seconds-from-dateTime(xs:dateTime("2006-08-15T10:30:23.5")) returns 23.5.

Related Functions

seconds-from-time

seconds-from-duration

Gets the normalized number of seconds in a duration

Signature

```
seconds-from-duration($arg as xs:duration?) as xs:decimal?
```

Usage Notes

This function calculates the seconds component of a normalized xs:duration value, as a decimal number between –60 and 60 exclusive. This is not necessarily the same as the number that appears before the S in the value. For example, if the duration is PT90S, the function returns 30 rather than 90. This is because 60 of those seconds are considered to be 1 minute, and the normalized value would therefore be PT1M30S.

Special Cases

- If $arg is a negative duration, the function returns a negative value.
- If $arg is the empty sequence, the function returns the empty sequence.

Examples

Example	Return value
seconds-from-duration(xs:duration("PT30.5S"))	30.5
seconds-from-duration(xs:duration("-PT90.5S"))	-30.5
seconds-from-duration(xs:duration("PT1M"))	0
seconds-from-duration(xs:duration("PT60S"))	0

seconds-from-time

<div style="text-align: right">Gets the seconds portion of a time</div>

Signature

```
seconds-from-time($arg as xs:time?) as xs:decimal?
```

Usage Notes

This function returns the seconds portion of an xs:time value, as a decimal number.

Special Cases

- If $arg is the empty sequence, the function returns the empty sequence.

Example

seconds-from-time(xs:time("10:30:23.5")) returns 23.5.

Related Functions

seconds-from-dateTime

starts-with

<div style="text-align: right">Determines whether one string starts with another</div>

Signature

```
starts-with($arg1 as xs:string?, $arg2 as xs:string?,
        $collation as xs:string) as xs:boolean
```

Usage Notes

This function returns an xs:boolean value indicating whether one string ($arg1) starts with the characters of another string ($arg2). Leading and trailing whitespace is significant, so you may want to use the normalize-space function to trim the strings before using this function.

Special Cases

- If $arg2 is a zero-length string or the empty sequence, the function returns true.
- If $arg1 is a zero-length string or the empty sequence, but $arg2 is not, the function returns false.
- If $collation is provided, the comparison uses that collation; otherwise, the default collation is used. Collations are described in Chapter 17.

Examples

Example	Return value
starts-with("query", "que")	true
starts-with("query", "query")	true
starts-with("query", "u")	false

Example	Return value
starts-with("query", "")	true
starts-with("", "query")	false
starts-with("", "")	true
starts-with("query", ())	true
starts-with(" query", "q")	false

Related Functions

ends-with, contains, matches

static-base-uri

Gets the base URI of the static context

Signature

```
static-base-uri() as xs:anyURI?
```

Usage Notes

This function returns the base URI of the static context. This may have been set by the processor outside the scope of the query, or it may have been declared in the query prolog.

The base URI of the static context is used for constructed elements and for resolving relative URIs when no other base URI is available. It is not the same as the base URI of any given element or document node. For more information, see "The base URI of the static context" in Chapter 20.

Example

static-base-uri() might return http://datypic.com/prod, if that is the base URI of the static context.

Related Functions

base-uri

string

Returns the string value of an item

Signature

```
string($arg as item()?) as xs:string
```

Usage Notes

If $arg is a node, this function returns its string value. The method of determining the string value of a node depends on its kind. Table A-6 describes how the string value is determined for each node kind.

If $arg is an atomic value, the function returns that value, cast to xs:string. For more information on casting a typed value to string, see "Casting to xs:string or xs:untypedAtomic" in Chapter 11.

Table A-6. String value based on node kind

Node kind	String value
Element	The text content of the element and all its descendant elements, concatenated together in document order. Attribute values are not included.
Document	The string values of all of the descendant elements concatenated together in document order. That is, the text content of the original XML document, minus all the markup.
Attribute	The attribute value
Text	The text itself
Processing instruction	The content of the processing instruction (everything but its target)
Comment	The content of the comment

When $arg is a typed node, there may be some differences in the formatting such as leading and trailing whitespace and leading zeros. This is because the implementation can optionally provide the canonical representation of the value instead of the actual characters that appear in an input document. For example, if <myInt> 04 </myInt> appears in an input document, and it is validated and annotated with the type xs:integer, its string value may be returned as 4 without leading or trailing spaces instead of 04 .

If you want the resulting value to be some type other than xs:string, you should use the data function instead. For example, if $myInt is bound to the myInt element from the previous prargraph, the expression data($myInt) returns the integer value 4.

Special Cases

- If $arg is not provided, the function uses the context item.
- If $arg is not provided, and the context item is undefined, the error XPDY0002 is raised.
- If $arg is the empty sequence, the function returns a zero-length string.
- If $arg is an element with empty content (e.g., <a> or <a/>), the function returns a zero-length string.

Examples

Given the fourth product element in our catalog:

```
<product dept="MEN">
  <number>784</number>
  <name language="en">Cotton Dress Shirt</name>
  <colorChoices>white gray</colorChoices>
  <desc>Our <i>favorite</i> shirt!</desc>
</product>
```

the string value of the product element is:

```
784Cotton Dress Shirtwhite grayOur favorite shirt!
```

assuming a schema is in place; otherwise, there will be additional whitespace between the values. The string value of the number element is 784 and the string value of the desc element is Our favorite shirt!.

Related Functions

data

string-join
Concatenates a sequence of strings together, optionally using a separator

Signature

string-join(**$arg1 as xs:string*, $arg2 as xs:string**) as xs:string

Usage Notes

The $arg1 argument specifies the sequence of strings to concatenate, while $arg2 specifies the separator. If $arg2 is a zero-length string, no separator is used.

Special Cases

- If $arg1 is the empty sequence, the function returns a zero-length string.

Examples

Example	Return value
string-join(("a", "b", "c"), "")	abc
string-join(("a", "b", "c"), "-")	a-b-c
string-join(("a", "", "c"), "-")	a--c
string-join("a", "-")	a
string-join((), "-")	A zero-length string

Related Functions

concat

string-length
Finds the length of a string

Signature

string-length(*$arg as xs:string?*) as xs:integer

Usage Notes

This function returns an xs:integer value indicating the number of characters in the string. Whitespace is significant, so leading and trailing whitespace characters are counted.

Special Cases

- If $arg is not provided, the function uses the string value of the context item.
- If $arg is not provided, and the context item is undefined, the error XPDY0002 is raised.
- If $arg is the empty sequence, the function returns 0.
- Unlike some programming languages, Unicode characters above 65535 count as one character, not two.

Examples

Example	Return value
string-length("query")	5
string-length(" query ")	9
string-length(normalize-space(" query "))	5
string-length("xml query")	9
string-length("")	0
string-length(())	0

string-to-codepoints

Converts a string to a sequence of Unicode code-point values

Signature

```
string-to-codepoints($arg as xs:string?) as xs:integer*
```

Usage Notes

This function returns a sequence of xs:integer values representing the Unicode code points.

Special Cases

- If $arg is a zero-length string or the empty sequence, the function returns the empty sequence.

Examples

Example	Return value
string-to-codepoints("abc")	(97, 98, 99)
string-to-codepoints("a")	97
string-to-codepoints("")	()

Related Functions

codepoints-to-string

subsequence

Extracts a portion of a sequence, based on a starting position and optional length

Signature

```
subsequence($sourceSeq as item( )*, $startingLoc as xs:double,
           $length as xs:double) as item( )*
```

Usage Notes

This function returns a sequence of $length items of $sourceSeq, starting at the position $startingLoc. The first item in the sequence is considered to be at position 1, not 0. If no $length is passed, or if $length is greater than the number of items that can be returned, the function includes items to the end of the sequence. An alternative to calling the subsequence function is using a predicate. For example, subsequence($a,3,4) is equivalent to $a[position() = (3 to 6)].

Special Cases

- If $startingLoc is zero or negative, the subsequence starts at the beginning of the sequence and still goes to $startingLoc plus $length, so the actual length of the subsequence may be less than $length.

- If $startingLoc is greater than the number of items in the sequence, the function returns the empty sequence.

- If $sourceSeq is the empty sequence, the function returns the empty sequence.

- The function will accept xs:double values for $startingLoc and $length, in which case they are rounded to the nearest integer. This is because the result type of many calculations on untyped data is xs:double. Accepting xs:double values allows the $startingLoc and $length arguments to be calculated and passed directly to the function.

Examples

Example	Return value
subsequence(("a", "b", "c", "d", "e"), 3)	("c", "d", "e")
subsequence(("a", "b", "c", "d", "e"), 3, 2)	("c", "d")
subsequence(("a", "b", "c", "d", "e"), 3, 10)	("c", "d", "e")
subsequence(("a", "b", "c", "d", "e"), 10)	()
subsequence(("a", "b", "c", "d", "e"), -2, 5)	("a", "b")
subsequence((), 3)	()

substring

Extracts part of a string, based on a starting position and optional length

Signature

```
substring($sourceString as xs:string?, $startingLoc as xs:double,
         $length as xs:double) as xs:string
```

Usage Notes

The $startingLoc argument indicates the starting location for the substring, where the first character is at position 1 (not 0). The optional $length argument indicates the number of characters to include, relative to the starting location. If no $length is provided, the entire rest of the string is included.

The function returns all characters whose position is greater than or equal to $startingLoc and less than ($startingLoc + $length). The $startingLoc number can be zero or negative, in which case the function starts at the beginning of the string, and still only include characters up to (but not including) the position at ($startingLoc + $length). If ($startingLoc + $length) is greater than the length of the string, the rest of the string is included.

Special Cases

- If $sourceString is the empty sequence, the function returns a zero-length string.
- If $startingLoc is greater than the length of the string, the function returns a zero-length string.
- The function will accept xs:double values for $startingLoc and $length, in which case they are rounded to the nearest integer.

Examples

Example	Return value
substring("query", 1)	query
substring("query", 3)	ery
substring("query", 1, 1)	q
substring("query", 2, 3)	uer
substring("query", 2, 850)	uery
substring("query", 6, 2)	A zero-length string
substring("query", -2)	query
substring("query", -2, 5)	qu
substring("query", 1, 0)	A zero-length string
substring("", 1)	A zero-length string
substring((), 1)	A zero-length string

Related Functions

substring-after, substring-before

substring-after

Extracts the substring that is after the first occurrence of another specified string

Signature

```
substring-after($arg1 as xs:string?, $arg2 as xs:string?,
              $collation as xs:string) as xs:string
```

Usage Notes

This function extracts all the characters of a string ($arg1) that appear after the first occurrence of another specified string ($arg2).

Special Cases

- If $arg1 does not contain $arg2, the function returns a zero-length string.
- If $arg2 is a zero-length string or the empty sequence, the function returns $arg1 in its entirety.
- If $arg1 is a zero-length string or the empty sequence, and $arg1 is not, the function returns a zero-length string.
- If $collation is provided, the comparison uses that collation; otherwise, the default collation is used.

Examples

Example	Return value
substring-after("query", "u")	ery
substring-after("queryquery", "ue")	ryquery
substring-after("query", "y")	A zero-length string
substring-after("query", "x")	A zero-length string
substring-after("query", "")	query
substring-after("", "x")	A zero-length string

Related Functions

substring, substring-before

substring-before

Extracts the substring that is before the first occurrence of another specified string

Signature

```
substring-before($arg1 as xs:string?, $arg2 as xs:string?,
             $collation as xs:string) as xs:string
```

Usage Notes

This function extracts all the characters of a string ($arg1) that appear before the first occurrence of another specified string ($arg2).

Special Cases

- If $arg1 does not contain $arg2, the function returns a zero-length string.
- If $arg1 is a zero-length string or the empty sequence, the function returns a zero-length string.

- If $arg2 is a zero-length string or the empty sequence, the function returns a zero-length string.
- If $collation is provided, the comparison uses that collation; otherwise, the default collation is used. Collations are described in Chapter 17.

Examples

Example	Return value
substring-before("query", "r")	que
substring-before("query", "ery")	qu
substring-before("queryquery", "ery")	qu
substring-before("query", "query")	A zero-length string
substring-before("query", "x")	A zero-length string
substring-before("query", "")	A zero-length string
substring-before("query", ())	A zero-length string

Related Functions

substring, substring-after

sum
Calculates the total value of the items in a sequence

Signature

sum(**$arg as xs:anyAtomicType***, *$zero as xs:anyAtomicType?*) as xs:anyAtomicType?

Usage Notes

The $arg sequence can contain a mixture of numeric and untyped values. Numeric values are promoted as necessary to make them all the same type. Untyped values are cast as numeric xs:double values.

The function can also be used on duration values, so the $arg sequence can contain all xs:yearMonthDuration values or all xs:dayTimeDuration values (but not a mixture of the two). The $arg sequence cannot contain a mixture of duration and numeric values.

The $zero argument allows you to specify an alternate value for the sum of the empty sequence. If $arg is the empty sequence, and $zero is provided, the function returns $zero. The $zero argument could be the empty sequence, the integer 0, the value NaN, a duration of zero seconds, or any other atomic value. The main use cases of $zero are (a) to supply numeric zero in the desired datatype, e.g., xs:decimal, and (b) to supply a zero duration if you are summing durations. Since the processor, in the absence of static typing, cannot tell the difference between a zero-length sequence of numbers and a zero-length sequence of durations, this is the only way to tell it which kind of value is being totaled.

Special Cases

- If $arg is the empty sequence, and $zero is not provided, the function returns the xs:integer value 0.
- If $arg contains any NaN values, the function returns NaN.
- If $arg contains untyped values that cannot be cast to xs:double, the error "Invalid value for cast/constructor" (FORG0001) is raised.
- If $arg contains values of different types, or values that are not numbers or durations, the error "Invalid argument type" (FORG0006) is raised.

Examples

Example	Return value
sum((1, 2, 3))	6
sum(doc("order.xml")//item/@quantity)	7
sum(doc("order.xml")//item/@dept)	Error FORG0001
sum((xs:yearMonthDuration("P1Y2M"), xs:yearMonthDuration("P2Y3M")))	P3Y5M
sum((1, 2, 3, ()))	6
sum((1, 2, xs:yearMonthDuration("P1Y")))	Error FORG0006
sum(())	0
sum((), ())	()

timezone-from-date

Gets the time zone of a date

Signature

timezone-from-date(**$arg as xs:date?**) as xs:dayTimeDuration?

Usage Notes

This function returns the time zone of an xs:date value, offset from UTC, as an xs:dayTimeDuration value between –PT14H and PT14H. If the time zone is UTC, the value PT0S is returned.

Special Cases

- If $arg is the empty sequence, the function returns the empty sequence.
- If $arg does not have an explicit time zone, the function returns the empty sequence. It does not return the implicit time zone.

Examples

- timezone-from-date(xs:date("2006-08-15-05:00")) returns –PT5H.
- timezone-from-date(xs:date("2006-08-15")) returns the empty sequence, regardless of the implicit time zone.

Related Functions

`timezone-from-dateTime, timezone-from-time`

timezone-from-dateTime

<div align="right">Gets the time zone of a date/time</div>

Signature

> `timezone-from-dateTime(`**`$arg as xs:dateTime?`**`)` `as xs:dayTimeDuration?`

Usage Notes

This function returns the time zone of an `xs:dateTime` value, offset from UTC, as an `xs:dayTimeDuration` value between –PT14H and PT14H. If the time zone is UTC, the value PT0S is returned.

Special Cases

- If $arg is the empty sequence, the function returns the empty sequence.
- If $arg does not have an explicit time zone, the function returns the empty sequence. It does not return the implicit time zone.

Examples

- `timezone-from-dateTime(xs:dateTime("2006-08-15T10:30:23-05:00"))` returns –PT5H.
- `timezone-from-dateTime(xs:dateTime("2006-08-15T10:30:23"))` returns the empty sequence, regardless of the implicit time zone.

Related Functions

`timezone-from-date, timezone-from-time`

timezone-from-time

<div align="right">Gets the time zone of a time</div>

Signature

> `timezone-from-time(`**`$arg as xs:time?`**`)` `as xs:dayTimeDuration?`

Usage Notes

This function returns the time zone of an `xs:time` value, offset from UTC, as an `xs:dayTimeDuration` value between –PT14H and PT14H. If the time zone is UTC, the value PT0S is returned.

Special Cases

- If $arg is the empty sequence, the function returns the empty sequence.
- If $arg does not have an explicit time zone, the function returns the empty sequence. It does not return the implicit time zone.

Examples

Example	Return value
timezone-from-time(xs:time("09:54:00-05:00"))	-PT5H
timezone-from-time(xs:time("09:54:00+05:00"))	PT5H
timezone-from-time(xs:time("09:54:00Z"))	PT0S
timezone-from-time(xs:time("09:54:00"))	()

Related Functions

timezone-from-dateTime, timezone-from-date

tokenize

Breaks a string into a sequence of strings, using a regular expression to identify the separator

Signature

tokenize(**$input as xs:string?**, **$pattern as xs:string**,
 $flags as xs:string) as xs:string*

Usage Notes

The $pattern argument is a regular expression that represents the separator. The regular expression syntax is covered in Chapter 18. The simplest patterns can be a single space, or a string that contains the separator character, such as ,. However, certain characters must be escaped in regular expressions, namely . \ ? * + | ^ $ { } () [and]. Table A-7 shows some useful patterns for separators.

Table A-7. Useful separator patterns

Pattern	Meaning
\s	A single whitespace character (space, tab, carriage return, or line feed)
\s+	One or more consecutive whitespace characters
,	Comma
,\s*	A comma followed by zero or more whitespace characters
[,\s]+	One or more consecutive commas and/or whitespace characters
\t	Tab character
[\n\r]+	One or more consecutive carriage return and/or line-feed characters
\W+	One or more nonword characters

The separators are not included in the result strings. If two adjacent separators appear, a zero-length string is included in the result sequence. If the string starts with the separator, a zero-length string is the first value returned. Likewise, if the string ends with the separator, a zero-length string is the last value in the result sequence.

The $flags argument allows for additional options in the interpretation of the regular expression, such as multi-line processing and case insensitivity. It is discussed in detail in "Using Flags" in Chapter 18.

If a particular point in the string could match more than one alternative, the first alternative is chosen. This is exhibited in the last row in the Example table, where the function considers the comma to be the separator, even though ",x" also applies.

Special Cases

- If $input is the empty sequence, or $input is a zero-length string, the function returns the empty sequence.
- If $pattern is not a valid regular expression, the error "Invalid regular expression" (FORX0002) is raised.
- If the entire $pattern matches a zero-length string, for example q?, the error "Regular expression matches zero-length string" (FORX0003) is raised.
- If $flags contains unsupported options, the error "Invalid regular expression flags" (FORX0001) is raised.

Examples

Example	Return value
tokenize("a b c", "\s")	("a", "b", "c")
tokenize("a b c", "\s")	("a", "", "", "b", "c")
tokenize("a b c", "\s+")	("a", "b", "c")
tokenize(" b c", "\s")	("", "b", "c")
tokenize("a,b,c", ",")	("a", "b", "c")
tokenize("a,b,,c", ",")	("a", "b", "", "c")
tokenize("a, b, c", "[,\s]+")	("a", "b", "c")
tokenize("2006-12-25T12:15:00", "[\-T:]")	("2006","12","25","12","15","00")
tokenize("Hello, there.", "\W+")	("Hello", "there", "")
tokenize((), "\s+")	()
tokenize("abc", "\s")	abc
tokenize("abcd", "b?")	Error FORX0003
tokenize("a,xb,xc", ",\|,x")	("a", "xb", "xc")

trace

Traces the value of an item for debugging or logging purposes

Signature

```
trace($value as item( )*, $label as xs:string) as item( )*
```

Usage Notes

This function accepts an item and a label for that item, and returns the item unchanged. The exact behavior of the function is implementation-dependent, but generally the processor puts the label and the value of the item in a logfile or user console.

Example

trace($var1, "The value of $var1 is: ") might write the string The value of $var1 is: 4 to a logfile.

Related Functions

error

translate Replace individual characters in a string with other individual characters

Signature

```
translate($arg as xs:string?, $mapString as xs:string,
        $transString as xs:string) as xs:string
```

Usage Notes

The $mapString argument is a list of characters to be changed, and $transString is the list of replacement characters. Each character in $mapString is replaced by the character in the same position in $transString. If $mapString is longer than $transString, the characters in $mapString that have no corresponding character in $transString are not included in the result. Characters in the original string that do not appear in $mapString are copied to the result unchanged.

Note that this function is only for replacing individual characters with other individual characters or removing individual characters. If you want to replace sequences of characters, you should use the replace function instead. This function is sometimes used for translating strings between lowercase and uppercase, but the upper-case and lower-case functions do this more robustly based on Unicode mappings.

Special Cases

- If $arg is the empty sequence, the function returns a zero-length string.

Examples

Example	Return value
translate("1999/01/02", "/", "-")	1999-01-02
translate("xml query", "qlmx", "QLMX")	XML Query
translate("xml query", "qlmx ", "Q")	Query
translate("xml query", "qlmx ", "")	uery
translate("xml query", "abcd", "ABCD")	xml query
translate("", "qlmx ", "Q")	A zero-length string
translate((), "qlmx ", "Q")	A zero-length string

Related Functions

trace

true
<div style="text-align:right">Constructs a Boolean true value</div>

Signature

 true() as xs:boolean

Usage Notes

This function, which takes no arguments, is useful for constructing the Boolean value true. XQuery uses the false() and true() functions instead of keywords false and true. This is most commonly used to supply a value in a function call where a Boolean value is required.

Example

The expression true() returns the xs:boolean value true.

Related Functions

false

unordered
<div style="text-align:right">Signals to the processor that order is insignificant</div>

Signature

 unordered($sourceSeq as item()*) as item()*

Usage Notes

In cases where the order of the results does not matter, the processor may be much more efficient if it does not have to keep track of order. This is especially true for FLWORs that perform joins. For example, processing multiple variable bindings in a for clause might be significantly faster if the processor can decide which variable binding controls the join without regard to the order of the results. A query author can tell the processor that order does not matter by enclosing an expression in a call to the unordered function.

Example

```
unordered(
for $item in doc("order.xml")//item,
    $product in doc("catalog.xml")//product
where $item/@num = $product/number
return
  <item number="{$item/@num}" name="{$product/name}"
        quantity="{$item/@quantity}"/>
)
```

upper-case
<div align="right">Converts a string to uppercase</div>

Signature

```
upper-case($arg as xs:string?) as xs:string
```

Usage Notes

The mappings between lowercase and uppercase characters are determined by Unicode case mappings. If a character in $arg does not have a corresponding uppercase character, it is included in the result string unchanged.

For English, you can do a case-blind comparison by writing upper-case($A)=upper-case($B) (or use lower-case instead). However this doesn't always work well for other languages. It's better to use a case-insensitive collation.

Special Cases

• If $arg is the empty sequence, the function returns a zero-length string.

Examples

Example	Return value
upper-case("query")	QUERY
upper-case("QUERY")	QUERY
upper-case("Query")	QUERY
upper-case("query-123")	QUERY-123
upper-case("Schloß")	SCHLOSS

Related Functions

lower-case

year-from-date
<div align="right">Gets the year portion of a date</div>

Signature

```
year-from-date($arg as xs:date?) as xs:integer?
```

Usage Notes

This function returns the year portion of an xs:date value as an integer.

Special Cases

• If the year is negative, the function returns a negative number.
• If $arg is the empty sequence, the function returns the empty sequence.

Example

year-from-date(xs:date("2006-08-15")) returns 2006.

Related Functions

year-from-dateTime

year-from-dateTime

Signature

year-from-dateTime(**$arg as xs:dateTime?**) as xs:integer?

Usage Notes

This function returns the year portion of an xs:dateTime value as an integer.

Special Cases

- If the year is negative, the function returns a negative number.
- If $arg is the empty sequence, the function returns the empty sequence.

Example

year-from-dateTime(xs:dateTime("2006-08-15T10:30:23")) returns 2006.

Related Functions

year-from-date

years-from-duration

Signature

years-from-duration(**$arg as xs:duration?**) as xs:integer?

Usage Notes

This function calculates the years component of a normalized xs:duration value. This is not necessarily the same as the integer that appears before the Y in the value. For example, if the duration is P1Y18M, the function returns 2 rather than 1. This is because 18 months is equal to 1.5 years, and the normalized value is therefore P2Y6M.

Special Cases

- If $arg is a negative duration, the function returns a negative value.
- If $arg is the empty sequence, the function returns the empty sequence.

Examples

Example	Return value
years-from-duration(xs:duration("P3Y"))	3
years-from-duration(xs:duration("P3Y11M"))	3
years-from-duration(xs:duration("-P18M"))	-1
years-from-duration(xs:duration("P1Y18M"))	2
years-from-duration(xs:duration("P12M"))	1

zero-or-one Verifies that a sequence does not contain more than one item

Signature

 zero-or-one(**$arg as item()***) as item()?

Usage Notes

If $arg contains zero or one items, $arg is returned. Otherwise, the error "fn:zero-or-one called with a sequence containing more than one item" (FORG0003) is raised.

This function is useful when static typing is in effect, to avoid apparent static type errors. For example, to use the number function on a particular price, you might be tempted to write the expression:

 number (doc("prices.xml")//prod[@num = 557]/price)

However, if static typing is used, this expression causes a static error. This is because there could be more than one price element that matches that criterion, while the number function requires that one zero or one item be provided. A static error can be avoided by using the expression:

 number (zero-or-one(doc("prices.xml")//prod[@num = 557]/price))

In this case, no static error is raised. Rather, a dynamic error is raised if more than one price element is returned by the path expression. For more information on static typing, see Chapter 14.

If static typing is *not* in effect, calling exactly-one is not usually necessary, but it does no harm. The effect is usually to make explicit a runtime type check that would otherwise have been done automatically.

Examples

Example	Return value
zero-or-one(())	()
zero-or-one("a")	a
zero-or-one(("a", "b"))	Error FORG0003

Related Functions

one-or-more, exactly-one

Built-in Types

This appendix describes all of the types that are built into XQuery via the XML Schema specification. For each type, it describes the set of valid values, as well as notes on comparing and casting values of these types. The types, depicted in Figure B-1, are listed alphabetically in this appendix.

xs:anyAtomicType

The type xs:anyAtomicType is a generic type that encompasses all atomic types, both primitive and derived, including xs:untypedAtomic. No values ever actually have the type xs:anyAtomicType; they always have a more specific type. As such, it does not have a corresponding constructor.

However, this type name can be used as a placeholder for all other atomic types in function signatures and sequence types. For example, the distinct-values function signature specifies that its argument is xs:anyAtomicType. This means that any atomic value of any type can be passed to this function.

This type isn't actually defined in XML Schema 1.0, although it's in the XML Schema namespace for convenience.

xs:anyType

The type xs:anyType is given to some element nodes without a more specific type. The difference between xs:anyType and xs:untyped is that an element of type xs:anyType may contain other elements that have specific types. Elements of type xs:untyped, on the other hand, always have children that are also untyped. An element is assigned the type xs:anyType if:

- Validation was attempted but the element was found to be invalid (or partially valid). Some implementations may allow the query evaluation to continue even if validation fails.
- The element is the result of an element constructor, and construction mode is set to preserve.

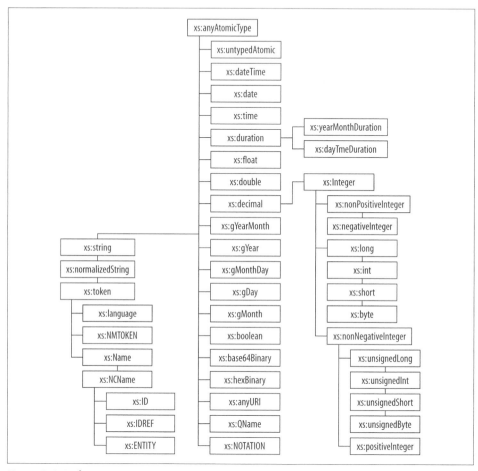

Figure B-1. Built-in types

xs:anyURI

The primitive type xs:anyURI represents a Uniform Resource Identifier (URI) reference. The value has to be a lexically valid URI reference. Since the bare minimum rules for valid URI references are fairly generic, most implementations accept most character strings, including a zero-length string. The only values that are not accepted are those that make inappropriate use of reserved characters, such as those that contain multiple # characters or have % characters that are not followed by two hexadecimal digits.

Some URI processors require that certain non-ASCII characters be escaped using a percent sign (%) followed by a two-digit Unicode code point. However, the xs:anyURI type *does* accept these characters escaped or unescaped. Table B-1 shows some examples of valid and invalid URI references.

For more information on URIs, see "Working with URIs" in Chapter 20.

Table B-1. Values of the xs:anyURI type

Values	Explanation
Valid	
http://datypic.com	Absolute URI (in this case, an HTTP URL)
http://datypic.com/prod.html#shirt	Absolute URI with fragment identifier
mailto:info@datypic.com	Absolute URI using mailto scheme
../%C3%A9dition.html	Relative URI with escaped non-ASCII character
../édition.html	Relative URI with unescaped non-ASCII character
../prod.html#A557	Relative URI with fragment identifier
urn:datypic:com	Absolute URI (in this case, a URN)
	Empty values are allowed
Invalid	
http://datypic.com#frag1#frag2	Too many fragment identifiers (# characters)
http://datypic.com#f%rag	% character followed by something other than two hexadecimal digits

Casting and Comparing xs:anyURI Values

Values of type xs:anyURI can be cast to and from xs:string or xs:untypedAtomic. No escaping or unescaping occurs when values are cast among these types. To escape reserved characters in URIs, use one of the functions iri-to-uri, escape-html-uri, or encode-for-uri.

In addition, xs:anyURI values are automatically promoted to xs:string whenever a string is expected by a function or operator. For example, you could pass an xs:anyURI value to the substring function, or to the escape-uri function, both of which expect an xs:string value as their first argument. This also means that xs:anyURI values can be compared to strings and sorted with them.

Two xs:anyURI values are considered equal if they have identical characters (based on Unicode code points). This means that if they are capitalized differently, they are considered different values, even if they may be seemingly equivalent URLs. For example, http://datypic.com/prod is not equal to http://datypic.com/proD, because the last letter is capitalized differently.

Values of type xs:anyURI that are relative URIs are also compared based on code points, and no attempt is made to determine or compare their base URI. For example,

../prod is always equal to ../prod, even if the two xs:anyURI values may have come from different XHTML documents with different base URIs.

xs:base64Binary

The primitive type xs:base64Binary represents binary data in base-64 encoding. The following rules apply to xs:base64Binary values:

- The following characters are allowed: the letters A through Z (uppercase and lowercase), digits 0 through 9, the plus sign (+), the slash (/), the equals sign (=), and XML whitespace characters.
- XML whitespace characters can appear anywhere in the value.
- The number of nonwhitespace characters must be divisible by four.
- Equals signs, which are used as padding, can only appear at the end of the value, and there can be zero, one, or two of them. If there are two equals signs, they must be preceded by one of the following characters: A, Q, g, w. If there is only one equals sign, it must be preceded by one of the following characters: A, E, I, M, Q, U, Y, c, g, k, o, s, w, 0, 4, 8.

Values of type xs:base64Binary can be cast to and from xs:hexBinary, xs:string, and xs:untypedAtomic. When cast to xs:string, an xs:base64Binary value is converted to its canonical representation, which contains no whitespace characters except for a line feed (#xA) character inserted after every 76 characters and at the end.

Note that these rules for acceptable base-64 values are rather strict, and processors are expected to enforce the rules strictly. This differs from practice elsewhere, and some software may generate "base 64" that doesn't meet these rules.

Table B-2 lists some values of the xs:base64Binary type. For more information on base-64 encoding, see *RFC 2045: Multipurpose Internet Mail Extensions (MIME) Part One: Format of Internet Message Bodies*.

Table B-2. Values of the xs:base64Binary type

Values	Explanation
Valid	
0DC7	
0 DC7 0F+9	Whitespace is allowed anywhere in the value
0F+40A==	Equals signs are used for padding
	An empty value is valid
Invalid	
DC7	Odd number of characters not valid; characters appear in groups of four
==0F	Equals signs can only appear at the end

xs:boolean

The primitive type xs:boolean represents a logical true or false value. The valid lexical representations for xs:boolean are false, true, 0 (which is equal to false), and 1 (which is equal to true). The values are case-sensitive, so TRUE and FALSE are not valid lexical representations.

Constructing xs:boolean Values

In addition to the standard xs:boolean constructor, xs:boolean values can be constructed using the true and false functions, which take no arguments and return the appropriate value. For example, true() returns the value true.

Boolean values are more often constructed indirectly, as:

- The result of a function that returns a Boolean value, such as exists($seq1)
- The value of a comparison expression, such as $price > 20
- The result of a path expression that is evaluated using its effective Boolean value, such as if (doc("catalog.xml")//product) ...

In addition, a function named boolean can be used to explicitly convert a sequence to its effective Boolean value. A sequence that is an xs:boolean value false, a single number 0 or NaN, a single zero-length string, or the empty sequence, evaluates to false. Otherwise, it evaluates to true. Note that it doesn't give the same result as the xs:boolean constructor—for example, xs:boolean("false") is false, but boolean("false") is true. More information on the boolean function can be found in Appendix A.

Casting xs:boolean Values

Values of type xs:string or xs:untypedAtomic can be cast to xs:boolean. The string false (all lowercase), or the string 0 is converted to the value false. The string true (all lowercase) or 1 is converted to true. Any other string value raises an error; other strings that may appear to be equal to 0 or 1, such as 0.0 or 01, are not accepted.

Values of any of the numeric types can also be cast to and from xs:boolean. A numeric value that is equal to 0 or NaN is converted to false; any other numeric value is converted to true.

Likewise, values of type xs:boolean can be cast to xs:string, xs:untypedAtomic, and any of the numeric types. When they are cast to xs:string or xs:untypedAtomic, they are represented as true and false, not their numeric equivalents.

xs:byte

The type xs:byte represents an integer between –128 and 127 inclusive. It is ultimately derived from xs:decimal, via xs:integer. Its value can be a sequence of digits, optionally preceded by a sign (+ or –). For example, –128, –1, 0, 1, and +127 are valid values.

xs:date

The primitive type xs:date represents a date of the Gregorian calendar. The lexical representation of xs:date is YYYY-MM-DD where YYYY represents the year, MM the month, and DD the day. The year value has to be at least four digits, but it can be more than four digits to represent years later than 9999. However, XQuery implementations are not required to support more than four digits. A preceding minus sign (–) can be used to represent years before 0001. A time zone can be added to the end, as described in "Time Zones" in Chapter 19.

Values of type xs:date can be cast to and from xs:dateTime, as described in the section on xs:dateTime. You can obtain the current date using the current-date function, which returns a value of type xs:date.

Table B-3 lists some values of the xs:date type. For more information on working with dates, see Chapter 19.

Table B-3. Values of the xs:date type

Values	Explanation
Valid	
2006-05-03	May 3, 2006
2006-05-03-05:00	May 3, 2006, U.S. Eastern Standard Time, which is five hours behind Coordinated Universal Time (UTC)
2006-05-03Z	May 3, 2006, Coordinated Universal Time (UTC)
Invalid	
2006/05/03	Slashes are not allowed as separators
05-03-2006	The value must be in YYYY-MM-DD order
2006-09-31	The date must be valid (September has 30 days)
	An empty value or zero-length string is not permitted

xs:dateTime

The primitive type xs:dateTime represents a combined date and time. The lexical representation of xs:dateTime is YYYY-MM-DDThh:mm:ss.sss, which is a concatenation of the xs:date and xs:time representation, with an uppercase letter T between them. The constraints described for the xs:date and xs:time types are also true for xs:dateTime. A time zone can be added to the end, as described in "Time Zones" in Chapter 19.

Table B-4 lists some values of the xs:dateTime type. For more information on working with dates and times, see Chapter 19.

Table B-4. Values of the xs:dateTime type

Values	Explanation
Valid	
`2006-05-03T13:20:00`	1:20 P.M. on May 3, 2006
`2006-05-03T13:20:15.5`	1:20 P.M. and 15.5 seconds on May 3, 2006
`2006-05-03T13:20:00-05:00`	1:20 P.M. on May 3, 2006, U.S. Eastern Standard Time
`2006-05-03T13:20:00Z`	1:20 P.M. on May 3, 2006, Coordinated Universal Time (UTC)
`2006-05-03T24:00:00`	Midnight the evening of May 3/morning of May 4
`2006-05-04T00:00:00`	Midnight the evening of May 3/morning of May 4 (equal to the previous example)
Invalid	
`2006-05-03T13:00`	Seconds must be specified
`2006-05-03`	The time is required
`2006-05-0313:20:00`	The letter T is required
	An empty value or zero-length string is not permitted

Values of type xs:dateTime can be constructed using the standard xs:dateTime constructor. In addition, a function named dateTime can be used to construct an xs:dateTime value from an xs:date and an xs:time. You can obtain the current date/time using the current-dateTime function, which returns a value of type xs:dateTime.

It is possible to cast some values to and from xs:dateTime, as shown in the examples in Table B-5. You can split an xs:dateTime value into its date and time components by casting it to xs:date or xs:time. Additionally, xs:date values can be cast to xs:dateTime, in which case the time components are filled in with zeros. Time zones are unchanged by the cast.

Table B-5. Examples of casting to date and time values

Expression	Result
`xs:dateTime("2006-05-03T10:32:15") cast as xs:date`	`2006-05-03`
`xs:dateTime("2006-05-03T10:32:15") cast as xs:time`	`10:32:15`
`xs:date("2006-05-03") cast as xs:dateTime`	`2006-05-03T00:00:00`

xs:dayTimeDuration

The xs:dayTimeDuration type is a restriction of the xs:duration type, with only day (D), hour (H), minute (M), and second (S) components allowed. Its lexical representation is PnDTnHnMnS, where an uppercase P starts the expression, n indicates the quantity of each component, and an uppercase letter T separates the day and time

components. For example, the value P3DT5H represents a period of three days and five hours. You can omit components whose quantity is zero, but at least one component is required.

All of the lexical rules for xs:duration also apply to the xs:dayTimeDuration type. This includes allowing a negative sign at the beginning of the value. Table B-6 lists some values of the xs:dayTimeDuration type.

 In previous versions of XQuery (including the Candidate Recommendation), dayTimeDuration was prefixed with xdt: instead of xs: because it was in a different namespace. Some processors still support the previous namespaces for these types instead.

Unlike the xs:duration type, the xs:dayTimeDuration type is totally ordered, meaning that its values can be compared using the operators <, >, <=, and >=. For more on working with durations, see Chapter 19.

Table B-6. Values of the xs:dayTimeDuration type

Values	Explanation
Valid	
P6DT11H32M20S	6 days, 11 hours, 32 minutes, 20 seconds
P2DT3H	2 day, 3 hours
PT40H	40 hours (the number of hours can be more than 24)
PT0S	0 seconds
-P60D	Minus 60 days
Invalid	
P2Y	Years and months may not be specified
P15.5D	Only the seconds number can contain a decimal point
P1D2H	The letter T must be used to separate day and time components
PT30S35M	Minutes must appear before seconds
	An empty value or zero-length string is not permitted

xs:decimal

The primitive type xs:decimal represents a decimal number. The lexical representation of xs:decimal is a sequence of digits that can be preceded by a sign (+ or –) and may contain a decimal point (.). Trailing zeros after the decimal point are not considered significant. That is, the decimal values 5.1 and 5.1000 are considered equal.

Table B-7 lists some values of the xs:decimal type.

Table B-7. Values of the xs:decimal type

Values	Explanation
Valid	
5.0	
-5.2	A sign is permitted
6	A decimal point is not required
0	
0006.000	Leading and trailing zeros are valid
Invalid	
5,6	The decimal separator must be a period, not a comma
1e6	Exponential notation is not allowed; use xs:float or xs:double instead
	An empty value or zero-length string is not permitted

Implementations vary in the number of significant digits they allow. They are free to round or truncate values to the number of digits they support. If overflow occurs during arithmetic operations on xs:decimal values, an error is raised. When underflow occurs, the value 0.0 is returned.

Casting xs:decimal Values

Values of type xs:decimal can be cast to and from any of the other numeric types. Casting among numeric types is straightforward if the value is in the value space of both types. For example, casting an xs:decimal value 12.5 to xs:float results in a value 12.5E0 whose type is xs:float.

However, some xs:float or xs:double values cannot be cast to xs:decimal. An error is raised if you attempt to cast to xs:decimal one of the special values NaN, INF or -INF, or a value that is too large or too small to be supported by the implementation.

You can cast xs:decimal values to xs:integer, in which case the value is truncated.

Values of type xs:decimal can also be cast to and from xs:string, xs:untypedAtomic, and xs:boolean. When cast to xs:string, the value will have no positive sign, no leading zeros, and no trailing zeros after the decimal point, except that there will always be at least one digit before the decimal point. If there is no fractional part, the decimal point is omitted. When cast to xs:boolean, the value 0 becomes false, and all other values become true.

xs:double

The primitive type xs:double is patterned after an IEEE double-precision 64-bit floating-point number. The lexical representation is a mantissa (a decimal number) followed, optionally, by the letter E (in upper or lowercase), followed by an integer

exponent. For example, 3E2 represents 3×10^2, or 300. In addition, there are three special values: INF, (infinity), -INF (negative infinity), and NaN (not a number).

Table B-8 lists some values of the xs:double type.

Table B-8. Values of the xs:double type

Values	Explanation
Valid	
-5E12	
44.56E5	
+23.2e-2	
12	
+3.5	Any value valid for xs:decimal is also valid for xs:float and xs:double
-0	Negative zero
INF	Positive infinity
NaN	Not a number
Invalid	
-5E3.5	The exponent must be an integer
37E	An exponent must be specified if E is present
	An empty value or zero-length string is not permitted

XQuery makes a distinction between positive and negative zero values for the xs:double type. 0 and -0 are considered to be equal but separate values.

The implementation has some flexibility regarding how to handle overflow or underflow during arithmetic operations on xs:double values. The processor may raise an error. Alternatively, in an overflow situation, it may return INF, -INF, or the largest or smallest possible value. For underflow, it may return the closest possible value to zero.

Casting xs:double Values

Values of type xs:double can be cast to and from any of the other numeric types. Casting among numeric types is straightforward if the value is in the value space of both types. For example, casting an xs:double value 12.5E0 to xs:float results in a value 12.5E0 whose type is xs:float.

However, some xs:double values are either too large or are otherwise not represented in the value spaces of xs:float, xs:decimal, or xs:integer. See the descriptions of these types for more information.

Values of type xs:double can also be cast to and from xs:string, xs:untypedAtomic, and xs:boolean. When cast to xs:string, if the value is between 0.000001 (inclusive)

and 1,000,000 (exclusive), the value is represented as a decimal. It will have no exponent, no positive sign, and no leading or trailing zeros, except that there will always be at least one digit before the decimal point. If there is no fractional part, the decimal point is omitted. If the value is outside that range, it is represented using an exponent as shown in the first three examples in Table B-8.

xs:duration

The primitive type xs:duration represents a duration of time. It allows you to specify a number of years (Y), months (M), days (D), hours (H), minutes (M), and seconds (S). The lexical representation of xs:duration is PnYnMnDTnHnMnS, where an uppercase P starts the expression, n indicates the quantity of each component, and an uppercase letter T separates the day and time components. For example, the value P3YT5H represents a period of three years and five hours.

The following rules apply to xs:duration values:

- A minus sign may appear at the beginning of the value (before the P) to indicate a negative duration.

- You can omit components whose quantity is zero, but at least one component is required.

- If no time components (hours, minutes, seconds) are specified, the T cannot appear.

- The numbers must be integers, except for the number of seconds, which can include a decimal point. XQuery implementations are required to support up to three fractional digits in the number of seconds, but may support more.

- If a decimal point appears in the number of seconds, there must be at least one digit after the decimal point.

Table B-9 lists some values of the xs:duration type. For more information on working with durations, see Chapter 19.

Table B-9. Values of the xs:duration type

Values	Explanation
Valid	
P3Y5M8DT9H25M20S	3 years, 5 months, 8 days, 9 hours, 25 minutes, 20 seconds
P2DT3H	2 day, 3 hours
P25M	25 months (the number of months may be more than 12)
PT25M	25 minutes
P0Y	0 years
-P60Y	Minus 60 years
PT1M30.5S	1 minute, 30.5 seconds

Values	Explanation
Invalid	
P16.3D	All numbers except the seconds must be integers
P3D5H	The T must be used to separate days and time components
P-40M	The minus sign must appear first
P1YM5D	The number of months is missing
	An empty value or zero-length string is not permitted

The xs:duration type is not totally ordered, meaning that values of this type cannot be compared because it is sometimes ambiguous. For example, if you try to determine whether the xs:duration value P1M is greater than or less than the xs:duration value P30D, it is ambiguous. Months may have 28, 29, 30, or 31 days, so is 30 days less than a month or not?

For this reason, XQuery defines two new types that are derived from duration: xs:yearMonthDuration and xs:dayTimeDuration. By ensuring that month and day components never appear in the same duration, the ambiguity is eliminated.

Values of xs:duration can be tested for equality (or inequality) with other values of the same type. Two xs:duration values will be considered equal if they have the same (normalized) number of months and seconds. For example, P1YT60S is equal to P12MT1M because they represent the same duration of time (12 months and 60 seconds).* However, you cannot compare them using the operators <, <=, >, or >=. These operators *can* be used on the two ordered subtypes.

xs:ENTITIES

The type xs:ENTITIES represents a whitespace-separated list of xs:ENTITY values. XQuery does not provide any special functions for this type. However, since xs:ENTITY is ultimately derived from xs:string, a value of type xs:ENTITIES can be treated like a sequence of xs:string values.

xs:ENTITY

The type xs:ENTITY represents a value that refers to an unparsed entity, which must be declared in the document's DTD. The xs:ENTITY type might be used to include information from another file that is not in XML syntax, such as images. XQuery does not provide any special functions for this type. However, since xs:ENTITY is ultimately derived from xs:string, xs:ENTITY values can be compared and used like strings.

* This is in contrast to the way they are handled in XML Schema validation, where they would be considered two different values.

xs:float

The primitive type xs:float is patterned after an IEEE single-precision 32-bit floating-point number. The lexical representation is a mantissa (a decimal number) followed, optionally, by the letter E (in upper- or lowercase), followed by an integer exponent. For example, 3E2 represents 3×10^2, or 300. In addition, there are three special values: INF, (infinity), -INF (negative infinity), and NaN (not a number).

Table B-10 lists some values of the xs:float type.

Table B-10. Values of the xs:float type

Values	Explanation
Valid	
-5E12	
44.56E5	
+23.2e-2	
12	
+3.5	Any value valid for xs:decimal is also valid for xs:float and xs:double
-0	Negative zero
INF	Positive infinity
NaN	Not a number
Invalid	
-5E3.5	The exponent must be an integer
37E	An exponent must be specified if E is present
	An empty value or zero-length string is not permitted

XQuery makes a distinction between positive and negative zero values for the xs:float type. 0 and -0 are considered to be equal but separate values.

The implementation has some flexibility regarding how to handle overflow or underflow occurs during arithmetic operations on xs:float values. The processor may raise an error. Alternatively, in an overflow situation, it may return INF, -INF, or the largest or smallest possible value. For underflow, it may return the closest possible value to zero.

Casting xs:float Values

Values of type xs:float can be cast to and from any of the other numeric types. Casting among numeric types is straightforward if the value is in the value space of both types. For example, casting an xs:float value 12.5E0 to xs:decimal results in a value 12.5 whose type is xs:decimal.

However, some xs:float values are either too large or are otherwise not represented in the value spaces of xs:decimal or xs:integer. See the descriptions of these types for more information.

Additionally, some special cases apply when casting xs:double values to xs:float. Values that are too large to be represented by xs:float are cast to INF, values that are too small are cast to -INF, and values that would cause underflow are cast to 0.

Values of type xs:float can also be cast to and from xs:string, xs:untypedAtomic, and xs:boolean. When cast to xs:string, if the value is between 0.000001 (inclusive) and 1000000 (exclusive), the value is represented as a decimal. It will have no exponent, no positive sign, and no leading or trailing zeros, except that there will always be at least one digit before the decimal point. If there is no fractional part, the decimal point is omitted. If the value is outside that range, it is represented using an exponent as shown in the first three examples in Table B-10.

xs:gDay

The primitive type xs:gDay represents a recurring day of the month. It can be used to specify, for example, that bills are sent out on the 15th of each month. It does *not* represent a number of days; to represent that, use the xs:dayTimeDuration type instead.

The lexical representation of xs:gDay is ---DD, where DD is a two-digit day number. An optional time zone may be used, as described in "Time Zones" in Chapter 19. Table B-11 lists some values of xs:gDay.

Table B-11. Values of the xs:gDay type

Values	Explanation
Valid	
---04	The fourth of the month
Invalid	
---41	It must be a valid day of the month
04	The three leading hyphens are required
---4	It must have two digits
	An empty value or zero-length string is not permitted

Values of xs:gDay can be tested for equality (or inequality) with other values of the same type, but they cannot be compared using the operators <, <=, >, or >=.

Values of this type can be cast from the xs:date and xs:dateTime types. For example, the expression xs:date("2006-05-30") cast as xs:gDay returns an xs:gDay value of ---30. They can also be cast to and from xs:string and xs:untypedAtomic.

xs:gMonth

The primitive type xs:gMonth represents a recurring month. It can be used to specify, for example, that year-end auditing occurs in October of every year. It does *not* represent a number of months; to represent that, use the xs:yearMonthDuration type instead.

The lexical representation of xs:gMonth is --MM. An optional time zone may be used, as described in "Time Zones" in Chapter 19. Table B-12 lists some values of this type.

Table B-12. Values of the xs:gMonth type

Values	Explanation
Valid	
--06	June
Invalid	
--06--	Because of an error in the first version of XML Schema, you will often see examples that use this format, but it is technically invalid
--15	The month must be a valid month
2006-06	The year cannot be specified
06	The two leading hyphens are required
--6	It must have two digits
	An empty value or zero-length string is not permitted

Values of xs:gMonth can be tested for equality (or inequality) with other values of the same type, but you cannot compare them using the operators <, <=, >, or >=.

Values of this type can be cast from the xs:date and xs:dateTime types. For example, the expression xs:date("2006-05-30") cast as xs:gMonth returns an xs:gMonth value of --05. They can also be cast to and from xs:string and xs:untypedAtomic.

xs:gMonthDay

The primitive type xs:gMonthDay represents a recurring day of the year. It can be used to specify, for example, that your anniversary is on the 30th of July every year.

The lexical representation of xs:gMonthDay is --MM-DD. An optional time zone can be used, as described in "Time Zones" in Chapter 19. Table B-13 lists some values of this type.

Table B-13. Values of the xs:gMonthDay type

Values	Explanation
Valid	
--05-03	May 3
--05-03Z	May 3, Coordinated Universal Time (UTC)
Invalid	
--05-32	It must be a valid day of the year
05-03	The two leading hyphens are required
--5-3	The month and day must have two digits each
	An empty value or zero-length string is not permitted

Values of xs:gMonthDay can be tested for equality (or inequality) with other values of the same type, but they cannot be compared using the operators <, <=, >, or >=.

Values of this type can be cast from the xs:date and xs:dateTime types. For example, the expression xs:date("2006-05-30") cast as xs:gMonthDay returns an xs:gMonthDay value of --05-30. They can also be cast to and from xs:string and xs:untypedAtomic.

xs:gYear

The primitive type xs:gYear represents a specific year. The lexical representation of xs:gYear is YYYY. A preceding minus sign (–) can be used to represent years before 0001. An optional time zone may be used, as described in "Time Zones" in Chapter 19. Table B-14 lists some values of the xs:gYear type.

Table B-14. Values of the xs:gYear type

Values	Explanation
Valid	
2006	2006
2006-08:00	2006, U.S. Pacific Time
12006	The year 12006
0922	The year 922
-0073	73 B.C.
Invalid	
99	It must have at least four digits
922	It must have at least four digits; leading zeros can be added
	An empty value or zero-length string is not permitted

Values of xs:gYear can be tested for equality (or inequality) with other values of the same type, but they cannot be compared using the operators <, <=, >, or >=.

Values of this type can be cast from the xs:date and xs:dateTime types. For example, the expression xs:date("2006-05-30") cast as xs:gYear returns an xs:gYear value of 2006. They can also be cast to and from xs:string and xs:untypedAtomic.

xs:gYearMonth

The primitive type xs:gYearMonth represents a specific month. The lexical representation of xs:gYearMonth is YYYY-MM. A preceding minus sign (–) can be used to represent years before 0001. An optional time zone may be used, as described in "Time Zones" in Chapter 19. Table B-15 lists some values of the xs:gYearMonth type.

Table B-15. Values of the xs:gYearMonth type

Values	Explanation
Valid	
2006-05	May 2006
2006-05-08:00	May 2006, U.S. Pacific Time
Invalid	
2006-5	The month must have two digits
2006-13	The month must be a valid month
	An empty value or zero-length string is not permitted

Values of xs:gYearMonth can be tested for equality (or inequality) with other values of the same type, but they cannot be compared using the operators <, <=, >, or >=.

Values of this type can be cast from the xs:date and xs:dateTime types. For example, the expression xs:date("2006-05-30") cast as xs:gYearMonth returns an xs:gYearMonth value of 2006-05. They can also be cast to and from xs:string and xs:untypedAtomic.

xs:hexBinary

The primitive type xs:hexBinary represents binary data as a sequence of binary octets. The type xs:hexBinary uses hexadecimal encoding, where each binary octet is a two-character hexadecimal number. Digits 0 through 9 and lowercase and uppercase letters A through F are permitted. For example, 0CD7 and 0cd7 are two equal xs:hexBinary representations consisting of two octets.

Table B-16 lists some values of the xs:hexBinary type.

Table B-16. Values of the xs:hexBinary type

Values	Explanation
Valid	
0CD7	
0cd7	The equivalent of 0CD7
	An empty value is allowed
Invalid	
CD7	An odd number of characters is not allowed; characters appear in pairs

Casting and Comparing xs:hexBinary Values

Values of type xs:hexBinary can be cast to and from xs:base64Binary, xs:string, and xs:untypedAtomic. When cast to xs:string, xs:hexBinary values are converted to their canonical representation, which uses only uppercase letters.

Two xs:hexBinary values can be compared using the value comparison operators = and !=. Two xs:hexBinary values are considered equal if their canonical representations are equal. This means that the case of the letters is not taken into account in the comparison. An xs:hexBinary value is never equal to an xs:base64Binary value, nor is it equal to an xs:string containing the same characters.

Because the type is not ordered, two xs:hexBinary values cannot be compared using the <, <=, >, or >= operators.

xs:ID

The type xs:ID represents a unique identifier in an XML document. It is most commonly used as the type of an attribute that serves as an identifier for the element that carries it. Example B-1 shows an XML document that contains some ID attributes, namely the id attribute of the section element, and the fnid attribute of the fn element. Each section and fn element is uniquely identified by an ID value, such as fn1, preface, or context.

The example assumes that this document was validated with a schema that declares these attributes to be of type xs:ID. Having the local name id is not enough to make an attribute an xs:ID; the attribute must be declared in a schema to have the type ID. In fact, the name is irrelevant; an attribute named foo can have the type xs:ID, and an attribute named id can be of type xs:integer.

Example B-1. XML document with IDs and IDREFs (book.xml)

```
<book>
  <section id="preface">This book introduces XQuery...
    The examples are downloadable<fnref ref="fn1"/>...
  </section>
```

Example B-1. XML document with IDs and IDREFs (book.xml) (continued)

```
  <section id="context">...</section>
  <section id="language">...Expressions, introduced
   in <secRef refs="context"/>, are...
  </section>
  <section id="types">...As described in
    <secRef refs="context language"/>, you can...
  </section>
  <fn fnid="fn1">See http://datypic.com.</fn>
</book>
```

The values of attributes of type xs:ID must be unique within the entire XML document. This is true even if two xs:ID values appear in attributes with different names, or on elements with different names. For example, it would be illegal for an fn element's fnid attribute to have the same value as a section element's id attribute. Values of type xs:ID follow the same rules as the xs:NCName type; they must start with a letter or underscore, and can only contain letters, digits, underscores, hyphens, and periods.

Because xs:ID is ultimately derived from xs:string, xs:ID values can be compared and used like strings. For more information on working with IDs, see "Working with IDs" in Chapter 20.

xs:IDREF

The type xs:IDREF represents a cross-reference to an xs:ID value. Like xs:ID, it is most commonly used to describe attribute values. Each attribute of type xs:IDREF must reference an ID in the same XML document. For example, the ref attribute of the fnref element in Example B-1 contains an xs:IDREF value (again, assuming it is validated with a schema). Its value, fn1, matches the value of the fnid attribute of the fn element. You can find all the xs:IDREF values that refer to a specific ID using the idref function.

Because xs:IDREF is ultimately derived from xs:string, xs:IDREF values can be compared and used like strings. For more information on working with IDREFs, see "Working with IDs" in Chapter 20.

xs:IDREFS

The type xs:IDREFS represents a whitespace-separated list of one or more xs:IDREF values. In Example B-1, the refs attribute of secRef is assumed to be of type xs:IDREFS. The first refs attribute contains only one xs:IDREF (context), while the second contains two xs:IDREF values (context and language).

Because xs:IDREF is derived by restriction from xs:string, a value of type xs:IDREFS can be treated like a sequence of xs:string values.

xs:int

The type xs:int represents an integer between −2147483648 and 2147483647 inclusive. It is ultimately derived from xs:decimal, via xs:integer. Its value can be a sequence of digits, optionally preceded by a sign (+ or −). For example, -223, -1, 0, 5, and +3367 are valid values.

xs:integer

The type xs:integer represents an arbitrarily large integer. It is derived from xs:decimal, and it is the base type for many other integer types.

The lexical representation of the xs:integer type is a sequence of digits. A sign (+ or −) may precede the numbers. Decimal points are not permitted in xs:integer values, even if there are no significant digits after the decimal point. Table B-17 lists some values of the xs:integer type.

Table B-17. Values of the xs:integer type

Values	Explanation
Valid	
231	
00231	Leading zeros are permitted
0	
+4	A sign is permitted
-4	
Invalid	
4.0	A decimal point is not permitted
	An empty value or zero-length string is not permitted

Implementations vary in the number of significant digits they support. If overflow or underflow occurs during arithmetic operations on xs:integer values, the implementation may either raise an error or return a result that is the remainder after dividing by the largest possible integer value.

Casting xs:integer Values

Values of type xs:integer can be cast to and from any of the other numeric types. Casting among numeric types is straightforward if the value is in the value space of both types. For example, casting an xs:float value 12 to xs:integer in results in a value 12 whose type is xs:integer. When casting a number with a fractional part to xs:integer, the fractional part is truncated (not rounded).

However, some xs:float or xs:double values cannot be cast to xs:integer. An error is raised if you attempt to cast to xs:integer one of the special values NaN, INF or –INF, or if a value is greater or smaller than those supported by the implementation.

Values of type xs:integer can also be cast to and from xs:string, xs:untypedAtomic, and xs:boolean. When cast to xs:string, the value will have no positive sign and no leading zeros. When cast to xs:boolean, the value 0 becomes false, and all other values become true.

xs:language

The type xs:language represents a natural language. It is often used for attributes that specify the language of the element. Its values conform to *RFC 3066, Tags for the Identification of Languages*. The most common format is a two- or three-character, (usually lowercase) language code that follows ISO 639, such as en or fr. It can optionally be followed by a hyphen and a two-character (usually uppercase) country code that follows ISO 3166, such as en-US. Additional dialects or country codes may be specified at the end of the value, each preceded by a hyphen.

Processors do not verify that values of the language type conform to the above rules. They simply validate based on the pattern specified for this type, which says that the value must consist of parts containing one to eight characters, separated by hyphens.

The xs:language type is most commonly associated with the xml:lang attribute defined in the XML specification; the value of this attribute may be tested using the lang function. Table B-18 lists some values of the xs:language type.

Table B-18. Values of the xs:language type

Values	Explanation
Valid	
en	English
en-US	U.S. English
en-GB	U.K. English
de	German
es	Spanish
fr	French
it	Italian
ja	Japanese
nl	Dutch
zh	Chinese
any-value-with-short-parts	Although this value is valid, it does not follow RFC 3066 guidelines

Values	Explanation
Invalid	
`longerThan8`	Parts may not exceed eight characters in length
	An empty value or zero-length string is not permitted

The `xs:language` type is derived by restriction from `xs:string`, so any functions and operations that can be performed on strings, such as `substring` and comparing using the `<` operator, can also be performed on `xs:language` values.

xs:long

The type `xs:long` represents an integer between −9223372036854775808 and 9223372036854775807 inclusive. It is ultimately derived from `xs:decimal`, via `xs:integer`. Its value can be a sequence of digits, optionally preceded by a sign (+ or −). For example, −9223372036854775808, 0, 1, and +214 are valid values. Because implementations are only required to support integers up to 18 digits, some may not accept the full value range of `xs:long`.

xs:Name

The `xs:Name` type is used to represent a lexically valid name in XML. However, this type is almost never used in XQuery or XML Schema. The `xs:QName` type is much more appropriate to fully represent names, whether they are in a namespace or not. For unqualified names or local parts of names, `xs:NCName` or even `xs:string` are also appropriate types.

xs:NCName

The letters `NC` in `NCName` stand for noncolonized. The type `xs:NCName` can be used to represent the local part of names, or even prefixes. An `xs:NCName` value must start with a letter and underscore (_), and may contain only letters, digits, underscores, hyphens, and periods.

Because `xs:NCName` is ultimately derived from `xs:string`, `xs:NCName` values can be compared and used like strings.

xs:negativeInteger

The type `xs:negativeInteger` represents an arbitrarily large integer less than 0. It is ultimately derived from `xs:decimal` via `xs:integer`. Its value can be a sequence of digits, preceded by a sign (−). For example, −1 and −1234123412341234 are valid values.

xs:NMTOKEN

The type xs:NMTOKEN represents a string that contains no whitespace. xs:NMTOKEN values may consist only of characters allowed in XML names, namely letters, digits, periods, hyphens, underscores, and colons. For example, navy, 123, and SENDER_OR_RECEIVER are all valid values. Leading and trailing whitespace is allowed but is considered insignificant.

Because xs:NMTOKEN is ultimately derived from xs:string, xs:NMTOKEN values can be compared and used like strings.

xs:NMTOKENS

The type xs:NMTOKENS represents a whitespace-separated list of one or more xs:NMTOKEN values. For example, navy black is a valid value that represents two different xs:NMTOKEN values. Because xs:NMTOKEN is derived by restriction from xs:string, a value of type xs:NMTOKENS can be treated like a sequence of xs:string values.

xs:nonNegativeInteger

The type xs:nonNegativeInteger represents an arbitrarily large integer greater than or equal to 0. It is ultimately derived from xs:decimal via xs:integer. Its value can be a sequence of digits, optionally preceded by a sign (+). For example, 0, 1, and +1234123412341234 are valid values.

xs:nonPositiveInteger

The type xs:nonPositiveInteger represents an arbitrarily large integer less than or equal to 0. It is ultimately derived from xs:decimal, via xs:integer. Its value can be a sequence of digits, optionally preceded by a sign (– or + if the value is 0). For example, 0, -1 and -1234123412341234 are valid values.

xs:normalizedString

The xs:normalizedString type is identical to xs:string, except in the way that whitespace is normalized in its values. This whitespace normalization takes place during validation, and also when values are constructed or cast to xs:normalizedString. For values of type xs:normalizedString, the processor replaces each carriage return, line feed, and tab by a single space. This is different from xs:string values, where whitespace is preserved. There is no collapsing of multiple consecutive spaces into a single space; this is done with values of type xs:token.

The whitespace handling of the xs:normalizedString type is different from that of the normalize-string function, which *does* collapse multiple adjacent spaces to a single space.

The xs:normalizedString type is derived by restriction from xs:string, so any functions and operations that can be performed on strings, such as substring and comparing using the < operator, can also be performed on xs:normalizedString values.

xs:NOTATION

The primitive type xs:NOTATION represents a reference to an XML notation. Notations are a way to indicate how to interpret non-XML content that is rarely used in the domain of XQuery and XML Schema. xs:NOTATION is an abstract type, and as such, you cannot construct values that have the type xs:NOTATION. It is possible to create user-defined types that are restrictions of xs:NOTATION, which do have type constructors associated with them. These type constructors have the constraint that they will only accept a literal string as an argument, not an evaluated expression.

xs:positiveInteger

The type xs:positiveInteger represents an arbitrarily large integer greater than 0. It is ultimately derived from xs:decimal via xs:integer. Its value can be a sequence of digits, optionally preceded by a sign (+). For example, 1 and 1234123412341234 are valid values.

xs:QName

The primitive type xs:QName represents an XML namespace-qualified name. In XQuery, xs:QName values have three parts: the full namespace URI, the local part of the name, and the prefix. The namespace and the prefix are optional. If a QName does not have a namespace associated with it, it is considered to be in "no namespace."

When used in a query or schema, the lexical representation of an xs:QName has just two parts: an optional prefix and the local part of the name. Based on the prefix, the context is used to determine the namespace URI. If the prefix is not present, either the name is in the default namespace or it is in no namespace at all.

Table B-19 lists some values of the xs:QName type.

Table B-19. Values of the xs:QName type

Values	Explanation
Valid	
prod:number	Valid assuming the prefix prod is mapped to a namespace in scope
number	Prefix and colon are optional
Invalid	
:number	An xs:QName must not start with a colon
prod:3rdnumber	The local part must not start with a number; it must be a valid NCName
	An empty value or zero-length string is not permitted

The prefix itself has no meaning; it is just a placeholder. However, the XQuery processor does keep track of a QName's prefix. This simplifies certain processes such as serializing QNames and casting them to strings.

One of the most common ways of getting an xs:QName is to use the node-name function, which returns the name of an element or attribute as an xs:QName value.

The xs:QName type has a standard constructor that allows a value to be cast from xs:untypedAtomic or from xs:string. However, it has a special constraint that it can only accept a literal xs:string value (not an evaluated expression) as its argument. The value may be prefixed, e.g., prod:number, or unprefixed, e.g., number. If a prefix is used, it must be declared.

Two additional functions can be used to construct xs:QName values: QName and resolve-QName.

Two xs:QName values can be compared using the = and != operators. They are considered equal if they have the exact same namespace URI (based on Unicode code points) and the exact same local name (also based on Unicode code points); the prefixes are ignored. Because the xs:QName type is not ordered, two xs:QName values cannot be compared using the <, <=, >, or >= operators. The xs:QName type is not derived from xs:string, so you cannot compare them to strings directly.

More information on working with qualified names can be found in "Working with Qualified Names" in Chapter 20.

xs:short

The type xs:short represents an integer between −32768 and 32767 inclusive. It is ultimately derived from xs:decimal via xs:integer. Its value can be a sequence of digits, optionally preceded by a sign (+ or −). For example, -32768, -1, 0, 1, and +32767 are valid values.

xs:string

An xs:string value is a character string that may contain any character allowed by XML. The xs:string type is a primitive type from which a large number of other types are derived. It is intended to represent generic character data, and whitespace in elements of type xs:string is always preserved.

It should be noted that xs:string is not the default type for untyped values. If a value is selected from an input document with no schema, the value is given the type xs:untypedAtomic, not xs:string. But it is easy enough to cast an xs:untypedAtomic value to xs:string. In fact, you can cast a value of any type to xs:string, and you can cast an xs:string value to any type (with restrictions for xs:QName and xs:NOTATION).

Chapter 17 provides an overview of all the functions and operations on strings. All of the operations and functions that can be performed on xs:string values can also be performed on values whose types are restrictions of xs:string. This includes user-defined types that appear in a schema, as well as the built-in derived types such as xs:normalizedString, xs:language, and xs:ID.

xs:time

The primitive type xs:time represents a specific time of day. The lexical representation of xs:time is hh:mm:ss.sss where hh is the hour, mm is the minutes, and ss.sss is the seconds. XQuery implementations are required to support at least three fractional digits for the number of seconds, but may support more. To represent P.M. values, the hours 13 through 24 should be used. Either of the values 00:00:00 or 24:00:00 can be used to represent midnight. These values are considered identical, which means that 24:00:00 is considered less than 23:59:59. A time zone can be added to the end, as described in "Time Zones" in Chapter 19.

Values of type xs:dateTime can be cast to xs:time, but the reverse is not true. This is described further in the section on xs:dateTime. You can obtain the current time using the current-time function, which returns a value of type xs:time.

Table B-20 lists some values of the xs:time type. For more information on working with times, see Chapter 19.

Table B-20. Values of the xs:time type

Values	Explanation
Valid	
15:30:00	3:30 P.M.
15:30:34.67	3:30 P.M. and 34.67 seconds.
15:30:00-08:00	3:30 P.M., U.S. Pacific Time

Values	Explanation
15:30:00Z	3:30 P.M., Coordinated Universal Time (UTC)
00:00:00	Midnight
24:00:00	Midnight (equal to the previous example)
Invalid	
3:40:00	All numbers must be two digits each
15:30	Seconds must be specified
15:70:00	It must be a valid time of day
	An empty value or zero-length string is not permitted

xs:token

The xs:token type is identical to xs:string, except in the way that whitespace is normalized in its values. This whitespace normalization takes place during validation, and also when values are constructed or cast to xs:token. In values of type xs:token, the processor replaces each carriage return, line feed, and tab by a single space. Subsequently, all consecutive whitespace characters are replaced by a single space, and leading and trailing spaces are removed. This is different from xs:string values, where whitespace is preserved. It is also different from xs:normalizedString, which replaces whitespace characters but does not collapse them.

A value of type xs:token *can* contain whitespace, despite the fact that "token" implies a single token. The xs:token type is derived by restriction from xs:string, so any functions and operations that can be performed on strings, such as substring and comparisons using the < operator, can also be performed on xs:token values.

xs:unsignedByte

The type xs:unsignedByte represents an unsigned integer between 0 and 255 inclusive. It is ultimately derived from xs:decimal via xs:integer. Its value can be a sequence of digits. For example, 0, 1, and 255 are valid values. A leading plus sign (+) is not allowed.

xs:unsignedInt

The type xs:unsignedInt represents an unsigned integer between 0 and 4294967295 inclusive. It is ultimately derived from xs:decimal, via xs:integer. Its value can be a sequence of digits. For example, 0, 1, and 4294967295 are valid values. A leading plus sign (+) is not allowed.

xs:unsignedLong

The type `xs:unsignedLong` represents an unsigned integer between 0 and 18446744073709551615 inclusive. It is ultimately derived from `xs:decimal` via `xs:integer`. Its value can be a sequence of digits—e.g., 0, 1, and 18446744073709551615 are valid values. A leading plus sign (+) is not allowed.

xs:unsignedShort

The type `xs:unsignedShort` represents an unsigned integer between 0 and 65535 inclusive. It is ultimately derived from `xs:decimal` via `xs:integer`. Its value can be a sequence of digits. For example, 0, 1, and 65535 are valid values. A leading plus sign (+) is not allowed.

xs:untyped

The generic `xs:untyped` type applies to all element nodes that are "untyped", i.e., have no specific type annotation. This includes element nodes that not were validated against a schema declaration. "Types, Nodes, and Atomic Values" in Chapter 11 describes how element nodes might come to be untyped.

 In previous versions of XQuery (including the Candidate Recommendation), `untyped` was prefixed with `xdt:` instead of `xs:` because it was in a different namespace. Some processors still support the previous namespaces for these types instead.

xs:untypedAtomic

The generic `xs:untypedAtomic` type applies to all attribute nodes and atomic values that are "untyped," i.e., have no specific type. An attribute node is untyped if it was not validated against a schema declaration. "Types, Nodes, and Atomic Values" in Chapter 11 describes how attribute nodes might come to be untyped.

An atomic value might have the type `xs:untypedAtomic` if it was extracted from an untyped element or attribute. Untyped atomic values can often be used wherever a typed value would. This is because every function and expression has rules for casting untyped values to an appropriate type.

 In previous versions of XQuery (including the Candidate Recommendation), `untypedAtomic` was prefixed with `xdt:` instead of `xs:` because it was in a different namespace. Some processors still support the previous namespaces for these types instead.

xs:yearMonthDuration

The xs:yearMonthDuration type represents a restriction of the xs:duration type, with only year (Y) and month (M) components allowed. Its lexical representation is PnYnM, where an uppercase P starts the expression, and n indicates the quantity of each component. For example, the value P3Y5M represents a period of three years and five months. You can omit components whose quantity is zero, but at least one component is required.

All of the lexical rules for xs:duration also apply to the xs:yearMonthDuration type. This includes allowing a negative sign at the beginning of the value. Table B-21 lists some values of the xs:yearMonthDuration type.

In previous versions of XQuery (including the Candidate Recommendation), yearMonthDuration was prefixed with xdt: instead of xs: because it was in a different namespace. Some processors still support the previous namespaces for these types instead.

Unlike the xs:duration type, the xs:yearMonthDuration type is totally ordered, meaning that its values can be compared. For more information on working with durations, see Chapter 19.

Table B-21. Values of the xs:yearMonthDuration type

Values	Explanation
Valid	
P3Y5M	3 years, 5 months
P3Y	3 years
P30M	30 months (the number of months can be more than 12)
P0M	0 months
Invalid	
P2Y6M3D	Days cannot be specified
P16.6Y	The number of years cannot be expressed as a decimal
P2M1Y	The years must appear before the months
	An empty value or zero-length string is not permitted

Error Summary

This appendix lists all of the errors that may be raised during evaluation of a query, in alphabetical order by name. The XQuery spec does not define any programming API defining how queries are executed from, for example, C# or Java; but there is an expectation that in any such API, you will be able to test these error codes to find out what went wrong. In most cases, you can also expect that the error code will be accompanied with an error message that gives much more detailed information.

Error names, which are in the namespace `http://www.w3.org/2005/xqt-errors`, are broken down into three parts:

1. A two-character prefix indicating the specification that defines the error, listed in Table C-1.

2. A two-character category that groups the error messages into their functional meaning. In the case of XP and XQ errors, the categories are ST for static errors, DY for dynamic errors, and TY for type errors.

3. A four-digit number.

Table C-1. Error prefixes

Error prefix	Meaning
FO	Functions and Operators
SE	Serialization
XP	XPath
XQ	XQuery

FOAR0001

Division by zero, which may be raised by the `div` or `mod` operator (if the operands are `xs:integer` or `xs:decimal` values) or by the `idiv` operator (regardless of the types of the operands). Using the `div` operator on values of type `xs:float` or `xs:double` will not raise this error; it will return `INF` or `-INF`.

FOAR0002

Overflow or underflow occurred during a numeric operation. This occurs when the result of an arithmetic operation or cast is a value that is either larger or smaller (that is, closer to zero) than the values supported by the implementation.

FOCA0001

An attempt was made to cast to `xs:decimal` a value that is too large or too small to be supported by the implementation.

FOCA0002

A value that is not lexically valid for a particular type has been encountered. This can be raised in two situations:

- When passing an invalid name to the `QName` or `resolve-QName` function; see the descriptions of these functions in Appendix A for details
- When attempting to cast one of the special values NaN, INF, or –INF to `xs:decimal` or `xs:integer`

FOCA0003

An attempt was made to cast to `xs:integer` a value that is too large or too small to be supported by the implementation.

FOCA0005

When multiplying or dividing a duration value by a number, the number supplied was NaN.

FOCA0006

When casting to `xs:decimal`, the value supplied has greater precision than is supported by the implementation.

FOCH0001

A code point passed as an argument to the `codepoints-to-string` function does not refer to a valid XML character.

FOCH0002

An unsupported collation was passed as an argument to a function. Functions that accept collations as arguments are compare, contains, starts-with, ends-with, substring-before, substring-after, index-of, distinct-values, deep-equal, max, and min.

FOCH0003

An unsupported normalization form was passed as an argument to the normalize-unicode function.

FOCH0004

A collation that does not support collation units was passed to a function that requires collation units. Functions that require collation units are contains, starts-with, ends-with, substring-before, and substring-after.

FODC0001

A node that is not part of a complete document (i.e., does not have a document node among its ancestors) was passed to the id or idref function.

FODC0002

When calling the doc or collection function, the processor could not retrieve a resource from the specified URI. See the descriptions of these functions in Appendix A for details.

FODC0003

When calling the doc or collection function multiple times with the same argument, stability of the results returned cannot be guaranteed.

FODC0004

An invalid URI or an unknown collection URI was passed to the collection function. See the description of the collection function in Appendix A for details.

FODC0005

An invalid URI or an unknown document URI was passed to the doc function. See the description of the doc function in Appendix A for details.

FODT0001

Overflow or underflow has occurred during an operation involving a date or time value. This occurs when the result of an arithmetic operation or cast is a value that is either larger or smaller than the values supported by the implementation.

FODT0002

Overflow or underflow has occurred during an operation involving a duration value. This occurs when the result of an arithmetic operation or cast is a value that is either larger or smaller than the values supported by the implementation.

FODT0003

An invalid time zone value was passed to one of the three adjust-xxx-to-timezone functions. This may occur if the value of $timezone is not between -PT14H and PT14H inclusive or if it does not have an even number of minutes (e.g., -PT2H30M30S).

FOER0000

A nonspecific unidentified error has occurred. This may arise if the built-in error function is called with no arguments.

FONS0004

An undeclared prefix was used in either:

- The argument to the xs:QName type constructor
- The first argument to the resolve-QName function

FONS0005

When calling the resolve-uri function, the $base argument is not provided and the base URI of the static context is undefined. Either add a $base argument or use a base-URI declaration in the query prolog.

FORG0001

An invalid value was passed to a type constructor or a cast expression. It might be invalid because it is too large or too small, or because it does not have the correct lexical form or it does not follow the validity rules for the target datatype. This can happen in several situations:

- When passing an invalid value to a type constructor, for example `xs:integer("abc")`
- When passing an invalid value to a cast expression, for example `"2006-13-32" cast as xs:date`
- When passing an untyped value to one of the sum, min, max, or avg functions and that value cannot be cast to `xs:double`

FORG0002

When calling the `resolve-uri` function, either the `$relative` or `$base` argument is not a syntactically valid URI.

FORG0003

A sequence of more than one item was passed to the `zero-or-one` function; the argument must be either the empty sequence or a single item.

FORG0004

An empty sequence was passed to the `one-or-more` function; the argument must be a sequence of one or more items.

FORG0005

An empty sequence or a sequence of more than one item was passed to the `exactly-one` function; the argument must be a single item.

FORG0006

An invalid argument was used in a function or operation. This can happen in three situations:

- You passed an argument sequence to one of the sum or avg functions that contains values that are not numbers or durations, or that are a mixture of numbers and durations.

- You passed an argument sequence to one of the `min` or `max` functions that contains values that do not support the ‹ and › operators, or that have a mixture of different types.
- You attempted to find the effective Boolean value of a multi-item sequence whose first item is an atomic value. Effective Boolean value is calculated when calling the `boolean` and `not` functions, but also in many different operations that do not involve functions, such as conditional (if-then-else) expressions, where clauses of FLWORs, and predicates of path expressions. Effective Boolean value is discussed in more detail in "Effective Boolean Value" in Chapter 11.

One common cause of this is using an expression like:

```
doc("catalog.xml")//product[1 to 3]
```

Although this expression is allowed by some XQuery processors, it is technically not valid because it attempts to find the effective Boolean value of a sequence of integers. Instead, you should use:

```
doc("catalog.xml")//product[position() = 1 to 3]
```

FORG0008

The two arguments passed to the `dateTime` function have different time zones. They should have the same time zone or none at all.

FORG0009

When calling the `resolve-uri` function, the `$relative` argument cannot be resolved relative to the `$base` argument. This might occur if, for example, `$base` itself is a relative URI.

FORX0001

The `$flags` argument passed to the `matches`, `replace`, or `tokenize` function includes invalid letters. Valid letters are lowercase s, m, i, and x, and they may appear in any order.

FORX0002

The `$pattern` argument passed to the `matches`, `replace`, or `tokenize` function is not a valid regular expression. This might occur if, for example, there are mismatched parentheses or unescaped special characters. Note that the regular expression language supported omits many constructs that may be familiar, for example, to Perl programmers.

FORX0003

The $pattern argument passed to the replace or tokenize function matches a zero-length string—for example, q?.

FORX0004

The $replacement argument passed to the replace function is invalid. This can happen in two cases:

- It contains a dollar sign ($) that is not followed by a digit and is not preceded by a backslash (\).
- It contains a backslash that is not followed by a dollar sign and is not preceded by another backslash.

FOTY0012

An attempt was made to find the typed value of a node that has no typed value. This occurs, for example, when you pass to the data function an element node whose type has element-only content. It may also be raised during atomization, which extracts the typed value of a node.

SENR0001

The results of a query contain attribute nodes that are not associated with any elements. This result cannot be serialized.

SEPM0004

The result has no single element node and consists of multiple text nodes or elements nodes. In this case, it is considered to be an XML entity that may be included in another XML document but cannot stand on its own. Therefore, it is an error to specify the doctype-system parameter, or to specify the standalone parameter with a value other than omit.

SEPM0009

If the omit-xml-declaration parameter has the value yes, it is an error if either:

- The standalone attribute has a value other than omit
- The version parameter has a value other than 1.0 and the doctype-system parameter is specified

SEPM0010

Undeclaring namespaces is not allowed in Namespaces 1.0. Therefore, if the output method is XML, it is an error if the value of the `undeclare-prefixes` parameter is `yes` and the value of the `version` parameter is `1.0`.

SEPM0016

A serialization parameter has an incorrect value. Generally, a more specific error message will be provided.

SERE0003

This is a general-purpose error message that indicates that the serializer is unable to create a well-formed XML document or entity.

SERE0005

The result includes an NCName that contains a character not permitted by the version specified by the `version` parameter. The characters allowed in names in XML 1.1 (and Namespaces 1.1) are different from those allowed in XML 1.0 (and Namespaces 1.0).

SERE0006

The result contains a character not permitted by the version specified by the `version` parameter. The characters allowed in XML 1.1 (and Namespaces 1.1) are different from those allowed in XML 1.0 (and Namespaces 1.0).

SERE0008

The result contains a character that cannot be represented in the encoding being used by the serializer, and it cannot be replaced by a character reference (because, for example, it appears in a name, where character references are not allowed by XML syntax).

SERE0012

The value of the `normalization-form` parameter is set to `fully-normalized`, but some text in the result (for example, names or element content) begins with a combining character.

SERE0014

The output method is set to HTML, but the result contains one of the control characters #x7F–#x9F. These characters are allowed in XML, but not HTML. The most likely cause of this error is that the encoding of your input document is incorrectly declared. Microsoft Windows uses codes in this range to represent special characters such as an em dash or a euro currency symbol. If your source XML document uses these Microsoft codes, it must declare this by specifying encoding="cp1252" in the XML declaration. Otherwise they will be taken to represent the Unicode control characters at these positions, which are not allowed in HTML.

SERE0015

The output method is set to HTML, but the result contains a processing instruction that has the character > in its content. This is allowed in XML, but not HTML, because HTML terminates processing instructions with >.

SESU0007

The value of the encoding parameter is not supported by the serializer. All serializers support, at a minimum, UTF-8 and UTF-16.

SESU0011

The value of the normalization-form parameter is not supported by the serializer. All serializers support, at a minimum, NFC and none.

SESU0013

The output method is set to HTML, and the value of the version parameter is a version of HTML not supported by the serializer.

XPDY0002

An expression relies on some part of the dynamic context that is undefined. Most often, this is a path expression or function call that relies on the current context item but the context item is undefined. This may be because you used a relative path, when no outer expression set the context for the path. For example, if your entire query is:

```
//catalog/product
```

and the context is not set outside the query by the processor, this error will be raised because the processor will not know what the path is relative to. Instead, start your path with a function call or variable that sets the context, as in:

```
doc("catalog.xml")//catalog/product
```

This error may occur when you use paths in a FLWOR expression and forget to start each path with a step that sets the context. For example:

```
for $prod in doc("catalog.xml")//product
where number > 500
return number
```

In this case, the processor does not automatically know to evaluate number relative to the $prod variable; it has to be explicitly specified, as in:

```
for $prod in doc("catalog.xml")//product
where $prod/number > 500
return $prod/number
```

This error might also occur if you forget to put the dollar sign in front of the variable name, causing the processor to interpret it as a path. For example:

```
for $prod in doc("catalog.xml")//product
return prod
```

With the dollar sign omitted from the beginning of prod in the return clause, the processor will interpret it as a relative path to a child element named prod.

A number of built-in function calls will raise this error as well if they require the current context item and none is defined. There are a number of built-in functions that operate on the current context item by default if no appropriate argument is passed. These functions are base-uri, id, idref, lang, last, local-name, name, namespace-uri, normalize-space, number, position, root, string, and string-length. For example, the function call name() (with no arguments) uses the current context item.

Finally, this error can be raised in another situation: if a global variable is defined as external, but it was not bound to a value outside the scope of the query, any references to that variable will raise this error.

XPDY0050

This error is raised in two separate cases:

- When a path expression starts with / or // and the current context node is not part of a complete XML document (with a document node at its root)
- When using a treat expression, if the operand of the expression does not match the sequence type specified

In the first case, you can fix the expression by starting with a call to the root func-
tion, which does not require the root to be a document node. For example, you
could use root(.)/descendant-or-self::product instead of just //product.

XPST0001

This is a general-purpose error that is raised if an expression relies on a component
of the *static context* that has not been assigned a value. In most cases, a more specific
error code and message are provided.

XPST0003

A syntax or parsing error has occurred. This may happen, for example, if there are
mismatched parentheses or invalid keywords.

XPST0005

If static typing is in effect, this error will be raised if any expression in your query
(other than () and data(())) will always return the empty sequence. Often, this is
the result of a misspelling or an invalid path. For more information, see Chapter 14.

XPST0008

An undefined name was encountered. This could be a variable name, an element
name, an attribute name, or a type name. It may be that you misspelled the name or
referred to it in the wrong namespace.

If it is a variable name, that variable may be referenced outside the scope for which it
is bound. One reason for this error is misplaced or missing parentheses. A common
case is when you attempt to return two items using a FLWOR expression, as in:

```
for $prod in doc("catalog.xml")//product
return $prod/number, $prod/name
```

In this case, the second reference to $prod on the last line is out of scope, because only
a single expression is included in the return clause. The rest of the line (, $prod/name)
is considered to be a separate expression that appears after the FLWOR expression.
This example can be remedied by placing parentheses around the return clause, as in:

```
for $prod in doc("catalog.xml")//product
return ($prod/number, $prod/name)
```

If an element, attribute, or type name raises the error, it appears in a sequence type
but is not part of the in-scope schema definitions. For example, the sequence type:

```
schema-element(prod, ProductType)
```

will raise an error if the in-scope schema definitions do not include a declaration for a prod element and a type definition for ProductType.

XPST0010

The processor encountered an unsupported axis in a path expression. Implementations are not required to support the following axes: following, following-sibling, ancestor, ancestor-or-self, preceding, and preceding-sibling. Misspelling an axis name is a possible cause of this error.

XPST0017

You have attempted to call a function that is not declared. This may be because:

- You are using the wrong function name.
- You are using the wrong namespace prefix for the function name.
- You didn't import the module in which the function is declared.
- You are passing an incorrect number of arguments to a function. When calling a function, there must be an argument for every parameter specified in the function signature.

XPST0051

A sequence type refers to a type (other than within the element() or attribute() constructs) that is not an atomic type in the in-scope schema definitions. Sequence types most commonly appear in function signatures, as in:

```
declare function local:xyz ($arg1 as xs:string*, $arg2 as prod:SizeType?) { }
```

where xs:string* and prod:SizeType? are sequence types that described the types of the arguments. This error might be raised if you:

- Misspelled or incorrectly capitalized the name of a built-in type, e.g., xs:String or xs:srting.
- Used a user-defined type name that is not declared in an in-scope schema—for example, if SizeType is not in an imported schema.
- Used a user-defined type name that is a complex or list type, not an atomic type—for example, if SizeType allows children. Using the sequence type element(*,SizeType) *would* be allowed.

XPST0080

A cast or castable expression refers to an undefined type, meaning one that is not an atomic type in the in-scope schema definitions. This error is also raised if one of the types xs:NOTATION or xs:anyAtomicType is used in a cast or castable expression. See error XPST0051 for more information on undefined atomic type names.

XPST0081

A qualified name (QName) in your query has a prefix that is not declared, or that is referenced outside the scope in which it is declared. Anything that appears before a colon in a name is considered to be a prefix, and it must be declared, either in the prolog or in an element constructor. This error is raised for path expressions, element and attribute constructors, element and attribute sequence types, pragma names, and option names. For example, the path expression:

```
doc("nscat.xml")//prod:product
```

raises an error if the prod prefix is not declared either in the query prolog or in an outer direct element constructor.

XPTY0004

This error is a general type error that is raised when a value has a type that is incompatible with the type expected by a function or other expression. This could be because the type of the value is incorrect for the expression, which is the case when you try to multiply two strings. It could also arise if the value is a sequence of fewer or more items than are expected, for example when you pass the substring function a sequence of multiple strings instead of just a single string.

Common cases that raise this type error are:

- Comparing values with incomparable types, for example, "abc" = 1.
- Attempting to compare sequences of more than one value using the value comparison operators, for example, (1, 2) eq (1, 2).
- Attempting arithmetic operations on values that are not numbers or dates, for example, "abc" + "def".
- Calling a function with arguments that have incorrect types, for example, substring(1234, 3), whose first argument is an integer instead of a string.
- Calling a function with too few or too many items in an argument, for example, substring(("a", "b"), 3), which passes a sequence of two items as the first argument instead of just one.

- Passing an invalid operand to a type constructor or cast as expression. This includes passing a nonliteral value when constructing a value of type xs:QName (or a type derived from xs:QName or xs:NOTATION). These types have a special constraint that they can only accept a literal xs:string value, not an evaluated expression.
- Using an order by clause that returns more than one item to sort on, for example, order by $prod/*.
- Specifying a value with an incompatible type in a type constructor or cast expression, as in 53 cast as xs:date.
- Supplying an element node that has not been validated to a function that expects a validated element node.
- Calling a function that relies on the current context node, when the current context item is an atomic value rather than a node. A number of built-in functions will operate on the current context node by default if no appropriate argument is passed. These functions are base-uri, id, idref, lang, local-name, name, namespace-uri, and root.

XPTY0018

The last step in a path expression is returning both nodes and atomic values, which is not permitted. It must return either all nodes or all atomic values. The reason for this rule is that "/" causes sorting into document order if the step delivers nodes, but not if it delivers atomic values. Therefore, it doesn't make sense to return a mixture.

XPTY0019

A step in a path expression (that is not the last step) is returning atomic values, which is not permitted. For example, the following expression:

```
doc("catalog.xml")//name/substring(.,1,3)/replace(.,'A','a')
```

is not permitted because the second to last step, substring(.,1,.3), is returning atomic values. It can be rewritten as:

```
for $shortName in doc("catalog.xml")//name/substring(.,1,3)
return replace($shortName,'A','a')
```

XPTY0020

You have specified a relative path expression, but the current context item is not a node. This might occur, for example, if you use a relative path in a predicate where the current context item is an atomic value, as in:

```
doc("catalog.xml")//product/substring(name,1,3)[@dept = 'ACC']
```

The path expression @dept is being evaluated relative to the substring of the name (an atomic value) rather than the product element. In this case, the predicate can be moved to the previous step, as in:

```
doc("catalog.xml")//product[@dept = 'ACC']/substring(name,1,3)
```

XQDY0025

You have attempted to add two attributes with the same name to a constructed element. XML does not allow two attributes with the same name on the same element.

XQDY0026

The content of a processing instruction contains the string ?>, which is not allowed.

XQDY0027

An element was determined to be invalid when a validate expression was applied to it.

XQDY0041

When constructing a processing instruction, its target (name) is a value that cannot be cast to xs:NCName. Processing instruction targets must be castable to xs:NCName, whose valid values are described in Appendix B.

XQDY0044

The name specified for an attribute constructor is xmlns, or a name whose prefix is xmlns, as in:

```
attribute xmlns:prod { "http://datypic.com/prod" }
```

This is not allowed; you cannot construct namespace declarations using computed attribute constructors. Instead, you should declare the namespace in the query prolog or in an outer direct element constructor.

XQDY0061

If the expression that appears in curly braces after the validate keyword is a document node, that document node must have exactly one child element node. It may also have as children zero, one, or many comment nodes and processing-instruction nodes, in any order.

XQDY0064

When constructing a processing instruction, its target (name) cannot be the letters XML (in any combination of uppercase or lowercase letters). If you are attempting to add an XML declaration to your results, this is controlled by setting the `omit-xml-declaration` serialization parameter to `no` rather than being constructed in your query. Consult the documentation for your XQuery processor to determine how to set the serialization parameter (it varies by implementation).

XQDY0072

A computed comment constructor results in a comment that contains two consecutive hyphens (`--`) or ends in a hyphen, which is not allowed.

XQDY0074

The name expression in a computed constructor cannot be cast to `xs:QName`, for example because it is an invalid XML name or an undeclared prefix is used.

XQDY0084

When evaluating a validate expression whose validation mode is strict, the processor could not find a global element declaration in the in-scope schema definitions or anywhere else. This may be because the schema was not imported or because the element was not globally declared.

XQDY0091

You have attempted to construct an attribute named `xml:id` with an invalid value. ID values must start with a letter or underscore and can only contain letters, digits, underscores, hyphens, and periods.

XQDY0092

You have attempted to construct an attribute named `xml:space` with a value other than `preserve` or `default`. Processors are not required to raise this error.

XQST0009

The processor found a schema import in the prolog, but it does not support the optional Schema Import feature.

XQST0012

One or more of the imported schemas contain definitions that are incomplete or invalid, or contain duplicate declarations.

XQST0013

The processor has recognized a pragma but determined that it contains invalid content as defined by the implementation. Consult the documentation for your implementation to determine what values are allowed for the pragma.

XQST0016

The processor encountered a module import, but it does not support the optional Module feature.

XQST0022

The namespace name used in a namespace declaration attribute (in a direct element constructor) uses an enclosed expression. It must be a literal value; it cannot be dynamically evaluated.

XQST0031

The processor has encountered a version of XQuery that it does not support in the version declaration. For XQuery 1.0, the version (if specified) should always be 1.0, as in:

```
xquery version "1.0" encoding "UTF-8";
```

XQST0032

The prolog contains more than one base URI declaration, which is not allowed. Base URI declarations start with `declare base-uri`.

XQST0033

The prolog contains more than one declaration for the same namespace prefix, which is not allowed.

XQST0034

You may have attempted to declare two functions with the same qualified name and the same number of parameters. The conflicting function signature may appear in a separate module that has been imported.

This error is also raised if you declare a function with only one parameter, and it has the same qualified name as a type that is in scope. For example, if you import a schema that contains a type named order in the namespace http://datypic.com/prod, you cannot also declare a function, with one parameter, named order in the same namespace. This is because each type has a constructor function that shares its name, and it would be impossible to distinguish between the type constructor and the user-defined function.

XQST0035

You have attempted to import two schema documents that have duplicate names for globally declared components such as elements, attributes, and types.

XQST0036

When you import a module, any type names that are used in variable names or function signatures of the imported module must be in the in-scope schema definitions of the main module. For example, suppose strings.xq contains the variable declaration:

```
declare variable $strings:LetterA as strings:smallString := "A";
```

where smallString is a user-defined type defined in stringtypes.xsd. If a main module uses the LetterA variable, it must import the stringtypes.xsd schema in addition to the strings.xq module. If the main module does not make any references to the LetterA variable, it can import strings.xq without importing stringtypes.xsd.

XQST0038

This error is raised in two situations:

- The prolog contains more than one default collation declaration. Default collation declarations start with declare default collation.
- The prolog refers to a default collation that is not supported by the implementation.

XQST0039

A function signature contains more than one parameter with the same name; the parameter names within a particular function signature must be unique.

XQST0040

A direct element constructor contains two attributes with the same qualified name. As with normal XML syntax, the attributes of an element must have unique names.

XQST0045

You have attempted to declare your own function in one of the following namespaces:

- `http://www.w3.org/XML/1998/namespace` (xml)
- `http://www.w3.org/2001/XMLSchema` (xs)
- `http://www.w3.org/2001/XMLSchema-instance` (xsi)
- `http://www.w3.org/2005/xpath-functions` (fn)

This is not permitted. Instead, use the prefix `local`, or declare a new namespace and prefix your function name with that namespace.

XQST0046

URI values (including namespace names) used in queries should be syntactically valid URIs, which can be URLs or URNs. A processor may optionally raise this error if a URI is not syntactically valid according to the rules, which are described in *RFC3986, Uniform Resource Identifiers (URI): Generic Syntax.*

This error may be raised by any of the following URIs used in a query:

- The namespace name in a namespace declaration (either in the prolog or in a direct element constructor)
- The module location or namespace name in a module import
- The target namespace of a library module
- The schema location or namespace name in a schema import
- The collation URI in a default collation declaration or in an order by clause
- The base URI in a base URI declaration

XQST0047

Two separate module imports specify the same target namespace, which is not permitted. Instead, specify multiple module locations for the same target namespace in a single import, using commas to separate them. For example, change this:

```
import module "http://datypic.com/strings"
            at "http://datypic.com/strings/lib.xq";
import module "http://datypic.com/strings"
            at  "http://datypic.com/strings/lib2.xq";
```

to this:

```
import module "http://datypic.com/strings"
            at "http://datypic.com/strings/lib.xq",
               "http://datypic.com/strings/lib2.xq";
```

XQST0048

One of the functions and variables declared in a library module is not in the target namespace. Every function and prolog variable declared in a library module must be qualified with the target namespace of that module. Generally, this means that they use the prefix that is mapped to the target namespace in the module declaration. For example, the following is not permitted because the variable maxStringLength is not in the target namespace:

```
module namespace strings = "http://datypic.com/strings";
declare variable $maxStringLength := 32;
declare function strings:trim($arg as xs:string?) as xs:string? {
  "function body here"
};
```

Instead, it must be prefixed with strings: to put it in the target namespace http://datypic.com/strings.

XQST0049

Duplicate prolog variable declarations were found. The qualified names of all variables declared in prologs must be unique across all modules that are used together. This includes the main module and any imported library modules.

XQST0054

Function and variable declarations with circular definitions were encountered; these are not allowed. For example, an initializing expression in a variable declaration cannot call a function whose body itself references the variable being initialized.

XQST0055

The prolog contains more than one copy-namespaces declaration, which is not permitted. Copy-namespaces declarations start with `declare copy-namespaces`.

XQST0057

A schema import that specifies a prefix has a zero-length namespace name, which is not allowed. For example, the following schema import is invalid:

```
import schema namespace prod = ""
            at "http://datypic.com/prod.xsd";
```

You can, however, import a schema with no target namespace if you make "no namespace" the default, as in:

```
import schema default element namespace ""
            at "http://datypic.com/prod.xsd";
```

XQST0058

Two separate schema imports specify the same target namespace, which is not permitted. For example:

```
import schema "http://datypic.com/strings"
            at "http://datypic.com/strings/str.xsd";
import schema "http://datypic.com/strings"
            at  "http://datypic.com/strings/str2.xsd";
```

Instead, you can specify multiple schema locations for the same target namespace in a single import, using commas to separate them. For example:

```
import schema "http://datypic.com/strings"
            at "http://datypic.com/strings/str.xsd",
               "http://datypic.com/strings/str2.xsd";
```

However, the semantics of this are somewhat implementation-defined because schema locations are just hints. A safer option is to create a schema document that includes the two other schema documents, and import that.

XQST0059

The processor cannot find a valid library module for the target namespace specified in a module import or a schema import. This might occur, for example, because it could not find a module or schema at all, or it found a module or schema with a different target namespace than the one specified in the import. Different processors have different strategies for locating query modules—for example, some might allow independent compilation of library modules.

XQST0060

A function is declared with a name that is not in a namespace. All function names must be in a namespace. Note that default element namespace declarations do not apply to function names.

To remedy this, revise your function name to include a namespace prefix. In a main module, you can use any prefix that is declared in the prolog or the predeclared prefix `local`. In a library module, you must use the prefix that is mapped to the target namespace of the module.

XQST0065

The prolog cannot contain more than one ordering mode declaration. Ordering mode declarations start with `declare ordering`.

XQST0066

The prolog contains more than one default element namespace declaration or more than one default function namespace, which is not allowed. Default element namespace declarations start with `declare default element namespace`, and default function namespace declarations start with `declare default function namespace`.

XQST0067

The prolog contains more than one construction declaration, which is not allowed. Construction declarations start with `declare construction`.

XQST0068

The prolog contains more than one boundary-space declaration, which is not allowed. Boundary-space declarations start with `declare boundary-space`.

XQST0069

The prolog contains more than one empty order declaration, which is not allowed. Empty order declarations start with `declare default order`.

XQST0070

This error is raised if a namespace declaration attempts to:

- Bind a URI to the prefix xmlns. This built-in prefix has special meaning in XML and cannot be used in a declaration.
- Bind the xml prefix to a namespace other than http://www.w3.org/XML/1998/namespace.
- Bind the http://www.w3.org/XML/1998/namespace namespace to a prefix other than xml.

This error could be raised by a standard namespace declaration, or by the namespace binding that occurs as part of a module declaration, module import, or schema import.

XQST0071

More than one namespace declaration attribute on a single element constructor uses the same prefix, which is not allowed. For example, the following is illegal because the prod prefix is mapped twice on the same element:

```
<product xmlns:prod="http://datypic.com/prod"
         xmlns:prod="http://datypic.com/prd">...</product>
```

XQST0073

A module cannot import itself, either directly or indirectly, unless all the modules in the chain have the same target namespace.

XQST0075

A validate expression was encountered by a processor that does not support validate expressions. Not all implementations support the validate expression; it is an optional feature.

XQST0076

The collation specified in an order by clause is not supported by the implementation.

XQST0079

An extension expression has no expression between its curly braces, and the processor does not recognize the pragma.

XQST0085

Namespace declaration attributes with prefixes whose values are zero-length strings, such as `xmlns:cat=""`, are only allowed if the implementation supports Namespaces 1.1.

XQST0087

The version declaration contains an invalid encoding value. Example valid values for the encoding include `UTF-8`, `UTF-16`, `ISO-8859-1`, and `US-ASCII`. Encoding names always start with a letter and may contain letters, digits, periods, underscores, and hyphens.

XQST0088

The target namespace specified in a module import or a module declaration is a zero-length string, which is not allowed.

XQST0089

A variable bound in a for clause has the same name as the positional variable used in that same clause. This is not permitted. For example, change:

```
for $x at $x in (doc("catalog.xml")//product)
```

to:

```
for $x at $y in (doc("catalog.xml")//product)
```

XQST0090

A character reference (e.g., ` `) refers to a character that is not a valid character in the version of XML that is in use.

XQST0093

A set of module imports is circular, in that module A directly depends on one or more other modules that themselves directly depend on module A. *Directly depends* means that a function or variable in module A references a function or variable in the next module in the import chain.

XQTY0024

In element constructor content, enclosed expressions that evaluate to attributes must appear first in the element constructor content, before any other kinds of nodes. For example, the following query is not valid because the second enclosed expression, {$prod/@dept}, appears *after* an enclosed expression that returns element nodes.

```
for $prod in doc("catalog.xml")/catalog/product
return <li>{$prod/number}{$prod/@dept}</li>
```

XQTY0030

The expression that appears in curly braces after the validate keyword must be a single document or element node. If it evaluates to a sequence of multiple items, another kind of node, or an atomic value, this error is raised.

XQTY0086

If you set the copy-namespaces mode to no-preserve, and the construction mode to preserve, there may be a conflict if your element *content* (or attribute values) contains namespace-sensitive values, such as qualified names. Namespaces used in content (as opposed to in element/attribute names) are not considered to be "used."

For example, suppose your input document (qnames.xml) looks like this:

```
<listOfQualifiedNames xmlns:prod="http://datypic.com/prod">
  <qName>prod:xyz</qName>
  <qName>prod:abc</qName>
</listOfQualifiedNames>
```

Suppose also that this document has been validated with a schema, and the qName elements are annotated with the type xs:QName. You might query the document with:

```
<myNewList>{doc("qnames.xml")//qName}</myNewList>
```

intending to return a new element that contains the two qName elements. If construction mode is preserve, the qName elements will still have the type xs:QName. But if the copy-namespaces mode is no-preserve, the http://datypic.com/prod namespace will not be preserved, because it is used only in content, not in element or attribute names. Therefore, the qName elements' content will have undefined prefixes and this error will be raised.

Index

Symbols

& (ampersand)
 && (and) full text operator, 286
 entity reference (&), 279
 escaping in element constructor
 content, 59
 escaping in string literals, 214
 separator character in URIs, 262
< > (angle brackets)
 < (less than) operator, 30
 comparing dates and times, 246
 comparing durations, 248
 comparing numeric values, 206
 comparing strings, 215
 entity reference (<), 229, 279
 SQL and XQuery, 297
 <!-- -->, XML comment delimiters, 29
 <![CDATA[and]]> CDATA section
 delimiter, 280
 <, escaping in element constructor
 content, 59
 << and >> operators, comparing nodes by
 relative position in document
 order, 91
 <= (less than or equal to) operator, 30
 comparing dates and times, 245
 comparing numeric values, 206
 comparing strings, 215
 SQL and XQuery, 297
 <? ?>, in processing instruction
 constructors, 271

> (greater than) operator, 30
 comparing dates and times, 246
 comparing durations, 248
 comparing numeric values, 206
 comparing strings, 215
 entity reference (>), 279
 SQL and XQuery, 297
>= (greater than or equal to) operator, 30
 comparing dates and times, 245
 comparing numeric values, 206
 comparing strings, 215
 SQL and XQuery, 297
' (apostrophe), entity reference ('), 279
* (asterisk)
 *? (reluctant quantifier), 236
 escaping in regular expressions, 229
 multiplication operator, 207
 multiplying durations by
 numbers, 252
 occurrence indicator, zero, one, or many
 items, 103, 107, 151, 152
 cast expression and, 157
 return type of function, 151
 quantifier, zero, one, or many
 occurrences, 227
 wildcard in path expressions, 6, 39, 43
@ (at sign)
 @*, copying attributes from an
 element, 111
 abbreviation for attribute axis, 45
 abbreviation for axes, 45
 returning attributes in path expressions, 5
 separator character in URIs, 262
\ (backslash)

We'd like to hear your suggestions for improving our indexes. Send email to *index@oreilly.com*.

arguments (function)
 conversion to expected type, 103
 empty sequence as argument, 107
 nodes vs. atomic values, 107
arithmetic operations, 207–211
 addition, subtraction, and
 multiplication, 209
 on dates, times, and durations, 249–252
 division, 210
 expressions, 27
 modulus (remainder), 211
 on multiple numeric values, 208
 numeric type promotion in
 expressions, 206
 precedence of arithmetic operators, 209
 SQL and XQuery, 298
 types and, 208
 XQuery 1.0 and XPath 1.0 and 2.0, 316
ascending or descending order, 87
assertions, type, 190
at keyword, 116
 namespace prefix mapping in module
 import, 165
atomic types
 built into XQuery, 143
 hierarchy, 144
 as sequence types, 153
atomic values, 22
 casting any type to xs:string or
 xs:untypedAtomic, 158
 casting between specific types, 158–159
 comparing, 30
 constructing with given types, 155
 enclosed expressions in direct element
 constructors evaluating to, 61
 nodes vs. in function arguments, 107
 returned by last step in a path, 46
 sequence types for function
 parameters, 103
 types, 145
 untyped, 438
atomization, 148
 function conversion rules, 150
 on operands of arithmetic
 expressions, 208
atoms (regular expressions), 226
 parenthesized subexpressions as, 227
attribute axis, 41
attribute nodes, 18
 (see also attributes)
attribute() kind test, 154, 183

attributes
 adding to an element, 111
 adding to query results, 9
 atomic values, 22
 computed attribute constructors, 70
 declarations in XML Schema, 173
 enclosed expressions in direct element
 constructors evaluating to, 61
 finding with path expressions, 5
 including with result elements, using
 enclosed expressions, 62
 from input document, including in query
 results, 57
 matching based on name, 183
 names, 21
 affected by namespace declarations in
 XQuery, 133
 namespaces, 24, 125
 declaration attributes, 131
 predeclared, 128
 prefixes, 124
 node hierarchy (family analogy), 19
 removing from an element, 111
 removing from an element and all
 descendants, 112
 specifying directly using direct element
 constructors, 62
 string and type values, 21
 types, 173
averages
 avg function, 95, 212, 324
 ignoring absent nodes, 96
 avg-empty-is-zero function, 97
 calculating with missing values, 198
axes, 41
 abbreviated syntax, 44
 forward, 41
 Full Axis feature, 289
 reverse, 41
 positional predicates and, 50
 using node() test with, 44
axis steps, 41
 node tests, 42–44

B

back-references, 237
base URIs, 259
 finding for a node, 260
 resolving URIs, 261
 specifying with xml:base attribute, 260
 of the static context, 261
base-URI declaration, 261

N

\n (line feed), in regular expressions, 229
N/A values, indicating default missing
 values, 198
name function, 21
names
 affected by namespace declarations in
 XQuery, 133
 choosing for clarity of queries, 194
 computed element constructors, 69
 conventions in XQuery, 27
 element and attribute nodes, 21
 elements from input document, changing
 in query, 114
 function, 100, 106
 reserved, 106
 local-name function, 21, 254, 256, 362
 name function, 21, 52, 254, 371
 node name tests, 42–43
 node-name function, 21, 254
 valid name in XML (xs:Name), 432
 variables, 28, 167
namespace declaration attributes, 131, 136
namespaces, 24, 123–140
 choosing prefixes for clarity of
 queries, 195
 copy-namespaces declarations, 138–140
 declarations in element constructors, 63,
 131
 declarations in prolog, 128–131, 161
 default namespace declarations in
 queries, 133
 elements, changing the namespaces
 of, 258
 error names, 440
 functions, 100
 impact and scope of declarations, 132
 in-scope, 357
 statically known namespaces
 vs., 135–137
 library module imports, 164
 multiple module locations for single
 namespace, 165
 names in XQuery, 27
 node name tests and, 43
 option names, 292
 predeclared, 128
 URIs (see URIs)
 user-defined function names, 106
 variables, 28

XML, 123–127
 attributes and, 125
 declarations and scope, 126
 declaring, 124
 default namespace declarations, 125
 URIs, 123
 XML Schema and, 175
 XML versions, 290
Namespaces in XML (W3C
 recommendation), 123
namespace-uri function, 254, 372
namespace-uri-for-prefix function, 259, 373
namespace-uri-from-QName function, 257,
 374
NaN (not-a-number), 205, 208
 comparisons, 207
 results for mod operator, 211
 sorting order, 87
native XML database, 2
NCName, 264, 432
 target for processing instructions, 272
ne operator (see not equal to operator)
negation operator (-), 207
negative durations, 246
negative infinity (-INF), 207
 results for mod operator when an operand
 is -INF, 211
nesting
 conditional expressions, 36
 expressions in XQuery, 302
 sequences and, 23
nil and empty values, 198
nilled elements, 295
nilled function, 375
node tests, 42–44
 node kind, 44
 node name, 42–43
 using wildcards, 43
node() kind test, 44, 111
 generic sequence type, 152
 processing instructions, 271
 text nodes, 276
 XML comments, 268
node-name function, 21, 254, 376
nodes, 18–22
 atomic values, 22
 comparisons, 30
 atomization, 148
 comment, 267
 comparisons, 34
 as context item, 40

W3C
 converter for XQuery to XqueryX
 conversions, 285
 Namespaces in XML, 123
 XML Schema (see XML Schema)
 XQuery Working Group
 Full-Text recommendation, 286
 XQuery Update Facility, 285
web sites
 backward compatibility between XPath
 1.0 and 2.0, 314
 official XQuery site, 17
 source code for functions, 34
 user-defined function examples, 103
 web page for this book, xiv
weight keyword, 287
where clause (FLWORs), 7, 73, 77
 composed of multiple expressions, 77
 scope of variables, 79
 three-way join, 83
 two-way join, 301
 using an order comparison, 91
 using instead of predicate, 83
 using predicates instead of, 202
whitespace, 27
 in direct element constructors, 65–67
 boundary whitespace, 65
 boundary-space declaration, 66
 forcing preservation of boundary
 whitespace, 67
 nonstring types cast to xs:string, 214
 normalize-space function, 377
 in regular expressions
 escaping, 228, 230
 ignoring, 239
 separating list of xs:IDREF values, 265
 space, character reference for, 278
 in strings, 222
 considering in string length, 217
 between tags in source XML with no DTD
 or schema, 275
 using for query clarity, 194
wildcards
 asterisk (*) in path expressions, 6
 schema, types and, 180
 using in node name tests, 43
word character (\w) in regular
 expressions, 230

X

x option ($flags argument), indicating
 ignoring whitespace
 characters, 239
XDM (XQuery 1.0 and XPath 2.0 Data
 Model), 17
XHTML, wrapping query results in, 8
XML
 CDATA sections, 280
 comments, 267
 constructing, 268
 data model and, 267
 included in queries, 29
 querying, 268
 sequence types and, 268
 data model, relational vs., 294
 documents, 272–274
 constructing document nodes, 273
 document nodes and data model, 273
 document nodes and sequence
 types, 273
 serialization of query results to, 289
 entity and character references, 278–280
 character reference examples, 278
 entity references, 279
 input documents, 15
 namespaces, 123–127
 attributes and, 125
 declarations and scope, 126
 declaring, 124
 default namespace declarations, 125
 names.xml document (example), 255
 URIs, 123
 using namespace declarations in
 XQuery, 136
 notations, 434
 processing instructions, 269–272
 constructing, 271
 data model and, 270
 querying, 270
 sequence types and, 271
 SQL/XML query, 306
 text nodes, 274–278
 constructing, 278
 querying, 276
 reasons for working with, 276
 sequence types and, 276
 XQuery data model and, 275
 version support in XQuery
 implementations, 290

About the Author

Priscilla Walmsley has been working closely with XQuery and XML Schema for years. She was a member of the W3C XML Schema Working Group from 1999 to 2004, and wrote the respected book *Definitive XML Schema* (Prentice Hall). Currently, Priscilla serves as Managing Director of Datypic (*http://www.datypic.com*), where she specializes in XML- and Service Oriented Architecture (SOA)-related consulting and training.

Colophon

The animal on the cover of *XQuery* is the satyr tragopan (*Tragopan satyra*), a member of the pheasant family and one of five tragopan species. This bird, sometimes called the crimson horned tragopan, inhabits the Himalayas, from Kashmir east up into Tibet and central China. Its two names are derived from the distinctive appearance of the male—his protruding fleshy outgrowths above the eyes, which look like horns, and his bright red plumage. Both plumage and horns are central to his courtship displays.

Tragopans feed on insects, leaves, sprouts, and seeds and are thought to be monogamous. Although incubation is done entirely by the female, the male may assist in tending the chicks. Most tragopans are good breeders in captivity, adapting well to various cold-weather climates and becoming quite tame.

Four of the five species of tragopans are in danger of extinction due to the destruction of their habitats. Unlike most fowl, tragopans live at very high elevations, ranging from 925 to 3650 meters. In the winter they are typically found in the thickest parts of pine trees, but during mating season they travel upward to the extreme limits of the forest. Finding a high branch, the male tragopan establishes a territorial perch from which he makes mating calls at five-minute intervals. His call, which some have described as similar to that of a goose or young lamb, can be heard for more than a mile.

The cover image is from *The Riverside Natural History*. The cover font is Adobe ITC Garamond. The text font is Linotype Birka; the heading font is Adobe Myriad Condensed; and the code font is LucasFont's TheSans Mono Condensed.

Better than e-books

Buy *XQuery*, and access the digital edition
FREE on Safari for 45 days.

Go to www.oreilly.com/go/safarienabled
and type in coupon code NEZJIXA

Search
thousands of
top tech books

Download
whole chapters

Cut and Paste
code examples

Find
answers fast

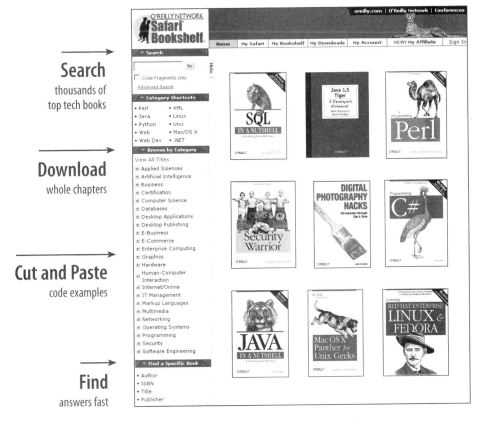

Search Safari! The premier electronic reference
library for programmers and IT professionals.